Transcultural Experiments

Transcultural Experiments

Russian and American Models of Creative Communication

Ellen E. Berry and Mikhail N. Epstein

St. Martin's Press
New York

TRANSCULTURAL EXPERIMENTS

Copyright © Ellen E. Berry, Mikhail N. Epstein 1999. All rights reserved. Printed in the United States of America. No part of this book may be used or reproduced in any manner whatsoever without written permission except in the case of brief quotations embodied in critical articles or reviews. For information, address St. Martin's Press, 175 Fifth Avenue, New York, N. Y. 10010.
IBSN 0-312-21808-7

Library of Congress Cataloging-in-Publication Data

Berry, Ellen E.
    Transcultural experiments : Russian and American models of creative communication / Ellen E. Berry and Mikhail N. Epstein.
        p. cm.
    Includes bibliographical references and index.
    ISBN 0-312-21808-7 (cloth)
        1. Intercultural communication.   2. United States—Relations—Russia (Federation)   3. Russia (Federation)—Relations—United States.   I. Epshtein, Mikhail N.   II. Title.
P94.6.B475   1999
302.2—dc21   99-14323
                                                                                  CIP

Design by Binghamton Valley Composition

First edition: October 1999
10 9 8 7 6 5 4 3 2 1

To improvisational communities
both actual and virtual.

Contents

Acknowledgments ix
Introduction
Berry and Epstein 1

Part I. HISTORY

1. From Culturology to Transculture (with Appendix)
   Epstein 15
2. Collective Improvisation and Transcultural Consciousness
   Epstein 31
3. Postmodern Avant-Gardes and Cultural Reinvention
   Berry 56

Part II. THEORY

A. Definitions

4. Transculture in the Context of Contemporary Critical Theories
   Epstein 79
5. From Difference to Interference
   Epstein 91
6. Transculture and Society
   Epstein 102
7. The Rehumanization of the Humanities
   Epstein 113
8. Nomadic Desires and Transcultural Becomings
   Berry 121

B. Infinitions

9. How Does Newness Enter the Postmodern World?
   Berry 142
10. The Permanence of Newness and Spaces for Difference:
    From History to Geography
    Epstein 152

11. The Ethics of Imagination
   Epstein — 164
12. A Transcultural Imaginary
   Berry — 169

Part III. PRACTICE

13. The Lawlessness of Genres
   Berry — 177

A. Genres

14. On the Birth of Genres
   Epstein — 184
15. An Essay on the Essay
   Epstein — 189
16. The Catalog of Catalogs
   Epstein — 195

B. Collective Improvisations

17. Improvisational Community
   Epstein — 201
18. Sample Sessions at Universities — 214
19. Nomads at Home: Improvisation in the Academy
   Berry — 229

C. Authorship

20. Hyperauthorship: The Case of Araki Yasusada
   Epstein — 240
21. Poetry as a State of Being: From the Notes of Ivan Solovyov
   Epstein — 256

D. The Internet and Creativity

22. InteLnet: Web Projects in the Humanities
   Epstein — 276
23. The Interactive Anthology of Alternative Ideas: An Introduction
   Epstein — 290
   In Place of a Conclusion: Transcultural Dialogue
   Berry and Epstein — 302
   Index of Names — 323
   Index of Subjects — 329

Acknowledgments

Above all, I would like to thank my co-author for his dedication to this project and his generosity in sharing his many, varied, and inspiring ideas. It has been a delight and a privilege to work with him, to see from his angle of vision: an experience that has irrevocably altered my own. Thanks go as well to Kent Johnson for first introducing me to Mikhail; to the Institute for Culture and Society at Bowling Green for its generous award of a fellowship to pursue this project; to Martin Prochazka and faculty at Charles University in Prague for their interest in this work; to Victoria Lees for her careful formatting of the manuscript and her diligent attention to preparation of the index; and to Karen Wolny at St. Martin's Press for her belief in this project.

—Ellen E. Berry

The transcultural project has developed through two stages, Russian (1982–89) and American (1990–98), each of which relied on the participation and contributions of many colleagues. I want to thank my friends and co-thinkers Vladimir Aristov, Iosif Bakshtein, Ilya Kabakov, Aleksei Mikheev, Liudmila Pol'shakova, Boris Tseitlin, Maria Umnova, Olga Vainshtein, and all those who participated in collective improvisations in Moscow and exemplified the spirit of improvisational community. I am also thankful to Sophia Olinova, Vladimir Tikhvinsky, Eduard Shul'man, and all those who helped to consolidate, both intellectually and organizationally, the Moscow interdisciplinary associations: the Club of Essayists, "Image and Thought," and the Laboratory of Contemporary Culture. Without the generous help and participation of these people no transcultural work or creative "interference" would be possible.

Regarding the American stage, I want to thank above all my co-author, whose work of integrating the transcultural project into the framework of contemporary cultural theories was inspiring and has stimulated many conceptual innovations. Ellen believed in the truly transcultural potentials of this project and did everything a friend, a colleague, and a co-thinker can do to bring it to full realization. Her participation in the production of the manuscript and in testing the American potential for collective improvisation was invaluable.

My special thanks go to Dmitry Shalin (University of Nevada), who read the manuscript at its critical stage and made an extensive, thoughtful commentary that led to its considerable improvement. My ongoing dialogue and collaboration with Kent Johnson (Highland Community College, IL) helped me immensely in formulating some ideas and hypotheses about the potentials of hyperauthorship as one of the transcultural practices. The interrogative reading of the project by Eve Adler (Middlebury College) helped me to reformulate some principal theses. I am grateful to Walter Reed (Emory University) and Mihai Spariosu (University of Georgia and the International School of the Humanities in Santiago de Compostela, Spain) for their valuable help in organizing improvisational sessions at these institutions, and I thank all creative participants of these experimental sessions.

I am grateful to Karen Wolny at St. Martin's Press for her enthusiasm and continuous care about this project, and to Victoria Lees of Bowling Green University for her help in the technical preparation of the manuscript.

—Mikhail N. Epstein

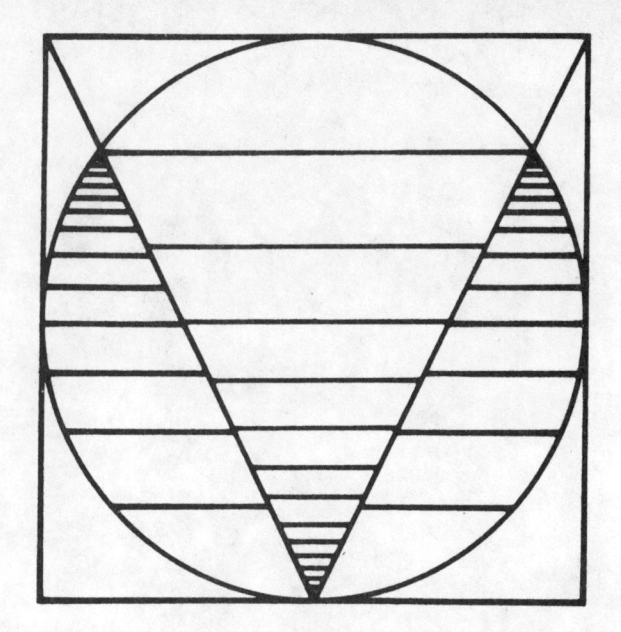

Figure I
The emblem of the association Image and Thought (Obraz I Mysl')

Figure II
A large (fractal) pyramid constructed from smaller pyramids
　　　which are constructed from smaller pyramids
　　　　which are constructed from smaller pyramids . . .

Introduction
Ellen E. Berry and Mikhail N. Epstein

This book aims to theorize and develop new modes of intercultural communication made possible in part by contemporary processes of globalization. As most studies of the nature and effects of postmodern globalization have focused almost exclusively on postcolonial interrelations between so-called first and third worlds, the need for transcultural investigations may be especially acute in the area of changing relations between first and second world cultures. Until quite recently, the U.S.-USSR nexus represented one of the most persistent and pernicious of global oppositions. Russia and the United States represented the Other to each other, the immense unknown, divided by the polarization of political ideologies and the imperial rivalry of the Cold War.

With the collapse of this dualistic narrative, it now becomes possible to rework the opposition between the former antagonists into a new resource for experiencing the multiple forms of otherness within each of these cultures, Americanness in Russian culture, Russianess in American culture. This book stages a series of comparisons and interferences between the Russian discipline of "culturology" and various Western postmodern theories and traditions associated with Anglo-American cultural studies. It suggests points of connection and divergence between these two very diverse traditions, and outlines a range of new cultural spaces and genres growing out of their interaction. Because the model proposed here is based on the perspectives of "difference" and "interference" between cultures instead of on outdated models of rigid national identities and global oppositions, it also suggests, we hope, a theoretical network appropriate to the post–Cold War period in the relationship between Russian and American cultures.

The book elaborates the origins of the Russian transcultural method as it was developed during the 1980s in several unique cultural institutions of the perestroika era: the Club of Essayists (1982–87), the association "Image and Thought" (1986–88), and the Laboratory of Contemporary Culture (1988–89). Highlighted here are a variety of new modes of cultural communication and interaction invented in these institutions, including concrete methods of collaborative writing and conceptualization of the material environment such as collective improvisation and the lyrical museum. We situate this history within and distinguish it from the tradition of Russian cultural theory, the project of the historical avant-gardes in both West and East, and Western postmodern approaches to culture. We also chart the emergence of contemporary theories of culture in the Anglo-American tradition, including especially theories of multiculturalism and globalization, and suggest how the Russian transcultural model illuminates and suggests solutions to some of the major theoretical impasses of this tradition.

Although the transcultural approaches developed in late Soviet Russia are a culturally specific response to a unique historical moment, they nonetheless help to expose some of the critical blind spots of the Western tradition. They do so in part by stressing the necessary interaction between critical theory and cultural practice and by employing terms that largely have been rendered suspect within the Western postmodern canon, among them *utopia, future, totality, newness,* and *authorship.* Our analysis of these terms involves critically reworking them from the perspective of the Russian transcultural tradition and putting them in dialogue with some newly emerging tendencies in Anglo-American cultural studies.

The transcultural interferential model proposed here responds to limitations inherent in some of the contemporary models circulating on the global stage. It is to be distinguished from an understanding of the global system as a collection of "discrete worlds" or "clashing civilizations" (as in Samuel Huntington's model). It also diverges from the older American "melting pot" metaphor in which cultural differences were assimilated to a national norm as well as a model of the contemporary global system as a totalized "universal cultural ecumene." Finally, it departs from the U.S. multicultural model that posits aggregates of discrete subcultures (based on racial, ethnic, sexual, or other differences), each of which seeks to constitute and maintain its cultural specificity in the face of a homogenizing dominant culture.

Transculture shares with multiculturalism a desire to dislodge a vision of culture as unitary and monolithic, but it does so by attempting to theorize and work within the interactions and interdependencies arising among cultural differences. Within a multicultural framework, differences are often promoted for their own sakes, resulting in a kind of cultural leveling that may transform differences into their exact opposite, leading to a relativistic and cynical "indifference" among cultures. In contrast, transcultural approaches assert the fundamental insufficiency and incompleteness of any culture and thus its need for radical openness to and dialogue with others.

The book thus represents an articulation of some new "post-poststructuralist," or rather "proto-interferential" concepts that serve as modes of "conceptive" (creatively conceptual) criticism, not simply as analytic tools. We explore the generative capacity of these concepts, such as "hyperauthorship" or "collective improvisation," their ability to activate experimental forms and concealed potentials within both known and unknown cultures. As a theory of communication among existing cultural differences plus a gesture toward those possibilities not yet actualized in any culture, the transcultural model opens new utopian spaces that respond to Fredric Jameson's call for a reinvention of the utopian vision in contemporary politics and the elaboration of a radically new type of internationalism. Transcultural models offer strategies for the invention of positive alternatives to the legacies of cultural antagonism and domination that have pervaded both Western and second world cultures. Donna Haraway has suggested that one of our most urgent tasks as cultural critics is to build "more powerful collectivities," to create the conditions for producing "an articulated world comprised of an undecidable number of modes and sites where powerful new connections can be made."[1] The spaces opened by experiments in transcultural thinking may well provide such sites.

What Is Transculture?

Currently there is no consensus about the meaning of the term "transculture," although it is used increasingly among a range of critics writing in the West and in relation to a number of disciplinary and cultural contexts. Tracing the historical emergence of the term—from its origins in the fields of sociology and anthropology to its contemporary uses in postmodern theory, postcolonial studies and, other areas—helps at least to clarify some of the multiple ways it has been adapted and disseminated and the distinctive emphases it is being given in this study.

Diane Taylor attributes the term "transculturation" to Cuban sociologist Fernando Ortiz, who first used it in the 1940s to describe Afro-Cuban culture and the processes of hybridization engendered within it by a fusion of indigenous and foreign cultural elements. Ortiz and others after him, such as the Peruvian ethnographer José Maria Arguedas, distinguished their theories from Western models of static "uni-cultures," which are unable to account for either the hybridized quality of the transcultural phenomenon or its dynamic processual nature that shifts through time and space. Taylor also insists on the inherently political nature of the process of transculturation within these early definitions. "The theory of transculturation ... delineates the process by which symbols, discourse, and ideology are transformed as one culture changes through the imposition or adoption of another, and examines the historic and socio-political forces that produce local meanings ... the theory of transculturation is [also] a political one in that it suggests the consciousness of a society's own historically-specific, cultural manifestations—in contact with but differentiated from other societies.... The issue of transculturation, then, is not only one of meaning. It is also one of political positioning and selection: which forms, symbols or aspects of cultural identity become highlighted or confrontational, when, and why?"[2] Taylor considers the strengths of these early theories of transculture to be their eschewal of oppositional binaries—especially center and periphery—and their emphasis on cultural identity as a dynamic, unstable, and ongoing construction.

Since at least the 1970s, the term "transculture" has most generally been applied to discussions of cultural exchange and change in colonial and postcolonial contexts. For example, in *Imperial Eyes: Travel Writing and Transculturation,* Mary Louise Pratt borrows the term "transculturation" from ethnography to describe "contact zones" or social spaces where "disparate cultures meet, clash, and grapple with each other, often in highly asymmetrical relations of domination and subordination—like colonialism, slavery or their aftermaths."[3] In *Colonial Inscriptions,* Carolyn Shaw analyzes the cultural narratives of subordination and domination in Kenya as an "intercultural" borderland between European and African knowledges and experiences: "[T]he notion of interculturality recognizes the power differential between the colonizer and the colonized, but also recognizes that arrows of influence may be drawn from the colonized to the colonizers, and thus that interactions with the African people and landscape reshaped European ideas, attitudes, and practices [as well]."[4] Pratt and Shaw's studies are just two of the many contemporary texts to explore processes of cultural production, interaction, and admixture in postcolonial contexts.[5]

Contemporary uses of the term "transculture" also are marked by awareness of the movements of multinational capital and global flows of other kinds. They share an interest in analyzing those new cultural forms and subjectivities arising within and as a response to global frameworks, forms that cannot be understood merely as products of bilateral exchanges between nation-states. "Transculture" here refers to the instabilities and complexities of cultural production within the conditions of transnationalism more generally, a global present that foregrounds and intensifies the latent interactivity of previous models and historical eras. Exemplary studies include those of Featherstone, Appadurai, Harvey, Buell, Jameson, Bhabha, which analyze transcultural flows from sociological, political, literary, and other perspectives. Often the term "third culture" is used in reference to this global context independent of considerations of those asymmetrical power relations between cultures—in distinction from feminist, postcolonial, and other politically interested uses of the term. Here it describes those cosmopolitan, occupational, or commercial cultures—made possible by media and multinationals and constructed from the decontextualized fragments of regional, national, and local cultures—that typically exist to facilitate negotiations between international organizations. Some critics note the often-sublimated but ever-present relations between these commercial cultures and the imperial past as well as their fundamentally standardizing or homogenizing tendencies.

In this regard, Ulf Hannerz's description of the global cosmopolitan refers to a particular new type of individual formed by transnational networks, a subjectivity based on the mobility and access afforded by certain occupations, such as intellectual, bureaucrat, politician, or business person. Roland Robertson focuses on the *consciousness* of the process of globalization, the perceived facticity of a single world, rather than economic determinants in his explanation of how the global has developed. He emphasizes that although few currently believe in the existence of a global transculture in the sense of a body of common values, ideas, etc. that are binding on a group, the globalizing process itself, the rendering of the world as a single place, constrains civilizations and societies to be increasingly vocal about their "global callings"—to articulate their unique geocultural and geomoral contributions to world history.

Finally, Bruce Robbins and other contributors to the recent anthology *Cosmopolitics* use the term "cosmopolitan" to describe (1) actually existing "habits of thought, feeling, attachment, and belonging shaped by particular supranational or translocal collectivities," styles of practical consciousness; and (2) a not-fully realizable ideal. The ideal cosmopolitanism is predicated on development of a kind of global empathetic and ethical capacity to extend ourselves imaginatively in relation to cultural Others. Such a capacity is a precondition for the development of transnational modes of citizenship free from the associations of rationalist universalism within which the term "cosmopolitan" historically has been entangled.

As subsequent chapters show, our book is in dialogue with current efforts to theorize the nature and consequences of global cultural flows in a contemporary moment. The contribution of the book to discussions of transculturalism is our infusion of the distinctive development of this term in the Russian context—a context that has largely been missing from discussions of globalization more generally—and our efforts to accentuate the transformative potentials of the term in relation to some specific practices and genres of creative communication.[6]

What Is an Experiment?

The epistemological status of an experiment in the postmodern age should be distinguished from both traditional notions of experiments in the natural sciences and the historical avant-garde's modes of experimentation within art. The task of scientific experimentation, in the most conventional terms, is to test an initial hypothesis and either confirm it as true or reject it as false. The dynamics of experimentation ideally lead, therefore, from epistemological uncertainty to affirmation of a truth.

In distinction from natural sciences, an experiment in culture has no reference point of verification, no means of being tested objectively in relation to external reality. It neither confirms nor rejects any preliminary postulate but aims to multiply and disseminate new forms of expression or new paradigms of knowledge. Experimentation in culture should be distinguished from creativity as the search for a unique form to suit a unique content or inspiration. Experimentation challenges organicist modes of creativity and departs from the realm of accomplished works of art into the realm of cultural possibilities through proposing various and complementary alternatives that need not find completed expression in the existence of a work as such.

One should discriminate further between the experiments of the historical avant-gardes and postmodern types of cultural experimentation. Avant-garde experiments were designed to challenge traditional forms and institutions of art; the avant-garde exercised an imperative modality in its experimentation and still operated in the realm of truth and accomplishment. Postmodernity, of a particular kind, develops a subjunctive modality in its experiments, attempting to broaden the range of possibilities and to transfer the status of experimentation from certainty to uncertainty, from "result" to "draft," in direct opposition to what is implied by experimentation in the natural sciences and in the historical avant-gardes. If science seeks to establish through experimentation what is, and the avant-garde tries to affirm what should be, postmodern experiments—as we are using this term—highlight the uncertainty and multiplicity involved in the process of experimentation to propose a range of possible cultural genres or cultural worlds, each valued in its own right as a *possibility*. The aim of an experiment in this sense of the term is to problematize a particular cultural symbol or system, to potentiate a series of alternative symbols rather than to solve a problem or to actualize a specific potential. In proposing these distinctions we are in accord with Jean-François Lyotard's proposition concerning the value of the "wasteful" or nonproductive time of speculation, which he distinguishes from the capitalist commodification of time that views the future as a fund of fixed returns against which the present may borrow. In contrast, cultural experimentation opens a space of delay—a utopian space—in which to imagine a future imperfect temporality. The concepts of the *experimental* and *interference* form the cornerstones of the transcultural method.

What Is Interference?

The problematic of difference has been a central one for cultural studies and general critical theory over the course of the last twenty years. In part the concept of difference was advanced to challenge the monolithic cultural canons that in distinct ways prevailed in both the first and second worlds, taking the rigid form of Soviet totalitarianism and the much milder but nevertheless compulsory forms of majority rule and majority canon in the West. The assertion of difference proclaimed the right of each subculture and each political, ideological, racial, and sexual minority to constitute its own sovereign realm of cultural expression.

However, such an understanding of difference has resulted in a multiplicity of self-contained and disconnected cultural worlds each assuming tolerantly indifferent positions toward the other. Subcultures tend to eliminate the prefix "sub-," which served as a reminder of belonging to some higher order of cultural integrity, and tend to isolate themselves, leaving no room for global or even national cultural spaces where exchange and interaction among cultures might take place. The expansion of subcultures, their transformation into distinct "cultures" of their own, and their desire to defend their specificity or integrity reduces the potential space of interaction between them and serves as a reminder of the cancerous potential of such a process in which a separate organ proliferates its cells to the degree that its connection with other organs and the functioning of the organism as a whole are destroyed.

Another outcome of this process of cultural detachment and isolation is that the only unifying thread among various cultures becomes their political and economic unity at the level of the state; it is the pragmatism of politics rather than the needs and desires of culture itself that dictates forms of unity in a culturally disintegrating world. Paradoxically, this increases the dangers of political totalitarianism precisely on the grounds of the cultural disintegration of society. People who live within their small isolated cultural worlds experience the unifying nature of humanity only in the form of alienated political power. Culturally estranged and disconnected, these groups meet only on the platform of political elections or legal regulations; thus the ground for unity becomes purely formal. Such is the outcome of extreme cultural diversification as it exists in the West and as it may also emerge in post-communist Russia, where the increasing pluralism of small cultural communities privileges the political role of a unifying central power and reduces the possibilities for intellectual dialogue. What remains national in these diversified cultures is only national government, national banks, and monopolies.

However, one can detect new possibilities borne within this impulse to emphasize cultural differences and simultaneously challenging the very category of difference as a self-justified and self-contained principle of contemporary cultural reformation. Unity of a totalitarian or canonical type evidently cannot and should not be restored; instead what is needed is a model of cultural interaction that would not unify cultures but diversify them further through their mutual interaction. What requires the utmost theoretical attention is the process of *interference* among various cultures that would increasingly complement their progressive differentiation. The term "interference" typically assumes negative connotations, alluding to the forceful interruption from the outside of an otherwise self-contained system. "To interfere" means to violate the laws of a given system, introducing the effect of a different, intervening system. However, the term "interference" also may be used in another sense, which can be productively applied to the spontaneous interaction between various kinds of cultural activity.

This effect is known to physical science and is responsible for the most beautiful, colorful patterns in the natural world, such as the butterfly's markings, or the rainbow colors of a film of oil on water, or iridescence on the surface of soap bubbles. Two or more flows or waves interact in such a way that the amplitudes of their frequency either reinforce or neutralize each other—which corresponds to "constructive" and "destructive" interference—and the result is a colorful pattern, with variable light and darker bands. According to *Webster's* (the authoritative edition of 1913), interference is "the mutual influence, under certain conditions, of two streams of light, or series of pulsations of sound, or, generally, two waves or vibrations of any kind, producing certain characteristic phenomena, as colored fringes, dark bands, or darkness, in the case of light, silence or increased intensity in sounds; neutralization or superposition of waves generally."[7]

"Interference" has the same Greek and Latin root as the word "difference" but while "differ" means to carry apart, "interfere" means to bear or bring between.[8] Within a transcultural model, spaces between diverging cultures are filled by the effects of their interference. Interference produces not unification but rather more diversification within existing diversity; differences no longer isolate cultures from each other but rather open between them perspectives of both self-differentiation and mutual involvement. Instead of isolated spots or separate points, interference produces polychromatic patterns. A transcultural vision of cultural space is three-dimensional and can be compared to holographic imaging, which is another effect of interference.[9]

Our use of the term "interference" is distinct from its application by Itamar Even-Zohar in what he calls "polysystem studies." In his article "Laws of Literary Interference," Even-Zohar defines interference as "a relation(ship) between literatures, whereby a certain literature A (a source literature) may become a source of direct or indirect loans for another literature B (a target literature)."[10] Thus, "interference" here is merely a synonym for one culture's influence on another. Although Even-Zohar recognizes that the influence can be bilateral, his understanding of interference as influence leads him to conclude that "interference is mostly unilateral" and that "interference occurs when a system is in need of items unavailable within itself."[11] For us, interference is not only a necessary, mutual, and multidirectional process, but also a wavy and fuzzy one (as the original scientific use of this term suggests) that transposes the borders of interacting cultures, mentalities, and disciplines in multiple directions. However, we do agree with Even-Zohar's proposition, in his article "System Dynamics and Interference in Culture: A Synoptic View," that "interference tends to be 'stronger' when systems are either in a state of emergence . . . or at turning points in their history."[12] The current moment is precisely a historical turning point from polarization to both pluralization and globalization that intensifies the interference among cultures on the threshold of the third millennium.

Thus this book aims to describe and intensify the processes of interference that arise from the existing differentiation of cultures. Paradoxically, the effects of interference are most strikingly manifested in the relationship between cultures that traditionally have exemplified the opposite poles of diversity—Russian and American ones. As Russian culture in the post-Soviet period assimilates models of American culture, including the value of pluralism and the role of multimedia, there is an increasing need in the opposite direction of interference. American culture may significantly benefit from the assimilation of Russian models of interaction between various cultural genres, professions, disciplines, and types of behavior.

In provoking processes of interference across existing cultural demarcations, this book also actively seeks to produce modes of creative estrangement that allow us to investigate our own culture in order to distance ourselves from it and to investigate a foreign culture in order to inscribe ourselves into it. Since transculture may be conceived both as a mode of existence or cognition on the borders of existing cultures, in their overlapping potential spaces, and a mode of cultural productivity involving the dialogue and interference between representatives of various cultural traditions, we also enact the transcultural method in the book's composition by using forms of dialogue and conceptual interference (parallel analysis of the same issue by the authors) to interrogate some central social, ethical, literary, and aesthetic issues in the contemporary humanities.

This book as a whole exists as one example of an interferential process since its two authors embody some of the same cultural differences that are described in the book: those of Russian-American, male-female, émigré-native, Jewish-Christian and Christian-Agnostic, non-Marxist and neo-Marxist—allowing for the fact that these are not necessarily stable oppositions but may represent internal differences within each author's identity. The book consists of alternations of two voices which rarely mingle in combined authorship but together produce interferential patterns. Interference results from the mutual effect of two or more waves passing simultaneously through a given region, producing reinforcement at some points and neutralization at other points; this book is precisely "a given region" in which two voices, two waves of different frequency, pass simultaneously, hopefully producing the effect of mutually reinforced judgment.

Interference between the authors' voices concerns not only the result but also the very process of their collaboration: Although our views remain distinct we provided each other with the most convincing arguments in support of one another's differing positions, indicated sources, and made editorial comments. It was a pleasure for both of us to think on behalf of the other, especially when the other's position or opinion differed most, and to assume potential positions that might be different or even opposed to our own actual position on an issue. This is an attempt at self-differentiation without losing one's own identity, an attempt that, it is hoped, will contribute to those processes of interference-through-difference that are the very subject of the chapters that follow.

Finally, the relationship among the terms that comprise the conceptual structure of this book also can be described as interferential. A variety of terms are employed that supplement each other in a chain of conceptual metaphors, such as "transculture," "transcultural imaginary," "transcultural desire," "interference," "self-differentiation," "nontotalitarian totality," "nomadism," "potentiation," "positive deconstruction," "infinition," "collective improvisation," "hyperauthorship," "reverse citation," "surplement," and "inteLnet," among others. All terms partially overlap with, but are irreducible to one another and are multiply contextualized throughout the book so that no single term prevails over others in a kind of logical hierarchy and hegemony. However no book, least of all a scholarly one, can dispense with a title, which is a hegemonic location for certain terms. Thus the term "transculture" takes this privileged position but only in the hope that it contains the internal conceptual movement that trans-cends this very hegemony.

Part I: History traces the origins of Russian culturology and the Russian transcultural method, and situates this history in relation to the historical avant-gardes, both Russian and Western, as well as in relation to some Western postmodern theories of cultural production.

Part II: Theory elaborates various aspects of transculture as a mode of critical thought and an analytic/generative practice by putting them in dialogue with a number of disciplinary perspectives and contemporary theories.

Part III: Practice presents examples of the transcultural genres that developed and continue to evolve in the Russian tradition generally, and in Mikhail Epstein's philosophy more specifically. It also speculates on the ways in which these practices might encourage—by providing a kind of training ground for—the development of a more constructive, cosmopolitan and trans-disciplinary spirit in traditional academic institutions as well as the development of new improvisational communities by transforming a divisive politics of identity into a politics of creative interference.

Notes

1. Donna J. Haraway, *Simians, Cyborgs, and Women: The Reinvention of Nature* (New York: Routledge, 1991): 192.
2. Diane Taylor, "Transculturating Transculturation," *Performing Arts Journal*, (May 1991): 91.
3. Mary Louise Pratt, *Imperial Eyes: Travel Writing and Transculturation* (New York: Routledge, 1992): 4.
4. Carolyn Martin Shaw, *Colonial Inscriptions: Race, Sex, and Class in Kenya* (Minneapolis: University of Minnesota Press, 1995): 23.
5. See additionally Chandra Mohanty et al., eds., *Third World Women and the Politics of Feminism* (Bloomington: Indiana University Press, 1991); Inderpal Grewal and Caren Kaplan, eds., *Scattered Hegemonies: Postmodernity and Transnational Feminist Practices* (Minneapolis: University of Minnesota Press, 1994); Gayatri Chakravorty Spivak, *In Other Worlds: Essays in Cultural Politics* (New York: Routledge, 1988, 1987); and Homi Bhabha, *The Location of Culture* (New York: Routledge, 1994), among others.
6. A concise introduction to the problems of transculture from a late-Soviet and post-Soviet perspective is given in Mikhail Epstein, "Culture—Culturology—Transculture," in *After the Future: The Paradoxes of Postmodernism and Contemporary Russian Culture* (Amherst: University of Massachusetts Press, 1995): 280–306.
7. In a contemporary edition, interference is defined as "the mutual effect on meeting of two wave trains of the same type so that such wave trains of light produce lines, bands, or fringes either alternatively light and dark or variously colored and such wave trains of sound produce silence, increased

intensity, or beats." *Webster's Third New International Dictionary of the English Language Unabridged* (Chicago et al.: Encyclopedia Britannica, Inc., 1986): 1178.
8. The cognates of the word "interference," derived from the Greek root "pherein" and Latin "ferre" (to bear), include "fertile," "confer," "defer," "prefer," "infer," "refer," "transfer," "offer," "suffer," and their derivatives. See Joseph T. Shipley, *Dictionary of Word Origins* (New York: Philosophical Library, Inc.: Dorset Press, 1945): 194, 343.
9. Instead of being a flat photographic image of an object, a hologram is an image of the interference pattern between two beams of light reflected off an object and its mirror image; when a hologram is illuminated, this interferential picture restores the three-dimensional quality of the original.
10. Itamar Even-Zohar, "Laws of Literary Interference," *Poetics Today: International Journal for Theory and Analysis of Literature and Communication* 11, no. 1 (Spring 1990): 54.
11. Ibid., 59.
12. Ibid., 93.

Part I

History

Chapter 1

From Culturology to Transculture
Mikhail Epstein

The Historical Context

Culturology is a specific branch of Russian humanities that found its earliest expression in the works of Nikolai Danilevsky (1822–85) and Pavel Florensky (1882–1937), culminating in the 1960s-80s with works by Mikhail Bakhtin (1895–1975), Aleksei Losev (1893–1988), Yury Lotman (1922–93), Vladimir Bibler (b. 1918), Georgy Gachev (b. 1929), and Sergei Averintsev (b. 1937). Culturology investigates the diversity of cultures and their modes of interaction and functions as a metadiscipline within the humanities, the aim of which is to encompass and link the variety of cultural phenomena studied separately by philosophy, history, sociology, literary and art criticism, etc.

The philosophy underlying culturology may be traced to the German intellectual tradition, particularly the views of Goethe, Herder, Windelband, Simmel, and Spengler on culture as an integral organism.[1] From this standpoint, culture embraces various kinds of cognitive and creative activity, including politics, economics, science, the arts, literature, philosophy, and religion. All of these fields find their roots in the primordial intuition, the "ur-phenomenon" of a given culture, which varies with specific historical and ethnic formations.

In Russia, this organicist concept of culture found its earliest expression in the work of Nikolai Danilevsky, a late-nineteenth-century Slavophilic thinker who half a century before Oswald Spengler outlined a certain number of cultural-historical types, including "European" and "Slavic." For Danilevsky, culture is the broadest concept that embraces four kinds of activities: religious, political, socio-economic, and cultural in the narrow sense (art, science, and technology).[2] Culturological topics were widely discussed in prerevolutionary Russian religious philosophy, where Nikolai Berdiaev, Dmitry Merezhkovsky, and Pavel Florensky speculated on culture as a complementary aspect of cult, that is, as a free creative response of man to God's act of creation. According to Berdiaev, "in social life, the spiritual primacy belongs to culture. The goals of society are fulfilled in culture, not in politics and economics."[3]

The concept of culture proved to be central for many important thinkers in post-Stalinist Russia as an alternative to the concept of society dominant in Marxist theory. While society is divided into classes and parties, each fighting for power and supremacy, culture has the potential to unite people and transcend social, national, and historical divisions. From a culturological standpoint, culture can be defined as a symbolic responsiveness: Any new artistic work or philosophical theory introduced into the system of culture changes the meaning of all other elements, and in this way not only does the past influence the present, but the present gives shape to the past. The model of history as a unidirectional vector, which long held sway over the Soviet mentality, was challenged by the concept of culture as a multidimensional continuum on which epochs are not successive steps in humanity's progress but coexist on equal terms and give meaning to each other.

A strong challenge to Marxism in the 1960s came also from structuralism, the methodology that must be credited with propelling the concept of culture to the forefront of the humanities. Though both structuralism and culturology consciously opposed themselves to orthodox Marxism, there are clear methodological distinctions between them. The structuralist project is predominantly scientific and attempts to introduce the standard of mathematics and natural sciences into the core of humanistic research, whereas culturology, as influenced by neo-Kantian and hermeneutic traditions, is careful to emphasize the specificity of cultural phenomena as inaccessible to rigorous analysis and calculation. According to such major representatives of culturology as Bakhtin and Averintsev, the inability of the humanities to achieve formal rigor is to their advantage rather than to their detriment. Since the very object of the humanities embraces the free will and spiritual activity that escapes mathematical or naturalistic definition, the humanities elaborate their own criteria of precision and challenge scientistic approaches to culture as a system of informational codes. Thus culturology emerged in the USSR as a kind of third force in the methodological dispute between Marxism and structuralism: Abandoning social and ideological bias in its approach to culture, culturology also attempted to overcome scientific and technological bias as another form of reductionism. The formation of culturology as a single disciplinary field occurred in the late 1960s, with the waning of the initial enthusiasm for structuralist rigor and the publication of the last works of Bakhtin and the first works of Averintsev, which were internally polemical with respect to technological rationalism. In his notes made in 1970–71, Bakhtin insisted on "[t]he study of culture (or some area of it) at the level of system and at the higher level of organic unity: open, becoming, unresolved and unpredetermined, capable of death and renewal, transcending itself, that is, exceeding its own boundaries."[4]

The advancement of culturology in the post-Stalinist period proved to be in consonance both with national traditions of universalism and with pluralistic and liberal modes of thinking. In culturology, "culture" is treated as a descriptive rather than a normative concept, the term itself being used both in the singular and in the plural. *Culture* as an integrity of disciplinary spheres presupposes the diversity of *cultures* as multiple national and historical types, each having its own formative principle, irreducible to others. While culturology is concerned with culture as a whole, it also recognizes the diversity of these "wholes" and is reluctant to discriminate among them in terms of value.

Thus the methodology of culturological research necessarily combines two procedures. First, it seeks to identify the broader underpinnings of diverse disciplines, to go beyond the specificity of any professional sphere. Mikhail Bakhtin, for example, in his meditations on the tasks of literary scholarship, insists that "[l]iterature is an inseparable part of culture and it cannot be understood outside the total context of the entire culture of a given epoch. . . . [N]arrow specification is alien to the best traditions of our scholarship. . . . In our enthusiasm for specification we have ignored questions of the interconnection and interdependence of various areas of culture . . . and we have not taken into account that the most intense and productive life of culture takes place on the boundaries of its individual areas and not in places where these areas have become enclosed in their own specificity."[5]

The second procedure presupposes a definition of cultural phenomena in terms of their historical and national specificity. If, within a given culture, various disciplinary and professional spheres are linked by a common intuition, then the uniqueness of this intuition serves to distinguish one culture from another on a global scale. This aspect of culturology was most thoroughly developed by Aleksei Losev in his extensive investigations of classical aesthetics, demonstrating that antiquity as a cultural phenomenon preserves its individuality on all levels of interpretation. Analyzing the most abstract theories of the dialectics of sameness and difference in Plato and the neo-Platonic school, Losev shows that behind these abstractions, and "penetrating all antiquity . . . , lies a powerful and inescapable intuition of a *universal organism,* or the intuition of all reality as a living organism."[6] For Losev, the principal goal of culturological research is to perceive the uniqueness of a given phenomenon as an "expressive faceness of being" (*vyrazitel'nyi lik bytiia*). "In exploring any fact from the culture of classical antiquity, I did not rest until I found in it a quality that sharply distinguished it from everything that is not classical. . . . 'Style' and 'worldview' must be integrated by any means; they must necessarily reflect each other."[7]

These two aspects of culturology, "diversity" and "integrity," are inseparable, but certainly their respective significance may vary within the works of a given thinker. Russian culturology, as it formed in the 1960s, found great living proponents for each aspect of the discipline in Bakhtin and Losev, both of whom had already laid the groundwork for this methodology in their earlier works of the 1920s. While Bakhtin stresses the dialogic nature of a specific culture in its internal and external differentiations, Losev is more inclined to theorize cultural identity as a multifaceted manifestation of one basic, primordial intuition.[8]

Culturology and Cultural Studies

The best way to introduce Russian culturology to an American audience is to juxtapose it point by point with what is known in the English-speaking world as "cultural studies."[9] We will take as a point of reference *Introducing Cultural Studies,* Ziauddin Sardar and Borin Van Loon's lucid summary of characteristic trends in the field. Five definitions that apply to cultural studies also reveal its parallels and contrasts with culturology.

1. "Cultural studies aims to examine its subject matter in terms of *cultural practices* and their *relation to power.* Its constant goal is to expose power relationships and examine how these relationships influence and shape cultural practices."[10]

* * *

Culturology aims to examine culture as the locus of all existing and possible practices that, taken as a whole, liberate humans from their natural conditions and physical dependencies, including the dependency of the weak on the strong, that is, the relation of power. Culture is everything created by humans and, in its turn, everything that creates humans in their distinction from and irreducibility to organic nature. By introducing a symbolic dimension to power relationships, culture mediates them through the liberating practices of signification, estrangement, deferral, and erasure of biological (racial, sexual) origins. Cultural practices cannot be reduced to power relationships as such and should not be seen as solely shaped and determined by them: Such reductionism is easily compatible with an oppressive and totalitarian politics of culture as an instrument of power.

2. "Cultural studies is not simply the study of culture as though it was a discrete entity divorced from its social or political context. Its objective is to understand culture in all its complex forms and to analyze the *social and political context* within which it manifests itself."

Culture exists in a social and political context but this context itself is only a partial aspect of culture and should not dominate the whole. Works of art and philosophy, spiritual practices and rituals, moral values, personal relationships, everyday practices of symbolic exchange and communication—all these multiple dimensions of culture prevent humans from being reduced to political animals. The task of culturology is to expose culture as an open totality surpassing and transcending any of its single constituents, including the political one. Culturology is the self-awareness of culture; its mission is not to govern culture through the institutions of power, as politics does, but to be its self-governing consciousness.

3. "Culture in cultural studies always performs two functions: it is both the *object* of study and the *location* of political criticism and action. Cultural studies aims to be both an intellectual and a pragmatic enterprise."

Culturology shares these two functions with cultural studies, but it presents culture not as the location of political criticism and action but rather as permanent dislocation of political practices through the further contextualization of their symbolic contexts. It is not only that a religious practice or an aesthetic device may be decoded to reveal an encrypted political message—alternative ways of deciphering political phenomena as encryptions of mythological or aesthetic codes would be equally relevant. Even narrow party activities may be seen through culturological prisms as refractions or paraphrases of ritualistic codes, language games, literary narratives, or psychological archetypes. Culturology does not allow any single code or discipline to be privileged over the others and to serve as the ultimate vocabulary or universal basis of interpretation. Culturology is not a "pragmatic enterprise" along with other modes of cultural activities; it is rather a "metapragmatic" consciousness that is critical of narrow pragmatism, isolationist and/or hegemonic claims of any specific practice and discourse.

4. "Cultural studies attempts to *expose and reconcile the division of knowledge,* to overcome the split between tacit (that is, intuitive knowledge based on local cultures) and objective (so-called universal) forms of knowledge. It assumes a common identity and common interest between the knower and the known, between the observer and what is being observed."

In its attempt to overcome the division of knowledge and extremes of specialization, culturology most closely cooperates with cultural studies. Culturology attempts to approach culture on its own terms and to develop a holistic language that avoids lapsing into politicism, scientism, aestheticism, moralism, or the absolutization of any single aspect of culture. This is why culturology departs also from the political accentuation of culture, which is predominant in cultural studies. If all other specialists work inside their own disciplines or realms of culture, unconsciously abiding by their rules and taboos, a culturologist makes his own culture the object of *definition* and thereby surpasses its confines, its *finiteness.*

5. "Cultural studies is committed to a *moral evaluation* of modern society and to a *radical line* of political action. The tradition of cultural studies is not one of value-free scholarship but one committed to social reconstruction by critical political involvement. Thus cultural studies aims to *understand* and *change* the structures of dominance everywhere, but in industrial capitalist societies in particular."

Russian culturology emerged in a socialist, totally politicized, and morally indoctrinated society and sought the most radical alternatives to the existing system not in political engagement or moralistic lamentations that would have conformed to the prevailing ideological codes, but rather in transgression of any established codes, including political and moral codes (such as "collectivism," "materialism," "the political hegemony of the working class," and "the moral supremacy of physical labor"). Culture was viewed not as an instrument of politics (to which it was actually reduced under socialism) but as the horizon of liberation from the limits of one cultural realm by reaching out to other realms. For culturology, science presented an escape from politics; art, an escape from science; religion, an escape from art; philosophy, an escape from religion; and finally, culture, an escape from all of them, the capacity of humans to release themselves from all physical and symbolic prisons.

Both cultural studies and culturology pursue goals beyond pure value-free scholarship. Since cultural studies is focused on politically invested forms of culture, or even culturally disguised forms of power, the aim of this discipline is primarily critical and deconstructive. This is generally characteristic of the postmodern Western humanities, in which deconstruction became the primary methodology of cultural research. Culturology, on the contrary, is focused on the constructive potentials of culture and aims to broaden and multiply the meanings of every cultural symbol beyond its literal and pragmatic meaning. Deconstruction, at least in its conventional form of academic poststructuralism, is mostly understood as "the undoing, decomposing, and desedimenting of structures," though, according to Jacques Derrida's own intention, it "was not a negative operation. Rather than destroying, it was also necessary to understand how an 'ensemble' was constituted and to reconstruct it to this end. However, the negative appearance was and remains much more difficult to efface.... That is why this word, at least on its own, has never appeared satisfactory to me."[11] Culturology is the art of explicitly *positive* deconstruction, which opens alternatives and free spaces within and beyond certain cultural practices.[12]

Culturology addresses the practices and institutions of power no less critically than cultural studies does, which is evidenced by the former's liberational message and explosive role in the networks of Soviet official culture. But culturology is not a form of political dissidentism. It does not criticize one cultural politics on behalf of another, more advanced and progressive politics. Rather it criticizes politics, as a type of discourse, as a relation of power, as a narrow pragmatism, from the standpoint of culture as a whole. Culturology is not about opposition, but about transcendence: How to transcend a given practice or theory using the symbolic capacities of culture, its infinitely rich, multileveled encodings and decodings of every human phenomenon.

Cultural studies and culturology developed almost simultaneously as the extensions of their respective cultures' distinct theoretical needs and priorities. The name "cultural studies" comes from the Center for Contemporary Cultural Studies at the University of Birmingham, established in 1964. In 1972, the Center published the first issue of *Working Papers in Cultural Studies* with the specific aim "to put cultural studies on the intellectual map."

It is more difficult to date the emergence of Russian culturology. It integrated Yury Lotman and his school's works on cultural semiotics (mid-1960s), the methodological notes of Mikhail Bakhtin (1960s–1970s), the research program of Vladimir Bibler and his scientific seminar "Arche" (from 1967), and the first publications of Georgy Gachev and Sergei Averintsev (mid- and late-1960s).

The founders of cultural studies—Richard Hoggart, Raymond Williams, Stuart Hall—were working-class intellectuals inspired by Old Left and New Left ideals and heavily influenced by Marxism. By the early 1970s, Marxism had lost almost all political battles in the West and was receding into the more quiet cultural realm attempting to transform it into a new political arena. Cultural studies emerged and continued, in essence, as political studies of culture and experiments in its social transformation. Culture appeared to present a more open and accessible area for socialist experiments than economics or practical politics.

In Russia, the situation was quite the opposite: For many years the official culture had been utterly politicized and reduced to ideological and propagandistic functions. Soviet Marxism was in a position to impose on culture as a "secondary superstructure" all the power of economic and social determinations. The principal goal of Russian culturology was to depoliticize culture, to rescue it from the narrow pragmatic context where it served as an instrument of power. Culture was explored as the ultimate resource of human freedom and creativity that transcends social limits and historical determinations.

Which of these two branches of "cultural science" presents more potentials for the future? At first sight, the collapse of Soviet Marxism has eliminated the totalitarian context in which Russian culturology emerged. But is not the very collapse of totalitarianism an argument in favor of the culturological approach to culture as the metasystem that survives and transgresses all political contexts, even so powerful a one as that which dominated the Soviet Union for 70 years? The culturological approach to culture as a nonsurpassable and all-surpassing totality successfully challenged Marxist-Leninist and other politicist, or moralist, or scientist approaches that attempted to reduce culture to one of its constituents. That is why culturology has become one of the main branches of humanistic scholarship in post-Soviet Russia, in fact, the leader in the methodology of research and teaching. In many universities, departments of culturology have replaced those departments of "scientific communism" and "Marxism-Leninism" that were previously responsible for the political supervision and utilization of all other disciplines.

Culturology and Transculture[13]

Though culturology is a scholarly discipline, it contains some possibilities that lead beyond the realm of scholarship, into certain practices that we call "transcultural." To use Bakhtin's words, culturology approaches culture as an "organic unity" that is capable of "transcending itself, that is, exceeding its own boundaries."[14] Culturology takes a distanced view of culture that propels culture's own self-distancing, a disruption of its self-identity. Culturology "estranges" and "defamiliarizes" culture, in the same sense in which the major Russian theoretician Viktor Shklovsky defined "estrangement" as the main technique of art. According to Shklovsky, our daily habits and perceptions tend to retreat into the area of the unconsciously automatic, as if they were natural, inevitable, and predetermined. "Habitualization devours works, clothes, furniture, one's wife, and the fear of war. . . . And art exists that one may recover the sensation of life; it exists to make one feel things, to make the stone *stony.* . . . The technique of art is to make objects 'unfamiliar,' to make forms difficult, to increase the difficulty and length of perception because the process of perception is an aesthetic end in itself and must be prolonged. *Art is a way of experiencing the artfulness of an object* . . ."[15]

In the same way, culturology is a way of experiencing the culturality of culture. If art, as a part of culture, deautomatizes our perception of objects, then culturology deautomatizes our perception of art and culture themselves, exposes their artificial constructs and contingencies and thus allows us to transcend their automatism. Culturology distances and "alienates" us from the culture to which we belong by birth and education, and thus prepares us for free cultural creativity. In this transcending capacity, culturology becomes a critique not only of specific branches and disciplines within a particular culture, but of any given culture as a whole. At this point culturology grows into transcultural theory and practice. Transculture is a way to transcend our "given" culture and to apply culture's transformative forces to culture itself. Transculture is the second order of "culturality" of culture, its capacity for self-cultivation and self-transcendence. If culturology is the self-awareness of culture, then transculture is the self-transformation of culture, the totality of theories and practices that liberate culture from its own repressive mechanisms.

This movement of transcendence starts within culture itself, as it liberates humans from natural dependencies through the system of symbolical mediations and replacements. Such cultural categories as "taste," "love," "word" constitute the realm of human freedom from the pressures of physical hunger and lust, from the physical presence of an object, etc. Simultaneously, cultural activity creates its own system of dependencies that are peculiar to a given culture, its ethnic, racial, social, or sexual determinants. In transposing their inborn qualities into a cultural dimension, humans still reproduce many of their physical conditions and identities on this symbolic plane. That is why many cultural activities, including literature, cinema, theory, and writing in general, are still designated by natural labels, such as white and black, male and female. Even ethnic labels—Russian, German, French—still connect culture with physical conditions, geographic regions, climates, landscapes, etc. Every culture has its own idiosyncrasies, manias, phobias, ideological assumptions and restrictions, modes of indoctrination, informational filters, etc.

By transcending the limits of these "natural," or "first order" cultures, the transcultural dimension opens the next level of human liberation, now from those symbolic dependencies, ideological addictions, patriotic infatuations that belong to us as members of a certain cultural group. To use Bakhtin's words, culture is capable of "transcending itself, that is, exceeding its own boundaries,"[16]—and therefore contains possibilities for transculture. Transculture can be defined as an open system of symbolic alternatives to existing cultures and their established sign systems.

This does not mean that all our cultural identities are to be forsaken for the sake of transcultural liberation. We cannot and should not get rid of our primary symbolic identities, which are relevant to some levels of behavior. The transition of humans from a natural to a cultural condition did not deprive them of their physical bodies; on the contrary, their bodies acquired new expressiveness and vigor through the cultivation of physical abilities and the exercise of symbolic activities, such as speaking, dancing, drawing, writing, training in various arts and trades, and sports. In the same way, transcultural activity does not deprive us of our symbolic bodies, our constitutive identities as Russians and Americans, males and females, biologists and novelists, chess players and soccer players. Transcultural practice is not a diminishment of or confrontation with our cultural selves but rather a way of expanding the limits of our ethnic, professional, linguistic, and other identities to new levels of indeterminacy and "virtuality." Transculture builds new identities in the zone of fuzziness and interference and challenges the metaphysics of discreteness so characteristic of nations, races, professions, and other established cultural configurations that are solidified rather than dispersed by the multiculturalist "politics of identity."

Although it is a theoretical extension of culturology, the transcultural model is not just a field of knowledge but also a mode of being, located at the crossroads of cultures. This transcultural dimension grows out of the potentialities of the global cultural network, seen as the next historical stage in humanity's liberation from deterministic mechanisms of both natural and cultural environments. The essential element and merit of culture is its capacity to free humans from the dictates of nature, its physical restrictions and necessities; but it is the capacity of transculture to free humans from the determinations of culture itself. Culture, by releasing us from physical limitations, imposes new limitations, of symbolic order, and transculture is the next step in the ongoing human quest for freedom, in this case liberation from the "prison house of language" and the variety of artificial, self-imposed, and self-deified cultural identities. In contrast to the European followers of Rousseau and the American proponents of a counterculture, what transculture suggests is not the escape from culture back to nature, to a primitive, precultural condition, but rather a progression beyond culture, into the postcultural condition that is technologically shaped by contemporary global communications.

Although transculture depends on the efforts of separate individuals to overcome their identification with specific cultures, on another level it is a process of interaction between cultures themselves in which more and more individuals find themselves "outside" of any particular culture, "outside" of its national, racial, sexual, ideological, and other limitations. I would compare this condition with Bakhtin's idea of *vnenakhodimost,* which means being located beyond any particular mode of existence, or, in this case, finding one's place on the border of existing cultures. This realm *beyond* all cultures is located *inside* transculture.

One of the prevailing arguments of contemporary cultural studies is that we are bound to the conditions and conventions of our cultures; we cannot transcend the contingencies of our sign systems. But even if we cannot rid ourselves of our "symbolic" body, we can integrate it into a more capacious transcultural dimension. Similarly, as we know, the creation of tools, signs, and values did not release humans from their physical bodies and natural instincts but added a new, "transnatural," specifically cultural dimension to their existence. Now that the boundaries of "native cultures" have become too narrow for humans, we are developing other new dimensions that we call here transcultural.

Notes

1. The term "culturology" (German "Kulturologie") was proposed, perhaps for the first time, by the distinguished German chemist and Nobel prize winner Wilhelm Ostwald in 1915 in his address "The System of the Sciences." For a brief history of the term, see Leslie A. White, *The Science of Culture: A Study of Man and Civilization* (New York: Farrar, Straus and Cudahy, 1949): 410–412.
2. N. Ia. Danilevskii. *Rossiia i Evropa* (1869) (Moscow: Kniga, 1991): 471–472.
3. Nikolai Berdiaev. "Filosofiia neravenstva," in his book *Sobranie sochinenii*, in 4 volumes (Paris: YMCA-Press, 1990 vol. 4): 556.
4. Mikhail Bakhtin. *Speech Genres and Other Late Essays,* ed. Caryl Emerson and Michael Holquist (Austin: University of Texas Press, 1986): 135.
5. Ibid., 2.
6. A. F. Losev. *Istoriia antichnoi estetiki. Poslednie veka.* Book 2 (Moscow: Iskusstvo, 1988): 379.
7. A. F. Losev. *Ocherki antichnogo simvolizma i mifologii*, vol. 1 (Moscow: Izdanie avtora, 1930): 690, 693.
8. To intimate the scope and diversity of Russian culturology, I am supplying a selective bibliography at the end of this chapter.
9. In the late 1940s, the outstanding American anthropologist Leslie A. White attempted to introduce the term and concept of "culturology" into Anglo-American scholarship. Characteristically, he viewed culturology as a discipline with a larger field and intellectual capacity than sociology because "culture" itself is a broader concept than that of "society": ". . . Instead of dealing with cultural determinants upon their own level, i.e., culturologically, sociology brought them down to the socio-psychological level . . . The attempts of sociologists to explain culture in terms of 'social process' or 'interaction' failed as of course it must" (Leslie A. White. *The Science of Culture: A Study of Man and Civilization*. New York: Farrar, Straus and Cudahy, 1949: 80, 81). At that time, H. L. Mencken, the distinguished authority on the American language, found "culturology" "a rather clumsy word, but nevertheless logical" (Ibid., 410). However, the term failed to achieve recognition in Anglo-American scholarship, obviously, for a deeper reason than mere "clumsiness." The concept of culturology, as it was elaborated by Leslie A. White and, independently, by Russian scholars, presupposes that culture is a comprehensive structure, "the extra-somatic continuum of symbol-borne events" (Leslie White) that is irreducible to social interactions and political contexts. "The explanation of culture is and must be culturological . . . 'Cul-

turology' specifies a sector of reality and defines a science. In so doing it trespasses upon the prior claims of psychology and sociology. It does more than trespass, of course; it expropriates as well. That is, it makes it clear that the solution of certain scientific problems does not properly lie within the provinces of psychology and sociology as previously supposed, but belongs to—i.e., can be solved only by—a science of culture . . . 'Sociology' . . . assimilates culture to its basic concept of interaction, making culture an aspect, or a by-product, of the social process of interaction whereas the structures and processes of human society are functions of culture" (Ibid., 393, 412, 414). In culturology, culture comprises the method, not only the object of research. The approach that dominated Anglo-American scholarship under the name of "cultural studies," on the contrary, gives priority to socio-political perspectives on culture. Thus the difference between "culturology" and "cultural studies" is methodological, not only terminological.
10. Ziauddin Sardar and Borin Van Loon, *Introducing Cultural Studies*, ed. Richard Appignanesi (New York: Totem Books, 1998): 9. The next four definitions are cited from the same page.
11. "Letter to a Japanese Friend" (1983), in *A Derrida Reader: Between the Blinds*, ed. Peggy Kamuf (New York: Columbia University Press, 1991): 272.
12. See more on the methodology of potentiation as "positive deconstruction" in the chapter "The Permanence of Newness . . ."
13. The relationship between culturology and transculture is explored more extensively in the chapter "Culture—Culturology—Transculture," in Mikhail Epstein, *After the Future: The Paradoxes of Postmodernism and Contemporary Russian Culture* (Amherst: University of Massachusetts Press, 1995): 280–306.
14. Mikhail Bakhtin. *Speech Genres and Other Late Essays,* ed. Caryl Emerson and Michael Holquist (Austin: University of Texas Press, 1986): 135.
15. Viktor Shklovsky. "Art as Technique," in *Contemporary Literary Criticism. Modernism Through Poststructuralism*. Edited and with Introductions by Robert Con Davis (New York and London: Longman, 1986): 55.
16. Mikhail Bakhtin. *Speech Genres and Other Late Essays*, ed. Caryl Emerson and Michael Holquist (Austin: University of Texas Press, 1986): 135.

Appendix

(compiled by Mikhail Epstein)

This very selective bibliography is organized according to my division of the discipline into nine major directions and thematic categories.

General

Filosofiia i kul'tura: ukazatel literatury, izdannoi v SSSR na russkom iazyke v 1974–1981 gg. (Moscow: INION, 1983).

Gurevich, Pavel. *Filosofiia kul'tury: uchebnoe posobie dlia studentov gumanitarnykh vuzov.* 2-e izd., dop. (Moscow: Aspekt Press, 1995).

Kagan, Moisei S. *Filosofiia kul'tury* (St. Petersburg: Petropolis, 1996).

Kul'turologiia: kratkii slovar. 2 izd. (St. Petersburg: Petropolis, 1995).

Kul'turologiia kak ona est' i kak ei byt'. Mezhdunarodnye chteniia po teorii, istorii i filosofii kul'tury, vypusk 5 (St. Petersburg: FKITs "Eidos", 1998).

Markarian, E. S. *O genezise chelovecheskoi deiatelnosti i kul'tury* (Erevan: Izd-vo AN ArmSSR, 1973).

Rabinovich, Vadim L., ed. *Krasnaia kniga kul'tury?* (Moscow: Iskusstvo, 1989).

Rozhdestvenskii Yu. V. *Vvedenie v kul'turovedenie. Uchebnoe posobie* (Moscow: CheRo, 1996).

Rozin, V. M. *Vvedenie v kulturologiiu* (Moscow: Mezhdunarodnaia pedagogicheskaia akademiia, 1994).

Skvortsov, L., and S. Levit, eds. *Kulturologiia XX vek: antologiia* (Moscow: INION, 1994).

Sokolov E. G. *Lektsii po kul'turologii. Chast' 1. Kul'tura. Formy kul'tury* (St. Petersburg: SPbGTU, Laboratoriia metafizicheskikh issledovanii, 1997).

Sokolov, E. V. *Kul'tura i lichnost'* (Leningrad: Nauka, Leningradskoe otdelenie, 1972).

Sokolov E. V. *Kul'turologiia. Ocherki teorii kul'tury. Posobie dlia starsheklassnikov* (Moscow: Interpraksis, 1994).

Marxist Approaches

Arnoldov, Arnold, ed. *Marksistsko-leninskaia teoriia kul'tury.* (Moscow: Politizdat, 1984).

Ilyenkov, Evald. *Filosofiia i kul'tura* (Moscow : Politizdat, 1991).

Lifshits, Mikhail. *Karl Marx. Iskusstvo i obshchestvennyi ideal* (Moscow: Khudozhestvennaia literatura, 1972).

Semiotic and Structural Approaches

Lotman, Yury M. *Kul'tura i vzryv* (Moscow: Gnozis, 1992).

Lotman, Yury M. *Universe of the Mind: A Semiotic Theory of Culture,* Trans. Ann Shukhman (Bloomington and Indianapolis: Indiana University Press, 1990).

Lucid, Daniel P., ed. *Soviet Semiotics: An Anthology*. (Baltimore & London: The Johns Hopkins University Press, 1988).

Dialogic Approaches

Arkhe. Kul'turno-logicheskii ezhegodnik, vypusk 1 (Kemerovo: Alef, 1993).
Bakhtin, Mikhail. *Speech Genres and Other Late Essays*. Trans. Vern W. McGee. Ed. Caryl Emerson and Michael Holquist. (Austin: University of Texas Press, 1986).
Bibler, Vladimir. *Mikhail Mikhailovich Bakhtin, ili poetika kul'tury*. (Moscow: Progress, 1991).
Bibler, Vladimir. *Ot naukoucheniia k logike kultury: dva filosofskikh vvedeniia v dvadtsat pervyi vek*. (Moscow: Politizdat, 1991).

Historicist Approaches

Batkin, Leonid M. *Ital'ianskoe vozrozhdenie v poiskakh individualnosti* (Moscow: "Nauka", 1989).
Batkin, Leonid. *Pristrastiia: izbrannye esse i stat'i o kulture* (Moscow: Oktiabr', 1994).
Gurevich, Aron Iakovlevich. *Categories of Medieval Culture* (London and Boston: Routledge & Kegan Paul, 1985).
Gurevich, Aron Iakovlevich. *The Origins of European Individualism* (Oxford: Cambridge, MA.: Blackwell, 1995).
Konrad N. I. *Zapad i Vostok. Stat'i* (Moscow: Glavnaia redaktsiia vostochnoi literatury, 1972).

Theological Approaches

Averintsev, Sergei. *Poetika rannevizantiiskoi literatury* (Moscow: Nauka, Glavnaia redaktsiia vostochnoi literatury, 1977).
Averintsev, Sergei. *Religiia i literatura* (Ann Arbor: Hermitage, 1981).
Men', Alexander. *Kul'tura i dukhovnoe voskhozhdenie* (Moscow: Iskusstvo, 1992).

Ethnological Approaches

Gachev, Georgii. *Natsional'nye obrazy mira* (Moscow: Sovetskii pisatel', 1988).

Gachev, Georgii. *Natsional'nye obrazy mira. Amerika v sravnenii s Rossiei i slavianstvom* (Moscow: Raritet, 1997).
Gumilev, Lev N. *Ethnogenesis and the Biosphere* (Moscow: Progress Publishers, 1990).
Gumilev, Lev N. *Etnosfera. Istoriia liudei i istoriia prirody* (Moscow: Ekopros, 1993).

Ecological Approaches

Genisaretskii, O. I., (ed.) *Ekologiia kul'tury* (Moscow: Nauchno-issledovatel'skii institut kul'tury, 1991).
Girionok, F. I. *Ekologiia, tsivilizatsiia, noosphera* (Moscow: Nauka, 1987).
Likhachev, D. S. "Ekologiia kul'tury" (1979), in his book *Proshloe—budushchemu. Stat'i i ocherki* (Leningrad: Nauka, 1985).

Poststructuralist Approaches

Berry, Ellen, and Anesa Miller-Pogacar, eds. *Re-entering the Sign: Articulating New Russian Culture* (Ann Arbor: University of Michigan Press, 1995).
Boym, Svetlana. *Common Places: Mythologies of Everyday Life in Russia* (Cambridge: Harvard University Press, 1994).
Epstein, Mikhail N. *After the Future: The Paradoxes of Postmodernism and Contemporary Russian Culture,* trans. and intro. Anesa Miller-Pogacar (Amherst: University of Massachusetts Press, 1995).
Epstein, Mikhail, Alexander Genis, Slobodanka Vladiv-Glover. *Russian Postmodernism: New Perspectives on Post-Soviet Culture* (New York and Oxford: Berghahn Books, 1999).
Miller-Pogacar, Anesa. *Transculture and Culturology: Post-Structuralist Theory in Late and Post-Soviet Russia* (Ph. D. Thesis, University of Kansas, 1993).

Chapter 2

Collective Improvisation And Transcultural Consciousness

Mikhail Epstein

Transcultural activity, as it emerged in Moscow in the early 1980s, was part of neither official Soviet nor oppositional dissident, nor underground avant-gardist cultures. The very meaning of "transculturalism" implies transcending differences among various cultures and bridging them across their borders. The transcultural project, as developed in the years 1982–90, before and during perestroika, played on those radical differences between official and nonofficial cultures that were later effaced by Gorbachev and Yeltsin's reforms, in the process of the de-ideologization and de-communization of Russian society.

Creativity and Communication

One aspect of transcultural practice is exemplified in "collective improvisation," a heuristic model that the author and some of his colleagues practiced in Russia. I will rely on my own memory and records in recounting the history of this transcultural project, which started as a creative enterprise among several friends. During the 1970s and 1980s I was fortunate to have among my friends representatives of various intellectual and creative fields: an artist, a sociologist, a physicist, a mathematician, a poet, and a philologist. We used to meet at each other's birthday parties and other similar celebrations. At that time, such gatherings were the strongest intellectual need of the late Soviet intelligentsia, increasingly alienated from society and the institutionalized cultural establishment. However, I had to admit to myself that socializing within our circle was not as intellectually rewarding and gratifying as our individual communications, which concentrated around the really important creative aspects of each others' work. While sitting at the festive table, we exchanged jokes, discussed general political issues, tried to witticize about commonplaces and expose our ironic attitude toward the trivialities of Soviet life. This was a kind of collective psychotherapy, but I suspect that each of us was slightly disappointed by the redundancy of conversation when there was not much to say.

I was puzzled by this paradox: The same people who were brilliant in their individual creativity and in private talks, proved to be much less colorful when gathering to converse. I imagined that by inviting artist A, writer B, critic C, and physicist D, and introducing them to one another, I would witness a feast of the gods as they appeared to be in their studios, laboratories, and journals. Instead they turned out to be rather common people when coming together, and the only mark of their individual distinction was that they felt uneasy about this mediocrity enforced by conventional forms of socializing. The simple rule of multiplication—four talented people and thus sixteen possible ways of inspired communication—did not work in this case. Instead what we observed was a process of division and diminishment, such that in the presence of four gifted people each of them became one-fourth (or even less) of himself.

The problem we encountered was that of the ambivalent relationship between *creativity* and *communication,* between the "vertical" and "horizontal" axes of human symbolical activity. Creativity is built on the uniqueness of each person, while communication usually involves those qualities that are common to people, and, therefore, the highest success in society often belongs to the most common of the people who succeed in being more spontaneously and ingeniously common than others. How could we tackle this problem? Was there any way to bring together the values of creativity and communication so that the presence of other people would not paralyze each person's inventive capacities but rather mobilize and stimulate them to new modes of creativity? Was there any way to engage the unique gifts of each individual in the process of communication so that their originality would not be dulled and discouraged?

First Collective Improvisations: Trialogues

In attempting to answer this set of questions, the idea of collective improvisations was born. In May 1982 we began to meet, at first three of us, the artist Ilya Kabakov, the sociologist Iosif Bakshtein, and I, for sessions of creative communication, and this moment could be identified as the inception of the Russian transcultural movement. Our first improvisation, though it may seem to be a simple coincidence, was devoted to a transcultural problem: the existence of poets of Jewish origin, such as Pasternak, Mandel'shtam, and Brodsky, within the Russian language and Russian culture, and the new creative possibilities generated by this transgression of ethnic boundaries. What was important about this first improvisation, however, was not its topic—more or less arbitrary—but this new structure of communication that could assimilate our professional and personal differences and even sharpen them through concentration on a common problem.

Perhaps the most magical instrument of this type of communication was *writing,* which allowed us to incorporate the possibility of thoughtful and articulate self-expression into the framework of dialogue or, more precisely, "trialogue," as we later called our regular sessions. The alternation of oral and written communication is related to the dialectic of selfness and otherness, which is undermined both in the seclusion of the study and in light party talk. After our essays were finished and we read them aloud, we agreed to write commentaries on one another's texts, and this was a new round of creativity turning into the next round of communication. Now our thoughts about Jewishness in Russian literature became intermingled and inseparable so that Kabakov's text could be fully appreciated and understood only in its overlapping with Bakshtein's commentaries and vice versa.

Transculture as I saw it at this stage was the experience of transcendence, in a specifically cultural rather than psychological, metaphysical, or religious sense. It was transcendence of professional, educational, and occupational boundaries in order to produce an interpersonal cultural work in the form of collaborative textual unities.

The Origins of the Club of Essayists

After we had conducted nine improvisational sessions devoted to such diverse topics as "the role of garbage in civilization," "hysterics as a feature of national character," "why Russians are so strong in hockey," and "the potential of the epic form in contemporary literature," a new opportunity emerged. At the end of 1982 the Moscow city authorities permitted the organization of a Cultural Center of Youth Leisure. Here we could test new modes of communication still absent in "adult culture," which was strictly specialized and divided into the so-called creative unions: one of writers, another of musicians, a third of artists, and so on.

I was invited to this center to do "something," and the first and actually the last thing that proved to be a success was the broadly publicized all-Moscow essay competition. The essay is a microcosm of cultural diversity, combining as it does philosophical generalization, artistic imagination, and historical or biographical authenticity.[1] Since our improvisations spontaneously acquired the form of the essay it was reasonable to expect that through public competition the circle of collective improvisations could be broadened and involve new participants. To put it briefly, improvisation is the communicative aspect of essay writing raised to the nth degree where n is determined by the number of participants. Improvisation is the social extension of essayism, which, starting in individual creativity, grows into a model of new community shaped across cultural boundaries.[2]

Invitations to the essay competition were distributed around the city; they hung in Moscow's most prestigious cultural institutions. About twenty-five people responded to this invitation, and as a result our second improvisational community arose, absorbing the winners of the essay competition. As distinct from the first trio, this one included a greater variety of professions and, especially important, individuals who had never met each other before.

The Transcultural Project

At that period, early 1983, I started to think more generally about the experimental possibilities of contemporary culture. It occurred to me that Soviet culture, not in spite of, but *due to* its collectivist and totalitarian nature, possessed some creative potentials that had never been realized before. The emergence of sots art and conceptualism, the postmodern trends in art and poetry of the 1970s and 1980s, clearly indicated the possibility of a "post-Soviet" mentality that challenged both official (apologetic, pro-Soviet) and dissident (oppositional, anti-Soviet) models of cultural activity. Though I enjoyed the textual eccentricities of Dmitry Prigov and especially the metaphysically provocative and shockingly "superficial" art of Ilya Kabakov at that time, I was not quite satisfied with the parodic and ironic bias that dominated conceptualism at that time as a "parrot" of Soviet ideology and "split mirror" of mass consciousness. I wanted to approach Soviet culture on its own terms, objectively and theoretically, and to disclose some potentials for its organic transformation in the future, not as a consequence of some social upheaval or political disruption, but as a matter of internal "creative erosion." This is how I came to formulate some vague ideas concerning transculture as reflected in my notes and letters of that period.

Diary Entries (May-June 1983)

Is politics a part of culture or culture a part of politics? And if they embrace each other, whose embrace is stronger, and which will force the other to relinquish its hold?

The multiplicity of cultural layers within Russia is the prototype of future global culture. We have a Buddhist people, a Christian religion, and an Islamic power.[3] We must understand how various elements of our culture—Western European, Judaic, Buddhist, Orthodox, Catholic, Chinese, Muslim—can be integrated in such a way that they might produce a creative synthesis, not an explosive mixture.

What to call it, "metaculture" or "transculture"? "Meta-" means beyond, "trans-" means across. They are related as goal and path, as target and arrow. Soviet culture is the point of departure, transculture is the path, metaculture is the culture of the beyond. Here-culture, where-culture, and there-culture.

It is necessary to treat Soviet culture even more seriously and solemnly than it treats itself. We should eliminate this intimacy and familiarity that contemporaries still feel towards their immediate surrounding, as if it were still alive. No, Soviet culture has deserved the solemnity of the burial ritual. This culture will die indeed when we start to do honor and render homage to it, as if it were dead.

Soviet culture should be understood as a rare and precious fossil, as a layer among archeological excavations of ancient millennial cultures—Egyptian, Chinese, Persian, Peruvian, and so on. It is unique as it has buried itself alive; it has died not from old age but from a lack of vitality. We should avoid any sarcastic denunciation or caustic humor towards this culture; it would be as inappropriate as sarcasm toward the Cheops pyramid or a mummy of the pharaoh. Let us at least pretend to have preserved some pious reverence towards the majestic remnants, and then they will turn out to be truly majestic.

Letter on Transculture (June 30, 1983)[4]

In the last half a year, beginning in January 1983, the contours of a new cultural movement, which I would call "transculture," are becoming clear. It is radically different from the counterculture, as the latter was produced in the West in the 1960s. I would also call transculture "reactive" (if not "reactionary"), emphasizing its distinction from the "revolutionary" counterculture. Marx called revolution "the locomotive of history" but it is clear that this mode of transportation has become obsolete long ago. Transculture uses rather the principle of a rocket that is driven through the air by its reaction to the rearward expulsion of gases: the transport of the late 20th century.

Transculture does not and cannot stand in revolutionary opposition to, let us say, monolithic, monocentric culture; it does not confront but oversteps, goes through, transcends the existing culture, cultivates its gaps and voids. Like the mirror-shield of Perseus, it reflects the dominant Medusian culture in a dual way: by reflecting and deflecting it simultaneously. Monoculture (dominant culture), when it recognizes itself in a mirror, loses its strength, freezes in awe, as if bewitched by its dead reflection. Perseus understood that he could not defeat Medusa with a "revolutionary" sword and instead resorted to a "reactionary" mirror. It is only Medusa's own reflection that can deaden Medusa. No external adversary can defeat this superpower, like no Hercules can defeat Medusa: It has to be turned to self-contemplation and be horrified by itself. Such is the mythic prototype of our cultural situation. Let's leave to others the heroic deeds of Hercules and Achilles, and let's take as our example resourceful and far-sighted Perseus.

Transculture has one crucial distinction: It is created in the integral form of culture rather than shaped by partial intracultural activities, like arts or sciences. This is a Russian tradition: The demarcations within culture always were perceived as less important than the position of culture on its frontier with nonculture (nature, religion, life, emptiness, nothingness . . .). Our gardeners cultivated not so much various species of trees but treeness as such, fruitness, gardenness. Culture existed among us as a quintessence of culturalness. Probably this is the sensibility of hermits—or nomads—in the desert for whom all distinctions between plants are negligent before the miracle and rarity of plant life as such. The rarity of culture makes it a miracle on this soil. Since the zone of a wasteland considerably expanded during the Soviet epoch, our perception of culture also became even more abstract, nostalgic, and holistic. Characteristically, in the 1920s and 1930s, the idiom "cultural person" became popular in the USSR. All differential descriptions—intelligent, educated, knowledgeable, skillful, polite, modest, organized, responsible, intellectual, erudite, and others—were condensed into one definition: "cultural." Culture persecuted by non-culture loses all its specifications and becomes quintessential: culture "as such."

We don't appreciate sufficiently the fact that in the twentieth century Russian culture ceased to be a spontaneously growing totality of creative acts and became an object and product of conscious creativity. Soviet art and science were of an inferior quality because all forces were mobilized for the construction of culture as a whole. But in the Soviet model, the formative force of culture was politics, one of its narrow and most ambitious constituents that worked destructively on the whole. This supremacy of politics has to be changed into the creation of culture by the forces of culture itself. Transculture will be total but not totalitarian, since its center will be located within culture itself, not within its special branches. Transculture deliberately constitutes itself not as a creativity within culture but as a creation of culture by the forces of culture itself. Transculture is culture's potential for self-awareness and self-transformation.

It is not by chance that the most productive contemporary genres are museum, storehouse, archive, trash, encyclopedia, catalogue, album, book, inventory, instruction, commentary, that is, genres of objectification, preservation, conservation, and even annihilation of culture. This is another aspect of transculture: It reappropriates all modes of its alienation. We have accumulated so many specific forms of the reification of culture, by transforming it into museum, encyclopedia, storehouse, archive, or trash, that transculture has now the broadest perspective of appropriation of all these forms.

Since transculture is the self-construction of culture, the project becomes its principal genre. The numerous projects of transculture comprise its major products whose merit does not depend on the fact of their realization. Realization is the category of history, projectivity is the category of culture. The genre of the project presupposes its realizability and thus is distinct from purely theoretical (nonrealizable) projections and purely practical (realized) plans. A project is a theory that justifies in advance a certain practice but does not predetermine its realization. There are a number of projects that exemplify the current stage of transculture: the "lyrical museum," the "ultimate work," "epistemological practice," "neo-lubok," "collective improvisation." In the next letter I hope to be able to describe them in more detail. Transculture is undergoing such a turbulent period of initial formation that, like an infant, its character changes from day to day. . . .

Public Improvisations

The first public performance, conducted in the Central House of Art Workers in July 1983, was probably the crucial test for the very idea of collective improvisation. Would people be inclined and able to write in the presence of others? Would it not be too heavy a responsibility—to express oneself in front of the group, to write coherently on a theme that one had never elaborated before, to complete the text within an hour, and to read it aloud to a large audience?

From about fifteen topics suggested by the audience one was chosen randomly, by drawing lots, and, amazingly, it was "a wreath"—a concept that corresponded perfectly to the very structure of collective improvisation, in which many individual approaches had to be interwoven, like flowers in a wreath. The sheets of paper were laid before each of us; we were left alone with our thoughts, and all of a sudden we felt (as we confessed later) something in the very structure of this improvisational space that impelled us to write and think in the presence of others. This co-presence proved to be unexpectedly inspirational, a magical space of communality where we no longer were obliged to pronounce common things in order to establish social contact with the others but could be justified and recognized in being ourselves, different from one another.

By positing a common topic, the improvisation from the very start gave necessary tribute to commonness, and from this moment on we were liberated to explore the most eccentric and idiosyncratic modes of interpretation. Usually in social communication the topic is never fixed in advance because to do so would seem to constrain the freedom of the speakers and to turn a time of relaxation into a more solemn occupation, a sort of scholarly dispute or conference panel. To follow the standards of politeness, people are ready to sacrifice their own interests, and the topic loosely wanders from the weather to shopping, from sports to politics, revolving around the "zero" point of neutrality and indifference. At improvisational sessions, as soon as the topic is fixed, all participants are free to develop it unpredictably or to digress from it meaningfully. What follows from the initial commonness is the imperative of individuation. At the same time, the collective improvisation never turns into a conference discussion because it displays individual rather than narrowly professional approaches to a common rather than a specialized theme.

The situation that originally seemed to threaten the participants with psychological stress, instead generated a state of inspiration that, as is known from the time of the Muses, comes as "otherness" to our mind, as if writing under somebody else's dictation. Here, this otherness was personified by the presence of others at the table, an interpersonal rather than a super-personal mode of transcendence.

After this first improvisation, we wondered whether in the process of co-thinking we had entered some flow of consciousness that was not limited to separate minds or to the simple sum of our ideas. When an electron is pushed from its orbit it emanates an energy that, adding to the energy of other displaced electrons, produces the most terrifying dynamics—thermonuclear energy. To use this as a metaphor, the displacement of cultural boundaries, the dislocation of separate concepts and images from their routine disciplinary orbits, produces an enormous discharge of transcultural energy, and this is what we permanently felt during the subsequent sessions. Some unfamiliar kind of intellectual energy was discharged by the transcendence of disciplinary borders.

Topics of Improvisations

Overall, in the six years from 1982 to 1987, we conducted seventy-two improvisations, approximately one per month. The most regular participants in our sessions were the literary scholar Olga Vainshtein, the physicist Boris Tseitlin, the mathematician Vladimir Aristov, the housewife Liudmila Pol'shakova, and the philologist Mariia Umnova. Also participating were the sociologist Iosif Bakshtein, the linguist Aleksei Mikheev, the mathematician Liudmila Morgulis, the poet Olga Sedakova, the theater critic Irina Vergasova, the cultural scholar Igor Iakovenko, and the artist Vladimir Suliagin. The sessions were occasionally visited by dozens of guest participants.

Generally, the preference was given to concrete and trivial topics, such as "sharp and cutting objects," "punctuation marks," "money," "hockey," and "jealousy," because they contained a richer scope of associations than topics already elaborated and exhausted in metaphysics, such as "good," "evil," or "freedom." The old logical rule says that the more narrow the concept, the richer its content; therefore, the most general concepts such as "substance" or "spirit" are almost empty. That is why we tried to approach issues belonging to ordinary life, to "no one's" territory in relation to specific sciences and disciplines. It was surprising to discover how much transcultural consciousness has in common with the ordinary, lying outside demarcated cultural borders.

For example, our first topic that caused unexpected animation was prompted by the fact that the session occurred in the springtime, when people changed their hats from heavy winter ones to lighter coverings. As we wrote about hats and how they can be viewed and used in heroic, tragic, comic, and idyllic modes, this juxtaposition of everyday objects with the categories of traditional aesthetics allowed us to achieve a double effect: On the one hand, high concepts were ironically estranged and reduced to the trivial; on the other hand, the trivial object was elevated to the rank of "eternal ideas." This "double-think," the ambivalence of ascending and descending interpretations, is one of the most enjoyable aspects of interdisciplinary communication. We called ourselves "metaphysical soldiers," implying that the "generals" of metaphysics like Kant or Hegel prefer to concentrate on the most general aspects of being and to observe it from the highest, "Olympian" perspectives as befitting commanders in chief, while we, rank and file, are thrown into the thickness of the ordinary and are responsible for the metaphysical explanation of the most trivial things, such as spoons and forks, fruits and vegetables, which will never attract the mind of a generalist.

A general concept, on a communicative plane, presupposes the ascension of various minds to a point of unity and universal harmony, which was believed to be the highest goal of metaphysical contemplation in Plato and Hegel. On the contrary, ordinary things are ordinary precisely because they cannot be reduced to one general idea. Interdisciplinary improvisation offered a variety of ideas that could resonate with the given object, but none of these ideas could encompass the object completely; therefore, difference in perspectives was justified by the opaque nature of the object itself. A man whipping his hat from his head and trampling it underfoot would be a gesture of heroic despair and determination, whereas the same hat put on the grass would signify an idyllic state of leisure where the top and the bottom are brought to the same level. All spatial polarities (tensions) are discharged (resolved) and what was meant to be on the head is brought to the level of the feet. These were only two of the numerous ideas that helped us to explain "the eternal essence" of the hat and still not exhaust it because the hat is far from being simply an eternal idea or a disciplinary term. No concept could be completely adequate to this ordinary object; rather its comprehension demanded the deployment of newer and newer concepts.

Below are listed some topics of Moscow improvisations:

1. Garbage
2. Hockey
3. Storehouse
4. Verbosity
5. Is the epic form still possible in contemporary literature?
6. Hats in tragic, heroic, idyllic, and comic aspects
7. Jealousy

8. Time—theater—space
9. Birthday parties
10. Sharp cutting tools
11. Berries
12. Alushi with blue legs (nonexistent species)
13. Shadow and sand (symbols of transitoriness)
14. Moods
15. Decorations
16. Animals in the city
17. Talking to oneself
18. Gestures and postures
19. Pain
20. Corridor
21. TV set
22. Solitude
23. Russian mind
24. Taboo and inhibition
25. Weather
26. Teacher and disciple
27. Myth and tolerance
28. A day as a life
29. Money
30. Punctuation marks

Techniques of Improvisation

We tried to alternate various modes of improvisational technique—gestures and postures in the intellectual dynamics of the communal body. The most regular kind of improvisation included six stages:

1. discussion of the topics suggested by all participants, choice of one of them, and distribution of its various aspects among participants (each chooses his or her own personal and professional angle on the subject) (approximately 30–40 minutes);
2. writing individual essays (1–1.5 hour);
3. reading and oral discussion of essays (1–1.5 hour);
4. writing a post-essay improvisation as a comment on or summary of what was written and discussed before (15 minutes);
5. reading and discussion of these meta-improvisations (20 minutes); and

6. collection of all written materials of the given session into a coherent whole, a "collective monograph," with a certain composition and order of individual "chapters" (10 minutes).

Another type of improvisation was more fragmented: Each participant started to write his or her own topic, without preliminary discussion. Ten or fifteen minutes later the sheets of paper moved from the left to the right and continued moving periodically until the topic initiated by each participant made the full circle, incorporating the contributions of all others. For example, one wrote about the perception of time, another about the theater scene, the third about domestic animals; and as a result six or seven topics came to be interpreted consecutively by six or seven participants. Thus instead of six or seven individual essays we produced thirty-six or forty-nine textual stripes or layers arranged in six or seven thematic rubrics (collages).

More challenging and sophisticated was the third type of improvisation, which complicated the task of the second type: Each participant had to interpret the themes of other participants by relating it to his or her own theme. For example, A started his round of writing by discussing the role of money in the contemporary world; B, quite independently from A, launched the topic "the attitude of a person toward his/her own name"; and C targeted the problem of the contemporary village as a remainder of the pre-urbanist type of mentality. When B received A's paper he had not only to continue A's discussion of money but to treat this problem through its association with naming, and C had to add the village aspect to the topics of money and names. Sometimes the connections proved to be artificial, but in a number of cases the improvisation succeeded in manifesting how a given problem contained logical or metaphorical intersections with all other problems, however arbitrary their initial choice was.

One of Anaxagoras's sayings can best explain the meaning of our endeavors: "In everything there is a part of everything." The same insight emerged almost at the same historical period from another part of the world, China: "There is no such thing that would not be that, and there is no thing that would not be this" (Chuang Tzu). The third aphoristic argument comes from the leader of French surrealism, André Breton: "Every thing can be described by means of any other thing." Indeed, in the third type of improvisation all topics, independently launched, had to be convincingly linked. The name proved to be the universal sign of social exchange in the same way that money was a universal sign of economic exchange; and the lack of money (banknotes) circulating in the village proved to be an analogue to the absence of surnames and the dominance of patronymics in the village community.

The Lyrical Museum

The next step in the evolution of collective improvisations was the project of the lyrical museum, which involved interpretation not merely of concrete concepts and images but of singular things, such as those all of us have in our possession. Like some of our other projects, the lyrical museum was first designed to be deployed in a public space, in a gallery, but a series of tacit political resistances led us finally to implement this project in the apartment of one of our participants, Liudmila Pol'shakova, to the benefit of the entire project.

A singular thing as compared with a class of objects is still more opaque to reflection; it is difficult to articulate the idea of a hat but it is practically impossible to spell out the idea of this unique hat that belongs to Liudmila or to Vladimir and hangs on the wall of her or his apartment, as a potential exhibit in the lyrical museum.

The ultimate impossibility of rational assimilation or representation of a specific object adds still another dimension to transcultural consciousness, which operates not only with signs and symbols but also with singularities inasmuch as they are transcendental to consciousness and therefore cannot be presented in the system of cultural symbols otherwise than through their own authentic being. In the lyrical museum, verbal descriptions of objects are presented along with the things themselves, so that through the diverse levels of their semiotic representation and through the varieties of metaphoric associations and conceptual readings, the singularities could be posited in their irreducibility to concepts and signs, as occupying a distinct trans-semiotic space.

This was, incidentally, our response to the Derridean critique of the signified and the "metaphysics of presence." I cannot speak for other participants, but for me Derridean pan-textuality ("there is no 'beyond the text'") always seemed to be not only a strong speculative assumption but also an evident contradiction to his own important notion of différance. It is generally accepted that the relationship between signs is based on their difference from each other—but what is different from signs themselves? Textuality is based on the principle of difference, which necessarily leads beyond textuality itself, into the realm of things as being radically different from words and all modes of signification.

Things are selected and presented in the lyrical museum on the following assumptions:

- not because they belong to some famous historical personalities;
- not because they are representative of certain historical periods or national traditions;
- not because they exemplify some rare species of nature, some unique or typical artifacts of past cultures;
- not because they are imbued with universal or extraordinary significance;
- but because they are what they are by virtue of their most ordinary belonging to the most ordinary individuals.

A traditional museum semioticizes things by rendering them as signs of other realities, such as ancient civilizations or great people's lives and achievements, whereas the intention of our museum was the desemioticizing of things, the disclosure of the irreducible gap between their silent singularity and those multiple signs that claim to represent and interpret them. The lyrical museum aims to discover in mundane objects, such as kitchen utensils or children's toys, the level of experience that resists metaphorization and even signification and, in so doing, allows us to escape conventional perceptual habits and restore the materiality of an everyday thing, typically shrouded in ideological or commercial projections. In the lyrical museum, descriptions of an object were presented along with the object itself—the actual spoon, or hat, or candy wrapper—so that through the diverse, multidisciplinary levels of semiotic representations and metaphoric associations, the singularities of these objects could be posited in their "thisness," irreducible to concepts and signs.

The purpose of these and other experiments was to reinvest the daily, the quotidian, with dignity, integrity, and wonder. During the collapse of communism—the most extraordinary utopia of the past—we felt it our duty to create a utopia of the ordinary rather than to reject utopianism as such.[5]

Why in Russia? Why in the 1980s?

In my reflections on transculture in the 1980s, I often proceeded from its comparison with the phenomenon of the counterculture as it emerged in the United States in the 1960s. The counterculture opposed itself to the social and cultural establishment, but the very possibility of such a legitimate opposition was sanctioned by democratic Western societies. In the USSR, we had no such open space within the society from which we could challenge the official culture. More importantly, we did not think that opposition could be culturally productive at all. By that time the Soviet intelligentsia already had acquired the experience of political opposition in the form of the dissident movement, but dissidentism finally proved to be anything but culturally productive. Opposition is not a creative mode of interaction with existing cultural conditions; consequently, the concept of "transcendence" was formulated as a type of cultural orientation distinct from opposition: Not to be "against" the existing and dominating culture but to take it as it is and to transcend it by acceptance and understanding; not to reject but to embrace and encircle.

This is why we were so strongly focused on the trivia of the Soviet lifestyle such as political myths, urban environments, storehouses, mass entertainments (like "parks of culture and rest"), sports (like hockey), and routine habits and customs (like birthday parties). Our intention was to test the limits of Soviet culture by inscribing it in the history of world cultures, by interpreting it as one of many possible cultural worlds, and by positing within it other cultural possibilities. From this perspective, Soviet civilization, instead of being simply rejected as a deviation from Western liberal canons, could be approached and even appreciated on its own, as one among many other great non-Western and "non-liberal" civilizations of antiquity and the Middle Ages, such as the Egyptian, the Babylonian or especially the Byzantine (huge bureaucracy, militarism, the synthesis of religion and politics, the role of books and scribes in culture, etc.).[6]

From a purely dissident point of view, such acceptance of the dominant culture instead of the unmasking of its repressive mechanisms could seem to be a betrayal or a compromise. I thought, however, that in the future such a transcultural vision of the phenomenon of Sovietism would be even more valid as this culture fades into the past. We felt ourselves to be not so much imprisoned by this repressive culture and therefore obliged to struggle against it, as situated on its border and thus capable of assessing it both from within and from without. To a certain degree, we projected ourselves at a space "beyond" this culture, in a post-Soviet space that surprisingly became a political reality much sooner than anybody could have expected: in the late 1980s and early 1990s. Unlike the "thaw" generation of the 1950s and 1960s who still believed in communism in their youth, we did not experience the moral obligation to become anti-communists in the period of Brezhnev's "frosts." We were not disappointed by communism because it never had enchanted us.

There was still another aspect of Soviet and more specifically Russian culture that made it an appropriate site for transcultural experimentation. In contrast with Western culture, it always emphasized the integrity of cultural capacities, not their specification. The very concept of an "intelligentsia" in distinction from Western "intellectuals" refers to the variety of cultural interests and holistic mentality that does not limit itself to certain professional areas. Intellectuals are most of all specialists in their respective fields, while the intelligentsia specializes in the universal. This integrative character of the Russian cultural tradition was partly to blame for the rise of Soviet totalitarianism with its forceful unification of culture under the guidance of politics and ideology, but we believed that the Russian inclination for cultural totality would finally prevail over its own perverse and immature form, political totalitarianism.

We did not see the fragmentation of culture as its most desirable and progressive tendency, and we were not satisfied with the extremely specialized orientation of the Western humanities. For example, Western philosophy during the twentieth century had been increasingly leaning toward the (self-)analysis of philosophical language and was losing the integrative character that it had in the writings of Nietzsche, Bergson, and William James. If even philosophy tends to become a specialized and a technical discipline, with a more limited vocabulary than chemistry or botany, where would the proper place for the general concerns of mind be? Which discipline could take upon itself the role that had been philosophy's in the past?

In response to these questions, various projects of a new humanist metadiscipline, which would be neither philosophy nor art nor science but would embrace the totality of various epistemological and disciplinary modes, originated at this time, and included "universics"[7] and "intelnetics."[8] If the essay and the catalog were transcultural genres of writing; and improvisation, the transcultural mode of communication; then universics had to become the transcultural mode of thinking. Its subject matter was "everything" and its methodological criteria "all," but it was far from abstract generalities, which in fact tend to be more specialized than the realm of concrete things and singularities. Even Hegel's universal philosophy of "Absolute Spirit" is limited by a professional jargon consisting of several dozen special terms—a poorer approximation of the richness of the universe than even meteorology or zoology, disciplines that operate with thousands of special terms. In universics, each word existing in the language, even the most concrete and object-oriented, such as "apple" or "hat," could be conceptualized in the same way that the words "unity" or "spirit" are conceptualized in philosophy, and consequently analyzed as categories of being (the "appleness" of spring, of paradise, of discord, and of the laws of gravity could illustrate some topics of research). In particular, universics had to fully use the potential of metaphors, which extend and multiply the meaning of each word. This is only one example of how the transcultural project challenged both opposite tendencies: cultural specialization of the Western type and political totalitarianism of the Soviet type.

Among the cultural formations of European history that most appealed to us was the group of fourteenth and fifteenth-century Italian scholars and artists who called themselves humanists, and the communities of German romantics in Jena and Weimar in the late eighteenth and early nineteenth centuries. American transcendentalism of the mid-nineteenth century also was an attraction for our transcultural group. The Russian Silver Age (the early twentieth century), though appealing in its cultural breadth and universality, had some objectionable features, such as messianic utopianism and eschatologism, which prepared the psychological ground for the Russian revolution.

What was so important for us in these experiences of the past was the consciousness of culture in its wholeness and the experiments in creating not just new works of art or science but new works of culture, (re)configurations of its entire field. For the Italian humanists and the German romantics, culture was as tangible and manageable a substance of creativity as a piece of marble is in the hands of a sculptor. These were rare and happy periods in history when in the rupture between two great epochs, such as the Middle Ages and Modernity in Italy, feudalism and capitalism in Germany, capitalism and communism in Russia ("the Silver Age"), culture dramatically manifested its wholeness, allowing for a conscious shaping of its future. In this sense, humanists, romantics, and Russian religious thinkers were transculturalists. For them culture was not something abstract and distant, as it was for citizens of more stable historical periods and participants in more isolated domains of arts and sciences. They were not just writers, sculptors, painters, or theologians, but workers in the field of culture as a whole.

We were not aware that we ourselves were living in the last years of the "communist formation," on the brink of its turbulent transition to "post-communism," but we did have the feeling that "the time was out of joint" and a dramatic break in historical continuity was imminent. This feeling was so intense that we perceived humanists and romantics as our "con-temporaries" living in the break between times.

The Interdisciplinary Association Image and Thought

With the advent of glasnost', the opportunities for transcultural activity expanded beyond our intimate circle. Though officially we bore the name the "Club of Essayists" and sometimes conducted improvisations in the Central House of Writers and the Central House of Art Workers, our primary bases were still the private residences of the participants. In May 1986, a new state decree permitted the organization of free associations and clubs for special interest groups which caused feverish activity among the intelligentsia. Among the very first newborns of glasnost', in October 1986, was the interdisciplinary association Image and Thought (Obraz i Mysl'), founded in the southwestern district of Moscow where the population of scientific and creative intelligentsia was especially dense.

The goal of the association as stated in its founding documents was to promote better understanding among the representatives of the humanities, arts, and sciences, and to elaborate a new mode of creative communication based on interactions among various disciplines.[9] The regular weekly sessions of the association took place in the district library and were open to everybody. The room accommodated approximately fifty persons but depending on the agenda it could attract twice or thrice as many. Naturally, such large audiences were not amenable to collective improvisations. Thus the two groups—the Club of Essayists, the improvisational group of six to eight permanent members, and the broader association Image and Thought, with about twenty or thirty more or less permanent members—continued to co-exist rather than merging, though some people were members of both.

The intellectual strategy elaborated for Image and Thought was that of opening new cultural spaces across the existing disciplines, or, as I tried to formulate it, the foaming and bubbling of the solidified substance of culture. It is noteworthy that the majority of people who used to visit our club preferred to express themselves in spheres different from their regular professions. This discrepancy between the person's "routine" profession and his or her "cherished" occupation (or way of life) was typical of the Soviet dualistic mentality, with its ubiquitous splits between the "official" and "nonofficial." If the profession was physics or mathematics, the occupation (and vocation) might be poetry (Vladimir Aristov) or literary criticism (Boris Tseitlin); if the occupation was stove setter or street sweeper, the profession might be metaphysics (Vitaly Kovalev) or poetry (Aleksei Parshchikov). One of our goals was to bring together these splintered aspects of personality.

It is true that the Soviet social system prevented people from the free pursuit of their intellectual aspirations and imposed forced divisions in their professional lives. But these divisions were not only false and forced; they had their positive aspects, stimulating those brilliant dilettantes who were not given a chance to test their gifts in narrow professional applications. Our club proved to be the repository for all these surplus intellectual values never solicited and utilized in Soviet society and perhaps even less applicable in those highly specialized Western societies where a person must concentrate narrowly in a certain profession in order to find an audience and achieve recognition.

The Bank of New Ideas

A special division established within Image and Thought was the Bank of New Ideas. It was designed to become a kind of patent bureau for those ideas in the humanities that rose above the boundaries of established disciplines and could be relevant for the culture as a whole. The traditional system of probation and defense of new ideas in the form of dissertation councils and university committees is usually even more narrow than those disciplines from which the corresponding ideas are advanced. As a rule, a dissertation presents a more specialized angle of knowledge than the discipline as a whole, and what is required from a doctoral candidate is not new ideas but a copious amount of read and cited materials. Thus, the Bank of New Ideas was established to accept, preserve, and disseminate the ideas that did not fit into separate branches of knowledge and that thus were unacceptable for specialized research councils. The Bank used as the primary motive of selection the novelty and the originality of the idea and its potential impact on the humanities as a whole.

The council designed for the assessment of new ideas consisted of representatives of various disciplines, and a list of seven criteria was elaborated according to which every idea had to be evaluated by each of the members of the Interdisciplinary Council. The first criterion was formulated in such a way that it would drive mad Soviet commissions for granting scholarly degrees: How wondrous is this idea? To what degree is it capable of surprising, of exploding the existing paradigms of knowledge? We did not invent this criterion arbitrarily but borrowed it from such a "respectable scholar" as Aristotle, who emphasized in his *Metaphysics* that the origin of knowledge is wonder. "For it is owing to their wonder that men both now begin and at first began to philosophize . . . a man who is puzzled and wonders thinks himself ignorant. . . ."[10] Epistemologically, wonder can be defined as the deconstruction of traditional modes of cognition and the change or reconfiguration of the paradigm of thinking within the scholarly community. The seven parameters devised for the evaluation of ideas will be discussed later in the chapter "InteLnet," devoted to the electronic forms of interactive intellectual "banking."

The first idea defended in our club and accepted for preservation in the Bank was "Diasophia," a discipline that would correspond to the latest stage of the self-development of the Hegelian "Absolute Idea." The author was Vitaly Kovalev, a follower of Hegel who attempted to explain the newest period of world history as a process of further self-realization of Absolute Reason beyond Hegel's own dialectical system; hence "diasophy" is literally "wisdom going across," transcending the border of the "ideal" in its reintegration with post-Hegelian historical reality. Later Kovalev published a book elaborating his ideas and became one of the most esteemed thinkers of his generation.[11]

There were other contributions to the Bank that allowed us not only to evaluate certain ideas but to work out principles of their evaluation from a transcultural perspective. An idea, according to this vision, is not an abstract notion but an "eidos," a multidimensional entity modeled in space, like a sculptural image, possessing its own plasticity. The proportion between inductive and deductive components of the argument, the relationship between general aspects of an idea and its concrete material applications—all this lays the foundation for quite a new discipline called "eidetics," or the "aesthetics of ideas," which would be different from purely logical, philosophical, or ideological approaches to ideas. Logic asks if an idea is coherent and noncontradictory; philosophy asks if an idea is true and corresponds to reality or to the laws of the universe; ideology asks if this idea is practically and politically useful and can be implemented in the transformation of reality. As regards aesthetics, it asks how beautiful an idea is and how its complexity correlates with its unity. One of the most beautiful ideas is Plato's idea of "idea"—a universal entity that is one in many things, that cannot be seen or touched but is present in a variety of tangible objects making them similar to each other though remaining different from all of them. If the "idea of ideas" is so beautiful, we have sufficient reason to judge ideas from an aesthetic point of view.

Specialization and Universality

One of the surprises following from my experience in Image and Thought was that the pursuit of transcultural consciousness was not an easy activity for the majority of our participants. Previously I believed that specialization is "unnatural," that it separates people and produces self-enclosed professional communities, whereas transdisciplinary consciousness could "naturally" bring them back to mutual understanding. My mistake was that I identified the advanced, synthetic stage of consciousness with its elementary, syncretic stage. Ordinary or trivial consciousness is common to the majority of people. All of us can discuss the weather, food, clothes, cars. Professional specialization divides this largest "trivial" community into smaller groups of initiated and competent "specialists."

But the next stage, transcultural consciousness, is not a mere return to the syncretic stage of everyday thinking. To a certain degree, it is even more specialized than the specialist's thinking, and only a few members of professional groups can overcome the boundaries of their disciplines to enter into productive intellectual exchange with members of other professions, without descending to the level of "commonness" and "triviality." The holistic unit of transdisciplinary thinking, "image-thought" (*mysleobraz*), is far from being as simple as a conventional unit of spontaneous, everyday thinking. Here is the crucial difference between the post-specialist, synthetic consciousness and the pre-specialist, syncretic one. Synthesis is always hypothetical and includes the space of uncertainty, the gap between those components that are brought together to form a new totality. Syncretic thinking is assertive, indicative in its modality, whereas the thinking of specialists can be characterized as conducted in an "imperative mood," that is, prescribing certain norms of professional methodology as a necessary prerequisite for obtaining new knowledge. Ordinary thinking describes, professional thinking prescribes, and only universalist thinking speaks in the subjunctive.

One of the problems is how to establish contact between universalist and ordinary thinking, and between people who are already crossing the limits of specialization and people who have not yet achieved the point of specialization. This is an issue of social and educational heterogeneity but also of personal growth and self-awareness. The "synthetic" and "syncretic" layers of thinking are mediated in our minds through professional thinking, and communication between these two poles may present an even more complex problem than communication between universalists and specialists.

The Laboratory of Contemporary Culture

Although people from various parts of Moscow and even from other cities used to come to Image and Thought, it formally stayed a district organization. With the progression of Gorbachev's reforms, the next step became possible, and in February 1988 a new transcultural body came into existence: the Laboratory of Contemporary Culture. It was a part of the Center for Creative Experimentation (*Eksperimental'nyi tvorcheskii tsentr*), located in the center of Moscow, and had the status of a citywide organization. The Center rented a spacious hall that accommodated about four hundred people; during some of our weekly meetings all seats were occupied and people even stood in the aisles.

The Laboratory was designed—as is implied by its name—as an experiment in various forms of transcultural activity, including discussions among the representatives of various disciplines and, most importantly, the refocusing of social life from political to cultural issues. This was an attempt to frame culture in the post-totalitarian epoch as a new type of totality that was no longer subdued by any of its components, such as politics or ideology—even the most liberal politics and democratic ideology, increasingly influential in the time of perestroika. We were equally reluctant to submit culture to any of its other constituents, to aestheticize or technologize culture, to subordinate it to the rule of religious beliefs or scientific rationality. The goal of the Laboratory was to advance culture's capacity for self-awareness and self-government as the growing totality among its multiplying divisions and specializations.

Religion, art, science, and politics, to the extent that they work to liberate a human being from the prison of nature, are forms of culture, mutually checking and restricting one another's power over society—power that, if unchecked, would monopolize and enslave the society. It is only through the mutual limitation of its various subspecies that culture maintains itself as a force of liberation, not only from the determinations of nature, but also from the usurping pretensions of each cultural realm trying to absolutize itself, such as religious fundamentalism and political totalitarianism, and also scientism, aestheticism, moralism, technocratism. It is not that culture, in dividing its constituent parts, rules over them, but, on the contrary, by integrating them, culture liberates humans from their restrictive supremacy. Culture functions not by the principle of "divide and conquer" but rather one of "unite and liberate": By unifying different spheres of consciousness, it liberates us from the dictates of each of them.

Thus, the depoliticization of culture was necessary but not sufficient; what was at stake was the culturalization of politics itself, and, more generally, the creation of an interdisciplinary community whose goal could be defined as the active self-awareness and "self-cultivation" of culture.

I will cite from the program of our Laboratory that was published as a poster and circulated around Moscow in 1988–89, not only in cultural institutions but also on the streets, in squares, and in other public places, indicating a new openness in the society to alternative ways of thinking. All formulations should be understood against the background of what Soviet culture imagined itself to be: existing beyond the limits of time, self-confident, indestructible, unsusceptible to any criticism from within and hostile to any criticism from outside.

> The subject of the Laboratory's investigation is contemporary culture which is aware of its place in time, is susceptible to crises, and is capable of self-criticism: culture as the laboratory of human creative potentials.
>
> Science and art, philosophy and religion—all this is the focus of our attention but only inasmuch as all these spheres themselves find their focus in the unifying concept of culture.
>
> Culture encompasses the interaction of different cultures: traditional and avant-gardist, popular and elitist, rebellious and academic, political and artistic. Our task is to intensify these differences and interactions, and to discover their hidden foundation in the growing openness of transcultural wholeness.
>
> We do not limit the meaning of the "contemporary" by chronological frames. The aim of the Laboratory is to explore those cultural traditions that nourish contemporaneity and are perceived as its anticipation and prototype. This relates to the cultures of the Far and Near East and to the epochs of the Middle Ages and the Baroque. Contemporaneity is to be read as con-temporaneity, as the coexistence of various times in the present.
>
> The main task of our Laboratory is the elaboration of contemporary culturological consciousness. Culturology is the tiny part of culture that contains the structure and the meaning of the whole like a seed contains the plan of the entire plant.
>
> Our goal is to develop the abilities and potentials of the culturologist in each member of the Laboratory. This can be achieved by his/her integration in different cultural worlds and overcoming of obsessive complexes, manias and

phobias peculiar to one limited culture, to its socio-historical determinism and its specific system of prescriptions and prohibitions.

We conducted about twenty-five sessions of the Laboratory, some of which were attended by hundreds of people, but by the beginning of 1990 I felt that the short period of pluralism in Russia had come to an end, and pluralities were reconfiguring into new polarities. Where recently productive differences had existed among groups, associations, and cultural movements, now hostile oppositions began to arise, especially regarding the relationship between liberal and nationalist camps. I felt this very sharply in my increasingly strained relationship with Sergei Kurginian, the head of the Experimental Center for Creativity, whose position quickly shifted to "White Communism," as he called his attempt to synthesize communism with the mysticism of the Eurasian "collectivist" spirit. In 1990 the Center evolved to the status of a thinktank for those pro-communist forces in Gorbachev's late government that organized the failed putsch of August 1991 and endeavored to preserve the political unity of the Soviet Union as a communist superpower. This drift to extreme nationalism and communist revivalism was one among several circumstances that impelled my departure from the Soviet Union in 1990.[12] After the fall of the Soviet Union in 1991, the Center remained the stronghold of the so-called spiritual opposition to Yeltsin's reforms, a political euphemism that unites nationalist and neo-communist factions.

Notes

1. See "An Essay on the Essay" in part III of this book.
2. See "Improvisational Community" in part III, especially the section "The Integrative Mode of Intellectual Activity. Essay and Trance."
3. What is meant here is the passive, unpractical traits of national character and the militant, aggressive character of the political regime.
4. Originally addressed to the art critic and philosopher Boris Groys, who emigrated to Western Germany in 1981. In our correspondence we exchanged news on the cultural trends emerging on both sides of the Iron Curtain. See another excerpt from this letter cited on p. 65.
5. For more detail on the history and theory of the lyrical museum see Mikhail Epstein, *After the Future: The Paradoxes of Postmodernism and Contemporary Russian Culture* (Amherst: University of Massachusetts Press, 1995): 253–279.
6. Viktor Krivulin, a poet and essayist, recalls the effect of the eminent culturologist and Byzantinologist Sergei Averintsev's public lectures at that time, in the 1970s and early 1980s: "At the public lectures of Averintsev on Byzantium, which occurred in the overcrowded halls, the atmosphere was far from

being academic. The problems of medieval theological debates, the enigmas of Byzantine aesthetics, and first of all, the specific understanding of the form and ritual, the metaphysical spirit of civil myth-construction—all this revealed to numerous listeners new modes of comprehension of Soviet daily life. Medieval Byzantium was becoming closer to numerous listeners than contemporary Europe or America. The Platonic, non-human beauty of the State existence that acquired bizarre, but stable and finished forms, was fascinating. . . . Averintsev's Byzantium attracted Russian intellectuals in the same way as the Winckelmann's idealized Greece attracted Germans in the eighteenth century." (Viktor Krivulin, "Konets epokhi Ryb," *Novoe russkoe slovo* [New York], [17 February 1995]: 36).

7. See "The Teachings of Yakov Abramov as Interpreted by his Disciples," compiled, commented upon, and edited by Mikhail Epstein, translated from the Russian by Anesa Miller-Pogacar, in *Symposion: A Journal of Russian Thought*, Vol. 3 (Los Angeles: Charles Schlacks, Jr., University of Southern California, 1999).
8. See the chapter "InteLnet" in part III of this book.
9. The club Image and Thought (Obraz i Mysl') still exists in Moscow, thirteen years after its founding in 1986. Its program reads as follows: "The idea that united the representatives of various professions—literary scholars and chemists, philosophers and mathematicians, sociologists, novelists and poets—is the elaboration of the interdisciplinary language of creative communication and the interconnection of various areas of culture." The club has its own emblem: the letters O and M inscribed into each other to symbolize the holistic, roundish pattern of Obraz (Image) and dividing, zigzag-like pattern of Mysl' (Thought) in their creative interaction (see figure I, p. xi). The syllable "OM"—the acronym of the club's name—is the traditional Indian symbol of the unity of all spiritual beings, of the Higher Self potential above in identity with the Deeper Self actual below—the ideal all of us are striving for." On the current program and events in the club see the Web site (in Russian): http://www.vavilon.ru/lit/office/obraz.html#adres.
10. Aristotle, *Metaphysics*. Book I, ch. 2 in J. L. Ackrill, ed., *A New Aristotle Reader* (Princeton: Princeton University Press, 1987): 258. On the relationship between scholarship, wonder, and imagination, and on the work of the Bank of New Ideas, see also Mikhail Epstein, "Theory and Fantasy," in his *After the Future*, 309–327.
11. Vitaly Kovalev, *Filosofiia postistorii* (Moscow: Alva-XXI, 1992).
12. I came to the United States at the invitation of Wesleyan University as Visiting Professor of Russian and later spent a year in Washington, D.C., as a fellow at the Woodrow Wilson International Center for Scholars.

Chapter 3

Postmodern Avant-Gardes and Cultural Reinvention

Ellen E. Berry

From Modern to Postmodern Avant-Gardes

As is true of the terms *modernism* and *postmodernism,* the concept *avant-garde* has proven to be a conceptually shifty one, full of definitional quagmires. It has been used to denote both the specific historical period from the romantics through the moderns, and a more generalized aesthetic sensibility that transcends any one specific era. It has been characterized as an attitude that links an artist's aesthetic innovation with his/her social antagonism toward existing orders, evidence of a more pervasive avant-garde desire to reintegrate life and art and so to transform the former through the latter. Alternatively, it has come to designate any pattern of self-conscious aesthetic innovation in the arts, regardless of its political intentions or effects. The term has expanded to become a general descriptor for anything new, from high art to high fashion, from food fads to art rock; conversely, it has narrowed to connote a fundamental philosophical/political category resolutely distinct from the realm of the popular.

Among the most vigorously debated issues raised within contemporary discussions are relations between the avant-gardes as they have been manifested historically and contemporary postmodern or neoavant-gardes, part of a more general question about the possibility of launching an effective oppositional critique from within a Western consumer culture of late capitalism. This debate merits fuller elaboration as it bears on my attempts here to situate and assess the status of the Laboratory of Contemporary Culture and allied institutions, such as the Bank of New Ideas, the history of whose formation and workings has been delineated in the previous chapter. I am especially interested in determining the degree to which these experiments in cultural innovation might open useful new directions for reconsidering the potentialities of a postmodern avant-garde impulse, including the possibilities of a transformative critical practice in the West.

A critic's position on the nature of a postmodern avant-garde obviously depends to some extent on his/her assumptions about the formation of a historical avant-garde and the context in relation to which this history is conceptualized. For example, in his early and widely influential study Renato Poggioli conflates modernist with avant-garde art, viewing both as exclusively modern phenomena that could arise only when art began self-consciously to contemplate itself from a historical perspective and only within "a climate where political liberty triumphs." He denies that aesthetic and political radicalism necessarily coincide within the avant-garde, concluding that "the only recurring political ideologies are libertarianism and anarchism," are, in other words, generalized stances of antagonism and extreme individualism. Poggioli does mention contemporary manifestations of an avant-garde spirit (such as the 1960s "Happenings"), but overall he concludes that the avant-garde as such has ceased to exist since it has become "the typical chronic condition of art" in a contemporary moment, institutionalized as an aesthetic norm rather than functioning as that which destroys such norms.[1]

Peter Burger disagrees with Poggioli on a number of points—most notably the importance of maintaining conceptual distinctions between modernist art of the type practiced by Ezra Pound, T. S. Eliot, James Joyce, or Franz Kafka, and avant-garde art such as dada, futurism, and surrealism; and the importance of greater historical precision and theoretical specificity in the genealogy of avant-gardism that Poggioli traces beginning with the romantics. Burger considers the genesis of the avant-garde to be a precise and dramatic shift away from late-nineteenth-century aestheticism—a movement in which art becomes problematic to itself, form becomes the preferred content of the work, and the separation of life and art that characterizes bourgeois society intensifies. The avant-garde arises when the artist recognizes the need to rejoin art and social praxis, and begins to comprehend and critically reflect on his/her own social status in bourgeois society. Thus, whereas modernist art attacked traditional aesthetic techniques in general, the avant-garde also launched its attack against the institution of art itself as a coherent system of production and distribution. This "system-immanent critique" ultimately failed politically in Burger's estimation since, over the course of the twentieth century, the avant-garde work itself has become institutionalized as art. This fact, in Burger's estimation, necessarily negates the work's genuinely avant-gardistic potential. Therefore, although he takes exception to a number of Poggioli's points, Burger shares Poggioli's pessimism about the possibility of new avant-gardes arising in a contemporary moment.[2]

While Jean Baudrillard does not offer a theory of the avant-garde as such, his widely influential analysis of the workings of postmodern consumer culture provides an important perspective from which to view the current possibilities for a socially transformative aesthetic practice. As Poggioli and Burger do, though for vastly different reasons, Baudrillard remains pessimistic about such possibilities. The Baudrillardian scheme posits that in advanced capitalist cultures—most especially in America—reality disappears in an incessant proliferation and dissemination of media simulations of reality, of signs that refer only to other signs. Having become indistinguishable from its simulation, reality itself becomes hyperreal. This implosion of sign and referent, this simulation of every social need, desire, or political interest, indicates for Baudrillard a radical breakpoint in the social symbolic that definitively and permanently alters previous conceptions of individual subjectivity or social relations, and negates the possibility of an effective oppositional stance; struggles for power and meaning persist only in simulated versions of themselves. As Baudrillard puts it, "[t]he Year 2000 has already happened," effectively negating the avant-garde's claims to being "en avant" and signifying the impossibility of genuinely critical thought and political engagement in a postmodern moment.[3]

Against these values—appropriate for a previous era—Baudrillard celebrates postmodern strategies of concealment and meaningless play, strategies of seduction. These are designed to accelerate the disappearance of the current order, the deepening of negative conditions, through substituting a fatal theory for critical theory. As Sadie Plant comments in her history of the Situationist Internationale,

> With the establishment of seduction as the new principle of the postmodern world, Baudrillard inverts the entire strategy of the old modern revolutionary [avant-garde] project. In place of desires for truth and real experience, the 'liberation' of meaning, the destruction of appearances, he promotes secrecy and

mediation, artifice and objectification . . . the object which refuses to bear meaning, the image which represents nothing, the sign which fails to signify, the commodified and silenced mass which refuses to participate.[4]

Plant points out that while Baudrillard's analysis of the workings of postmodernity is difficult to refute, one need not inevitably reach the same conclusions that he does. She defends the possibility of a transformative postmodern aesthetico-political practice by focusing on the work of another theorist, Guy Debord, whose analysis of the causes and consequences of spectacular postmodern culture shares features with Baudrillard's but whose political conclusions differ markedly. Whereas Baudrillard has "happily accepted" postmodern culture's own account of itself and thus finds no conceivable critical space outside of it, Debord argues that it is still possible and vitally necessary to unmask, critically analyze, and thus potentially escape/dislodge the workings of the society of the spectacle. As Plant puts it, "the recognition that even the most radical of gestures is implicated in [the] process [of spectacularization, simulation] cannot be allowed to lead to petrification and silence. It must, on the contrary, serve as a springboard for subversive strategies of interruption and provocation."[5]

Baudrillard remains the most extreme pole of the positions represented by both Burger and Poggioli, who also reject (though again for very different reasons) the possibility of any genuinely avant-gardistic impulses existing in a postmodern moment; postmodernism can only be a pale imitation of an earlier avant-garde. These positions all focus on a postmodernism of complicity or reaction, what has been called a "ludic" postmodernism, appropriate to a world in which everything has been done and said, in which no reality is recoverable outside the hyperreal simulations of consumer culture, where any gesture of opposition is immediately commodifiable. Within such a set of assumptions, all that remains is to "play with the fragments," as Baudrillard puts it.[6]

Debord suggests another position in the debate: a resistance postmodernism that remains effectively if only partially critical despite a recognition of its complicity with what it critiques. Several important recent critics, Plant among them, elaborate the conditions of possibility for such a postmodern practice through reference to neo-avant-gardistic works and artists. Of these Charles Russell remains the most tentative about the significance of the current wave of postmodern experimentation, arguing that it bears only "an ambiguous relation" to the stylistic inventiveness of the historical avant-garde. This is largely because while postmodern art may be antagonistic or experimental in an avant-garde sense (he cites the work of William S. Burroughs and Monique Wittig as exemplary), "it fails to offer any principle upon which a significantly different art or social vision might be created." [7] The avant-garde's commitment to radical stylistic innovation, its imperative to make it new, has been thoroughly compromised by consumer culture's fetishization of novelty. And its belief in the necessity and the possibility of social revolution has been discredited by the example of the Soviet Union as well as by a general postmodern undermining of progressive metanarratives. At best, the postmodern artist can struggle (largely unsuccessfully) against the status quo while he/she acknowledges the social and linguistic determinism of a postmodern moment; the postmodern avant-garde remains more potentially than actively radical.

As Russell does, Walter Kaladjian acknowledges the partiality and contingency of postmodern value systems; its confusing play of networks, codes, discourses, and simulations; and the dominance of its consumer culture, capable of reducing the most radical avant-garde gestures to so many postures or styles. But, in Debord's spirit, he views this condition not as cause for paralysis, ludic celebration, or nostalgia for a more properly avant-garde moment. Rather such are simply the conditions of possibility within which a postmodern avant-garde must operate, continually inventing new tactics of contestation appropriate to the world in which it finds itself. Kaladjian links postmodern avant-gardes to an American tradition of socially engaged art and writing that emerged in the 1930s, a tradition obscured by the canonization of high modernism. The postmodern avant-garde, like its predecessor, mixes formalism and populism, high and low aesthetic modes to launch a "'war of position' within, not outside, today's conglomerate mass media." Kaladjian focuses in particular on the emergence of those new social movements in the post-Vietnam era that represent the experiences of those most marginalized by dominant culture, among them women, racial and ethnic minorities, lesbians and gays. He details the possibilities for aesthetic and cultural activism arising from these "new antagonisms to dominant forms of subordination," gestures that are necessarily staged through the very spectacles and popular entertainment flows that we associate with the conglomerate media. Building on Foucault's observation that strategies of power always generate micropolitical tactics of resistance, Kaladjian analyzes the work of individual artists such as Jenny Holtzer and collectives such as ACT-UP, which "agitate along the fault lines and zones of stress that fissure the mainstream myths, icons, and imaginary representations which legitimate advanced capitalism . . . ," opening "outrageous postmodern breaches in the administered facade of the so-called 'new world order.'"[8]

These descriptions and assessments of a postmodern avant-garde share a conception of avant-gardism as, by definition, oppositional to dominant values whether the artist expresses this adversarial stance primarily in relation to aesthetic tradition or also in relation to a sociopolitical realm. As the historical avant-gardes did, contemporary versions assert a desire to effect changes in dominant symbolic practices and/or sociopolitical realms even if they fail to offer or even necessarily to imply a coherent vision for this change. As an adversarial oppositional force, the postmodern avant-garde is nonetheless by definition implicated in that which it critiques, and it draws its energy, its raison d'être, from this oppositional stance, as all avant-gardes do. But unlike previous avant-gardes it self-consciously acknowledges as part of its project its inescapable participation in these structures. (Perhaps this suggests a new stage of artistic self-consciousness that logically follows Burger's analysis of aestheticism and the modernist avant-garde.) It is therefore more reactive than creative; it undertakes, even parodies, a modernist quest for the new from within the realm of the already-said. It seeks to expose the constructed nature of cultural representations and signifying systems as well as their investment in certain strategies/structures of domination. But it also acknowledges its own status as equally constructed by and implicated in that which it seeks to undermine, implying the inescapability of these constructions even as it seeks to dislodge their dominance. It aims to demystify and expose the limits of systems and discourses that pretend to be comprehensive or universal or wholly liberatory. It equally calls attention to its own partiality as a discourse of truth or originality. Only ever momentarily effective, it is forced to adopt ever-new strategies of resistance and subversion as its efforts become anticipated, commodified, and incorporated into the workings of a flexible, mutable, and expanding consumer culture. The defining feature of postmodern avant-gardism lies in its compromised stance, its self-conscious paradoxical oscillation between complicity and critique; its mode is interrogative and not declarative. Whether this suggests only the latest mutation of an avant-garde sensibility, one appropriate to these times; signals the absolute demise of avant-gardism as such; or points to the partial emergence of new modes and sensibilities remains open to debate.[9]

Whatever their stance on the question of postmodern avant-gardism, these theories also share an analysis that links the development of the avant-garde in its historical and current manifestations with a culturally specific critique of the workings of Western bourgeois capitalist culture, including its processes for producing, transmitting, receiving, evaluating, and commodifying art. The visions of possibility for art in a postmodern era are both conditioned and limited by this particular framing.

Within most of these theories, Russian culture in the early years of the century is seen as forming a vital part of the historical avant-garde's development since, during the early twentieth century, Russia was the site of multiple and significant avant-garde experiments—among them suprematism, constructivism, futurism—that influenced and in turn were influenced by an international avant-garde. Charles Russell in fact considers the Russian futurists to be the only successful attempt to join aesthetic and social revolution, poetic and collective identity, art and everyday life—the goals of all avant-garde gestures, in his estimation. Avant-garde groups such as the futurists initially had a strictly aesthetic orientation, but as most avant-gardes did they believed that new symbolic forms would inevitably create new social realities. This emphasis on new social orders became more pronounced after the 1917 revolution—which seemed a fulfillment of the avant-garde dream of radical social transformation—and ushered in a period of urgent public discussion about the role of art in the new society, including "its bases of production, its formal and thematic concerns, its economic determinants, its relation to the former bourgeois, educated audience, and to the potential audience of workers and peasants, and, finally, its relationship with the Communist Party."[10] Of course Soviet party orthodoxy did not develop in sympathy with the programs of the avant-gardes—whose projects came to be viewed as unintelligible to the masses and as hopelessly tied to a critique of the bourgeois culture that communist society had supposedly rendered obsolete.

There surely is an enduring irony in the Russian example. Here, avant-gardism achieved perhaps its purest from, its greatest actual success, in that its goal to join artistic and social revolution was fully realized, if only momentarily. Here, avant-garde art found itself taken seriously enough to be censored and banned rather than simply commodified, normalized, and institutionalized as has been the case in Western culture. In the Soviet years, politics came to be privileged over art resulting in what might be called an *over*-integration of life and art—a forced integration.

While precise connections between the Western historical avant-gardes and their contemporary manifestations are open to debate—as I have suggested—it is still possible to trace a rough line of descent, whether to distinguish the two in their intentions and effects or to map parallels and continuities between them. Constructing such a genealogy becomes more problematic in the case of the former Soviet Union as the history of artistic production outside of official socialist realist channels until quite recently has remained shadowy and difficult to recover. Celebrated cases of an overtly dissident art—such as Solzhenitsyn's, whose *Gulag Archipelago* brought him international attention in the 1970s—are, of course, well known, as are accounts of unofficial or parallel cultures that existed throughout the Soviet years. Beginning in the 1960s and 1970s, a moralizing literature—sincere, confessional, indicting—of semi-approved nonconformism was also popular. Such "centered" prose is largely realistic, with a definite authorial voice and position and a belief in the power of language to represent reality and to reveal truth. Whether publicly censored or not, such dissident art expresses the avant-garde spirit of opposition and critique if not its mandate for formal experimentation.

Vestiges of this dissident tradition remain in the current post-communist context, which might be thought of as analogous to a Western postmodernism or as symptomatic of larger global processes of postmodernization.[11] For example, conceptualist art, literature, and film seek to be actively anti-ideological and post-utopian in relation to the legacy of Soviet totalitarianism rather than anti-totalitarian, as in dissident art proper, or engaged in ideo-social battles more generally, as in centered prose. Conceptualism emerged from the recognition that in the Soviet context ideas—denuded of a material referent—were in fact the only genuine substance of the Soviet lifestyle and, based on this recognition, it plays with the empty signs and fictions of an outmoded ideology, as well as with linguistic structures more generally. For example, sots art, a form of conceptualism, takes as its subject the quotidian aspects of Soviet daily life. In a manner similar to American pop artists, who ironically appropriated the signs and clichés of commercial culture so as to critique their cultural dominance, sots artists reacted to the "advertising" of socialism. As Elena Izumova puts it, "The countless slogans, quotes and monotonous posters surrounding a Soviet person during his life had lost their original meaning and turned into a part of the scenery, like, for example, an advertisement for Coca-Cola in American towns."[12] Conceptualism is an example of what has been called eccentric art that developed in an "internal polemic" with previous centered art. Whereas centered writing aimed at "seriousness itself and love of truth," eccentric prose was devoted to play, spectacle, and carnival; it acted as a mirror to re- and deflect dominant culture. Yet in ridiculing official ideology in this way, and therefore in part acting to reinscribe it, conceptualism also became outmoded as a critique. As Epstein puts it, "how is it possible to hold up for ridicule an ideology that no longer exists, that has long been laughing at itself? . . . What is ideological in conceptualism is out of date, a relic of anti-communism in the epoch of post-communism. It's absurd."[13]

The example of conceptualism points to the difficulty in a post-communist moment of working in a deliberately oppositional mode or genre; that is, with any kind of directedness "for" or "against." Instead, the most representative art of the post-communist era might well be considered an art of the "rear-garde", which is, according to Epstein, a term meant to signal its distance from the projects of oppositional and complicitous critique associated with modernist and postmodernist avant-gardes both Western and Eastern. As Epstein explains it,

> [O]ur old avant-garde, which flourished in the teens and twenties . . . was a utopian avant-garde. It tried to invent patterns for the future: the suprematism of Malevich or the futurism of Mayakovsky and Khlebnikov. . . . They tried to bring the future into the present, or to move the present into the future, and all of their schemes and constructions fit some kind of normative intention. Or else they assumed a very critical distance from existing society, which is the other side of utopian consciousness: to undermine, destroy, and ridicule. The early decades of the century were possessed of a superiority complex. Then, on the edge of exhaustion, the century began to appreciate lack of form; inferiority was just the thing. The all-accepting bottom of the universe swallows the sublime forms and great ideas of previous epochs. They've been digested and expelled as in the lavatory pan—and this bottom becomes the top of our rear-garde art. It is post-utopian or anti-utopian, and it doesn't proclaim any communistic 'shining heights.' . . . Art is now tired both of realism, which tries to coincide with reality, and of the avant-garde, which rushes forward and leaves reality behind . . . the rear-garde . . . falls behind deliberately, inventing aesthetic forms of backwardness. Art lags behind, collecting the remainders of the accelerated historical process, its trash, dust, rubbish.[14]

From a rear-garde perspective, the postcommunist moment signifies the death of both past and future, a "zero level of being and writing" after and beyond history. The rear-garde poses but in no way attempts to answer the cultural question "How to live after one's own future, or, if you like, after one's own death?" In a moment when "there is nothing to take from history into the future and nothing to be proud of in the past. . . . When there is simply no faith left in an ideal concord . . . nothing is left to defend." Characteristics of rear-garde art include this paradoxical post-communist atemporality; lack of attachment to reality or attempts to recreate it; dehumanization expressed as the absence of the human from life, or the figure of the collective being "who has departed from reason and history"; genrelessness/formlessness and desemanticization; a movement toward silence and stasis. As Epstein puts it, "The literature of the rear-garde has a reliable remedy against being infatuated by the idea, against the totalization of any style or outlook: a 'loaded' boredom, which selects the most secondary of words and proliferates a multitude of secondary meanings."[15] This is an absentminded prose, devoid of the seriousness of the centered or the playfulness of the eccentric; it calls for nothing, refers to "nothing." It eliminates primary meanings without creating secondary ones, in the zero-degree zone of writing.[16]

In distinction from an earlier modernist avant-garde moment in which a historical subject assumed a positive line of strategic resistance through appeals to liberation, emancipation, or absolute self-expression, and in distinction from a Western postmodernist avant-garde that views its critique as always already compromised, implicated within the system it seeks to expose and dislodge, within post-communist rear-garde art (a distinctly Baudrillardan kind of art), a strategic refusal of meaning and the word, an ironic and neutral resistance of the object recording the shadows of the system's disappearance, turns out to be most appropriate.

From Cultural Critique to Cultural Reinvention

In his 1983 "Letter on Transculture," Epstein writes: "Now we live as if after the death which lasted more than half a century. All tissues of our previous culture have rotted and decomposed and now we expect a revival in new, transparent flesh which we will have to name and cultivate. This is culture after culture as there is life after life in other transcendent dimensions. And as if newly resurrected we learn how to speak anew or more precisely to invent a still non-existent language of after-death culture." With this statement, Epstein gestures toward a moment beyond the rear-garde's zero level of being, thereby suggesting a tentative answer to the question "What comes after an art of the end?" It is toward this provisional uncertain space "beyond" that institutions such as the Bank of New Ideas and the Laboratory of Contemporary Culture directed themselves; it is culture after the death of one extremely powerful cultural system that they sought to (re)construct.[17]

Most generally, these organizations aimed to investigate culture in its totality, culture as a totality, by constructing modes of knowledge production capable of transcending individual disciplines or genres so as to open new intercultural territories—both actual and imagined. They also proposed a number of more specific goals, among them an archival one: to recover an ignored and repressed cultural history, to search for all those surplus cultural values never required or used in Soviet society. As Epstein puts it, "Soviet civilization exiled not only people to Siberia but also literary and philosophical movements, creative ideas, spiritual insights, cultural possibilities. The greatest land of the unconscious—a psychological and artistic Siberia—thus had been formed inside of us."[18] Acknowledging and confronting this repressed cultural history, this historical unconscious—an interesting variant of Fredric Jameson's political unconscious—resulted in a kind of mental "past shock," occasioned by meeting an unfamiliar Russian past—newly uncensored—and that of all humanity. From within this trauma, however, euphoria arose from a recognition that all cultures—Soviet, post-Soviet, global—now potentially were available as a sort of immense archive in which previously inexpressible forms and styles might commingle. In this respect one might say that the Laboratory of Contemporary Culture functioned as a local instance filtered through an imaginative reconstruction of the global, forming a kind of post-communist transcultural sublime, a topic I take up in a later chapter.

Cultural reinvention also was a goal; the Laboratory sought to develop new approaches to the analysis and production of culture—including a variety of new genres, such as the "lyrical museum" or collective improvisations—that would break dualities between self and other, public and private, performer and audience, known and unknown, speech and silence in order to form new social subjectivities and more authentic collectivities. "We tried," Epstein writes, "to produce modes of improvisational technique that were like different poses and gestures of the communal body. These techniques created forms of communality that preserved the right of each individual to be different."[19] In performing publicly new forms of the cultural body, participants were, in essence, reinventing forms of a genuinely public culture, enacting new social identities, creating new public dimensions for discourse, and providing new spaces for creativity itself to reemerge and be "tested."

The Lab also helped to heal the rift between an official and publicly visible culture and what Maurice Blanchot calls the "everyday," that most democratic realm of banal experience at the furthest remove from the gaze of official culture. Most often, the various experiments performed at the Laboratory involved people from a broad range of backgrounds writing collaboratively in large groups on collectively chosen topics—typically the most trivial-seeming ones, which, it was argued, contained a more fertile scope of associations than those ideas already elaborated and exhausted in a metaphysical tradition and within the Soviet system. To improvise meant to create unpredictably in the presence of others, to liberate creativity and forms of cultural potentiality in the process of communication, and thus to make visible the importance of daily, concrete, and immediate experience that typically exists outside of demarcated cultural borders. Essentially, this involved an imaginative reconstruction of culture from the ground up. Similarly, the lyrical museum aimed to discover in mundane objects such as hats or children's toys a level of experience that resists metaphorization, perhaps even signification and, in so doing, exceeds conventional perceptual habits and restores the materiality of an everyday typically shrouded in ideological projections. The purpose of these and other experiments in everyday life was not so much to radicalize life from a perspective outside of the everyday—a typically avant-garde gesture—as it was to reinvest the daily, the quotidian, with dignity, solidity, integrity, and wonder. In a time of the collapse of the communist utopia, it fell to these groups to create a utopia of the ordinary rather than to reject utopianism as such.

In this regard, then, the experiments in public cultural innovation as they existed in various incarnations from their inception in 1983 until the Laboratory's dissolution in 1990 differed in significant respects from both a rear-garde stance of refusal and negation and an avant-garde stance of dissidence and direct opposition. Instead, the Lab assumed a strategy of overstepping or encircling existing culture, assimilating and reworking the modes of its alienation. More proactive than reactive or oppositional in the conventional sense, it assumed a compensatory or supplementary place in relation to a repressive dominant culture, existing at once within and beyond it—elsewhere—gesturing outside its borders to the possibility of a global conversation. Estranged from a society that sought to subsume all of cultural life to a political goal, it used its alienation not to directly critique such a goal but instead to open spaces for the construction of new cultural fields and new modes of sociality.

In some respects, the Lab can be said to share features with earlier avant-garde agendas: its urge to invent culture anew, its belief that culture can have a socially transformative role, its sense of being poised at a new historical moment, its recognition of the need to invent new forms and methods adequate to respond to this moment, in short, its utopianism. But—crucially—these features were qualified by and shaped in response to the history (and failed utopianism) of the Soviet years, redefined for a post-communist moment. Not a conceptualist anti-utopianism or a rear-garde post-utopianism, not, in other words, the elimination of utopia as a category of possibility but rather a utopianism arising with full knowledge of the death of one "utopian" scheme and a commitment to moving beyond it. Existing in a moment between the waning of communism as a belief system and its actual dissolution, the Lab occupied a liminal moment and a heterotopic space in which the future could be hazarded as a category that must be pluralized, rendered indeterminate, made intransitive. As Epstein puts it, "Utopianism imposes a certainty on the future and presents it as an obligation and necessity rather than a possibility; one has to restore one's love of the future, not as a promised State but as a state of promise, as expectation without determination."[20] This provisional state applies to the Lab's liminal spatial position as well. Both Soviet totalitarianism and historical avant-gardism were teleological; both tried to locate the future in time. Epstein argues that a redefined utopianism must be returned to space, transformed into part of a geography that may be more imaginary than actual, the space of the not-yet-embodied or even necessarily embodiable.

This desire for "utopianism" after utopia, for acts of cultural reinvention born of cultural devastation positions the Lab in a distinct zone, one that differs in important respects from the cultural positioning of the Western postmodern avant-garde, which I also take to include critical left intellectuals. However, although their embodiments may differ in response to the specific cultural situations and traditions from which they emerge, they share a paradoxical doubleness, a sense of impossible possibilities, that is perhaps distinctly postmodern: for Western postmodernism a critique rendered "impossible" by its complicity with the system it seeks to dislodge; for Russian postcommunism a mistrust of utopian ideals and grand-scale plans coexisting with an "impossible" desire to thoroughly reinvent a cultural imaginary and forms of public sociality. The Lab sought nothing less than to secure a new dominance for culture itself by refocusing the entire life of society from the political to the cultural, thereby ending the dominance of politics over culture operative in the Soviet years. In this way culture might once again become a "laboratory of human creative potentials."

The experiments in cultural reinvention pioneered by Epstein and other critical intellectuals in the perestroika era contain several important lessons for Western artists and culture studies scholars, and I will close this chapter by briefly mentioning some of them. As does Russian culturology, culture studies, as it is practiced in the West, rejects a narrow view of culture as a privileged space apart from everyday life; instead, culture comes to refer to an array of a society's arts; beliefs; practices; and material, intellectual, and spiritual ways of life. It studies cultural practices and texts in relation to their social, political, historical, and geographical contexts of production and reception. In particular, within this tradition, cultural practices are examined from the point of view of their interactions with and within relations of power, including the ways in which audiences disrupt and reinvent the texts of a dominant culture. Moreover, in many cases, critics working within this tradition aim to move from simply analyzing cultural production and reception to discovering sites for political critique and intervention as well. As they are for postmodern avant-garde artists, radical social and cultural transformation are often overt foci and goals of the culture studies critic, who seeks not just to chronicle change but also to enable it.

Despite its emphasis on strategies of resistance and transformative cultural practices, however, Western critics working within the culture studies tradition also more directly problematize the possibilities of operating progressively within historical, social, economic, class, race, gender, sexual, and other determinants through their emphasis on the subject's resolute historical embeddedness and embeddedness in the power relations of capitalist culture. As a result, processes of contestation and struggle receive great emphasis, as do various strategies of disruption, appropriation, and recoding. Such emphases are given in the name of untangling the multiple problematics involved in articulating cultural differences and the modes/sites of cultural inscription. This reflects one of the primary impasses, one of the "impossibilities" of the culture studies tradition: incommensurability between its epistemological assumptions (we remain thoroughly embedded within, if not wholly determined by, the structures of our culture) and its progressive goals, claims, and desires.

Another difficulty is posed by the fact that culture studies wishes to examine the production of culture in a comprehensive sense—culture as a whole way of life—but, by and large, it does so from within the institutions of the academy, which are for the most part still limited to disciplinary perspectives and institutional standards for knowledge production. There is even now very little tradition of the public intellectual in American culture. In contrast with Western culture, Russian and Soviet cultures always tended to emphasize the integrity of cultural abilities, rather than their specification. As Epstein points out, the very concept of an intelligentsia in Russia, as distinct from Western intellectuals, refers to a "syncretic mentality" that is not necessarily confined to one area of professional achievement. Whereas intellectuals are most of all specialists in their respective fields, the intelligentsia specialize in the general. The integrative nature of the Russian cultural tradition was, of course, partly to blame for the rise of Soviet totalitarianism with its forceful unification and subordination of culture to ideology. But, as Epstein also notes, the Russian inclination for cultural unification also suggested other possibilities than its "perverse manifestation" in Soviet political totalitarianism, namely, the invention of "universics," a term meant to describe a new metadiscipline—neither philosophy nor art nor science—that would embrace the totality of various epistemological and disciplinary modes.

The critical assumptions and analytic goals of Western cultural studies limit its transformative social project in a number of other ways. First, as certain movements in Russian culture do, it tends to remain locked within a binary oppositional mode of oppression and momentary transgression, which can in fact paralyze meaningful action by producing what Dick Hebdige identifies as a pervasive mood of critical fatalism. Second, there is a kind of circularity to the approach whereby cultural studies becomes a critical practice that merely rediscovers its own operating assumptions, rediscovers what we already know—that, for example, cultural production is constrained in more or less predictable ways by the race, class, and gender determinants of an existing dominant culture. This recalls Epstein's warning about the dangers of becoming trapped in the "complexes, manias, and phobias peculiar to one limited culture, to its socio-historical determinism and its specific systems of prohibitions and prescriptions," pathologies that transcultural approaches mean to overcome.[21]

If we are to begin thinking beyond these limitations we need, among other things, models of transformative practice. One aspect of constructing such models involves hazarding the future as a category of open possibility rather than as something already determined in advance and thinking of theory as a place of speculation, of the hypothetical, rather than only as an attempt to describe what already exists. Here I follow

Jean-François Lyotard's suggestion that we consider the importance of the wasteful or nonproductive time of speculation, which exists as a hiatus between present and future. The time of speculation is to be distinguished from a capitalist commodification of time, which imagines the future as a fund of fixed returns and values against which the present may borrow, and from the communist determination of time, which tried to install the future in the present. Theory as speculation opens a space of delay—a utopian space—in which to think a future imperfect temporality, disclosing what might be called a postmodernism of the possible rather than a postmodernism of the already-said. In a similar vein, David Harvey stresses our need at this moment to work toward changes in shared fictions, values, and beliefs, a project that might be started by marking alternative values in the discursive and imaginative realms first. Finally, Donna Haraway argues that one of our most important tasks as cultural critics is to build more powerful collectivities, to create the conditions for producing what she calls "articulated worlds" comprised of an undecidable number of modes and sites where powerful new connections might be made. Too often, however, these are simply calls for such practices to be developed—in the future. The practices pioneered at institutions such as the Bank of New Ideas and the Laboratory of Contemporary Culture, including the public cultural role assumed by intellectuals there, may well provide more concrete examples than those currently available within a Western culture studies tradition.

For example, the models of communal interaction practiced at these Russian institutions may suggest one response to the current difficulty among politically engaged Western scholars in conceiving of new nontotalizing and noncoercive models of collectivity: The problem of how to reconcile a commitment to difference with the construction of new forms of interrelatedness and collective political projects. This problem itself might be seen as one specific manifestation of a global postmodern transformation, a "widespread apprehension that the old forms of collectivity are disappearing" in the face of the multiple dislocations that characterize contemporary sociality and in the face of the postmodern critique of totalizing structures more generally.[22]

Jean-Luc Nancy offers a particularly direct expression of this crisis in the opening paragraph of *The Inoperative Community:* "The gravest and most painful testimony of the modern world, the one that possibly involves all other testimonies to which this epoch must answer . . . is the testimony of the dissolution, the dislocation, or the conflagration of community."[23] In his effort to respond to this contemporary dissolution of forms of communality so as to redirect the current crisis, Nancy critiques two older ways of conceiving community. The first grows out of the Western philosophical tradition, whose historic inability to think beyond the unitary subject as its organizing category and founding principle has led to hierarchical notions of community with a head or ruler—the one who stands for the many. The second emerges from political philosophy and similarly assumes a prior constitution of self-determining subjects who freely choose to aggregate, an assumption that erases those differences between subjects "that complicate the presumption of their absolute equality." As George Vanden Abbeele points out, both theories conceal "the essentialism of a subject immanent to itself"; both function through a logic of identity that reduces or eliminates social and other differences, in turn fueling the contemporary sense of the loss of community. The Christian notion of communion and the Marxist narrative of communism also are predicated on idealized, essentialized communities in which differences must be suppressed or overcome so that the community may be unified, may, in other words, be constituted *as* a community. Moreover, as Iris Marion Young points out, and as contemporary global events make painfully clear, the traditional desire for community "relies on the same desire for social wholeness and identification that underlies racism and ethnic chauvinism on the one hand and political sectarianism on the other."[24] That is, the precondition for the existence of community is an identification premised on the community's oppositional difference from other groups; indeed, one of the primary functions of community may be the management and consolidation of an otherwise unregulated (and therefore threatening) play of differences.

In *The Inoperative Community,* Nancy calls for and begins to develop new modes of thinking that both acknowledge our deep need for communal forms and seek to overcome the serious limitations of previous models. First, Nancy posits an original intersubjective relation, what he calls our "being-in-common," to replace the Western tradition's reliance on the individual bounded subject as a foundation for thought. This relation consists not of a "mutual interpellation" between two already (previously) constituted subjects but rather of the appearance of the between as such, considered "the place of a specific instance of being-in-common which gives rise to the existence of being itself." Being-in-common is not just what we all have in common but what we share in common at the limit of commonality: "the incommunicable commonality of our finitudes—birth, death and no doubt a good deal in between."[25]

Nancy's model offers an important refinement of the self-other relation, which traditionally has resulted in a logic that either pathologizes and excludes difference or reduces it to the self-same. In Nancy's formulation, "I do not rediscover myself in the other: I experience the other's alterity or I experience alterity in the other together with the alteration that in me sets my singularity outside me and infinitely delimits it." Within the communal relation as Nancy imagines it, the subject is "inclined outside itself, over the edge that opens its being-in-common," leading to "a ravishing of the singular being that does not cross over into death." The communal thus becomes the search for a bond that forms ties without forming attachments or wholes, that unbinds by binding.[26]

Importantly, Nancy insists that his community has neither essence nor telos, since the community "that becomes a single thing necessarily loses the 'in' of being-in-common: it yields its being together to a being of togetherness." Thus, according to Nancy, one cannot work to institute or realize the thought of community in his sense of the term; one can only try to communicate the sense of community and critique those ideologies that hide its contemporary absence. In this respect, the political is redefined as the site where what it means to be in common is open to free contestation; it is a way of opening community to itself rather than to a particular destiny or future or to the nostalgic desire for a lost community that might be redeemed and restored.[27]

Not a community of individual subjects whose subjectivity precedes their being in relation, not a merging of individuals into some greater totality or essence, not a collective will or reference to a common origin, not a promise of immanence or the product of projected labor, community for Nancy is precisely what is disseminated and unworked as "the irrepressible but unsublatable liminality of social interaction." Inaugurated and sustained in difference rather than in the overcoming of differences, such a transformed thought of community would be nonhierarchical, affirmative, contestatory, nonteleological, nontotalizable, and based on a nonbinary, nonexclusive logic—thereby mirroring the incomplete, open character of every identity, every social interaction, every culture.

Nancy's theory represents nothing less than a call to reinvent the bases of our social imaginaries in relation to a new thought of difference and a new communitarian logic that attempts to "think from the communal" in its redefined sense and not simply about it. Even if we bracket for the moment Nancy's insistence that we cannot work to institute or realize the thought of community, such an imperative is difficult indeed, a difficulty arising in part from having to operate within old conceptual frameworks and traditions while trying to rework and displace them. However, predicated as they were on a simultaneous copresence of participants working in common, the practices of communal creation that occurred at the Laboratory of Contemporary Culture resonate in interesting ways with Nancy's intersubjective notion of identity and his call for new communitarian logics. The ephemeral nature of the Lab's improvisational space also echoes his call for sites where community may be opened to the process of its own unfolding rather than to a particular ideology or telos. Finally, in its reassertion of those collaborative artistic impulses repressed by the academic institution of modernism (with its cult of the individual genius), as well as by the structure of the contemporary U.S. academy, and in its reinvigoration of a concept of the communal as a desiring space ruined by the Soviet system, the Lab presents a vision of community and the creation of culture in which what it means to be in common is open to genuine contestation through an ongoing encounter with the other's difference.

Although the innovative Russian institutions that Epstein helped to pioneer were a culturally specific response to a unique historical moment, their example helps to expose other critical blind spots in contemporary cultural theory, in part by working with terms that have been rendered currently unthinkable within it, such as "individual," "universality," and "totality" (which Epstein is careful to re-figure as a "nontotalitarian totality"). The Lab may also provide an important perspective on some of our most pressing cultural limitations. For example, many American critics identify a particular manifestation of the contemporary crisis of community in the loss of an ideal of participatory democracy in contemporary society, the loss of a genuinely representative public sphere—defined as an institutionalized arena of discursive interaction (and not market relations) within which full participation is theoretically possible. In part this crisis arises as a result of the manufacturing of public opinion through the media as well as the fragmentation of a unified public sphere into a host of competing counterpublics, part of an increasingly global postmodern condition. Critics such as Nancy Fraser and Michael Warner note the urgent need to construct alternative models of democracy in postmodern America, to expand the availability of discursive space and the possibilities of discursive contestation among these competing publics. In offering models of public cultural interaction that could be thought of as forms of almost-pure democracy, these Russian cultural institutions may help us to see more clearly the limits of democratic institutions as they currently exist in late capitalist societies and may provide new perspectives on the project of rethinking the ways in which notions of the public sphere currently operate in Western culture. In part, I offer this and the other suggestions against the widespread insistence that the post-communist moment automatically signals an uncritical triumph of Western democracy and an implicit justification for the superiority of Western ways of life more generally.

I also present these final points as speculations, lines of thinking that might open rather than foreclose genuinely new critical possibilities. As subsequent chapters will make clear, my larger intention is to argue for the value of such speculations in creating more expansive critical agendas in a contemporary moment. Ultimately they might lead to the development of more enabling models and metaphors, to the discovery of anticipatory forms of cultural production, and to the invention of new models of comparativism, ones that would encourage genuine exchange—change on both sides of the comparison—rather than merely static confrontation between two rigid and unchanging points of view. Such models of cultural production and interaction—inspired by the history told here—might then also lead to more expansive and genuinely liberatory critical and cultural practices.

Having said this, however, I don't mean to suggest that either the impulse to develop or the actual development of new methods of cultural reinvention are unique to Russian culture. As I discuss in later chapters, new transcultural methods of inquiry and experimentation are emerging in the West as well, particularly in response to the fact of a vastly more complex, increasingly interdependent, globalized world. Nonetheless, I do think that a number of factors conditioned the specific forms taken by these Russian cultural institutions, and that these cultural forms and institutional modes—in the particularity of their cultural difference—are useful for Western scholars to consider for the reasons I have elaborated.

First, the historical moment of perestroika encouraged experimentation in a particularly direct way—indeed, made it vitally necessary to seize an opportunity to push cultural limits that might at any moment disappear. Both the nature and the magnitude of this cultural imperative, if you will, have no direct corollary in recent American history. Second, the Russian tradition of thinking about culture in a holistic sense that Epstein has elaborated, along with the damaging legacy of an imposed ideological correctness in all realms, including the cultural, make it more likely that theories with the sweep of culturology and transculture (in its Russian variant) would develop in the former Soviet Union. As Western scholars, we may have difficulty accepting the claims made for transcultural transformation, among other reasons because of our tendency to think of cultural production and cultural analysis as distinctly separate activities; because of the nature of intellectual activity in the United States, most of which is confined to the academy; and because of our suspicion of grand-scale plans or claims of any kind, questions/limitations I take up more extensively in later chapters. On the other hand, perhaps it is the case that one aspect of the complex process of cultural interference that we describe and enact in this book involves a kind of reverse cultural chauvinism, in which we find it easier to recognize in the experience of another culture solutions to the most pressing problems of our own.

Notes

1. Renato Poggioli, *The Theory of the Avant-Garde*, trans. Gerald Fitzgerald (Cambridge: Harvard University, 1968): 94, 96, 227.
2. Peter Burger, *Theory of the Avant-Garde* (Minneapolis: University of Minnesota, 1984).
3. Jean Baudrillard, "The Year 2000 Has Already Happened," in Arthur and Marilouise Kroker, *Body Invaders* (New York: St. Martin's Press, 1987): 43.
4. Sadie Plant, *The Most Radical Gesture: The Situationist International in a Postmodern Age* (London: Routledge, 1992): 163, 40.
5. Debord, in Plant, 183.
6. Quoted in Plant, 154.
7. Charles Russell, *Poets, Prophets and Revolutionaries: The Literary Avant-Garde from Rimbaud through Postmodernism* (New York: Oxford University Press, 1985): 238.
8. Walter Kaladjian, *American Culture Between the Wars: Revisionary Modernism and Postmodern Critique* (New York: Columbia University Press, 1993): 3, 18.
9. See, for example, Rosalind Krauss's argument that postmodern art makes a decisive break with both modernism and avant-gardism in its deconstruction of the notion of origin and originality in, "The Originality of the Avant-Garde: A Postmodernist Repetition," *October* 18 (Fall 1988): 47–66.
10. Russell, 172.
11. For an elaboration of connections between post-communism and postmodernism, see Epstein's "The Origins and Meaning of Russian Postmodernism," and my "Postmodernism East and West" in Ellen E. Berry and Anesa Miller-Pogacar, eds., *Re-Entering the Sign: Articulating New Russian Culture* (Ann Arbor: University of Michigan Press, 1995); and Jerome McGann et al., eds., "Symposium on Russian Postmodernism," *Postmodern Culture* 3: 1 (1994).
12. Elena Izumova, unpublished manuscript.
13. Ellen E. Berry, Kent Johnson, and Anesa Miller-Pogacar, "An Interview with Mikhail Epstein," *Common Knowledge* 2: No. 3 (1993): 112, 116–17.

14. Epstein, unpublished interview with the author, May 1995. Cf. M. Epstein, *After the Future* . . ., pp. 89–90.
15. For an analysis of one of the rear-garde's most vivid and extravagant manifestations see Ellen E. Berry and Anesa Miller-Pogacar, "A Shock Therapy of the Social Consciousness: The Nature and Cultural Function of Russian Necrorealism," *Cultural Critique* 34 (Winter 1997).
16. Mikhail Epstein, *After the Future: The Paradoxes of Postmodernism and Contemporary Russian Culture* (Amherst: University of Massachusetts Press, 1995): 93. On the three types of prose (centered, eccentric, and decentered) and on the concept of the rear-garde, see pp. 88–94 of the same book.
17. Epstein, unpublished interview with the author, May 1995.
18. Ibid.
19. Epstein, unpublished interview with the author, May 1995.
20. Epstein, *After the Future* . . ., pp. 334–335.
21. Miami Theory Collective, *Community at Loose Ends* (Minneapolis: University of Minnesota Press, 1991), ix.
22. Jean-Luc Nancy, *The Inoperative Community* (Minneapolis: University of Minnesota Press, 1991), 1.
23. Iris Marion Young, "The Ideal of Community and the Politics of Difference" in Linda J. Nicholson, ed., *Feminism/Postmodernism* (London: Routledge, 1990), 302.
24. Nancy, 30.
25. Ibid., 33, 34.
26. Ibid., 41.
27. Ibid., 42.

Part II

Theory

A. Definitions

Chapter 4

Transculture in the Context of Contemporary Critical Theories

Mikhail Epstein

The following notes intend only to delineate the territory of transculture on the map of contemporary theories, not to present it in color and detail.

Deconstruction and Multiculturalism

The project of transculture as applied to the Western postmodern condition grows from the latter's internal tensions and contradictions. There are two principal aspects of postmodern theory that are increasingly found to be in fundamental disagreement: deconstruction and multiculturalism.

The focus of deconstruction is the critique of essentialism, the refutation of the metaphysics of presence and origin. As we can read in Jacques Derrida and his followers, neither writing nor any system of signs, including culture as a whole, has any historical or physical origin that can be fixed in a certain moment of time or in the presence of some material body. Signs have relationship only with one another, and even the difference between signs and nonsigns constitutes still another level of the sign system and its internal division and multiplication. There are no origins, only traces left by these presupposed origins, only copies of the "original," and there is no end to the progression or regression of signs to the openness of the future or the past. "The trace is not only the disappearance of origin—within the discourse that we sustain and according to the path that we follow it means that the origin did not even disappear, that it was never constituted except reciprocally by a nonorigin, the trace, which thus becomes the origin of the origin."[1] From this perspective cultures do not reproduce or represent any natural condition, but rather constitute their own origin, beyond any initial physical parameters. If these parameters, like blackness or whiteness, maleness or femaleness, are invoked in the progression of culture, it is not because of their original essence, but because a certain author constructs his/her cultural personality in this way. Deconstruction, followed to its logical end, opens in its every object the capacity to endlessly reconstruct and redefine itself. The "origin" is never present as a determination of cultural identity; on the contrary, from the very beginning it is constructed culturally.

The axiomatics of deconstructionist theory come into contradiction with the axiomatics of another theory that is equally considered to be a foundation of the postmodernist paradigm: that of multiculturalism. Among various currents within multiculturalism, I refer mostly to those promoting essential and even essentialist connections between cultural production and ethnic and physical origin, including the institutionalized multiculturalism of the mainstream curriculum in American academia. Even the so-called strategic essentialism advocated by thinkers such as Gayatri Spivak, though accepting essentialism only as a temporary remedy, still clearly exemplifies this "other side" of the postmodern paradigm, in its sharp contradiction with the Deleuzean and Derridean theories of cultural "deterritorialization" and "the lack of origin."

Given these qualifications, multiculturalism proceeds from the assumption that each cultural formation can and should be explained in relation to its racial, sexual, or ethnic origin that gives rise to the particular system of social signification. As Toni Morrison, a Nobel prize-winner in literature, puts it, "Of course I'm a black writer. . . . I'm not just a black writer, but categories like black writer, woman writer and Latin American writer aren't marginal anymore. We have to acknowledge that the thing we call 'literature' is more pluralistic now, just as society ought to be. The melting pot never worked. We ought to be able to accept on equal terms everybody from the Hasidim to Walter Lippmann, from the Rastafarians to Ralph Bunche."[2] From this point of view there is no such abstract thing as a masterpiece of world literature but only a variety of specific canons, each reflecting the cultural dispositions of a given racial or sexual subject. Therefore the very definitions of multiple cultures necessarily include references to their point of physical origin as is true in "white male" culture, or "black female" culture, or "homosexual" culture.

If deconstruction and multiculturalism are two complementary aspects of the postmodernist paradigm, should we remain unaware of this basic contradiction that agonizes the entire postmodernist project? The stress on ethnic and sexual origins disables and undermines the deconstructionist approach, and vice versa: The more consistently we denounce any talk of physical presence or historic origin behind the cultural system of signs, the more futile is the multiculturalist insistence on the deduction of cultural heritage from the peculiarities of a given race and sex.

Jacques Derrida recently touched on this contradiction by setting up deconstruction against those multicultural theories that stress an external difference between self-enclosed cultural identities instead of looking into the internal difference that infuses and dynamizes all forms of identity.

> We often insist nowadays on cultural identity, for instance, national identity, linguistic identity, and so on. Sometimes the struggles under the banner of cultural identity, national identity, linguistic identity, are noble fights. But at the same time the people who fight for their identity must pay attention to the fact that identity is not the self-identity of a thing, this glass, for instance, this microphone, but implies difference within identity. That is, the identity of a culture is a way of being different from itself; a culture is different from itself; language is different from itself; the person is different from itself. Once you take into account this inner and other [outer?] difference, then you pay attention to the other and you understand that fighting for your own identity is not exclusive of another identity, is open to another identity. And this prevents totalitarianism, nationalism, egocentrism, and so on.[3]

The tension between deconstruction and multiculturalism is further accentuated by those thinkers who recognize the validity of deconstruction but still find essentialism to be a useful strategy to pursue the rights of minorities and the politics of identity. According to bell hooks, ". . . we cannot cavalierly dismiss a concern with identity politics. . . . The unwillingness to critique essentialism on the part of many African-Americans is rooted in the fear that it will cause folks to lose sight of the specific history and experience of African-Americans and the unique sensibilities and culture that arise from this experience."[4]

These two views—the multiculturalist, stressing "collective identities," and the deconstructionist, stressing "internal diffferences"—become increasingly incompatible within one theoretical paradigm. What is needed now is further thinking about the possible resolution or at least conscious elaboration of this contradiction. Is there any theoretical possibility of combining the theory of cultural origins with the theory of deconstruction and dis-origination as the specific model of cultural creativity?

I would like to consider the work of Merab Mamardashvili (1930–1990) as a different voice from an ethnic minority. Mamardashvili was a major Russian philosopher of Georgian origin, who spent his last years in his native Tbilisi, where he suffered through the excesses of Georgian cultural and political nationalism exacerbated by the downfall of the Soviet empire. Mamardashvili sympathizes with multiculturalism as a mode of liberation from a monolithic cultural canon, but objects to the glorification of ethnic diversity for its own sake. Parroting a typical argument: "Each culture is valuable in itself. People should be allowed to live within their cultures,"—Mamardashvili objects that, "The defense of autonomous customs sometimes proves to be a denial of the right to freedom and to another world. It seems as if a decision were made for them: you live in such an original way, that it is quite cultural to live as you do, so go on and live this way. But did anyone ask me personally? . . . Perhaps I am suffocating within the fully autonomous customs of my complex and developed culture?"[5]

Thus, what needs to be preserved, in Mamardashvili's view, is the right to live beyond one's culture, on the borders of cultures, to take "a step transcending one's own surrounding, native culture and milieu not for the sake of anything else. Not for the sake of any other culture, but for the sake of nothing. Transcendence into nothing. Generally speaking, such an act is truly the living, pulsating center of the entire human universe. This is a primordial metaphysical act." Mamardashvili understands metaphysics to be the movement beyond any physical determination and liberation from any social and cultural identity: "This understandable, noble aspiration to defend those who are oppressed by some kind of culture-centrism, for example Eurocentrism or any other—this aspiration forgets and makes us forget that there exists a metaphysics of freedom and thought that is not peculiar to us alone. This is a kind of reverse racism."[6] This type of racism can be described as a variety of reductionism, which includes not only the reduction of a diversity of cultures to one privileged canon, but also the reduction of a diversity of personalities to their "origins," their "genetic" culture. To transcend the limits of one's native culture does not constitute betrayal, because the limits of any culture are too narrow for the full range of human potentials. From this standpoint, transculture does not mean adding yet another culture to the existing array; it is rather a special mode of existence spanning cultural boundaries, a transcendence into "no culture," which indicates how, ultimately, the human being exceeds all "genetic" definitions.

Thus, to reduce culture to its racial or sexual origin means to ignore what makes culture different from nature. We can rephrase T. S. Eliot's famous passage in "Tradition and the Individual Talent": "Culture is not a turning loose of nature, but an escape from nature."[7] Culture in general can be described as the process of denaturalization and de-origination, which bears a connection with its origin only through the series of its erasures and subversions. This does not mean that the origin does not exist at all, that, as Derrida put it, "the origin did not even disappear, that it was never constituted except reciprocally by a nonorigin."[8] Such a radical denial would eliminate the dramatic tension that connects culture with its natural origins in the dialectics of departure and return, erasure and recognition. To expose physical origins as only retroactively "constructed" and entirely determined by subsequent cultural "self-images" would be a mere inversion of the derivation of culture from physical origins, i.e. a reverse form of determinism, now imposed from the present onto the past.

We cannot simply deny the role of inborn conditions, or genes in cultural formations. No escape or "deterritorialization" would be possible without the initial territory occupied by ethnic origins, gender, etc. Origins need to be clearly stated in order to be vigorously transcended. The location of the prison certainly predetermines the route of flight from the prison, and such "determinism" is a prerequisite for liberation. Natural origins are overstepped in cultural evolution and simultaneously reinscribed into its sign systems, as "whiteness" or "blackness," "masculinity" or "femininity" of cultural practices and rituals. We have to recognize the truth of multiculturalism in order to proceed with the task of deconstruction. Though an escape from nature, culture is still too natural, too essentialist, too deterministic; it carries further the racial, ethnic, and sexual limitations imposed by nature and therefore calls for new efforts of liberation.

Therefore we need to re-historicize the project of deconstruction, inscribing it within the future perspectives of cultures rather than denying their natural origins in the past. Cultures do have origins and are indeed sustained and determined by these origins. Only by accepting these origins can we posit the goal of dis-origination, the flight from origins as an emerging historical possibility. Instead of a theoretical denial of origins, we envision their historical overcoming. Deconstruction of the past should not diminish our historical labor in constructing the future.

It is in this space of internal tension between multiculturalism and deconstruction, between origins and disorigination, where the transcultural movement evolves. Transculture presumes the enduring "physicality" and "essentiality" of existing cultures and the possibility of their further transcendence, in particular through interference with other cultures. To be cultural means to rise above one's inborn identity, such as "white, adult male," through the variety of self-deconstructions, self-transformations, and interferences with other identities, such as woman, black, child, disabled. For this purpose books, films, and all sign systems are created: to dissolve the solidity of one's nature, one's identity and to share the experience of "the other."

Identity may be formed both on biological and symbolic levels, for example, as "natural sex" and as "cultural sexism," which correspond to the two possible movements of their subversion, cultural and transcultural. This can be illustrated by one passage from Julia Kristeva's "Women's Time"(1979). In her challenge to the concept of "gender identity" that had been cherished by the previous generations of feminists, Kristeva finds it necessary to "bring out—along with the *singularity* of each person and, even more, along with the multiplicity of every person's possible identifications . . . —*the relativity of his/her symbolic as well as biological existence. . . .*"[9] Gender identity makes way for a multiplicity of personalities, each with its own potential for further multiple identifications. The crucial role in this "relativization" of both biological and symbolic identities belongs, according to Kristeva, to "aesthetic practices" designed to "demystify" the ideological uniformity of gender and therefore to provide the symbolic "retreat from sexism (male as well as female)." Here we need to accentuate a distinction between the two levels of "relativization" implicitly inscribed in Kristeva's passage. Biological existence is relativized in symbolic practices of replacement and mediation that allow humans to transcend their original identities. But the same practices subsequently reestablish some "symbolic bond" or "community of language" among the representatives of the same biological identity, which corresponds to the strategies of "old feminism" as criticized by Kristeva. These symbolic identities should be "relativized" in their own turn, and Kristeva emphasizes this transcultural aspect of aesthetic practices by her call "to demystify the identity of the symbolic bond itself, to demystify, therefore, the *community* of language as a universal and unifying tool, one which totalizes and equalizes."[10]

Culture relativizes natural identities, whereas transculture demystifies cultural identities. This process has no limit. From a transcultural perspective, multiculturalism is right in asserting the natural origins and physical essences of existing cultures, whereas deconstruction is equally right in demystifying these origins and essences. It is not merely a contradiction within the postmodern paradigm but the very engine of its further transformation. Origins need to be acknowledged in order to be exceeded in the transnatural movement of culture that at a certain stage passes into transcultural movement.

Thus transculture arises from the internal paradox of postmodernity, not as a denial of this paradox but as an attempt at its conscious resolution.

Counterculture and Transculture

The countercultural model, which theoretically was elaborated by Herbert Marcuse and other New Left thinkers, underscored the role of marginalized strata and minorities in the transformation of the society. Racial and national minorities, students and intellectuals, lumpenized/declassed elements of the proletariat, and presumably even criminals had to unite against the capitalist system and to initiate social revolution.

The subsequent development of Western critical theory has tamed this revolutionary zeal of Marcusean reasoning but reaffirmed the appeal to minorities. Instead of instigating these minorities to radical actions against the entire system, as in the 1960s, critical theorists of the 1980s, such as Cornel West, bell hooks, and Homi Bhabha, propose the construction of a multicultural or "minoritized" society in which no group could claim the status of the ruling majority and each group would enjoy equal rights and respect for its national, racial, or gender identity. The theory of a counterculture in this sense can be regarded as a transition from the unitary conception of society ("living organism" or "melting pot") to multiculturalism ("mosaics," "rainbow" etc.). The concept of revolution had to connect multiple groups marginalized by or isolated from the society with the unitary ideal of the transformation of society as a whole. Paradoxically, the concept of revolution as a total destruction of the existing system turned out to be the last theoretical representation of the society as one whole, if only on the grounds that the society had to become the total object of annihilation.

As soon as the Marxist-Maoist-Marcusean ideal of revolution was abandoned in the mid-1970s, Western society had no more critical theories based on the unitary vision of society. After that, "unitary" and "critical" proved to be mutually exclusive terms. Critical theory now pursued not the transformation of the entire society but rather the growth of its internal diversity. The multiplicity of cultures and "subsocieties" had to replace the ideologically produced illusion of unity. Such a "minority rule" does not leave a social space for majorities, and even "white male culture" is reduced to the status of the *largest minority* as compared with the population of all other minority groups taken together (women, blacks, children, etc.). Subsequent divisions within the white male population, such as heterosexual and homosexual cultures, or youth and adult cultures, make for the further minoritization of any segment of the society.

The transcultural is based on the fact that many of the differences haunting Western and especially American society can be found within individuals.[11] This model takes into account the multiple identities of each individual and therefore is distinct both from the revolutionary model of the New Left and the multicultural model of collective identity politics. For example, youth culture can be viewed not as a separate stratum of the population but as each adult's inner experience and a transcultural drive. Adults who are faithful to their youthful commitments, friendships, and aspirations are not easily socialized in the way that the economic or ideological establishment requires them to be. Absolute socialization would mean that each person has his or her own strictly demarcated function in the mechanisms of economic and political productivity; however, each person has experiences and horizons that transcend this ideal of social unification. Among these transcultural experiences one can mention the experience of childhood, the experience of illness, the experience of love. We do not need to postulate the culture of "differently abled" people as a separate group only because almost all of us, or at least the vast majority of us, has at one time or another belonged to this group, has had the experience of illness, suffering, alienation.

In this sense, the majority of people, for shorter or longer periods, acquire different identities and belong to many actual or virtual minorities. Through love, we acquire the identity of our beloved, man or woman; through emigration or travel, the identities of foreigners . . . "Strangely, the foreigner lives within us: he is the hidden face of our identity, the space that wrecks our abode, the time in which understanding and affinity founder. By recognizing him within ourselves, we are spared detesting him in himself."[12] Julia Kristeva's dramatic description should be inverted: It is precisely this interior foreignness that grounds our understanding and affinity with the other. It is through the diversity of an individual experience that such distinct groups as men and women, adults and children, healthy and disabled, natives and foreigners can interact and find otherness within themselves.

One of the strongest factors resisting socialization in totalitarian states like the Soviet Union is people's attachment to their homes, but we do not need to establish a separate group of "homebodies" as a special minority because, again, they amount to the majority of the society. The task is not to dissect society into different organs, equalized and isolated "cultural castes," but to emphasize those multiple and fluid identities of each individual that allow him or her to transcend all group identities. This is the goal of transculture: to activate and mobilize transcultural elements in the society by invoking the value of those experiences and potentials that cannot be culturally stratified.

Instead of the revolutionary model, which opposes marginal elements to the social establishment; and instead of the differential model, which posits the multiplicity of collective identities, tolerant of but not interested in each other; transculture proposes the model of inherently "multicultural" individuals capable of crossing the borders of collective cultural identities. It is still possible to apply the term "critical theory" to transculturalism, but I would prefer to call it the theory of *positive otherness* because it does not so much criticize the unitary society or the dominant canon as it gives positive value to the experience of transcendence, not as an escape into the other world but as the *othering of this world:* via the experiences of childhood, youth, love, illness, loneliness, emigration, and pilgrimage . . .

The Marxist-Leninist Approach

The division of culture into "progressive" and "reactionary," or "the oppressive culture of the majority" and "the oppressed cultures of minorities" is still popular in contemporary politicized Western critical theory, after it dominated the now-extinct system of Soviet ideology for many decades. The division of one national culture into two opposing cultures was proposed by Lenin in his famous article "Critical Notes on the National Issue" (1913), later recognized as a model of Marxist discourse on culture. "There are two nations in each contemporary nation. . . . There are two national cultures in each national culture. There is [reactionary] Russian culture of Purishkevichs, Guchkovs and Struves,—but there is also [progressive] Russian culture characterized by the names of Chernyshevsky and Plekhanov. The same two cultures are in the Ukraine, in Germany, France, England, among Jews, etc."[13] Though unified by one national language, each culture, according to Lenin, is composed of two class subcultures: one of the oppressors—aristocratic and bourgeois culture, and another of the oppressed—democratic and revolutionary culture.

Though Lenin's hypothesis allegedly sought to diversify culture by having at least two of them instead of one, almost none of those figures he mentions as exemplifying these two cultures belonged to culture at all. Purishkevich, Guchkov, Struve, and Plekhanov were politicians of various orientations, from extreme nationalism and liberalism to Marxism. Chernyshevsky, a revolutionary writer of the 1860s, the author of the topical novel *What is to Be Done?*, also was more famous for his political ideas than aesthetic achievements. Is it just a coincidental choice of names on Lenin's part? Why did he not mention Pushkin or Gogol, Tolstoy or Dostoevsky, Glinka or Tchaikovsky, the indubitable representatives of Russian culture? Unfortunately for Lenin's theory, none of these creators could exemplify this class division; none belonged to either an oppressive or an oppressed culture, the exploiters or the exploited, probably because culture cannot be described in these terms at all.

In the same way the division of Western culture into two poles, "majority" and "minorities," "canon" and "margins," ignores the multidimensionality of cultural systems and reflects its sociological or political simplification and leveling. "Oppressing" and "oppressed," "progressive" and "reactionary" are political or even partisan categories externally imposed on culture and useful indeed for understanding what culture is not. Culture is "cultural" to the degree that it transcends those barriers and oppositions that permeate the society and the struggle of political parties. Leo Tolstoy's art had value not because it was aristocratic or antiaristocratic but because it transcended the boundary of "aristocratic-democratic." Both terms are derived from the sphere of politics and are applicable, in their proper sense, only to political regimes, the establishments of power, "-cracies." Can we apply, then, the definitions "aristocratic" or "bourgeois" to cultures as a whole?

The assumption that the entire culture, including ethics and philosophy, science and poetry, is centered in the issue of power continues to dominate neo-Marxist and neo-Nietzschean discourse in the Western humanities of the late twentieth century. According to Michel Foucault, "the intellectual has a three-fold specificity: that of his class position (whether as petty-bourgeois in the service of capitalism or 'organic' intellectual of the proletariat); that of his conditions of life and work, linked to his condition as an intellectual (the field of research, his place in a laboratory, the political and economic demands to which he submits or against which he rebels, in the hospital, in the university, etc.); lastly, the specificity of the politics of truth in our societies."[14] To put it briefly, first, second, and third, the specificity of being intellectual is to be a politician.

This is exactly the fallacy about which culturology warns us: the identification of culture as a whole with one part of it, such as politics. The very term "transculture," as used in this section, could be easily replaced simply with "culture" if our notion of culture itself had not suffered so much from its political and other reductive adaptations. The prefix "trans-" is added in order to revitalize the meaning of culture in its dynamic and trans-formative quality, and to restore the integrative meaning of culture after it underwent a number of dissections, such as the one that we have cited from Lenin. If culture is reduced to the category of "social value," or "dominating canon," or "ideological superstructure," or "instrument of class struggle," then the notion of "transculture" is necessary at least to reinstate the domain of culture to its full dimension.

Notes

1. Jacques Derrida, *Of Grammatology*, trans. Gayatri Spivak (Baltimore: The Johns Hopkins University Press, 1976): 61.
2. Quoted in *Newsweek*, 30 March 1981.
3. Jacques Derrida, *Deconstruction in a Nutshell: A Conversation*. (Roundtable on 2 October 1994, at Villanova University), ed. with Commentary by John D. Caputo (New York: Fordham University, 1997): 13–14.
4. bell hooks, "Postmodern Blackness," in *The Truth about Truth. De-confusing and Re-constructing the Postmodern World*, ed. Walter Truett Anderson (New York: Jeremy P. Tarcher/Putnam, 1995): 120, 122.
5. Merab Mamardashvili, "Drugoe nebo" (Another sky), in his book *Kak ia ponimaiu filosofiiu* (How I understand philosophy). (Moscow: Progress, izdatel'skaia gruppa "Kul'tura," 1992): 335, 337.

    A similar "internal" resistance to what later became known as multiculturalism can be detected in black writing. Charles W. Chesnutt (1858–1932), one of the first African American novelists whose books deal with race prejudice, observed as early as 1905: "We are told that we must glory in our color and zealously guard it as a priceless heritage. . . . Frankly, I take no stock in this doctrine. It seems to me a modern invention of the white people to perpetuate the color line. It is they who preach it, and it is their racial integrity which they wish to preserve: they have never been unduly careful of the purity of the black race. . . . Why should a man be proud any more than he should be ashamed of a thing for which he is not at all responsible? . . . Are we to help the white people to build up walls between themselves and us to fence in a gloomy back yard for our descendants to play in?" Charles W. Chesnutt, "Race Prejudice: Its Causes and Its Cures: An Address Delivered before the Boston Historical and Literary Association," *Alexander's Magazine*, 1 (July 1905): 25.

6. Ibid., 336.
7. T. S. Eliot wrote: "Poetry is not a turning loose of emotion, but an escape from emotion; it is not the expression of personality, but an escape from personality." *Critical Theory since Plato*, ed. Hazard Adams (Fort Worth: Harcourt Brace Jovanovich College Publishers, 1992): 764.
8. Jacques Derrida, *Of Grammatology*, trans. Gayatri Spivak (Baltimore: The Johns Hopkins University Press, 1976): 61.
9. *Critical Theory Since 1965*, ed. Hazard Adams & Leroy Searle (Tallahassee: Florida State University Press, 1990): 484.
10. Ibid., 484.
11. On the psychological and social significance of multiple cultural identities see Robert Jay Lifton, *Boundaries: Psychological Man in Revolution* (New York: Random House, 1970); Kenneth Gergen, *The Saturated Self: Dilemmas of Identity in Contemporary Life* (New York: Basic Books, 1991).
12. Julia Kristeva, *Strangers to Ourselves*, trans. Leon S. Roudiez. (New York: Columbia University Press, 1994): 1.
13. *Istoriia estetiki. Pamiatniki mirovoi esteticheskoi mysli* (Moscow: Iskusstvo, 1970): Vol. 5, 210.
14. "Truth and Power" (interview), in Michel Foucault, *Power/Knowledge: Selected Interviews and Other Writings, 1972–1977*, ed. Colin Gordon (New York: Pantheon Books, 1982): 132.

Chapter 5

From Difference To Interference
Mikhail Epstein

From Identity/Opposition to Difference

The concept of difference stands between two related categories of identity and opposition. Opposition was the most powerful theoretical instrument of Hegelian and Marxist theory as based on the dialectical relationship between thesis and antithesis. The Marxist "class struggle" was the exemplification of this logical opposition in the history of society. The principle of identity is deeply connected with the principle of opposition and cannot be divorced from it. If opposition is the basic model of relationship between social groups then each individual is bound to identify with one of these groups. If the meaning of history lies in the opposition (struggle, antagonism) of exploited and exploiters, or North and South, or East and West, or imperialist and colonized, then one can participate in history only through identification with one of these polarized groups. Thus the quest for identity entails the construction of real or imaginable oppositions. I join one party, evidently, in order to oppose another party; I identify myself as a democrat in order to oppose myself to aristocrats or communists.

However, the categories of opposition and identity, though complementing each other, do not preclude the significance of the third category, which is difference. In fact, both identity and opposition are only ideational or ideological projections of difference. We can, for example, oppose black and white because these are not real entities but abstract qualities; however, we cannot oppose real things, such as rain and table or lake and lion, because these entities are composed of many qualities. Though each of these qualities can be opposed to the corresponding quality of other entities (liquid rain—solid table, black coal—white sugar, etc.), the very fact that each entity is endowed with many qualities makes them different from but never opposite to each other. For example, two people, A and B, can be opposed by the color of their skin, but each of these individuals still possesses many other qualities: one is thirty-seven years old, the other is twenty-one; one likes cinema, the other likes basketball; one is Republican, the other is not a member of any party; one prefers meat, the other is a vegetarian. Each of these qualities in their abstractness can be opposed to each other: black and white, meat and vegetables, mature and young; but the specific bearers of these qualities, A and B, do not comprise opposites—they are simply different. In the same way, a person can never fully identify herself with any one of her qualities; to say "I am black" or "I am white" is a way of partial identification that becomes false when it claims to be full and exhaustive. "I" has no color, like the eyes into which we are looking have no color. The principle of difference can be formulated in this way: to oppose oneself to nobody, to identify oneself with nothing. As soon as we eliminate oppositional components in our self-definition, the component of identification will also be abandoned, and vice versa.

Meanwhile, "opposition" and "identity" not only come from the same categorial nest, but in the contemporary humanities they tend to conflate again, which confirms their interdependent nature. For example, in Honi Fern Haber's elaboration of "the politics of difference," which she uncritically identifies as "oppositional" politics, we can find such oxymoronic expressions as the call "to achieve oppositional identities."[1] The goal of postmodern theory, as set by this author, is "oppositional identity formation." This is quite a coherent conclusion, based on her assumption that "the subject must be seen as being formed within communities—many communities and changing communities."[2] Such is the theoretical limit of social determinism: It is ready to acknowledge the variety of communities, but still insists on the entirely communal nature of the subject. What is the driving force of "changing communities," then, if the individual as such is recognized only as a member of the community, or, according to Haber's words, if "our interests are always the interests of some community or another?"[3]

No wonder such an emphasis on collective identity reinforces the oppositions among communities and leaves no space for difference as a category that is itself different from both identity and opposition. The misunderstanding goes as far as to equalize these two notions, "opposition" and "difference," and to use them as synonyms: "My overall project . . . attempts to create a space for oppositional politics that can also be described as a 'politics of difference' . . ."[4]

It appears that a "politics of difference," by its very definition, cannot be oppositional, but should be consistently differential, which means avoiding both extremes of identity and opposition. The "differential" interaction between people emphasizes their personal differences, preventing them from making a "group identity," but also stopping short of stiffening these differences into oppositions (ideological, cultural, social, etc.). The differences complement each other and create a new interpersonal totality to which people belong, not because they are similar, but because they are different.

Certainly, a "politics of difference," in this particular sense, as a truly differential politics, will have to differentiate itself, first of all, from politics understood exclusively as the technology of power. The latter hardly can be "differential" rather than oppositional, because power, by its very definition, is power of one group of people over other group(s) and therefore presumes the opposition between the subject and the object of power. In this case, all claims of politics to be "differential" are purely utopian. But if it is still possible to define politics, or at least a branch of it, as a creative organization of public life or constructive participation in public affairs, then, outside the domain of inherently oppositional power relations, a "politics of difference" can be pursued quite effectively.

The problem with multiculturalism is that it halts the endless play of self-differentiation, with its potential for new creative unities, for the sake of extensive production of self-enclosed and highly oppositional identities. One cannot but agree with Karl Kroeber, who writes in his manifesto for "ecological literary criticism" :

> The importance of diversity, and ultimately of uniqueness, has been threatened by recent separatist critics as seriously as by earlier modernist proponents of 'universals'—which in fact turn out to be no more than the generalizations of Western European modes of thought. Ecological criticism, rejecting the popular reductionism that goes no farther than 'otherness,' specifies the significance of concrete distinctions—thereby making possible a dynamically complex cosmopolitan vision capable of liberating criticism from endlessly subdividing itself into defensive parochialisms of spirit.[5]

What Kroeber calls "ecological criticism" is a fruitful attempt to avoid the dilemma of old-fashioned modernist "universals" and postmodern "multiple identities;" the natural environment, however, hardly can be presented as the only or the most important target of such an approach. Another attempt in the same direction leads to the notion of "mixed" or "hybrid" forms of identity. It is quite understandable that a person with several ethnic backgrounds or an immigrant would try to substantiate his/her new identity through the synthesis of two or three cultural traditions. What is important, however, is to form new mixed identities in a way that differs from the way traditional mono-identities were formed. The "third zone," as Homi Bhabha puts it, is still a zone separated from the first or the second zone while transculture questions the very principle of zoning. The attempts to annunciate still another zone or identity actually reinforces the traditional way of thinking in "zones" and "segments" by dividing and multiplying this category rather than transcending it. If a person says that he is no longer simply an American but instead wants to be called an Asian American or a Russian American, he nonetheless still remains trapped within identity-based thinking.

Transcultural thinking does not add new categories to the existing list of identities but moves beyond the notion of identity, whether it is a single, or double, or multiple (hybridized) identity. The question is not who I am but who I might become and how I am different from myself. The category of identity is essentialist and naturalistic, derived from the kingdom of natural forms identical to themselves, including hybridized forms, transitional between various species and kingdoms. Hybridization and mutation, even if these categories are taken as metaphors, are still attached to the notion of species, stable essences as they are manifested in nature.

Beyond Struggle and Power

Contemporary cultural studies in the West is preoccupied with issues of power, empowerment, and political struggle. "There is no sign or thought of a sign that is not about power and of power," writes Jean-François Lyotard.[6] "Truth is linked in a circular relation with systems of power which produce and sustain it, and to effects of power which it induces and which extend it," says Michel Foucault.[7]

Power and struggle are based on *abstract* relationships among people, using the term "abstract" in a Hegelian sense, as both "devoid of rich specifications" and "historically immature." Although the call for struggles to overcome inequitable power relationships is most often made on the basis of quite concrete material realities, the struggle itself, as the engagement of an entire human being into an opposition to another human being, is an abstract relationship in the sense that it reduces all human differences to one particular issue that divides them. Both power and struggle usually insist meticulously on some very specific demands and tend to produce their detailed lists, but the type of relationship they inaugurate, that of opposition, renders people only schematic illustrations of some abstract principles: "good and bad," "rich and poor," "oppressors and revolutionaries."

Hegel asserted that the world makes permanent progress from the abstract to the concrete state of the Absolute Idea, and the same law operates in the history of human consciousness. He called this law "the ascension from the abstract to the concrete." On the abstract level, general properties determine the relationship between people. These generalities operate, on the one hand, as struggle or violent opposition; on the other hand, as power or enforced unity. Struggle is the social manifestation of abstract opposition, while power manifests the pretension to abstract unity. Both struggle and power are abstract because people are opposed or united on the basis of one general quality that is alienated from them and dominates them, such as their national identity, class origin, or ideological commitment. The more concrete the relationships between people, the more they abandon both abstract oppositions and abstract identities and base their interactions on difference.

The evolution from the unity-opposition mode to the difference mode follows this course of ascension from the abstract to the concrete that was elaborated by Hegel. Not surprisingly, however, this process of "ascension" finally transcends Hegel's own philosophical system, which logically is still based on the dialectics of opposition and unity, on the "struggle and unity of opposites," as the first and main law of dialectics is called. Marxism was an attempt to concretize this dialectics not only theoretically but practically and to integrate it into the variety of earthly social relationships among people. Marxist intervention in history, however, did not lead to the concretization of the dialectical law but to the increasing abstraction of history itself, which resulted in the absolute power of the totalitarian state and its antagonistic opposition to the rest of the world.

Presumably this paradoxical experiment in historical implementation of dialectics was useful in order to perceive the abstractness of dialectics itself that can never be concretized but renders abstract any living historical situation and reconfigures it along the lines of opposition and unity, struggle and power. Such an outcome, the greatest historical surprise of the twentieth century, could be predicted from the very premise that both unity and opposition, as basic categories of Hegelian and Marxist dialectics, operate only with general qualities, such as "thesis and antithesis," "antagonistic classes," "progressive and reactionary parties," etc., abstracted from individuals who in reality are neither identical nor opposite to each other but merely different. Dialectics, born from the logical plays of generalities, reproduced the same generalities on the level of historical forces at play: on the one hand, the most unified state in history, solidified by the terror and dictatorship of one party; on the other hand, the most stark and irreconcilable opposition between two world systems and superpowers, between "communist" and "capitalist" camps.

That is why the failure of the Marxist experiment requires the reconsideration of dialectics as such and its fundamental categories, "unity" and "opposition." Instead of concretization of dialectical laws, what appears on the intellectual agenda is the removal or "sublation" of dialectics itself and the search for the principle that would escape the abstractness of unity and opposition. This "third" principle, which provides for a more concrete approach to individuals and totalities than dialectics does, can be formulated as "difference." Difference does not operate with abstract qualities of people and objects but relates to the totality of various qualities, in such a way that this totality cannot be opposed to or identified with any other totality but is only different from them.

Difference in itself, however, also can operate as an abstract principle if it does not bring with it the potential for further internal differentiation. If opposition and unity as abstract principles have led in their historical manifestation to class antagonisms and totalitarian regimes, then the principle of difference, applied abstractly, can lead to complete mutual isolation and self-containment of the differentiated entities and their fixation in the state of *indifference* to each other. The principle of difference, such as it is, opens only a possibility for concrete thinking and concrete historical action, but in its first, most abstract application that is characteristic of postmodernist theory and practice, it generates "indifferent multiplicity," the pure "diversity" of those racial, ethnic, and gender groups that in a contemporary pluralistic society tend to ignore or become estranged from each other.

Therefore the next step of transition from the abstract to the concrete can lead to the fourth principle proceeding from difference but not limited to it. This principle that we call "interference," or "nontotalitarian totality," lies at the foundation of the transcultural project.

What is Different from Difference?

Now that Soviet totalitarianism has receded into the past, the desire and dream for new, nonviolent totalities intervenes into poststructuralist theory. The concept of difference worked successfully and progressively in the 1970s and 1980s, so far as political totalitarianism dominated in the East and a monolithic cultural canon dominated in the West. But in the 1990s, since the fall of the iron curtain, theory has had to respond to the radical changes in a world that is now more multicultural than ever, and more pluralized than polarized.

Transculture is the next stage of multicultural development, when the tendency for unification does not oppose itself to the diversity of cultures but issues from this diversity. The kind of pluralism that prevailed in multiculturalism can be called "passive" or "quantitative" since it recognized the pure, unqualified multiplicity of cultures without positing any ways for them to interact meaningfully and constructively. This pluralism was based on the ethical impulses of *pride*—in relation to one's one identity, and *tolerance*—in relation to other cultures.

What is at stake now is not whether different cultures can tolerate one another but whether they can be creatively involved with one another. From the multicultural perspective, each culture is perfect in its own way, as a self-enclosed and self-sufficient entity; from the transcultural perspective, each culture has some basic incompleteness that opens it for encounters with other cultures. The value of "pride" may be reconsidered in the light of another ethical disposition, "humility," which recognizes one's own deficiencies and the advantages of other(s). Consequently, "tolerance" gives way to active engagement and involvement with other cultures.

Transcultural theory is far from undermining the principle of difference; on the contrary, it pushes difference to the next stage of "differentiation from difference." As the principle of difference is accepted and shared by the major trends of poststructuralist thought, we can now assume the ensuing perspectives of self-differentiation as the foundation of a new, interferential model. Difference should not freeze into a one-dimensional state of self-identity, as a plain difference, or, as it does in many cases, as a catchy label for a simple opposition, like "black and white," or "culture and nature."

Even the classic works of Jacques Derrida on *différance* evidence the permanent danger of relapsing from a differential to an oppositional mode, as many of his favorite illustrations indicate. In discussing the effects of *différance* Derrida invariably cites the examples of the most traditional oppositions: intelligible/sensible, concept/intuition, etc. "Thus one could reconsider all the pairs of opposites on which philosophy is constructed and on which our discourse lives, not in order to see opposition erase itself but to see what indicates that each of the terms must appear as the *différance* of the other, as the other different and deferred in the economy of the same (the intelligible as differing-deferring the sensible, as the sensible different and deferred; the concept as different and deferred, different and deferring intuition; culture as nature different and deferred, different and deferring . . .)"[8] Or: ". . . the trace whereof I speak is not more *natural* . . . than *cultural*, no more physical than psychic, biological than spiritual. It is that starting from which a becoming-unmotivated of the sign, and with it all the ulterior oppositions between *physis* and its other, is possible."[9] Why does "something and its other" fall here under the category of "ulterior opposition," not that of difference; and why are the well-established binary oppositions of "natural and cultural," "physical and psychic" chosen to illustrate the play of the trace, the mark of difference?

Thus even the differential model, though highly acclaimed and prioritized in the contemporary humanities, still needs to be delimited more clearly from the oppositional model. The point is that difference, when relying on its own "selfness" and stability, on the value of difference as such, is easily susceptible to oppositional adaptations, as evidenced by the advancement of pure oppositions, like "male/female," "black/white," "heterosexual/homosexual," under the banners of cultural difference and diversity. That is why recently Jacques Derrida found it timely to warn against the reduction of difference to the model of opposition-identity. It is not sufficient to theorize the difference between certain identities; rather, one must explore their capacity for self-differentiation, which will provide their common ground with other identities. "[I]n the case of culture, person, nation, language, identity is a self-differentiating identity, an identity different from itself, having an opening or gap within itself. . . . It is because I am not one with myself that I can speak with the other and address the other."[10]

In order to confirm and expand its intrinsic value, difference must differ from itself, which means to posit new creative totalities in the act of progressive self-differentiation. The question, therefore, could be put in this way: How can the value of difference be reinscribed into the enhanced framework of a new wholeness? Is there any prospect for nontotalitarian totalities that would embrace rather than eliminate the differences among cultures?

We call "interference" this type of relationship between different entities that is different from their difference. As difference has the potential of maturation, it grows into interference, the "wavy" and "fuzzy" intersections and overlappings of two or more cultural entities, mentalities, principles, intuitions. It is a kind of wholeness that acknowledges difference but can be reduced neither to external differences between entities, nor to their predifferential unity. "Interference" leads to the construction of a "non-totalitarian totality" that is produced by the second order of difference—its differentiation from itself.

If we look at some of the most beautiful cultural patterns, such as the architecture of St. Petersburg or Russian literature of the nineteenth century (I take familiar examples), we find the intersection of several cultural flows, such as the Russian communal spirit, Western individualism and rationalism, Byzantine formalism and ritualism, and Oriental spiritual resignation. It is interference rather than merely difference (or an all-embracing and unifying "synthesis") that defined for two centuries the "wavy" patterns of Russian-Eastern-Western cultural interaction. And even the Cold War can be seen as a period of "destructive interference" between the two worlds when the collectivist impulses coming from one pole extinguished the impulses of individualism coming from the other. We know from physics that interference can go through constructive and destructive stages marked by the alternation of light and dark bands on a colored surface or by alternation of increased sounds and silent intervals.[11] Perhaps the same alternation occurs in the history of cultural interference, with its periods of light and dark, excessive brightness and emphatic silence, mutual reinforcement or neutralization of cultures.

The new totalities, or transcultural ensembles, that can be envisioned in the near future in the place of "collective identities" issue from the processes of self-differentiation maturing into interferences. In this case differences strengthen our need for each other. Some of our differences are neutralized (in order not to become oppositional), others are intensified (in order to avoid group identification). Interference is what we perceive as the joy and play of communication that reinforces some of our differences and neutralizes others in the play of non-totalitarian totalities. Generally, totality can be developed in two directions: (1) as *opposed* to difference and therefore eliminating all particular differences, as in a totalitarian state; (2) as truly *different* from difference and therefore preserving and nourishing all particular differences, as in an interdisciplinary community.

These new totalities will shape the transcultural world, which has not yet received any satisfactory theoretical articulation. Deconstruction may prove methodologically inadequate to this emerging class of totalities that could be detected as transcultural communities, or as transmetaphysical systems, as trans-utopian visions, or as transsocial groups. Deconstruction operates through the theoretical differentiation of existing unities while what is in question now is the new integration of differences, the construction of *trans-differential* cultural, social, epistemological totalities.

For example, deconstruction has demystified the so-called metaphysics of presence and revealed the basic inconsistency and even impossibility of rationally unified metaphysical systems. Does this mean that metaphysics is dead forever and will never rise again? Or that new varieties of metaphysics (or rather metaphysic-s, in the plural) may proliferate precisely on the basis of their inconsistency and impossibility? The same relates to utopias criticized as metaphysical projections of the present into the future. As soon as utopias are demystified and the shock of their partial realization has passed away, they will proliferate as utopias no more obliged to be realizable, consistent, or even progressive.

Here is what contemporary Moscow artists and art scholars have to say about the subject: "It is crucial that the problem of the universal be raised as a contemporary issue. I understand that it is a utopia. It is done completely consciously, yes, utopia is dead, so long live utopia. Utopia endows the individual with a more significant and wider horizon" (Viktor Miziano). "The future of contemporary art is in the will to utopia, in the breakthrough into reality through a membrane of quotations, it is in sincerity and pathos" (Anatoly Osmolovsky).[12] The subject here is the resurrection of utopia after the death of utopia, no longer as a social project with claims of transforming the world, but as a new intensity of intellectual vision and a broader horizon for the individual.

This type of mentality can be called "trans-utopian" and "trans-metaphysical," in agreement with the general vector of the transcultural movement. These "trans-utopias" will not be visionary or conceptual unities in the traditional sense. They will not reduce the variety of facts and possibilities to one basic principle or one predominant desire; rather, they will demonstrate the diversity of desires and principles, each of which is sufficient to ground one of possible worlds.[13]

Notes

1. Honi Fern Haber, *Beyond Postmodern Politics: Lyotard, Rorty, Foucault* (New York and London: Routledge, 1994): 134.
2. Ibid., 134.
3. Ibid., 1.
4. Ibid., 2.
5. Karl Kroeber, *Ecological Literary Criticism: Romantic Imagining and the Biology of Mind* (New York: Columbia University Press, 1994): 141.
6. *The Lyotard Reader*, ed. Andrew Benjamin (Oxford and Cambridge [MA]: Blackwell, 1992): 3.
7. Michel Foucault, *Power/Knowledge: Selected Interviews and Other Writings, 1972–1977,* ed. Colin Gordon; trans. Colin Gordon et al. (New York : Pantheon, 1981): 133.
8. "Différance," in Jacques Derrida, *Margins of Philosophy*, trans. Alan Bass (Chicago: The University of Chicago Press, 1982): 17.
9. Jacques Derrida, *Of Grammatology*, trans. Gayatri Chakravorty Spivak (Baltimore: The John Hopkins University Press, 1976): 47–48.
10. Jacques Derrida, *Deconstruction in a Nutshell: A Conversation.* (Roundtable on 2 October 1994 at Villanova University), ed. with Commentary by John D. Caputo (New York: Fordham University, 1997): 14.
11. *Constructive interference* occurs at a point where two overlapping waves of the same frequency are in phase, that is, where the crests and troughs of the two waves coincide. In this case, the two waves reinforce each other and combine to form a wave that has an amplitude equal to the sum of the individual amplitudes of the original waves. *Destructive interference* occurs when two intersecting waves are completely out of phase, that is, when the crest of one wave coincides with the trough of the other. In this case, the two waves cancel each other out. The present book concentrates almost exclusively on the possibilities of constructive interference, which in the realm of cultural flows and influences comprises the phenomenon of transculture. Transculture can be defined as the sum total of constructive interferences among different cultures and cultural domains (disciplines, arts, modes of creativity, and communication).
12. *Kto est kto v sovremennom iskusstve Moskvy (Who's Who In Contemporary Moscow Art).* (Moscow: "Album," 1993) [without pagination]. Viktor Miziano (b. 1957) is an art critic and curator of the Centre of Contemporary Art in Moscow. He is the editor in chief of the *Khudozhestvennyi zhurnal* (Art Journal). Anatolii Osmolovsky (b. 1969) is the leader of the anti-Conceptualist movements of E.T.I. and the "Revolutionary Rival Program NET-SEZUDIK."
13. On the category of the possible and its implications for the future of metaphysics, see my article "K filosofii vozmozhnogo. Vvedenie v postkriticheskuiu epokhu" (Toward the Philosophy of the Possible. An Introduction to the Post-Critical Epoch), *Voprosy filosofii* (Moscow, 1999).

Chapter 6

Transculture and Society
Mikhail Epstein

Transsociality

The transcultural project emerged in the society with the highest level of social determinism. The Marxist idea that social existence determines social consciousness and in the final analysis individual consciousness, and Lenin's idea that one cannot live in a society and be free from the society, were the governing assumptions of Soviet ideology. Since Soviet society was so persistently and forcefully homogenized it was impossible for any social group to challenge the foundations of the society or to oppose itself to the society as a whole. As a result, the project of transculture from its conception aimed to activate the transsocial potentials inherent in human individuals rather than those oppositional or revolutionary elements pertaining to specific social groups.

One of the sociological anticipations of the transcultural mode can be seen in the figure of the "stranger" as described in the works of the German philosophers and sociologists Georg Simmel and Alfred Schutz. I shall cite some sociological definitions in order to make clear the specificity of the transcultural experience.

> The stranger, like the poor and like sundry 'inner enemies,' is an element of the group itself. His position as a full-fledged member involves both being outside it and confronting it . . . In trade, which alone makes possible unlimited combinations, intelligence always finds expansions and new territories, an achievement which is very difficult to attain for the original producer. . . . The

classical example is the history of European Jews. The stranger is by nature no 'owner of soil.' . . . He is not radically committed to the unique ingredients and peculiar tendencies of the group, and therefore approaches them with the specific attitude of 'objectivity.' But objectivity does not simply involve passivity and detachment; it is a particular structure composed of distance and nearness, indifference and involvement . . . Objectivity may also be defined as freedom: the objective individual is bound by no commitments which could prejudice his perception, understanding, and evaluation of the given.[1]

. . . [T]he cultural pattern of the approached group is to the stranger not a shelter but a field of adventure, not a matter of course but a questionable topic of investigation, not an instrument for disentangling problematic situations but a problematic situation itself and one hard to master.[2]

Sociologically, the quality of being a stranger belongs to a certain person or a group of persons. Strangeness is a category of group identity, though this group, by its very definition, is dispersed among other groups. From a culturological standpoint, strangers do not constitute a separate group of people, but strangeness is incorporated into the entire cultural structure of society and is characteristic of the majority of individuals. Strangeness is our cultural distancing from that very society in which we are fully legitimate and recognized members. All people have gone through the experience of childhood and adolescence, with their antisocial drives and countercultural sensibility. Similarly, the majority of people have gone through the experiences of loneliness and boredom, sickness and suffering, mad love and mad inspiration that challenge stable social and cultural values. Therefore, temporary, or periodical, or partial "estrangement" from the society is inscribed in the very structure of cultural life, as a resource of its permanent innovation, and is not limited to some minorities or marginal groups.

This "majoritarian" strangeness accounts for transcultural activity, as different from multicultural activity, which is based on the self-awareness of minorities. The concept of transculture can serve as a theoretical framework for the long-needed exploration of this strangeness dispersed among cultural majorities. Usually we oppose "minorities" (in the plural) to the "majority" (in the singular), whereas I prefer to speak about variously delineated majorities: the classes of people who have experienced love, suffering, illness, aging, inspiration, and other states "transcending" their identities. What I mean by "majority," therefore, is not any divisive category, like "white heterosexual male," but the dimension of trans-social and transcultural experience that unites the vast majority of people across their ethnic, racial, sexual, and gender boundaries. Whites and blacks, men and women have the resource of their transcultural activity in their personal experiences of childhood and adolescence, suffering and creativity. These are majoritative transcultural formations, which intersect with minoritarian multicultural formations and need their recognition in the context of global communications.

The "stranger" as a sociological category is a divisive idealization: Some people are "settlers," other "strangers." People, however, always combine, in a certain proportion, features of "strangeness" and "settledness" in themselves. All of us are "strangers to ourselves," to use the expression of Julia Kristeva, not only because we come to America from Russia or to Russia from Central Asia, but because we come to a given society from our childhood, from our loneliness, from those extracultural and countercultural niches that are common to the majority of people all over the world. There are nonsocial and nonsociable elements within each personality, as well as a certain feeling of cultural anxiety, which accounts for the transcultural activity available to everybody, not only to underprivileged minorities or to those privileged and "romantic" individuals named "strangers."

The Cultural Middle Class

One of the striking peculiarities of American culture as compared with Russian is the absence or scarcity of what can be called a *cultural* middle class. This statement may be seen as absurd or shocking considering the economically prosperous American middle class as compared with the lack of such a social stratum in Russia. All failures of Russian democracy in the twentieth century are often explained by a deficit of the middle class in the structure of Russian society, which traditionally was sharply divided into the poles of the high aristocracy and the bourgeoisie and low-paid workers and peasants (serfs). This antagonism led to the Bolshevik revolution, to civil war, and to the establishment of a totalitarian regime for the larger part of the twentieth century (1917–91). Now in the post-Soviet period the foremost task of the newly born democracy is to develop its social and economic foundation—the middle class of proprietors who are interested in political stability to secure private property.

However, in Russia there did exist a kind of cultural middle class whose task was to mediate between the rulers and the popular masses. In most cases this class is called the intelligentsia. Because of its intermediate position, it was variably defined as the intellectual leader, the conscience and consciousness of the nation, and also as "the shit of the nation" (Lenin), a servant of the ruling classes. Now the intelligentsia is severely criticized in Russia for its "parasitic" character and for its compliance in the terrors of an ideocratic regime. In the time of ideocracy, the intelligentsia in fact was both the most privileged and the most persecuted of all social strata because its predominant task was the elaboration and propagation of the ideas ruling this society. The current demolition of the ideocratic regime puts into question the very existence of the intelligentsia and allegedly presupposes the formation of the economic middle class on the model of American society.

From an American perspective, the intelligentsia may be viewed as a useful cultural extension of (rather than an alternative to) the American notion of the middle class. American society is so divided culturally and professionally that the absence of mediating values makes more and more urgent the task of forming an American intelligentsia, or what can be called the *cultural middle class*. Today intellectual life is divided among professional circles and ethnic groups, though the sharpness of this division is moderated by the fact that members of the same ethnic circle are professionally diversified and members of the same professional circle may belong to various ethnic groups, in such a way that the two divisions intersect and complement each other.

Nevertheless, American society increasingly finds itself dissociated and dispersed into isolated circles of mutually indifferent or antagonistic groups. The role of mediators is entrusted to politicians and bankers, or to the mainstream media, not to cultural figures. There are practically no bridges between elitist intellectual circles and the general public—the role that in Russia and in the Soviet Union was fulfilled by the intelligentsia. The intelligentsia is the class of intellectual mediators that can incorporate and translate the values of various professions. A mathematician interested in poetry, or an engineer fascinated with abstract painting, or a teacher of physics writing literary essays: This versatility of cultural interests and dispositions constitutes what can be called the cultural middle class. "High" class can be identified with reputable professionals in various fields of creative endeavor, whereas "low" class is represented by people whose profession and mode of existence have nothing to do with cultural values. But values are really human values when they have the widest possible circulation across social and economic strata. Is it a normal condition for a culture when, for example, books on poetry written by university professors are read exclusively by university professors, and therefore poetry becomes a matter of purely professional "autocommunication," or, in the case of pulp fiction, a matter of mere entertainment? However incompatible the poles of elitist writing and mass entertainment might seem, they have in common the alienated and distanced mode of perception of cultural values, as an object of scholarly investigation or an instrument of passive leisure. Literature becomes divided into literature for research and literature for entertainment, and loses its nerve and hope to be read by a variety of people for whom it is designed and who might be changed and "cultivated" by this reading.

The cultural middle class is not simply a distributor of values from professionals to the ignorant—this was perhaps the fatal error of the Russian intelligentsia, to regard itself as only a servant of the toiling people or to function only as a servant of the ruling ideologies. The middle class is exactly this site where cultural values find their ultimate destination and designation. This class has the potential to gradually assimilate other layers of society, both "highbrows" and "rednecks" who, through research or entertainment, could be involved in the process of making values available to everybody and sharing them with the creators.

There is no necessary opposition or mutual exclusion between the economic and cultural categories of the middle class. The general purpose may be viewed as twofold: to instantiate the Russian intelligentsia as an economic entity, and to instantiate the American middle class as a cultural entity. Thus the American dream can acquire still another dimension, the class of proprietors becoming also the class of intellectuals.

The Advantages of Commodification

Among left Western intellectuals, commodification is often regarded as the greatest danger for the survival of culture in the age of mass production and mass consumption. This typical view is expounded by Fredric Jameson, who explains the entire phenomenon of postmodernism as the successful completion of the capitalist commodification of culture: "What has happened is that aesthetic production today has become integrated into commodity production generally . . . [L]ate or multinational or consumer capitalism . . . constitutes . . . a prodigious expansion of capital into hitherto uncommodified areas."[3] That is why the only way to dynamize culture and protect it from the leveling of mass consumption is thought to be countercultural movements, which are intended to be opposite to what the term indicates, not countercultural but pro-cultural, directed against the institutionalized and massified exploitation of culture. The traditional duty of left intellectuals is to position "the cultural act outside the massive Being of capital, from which to assault this last."[4]

Commodification, as a clearly negative term, signifies in the Marxist tradition an alienated state of a cultural product. However alienation as such is not an adversary to culture. Any cultural product is the result of alienation: In producing a work we exteriorize what had been deeply hidden within our mind and soul, to use a romantic figure. Indeed, many artists confess that the transformation of their internal vision into a product—a manuscript, a painting, a musical composition—makes them feel psychologically abused, tormented, and self-alienated. As Kafka put it, he writes differently from what he speaks, speaks differently from what he thinks, thinks differently from what he is, and so forth, to the darkest depth of selfness. It is impossible to precisely fix the border where the self ends and alienation begins; and if we nonetheless try, the demarcation line would not be essentially between the artistic production of the work and its market circulation but between the living of one's life and the production of the work. Creativity is a more self-alienating process than the book trade or artistic market.

Contrary to his own prolific writing, Plato, as is well known, condemned writing as the silliest occupation in the world because the written word does not belong anymore to the author, as distinct from the oral utterance, whose addressee can be chosen. The book most frequently is consumed by people with whom the author would never wish to speak. Since our culture is based on writing, should one be surprised or indignant at the subsequent commodification of the product that from the very beginning was designed to circulate among people? Thus, commodification seems to be built into the very enterprise of culture as one of its (self-)transcending dimensions. Thought transcends itself in the writing about this thought; writing transcends itself in the reading of this writing; reading transcends itself in a spatial object—the book—designed for market circulation. Thus commodification is a name for only one latest stage of this continuous exteriorization of culture whose destiny is to transcend its own origin.

In principle, culture is able to absorb and assimilate all revolutionary challenges to this mechanism of commodification, as can be seen in the countercultural activity of Western marginalized intellectual groups or, more impressively, in the endeavors of an ideocratic state, such as the Soviet Union, to establish a global site of noncommercialized cultural activity. These two challenges to the commodification of culture are to a certain degree opposite to each other. Counterculture is a gesture of interiorization that can mean many different things, for example, limitation of the audience to the circle of close friends and acquaintances of the artist; elimination of the stage and the curtain between the performer and the audience; deverbalization of the cultural product and emphasis on irrational or illogical, purely sensory components of art; choice of noncultural and even nonartistic ways of spiritual contemplation, such as hallucinations induced by narcotics, or a peaceful retreat into nature. Finally it may turn out that merely silence or an attempt at nonwriting, nonspeaking, and even nonthinking is the most radical challenge to exteriorization with its commodifying tendencies and temptations.

The weak point of this radical challenge to the world of commodities is that it is easily commodified in turn. The counterculture of the 1960s was not defeated in a trivial sense of this word; it was not banished, oppressed, or eliminated, but it was eroded by its acceptance and the commercial use of the same songs, melodies, modes of contemplation and meditation that were intended as an opposition to the culture of commodities. This was a decisive test for the comparative strengths of the commodity and its countercultural denial: The denial itself turned into the act of commodification.

This story would be too sad if we did not try to consider the other side of this problem. If challenge is transformed into a commodity, cannot a commodity itself be regarded as a challenge, perhaps the greatest challenge of all that culture can offer? Challenge to what? The answer comes from the history of another anticommercial experiment, the Soviet civilization in which decommodification led culture into the trap of ideologization. Culture stopped being what people want to read, view, and listen to, and for which they are ready to pay. It became what people are obliged to read, view, and listen to in order to think and feel in the way that the state wants them to. The Soviet system struggled with the exteriorization of the internal life, the process that at a certain point generates art as commodity. What the Soviet system required was, on the contrary, the interiorization of social life, of the officially approved artistic works, mythological schemes, philosophical concepts, and political imperatives that the state imposed on people.

Such is the decisive difference between culture, which is the voluntary exteriorization of the internal, and ideology, which is the forcible interiorization of the external. In this opposition between culture and ideology, commodification certainly works in support of culture. Consequently, a commodity can be regarded as a grass-roots challenge to all kinds of totalitarian uses and abuses of culture. Insofar as culture is sold and bought, it still reflects the needs of some people and the abilities of other people to satisfy these needs. The status of the commodity secures freedom in the relationship between those who produce and those who consume. As soon as culture is decommodified it becomes subject to exploitation by the power that is indifferent to what people want to receive and are able to produce. Totalitarian culture, if this combination of words is meaningful at all, is a pseudo-community devoid of any talent and taste for creative communication, since ungifted producers offer unwanted products to uninterested consumers.

Western society has become too accustomed to the material condition of commodification to appreciate its cultural depth, in particular, the cultural challenge that people from the Eastern bloc assigned to the glossy designs and labels of those goods that sometimes reached them behind the iron curtain. From the Western perspective, this expansion of commodities was the degradation and profanation of culture, while for many people from the East it was their first encounter with genuine culture, the culture of the free world. Of course they had the possibility to read Pushkin and Tolstoy, or to listen to Mozart and Tchaikovsky, or to look at the paintings of great Renaissance masters, but strange as it may seem, this great culture of the past, which was permitted and even supported in a totalitarian state, acquired a compromised quality of "being permitted," "being official." "Permission" meant serving the state in its unchallenged supremacy in such a way that even Tolstoy was utilized to teach readers how to sacrifice their lives for the sake of the Motherland, and Pushkin was perceived as the great fighter against autocracy and forerunner of the happy Soviet present. Foreign labels, these marks of commodification, served as signs of liberation for Soviet people, and also as signs of culture because culture is everything that is beyond permission, that transcends the boundaries of the allowable. What was cultural about these trivial imports was that they were designed to meet people's desires and expectations; they were not indifferent and not arrogant toward people's needs but in a friendly manner asked for interest and participation.

Totalitarian society is responsible for this unbelievable paradox: Jeans with a fashionable label were in a certain respect more representative of culture than Tolstoy with all his works of genius. This is not Tolstoy's guilt and not Levi-Strauss's accomplishment; it was the anticultural stance of totalitarianism that reversed and perverted aesthetic values. Even Tolstoy, when ideologized, proved to be less a cultural phenomenon than a trivial commodity when freely produced, freely circulated, and freely consumed. Culture is everything that is done freely by people and that further expands and nourishes their freedom. This explains a great deal about the comparative cultural values of commodity and ideology. The status of a commodity transforms even a trivial object into a cultural phenomenon, though minimally cultural, whereas the ideological function transforms even the greatest genius into a noncultural entity, a tool of moral and political enslavement.

Here in the United States, I still feel a spark of inspiration coming from those innumerable shining commodities that surround me everywhere. I do not like them; I am tired of them; I hate to make the decision of which to choose. But at the very core of their loud existence I still perceive the defiance that they address to my past, to the regime of power that attempted to reduce me to functioning as a model citizen in a model state. I believe that this challenge to the structures of power is what the greatest creations of art share with the most trivial products of commodity culture.

The Need for Ordinariness

Transcultural experience is deeply connected with everyday life. It is the ordinary that is probably in the shortest supply in Western civilization, and it was the ordinary whose value I reassessed most of all after my move to the United States from Russia. Life in the West is so rigorously categorized that the dispersion of signs and vagueness of meanings are regarded as anomalies and disturbances and tend to be eliminated as soon as possible. The ordinary can be defined as something undefinable that exists in the gap, in the pause, in between cultural categories. In Russia, there are huge semi-developed territories where culture and nature are so confused and diffused in each other that one feels this inordinate place is the true place of the ordinary.

For example, in American national parks or wilderness areas the boundary between culture and nature is drawn very strictly with an exactitude of several centimeters. There are special trails that delineate the route of penetration of culture into the domain of nature. But neither cultural nor natural areas in themselves create the feeling of ordinariness that is the erasure of structural oppositions, the zone of semiotic silence or rustle or whisper where the flow of information is interrupted and superseded by a natural noise. "Natural" not in a sense that nature is opposed to culture but natural in the sense of ignoring or transcending this opposition.

In Russia, the insufficiency of mapping, of cultural demarcations, makes life more dangerous and uncomfortable than it is in the West. You do not know where you are, on the edge of a forest or on the site of a future building: Nature is polluted and culture is diffused due to neglect and devastation. But this is what creates ordinariness; Russia is perhaps the largest ordinary place in the world. When you go through a meadow you always find several narrow paths that were not designed by the developers of this territory but spontaneously created by people who need to make a shortcut from one village to another. While walking these paths you feel the blessed meaning of the ordinary that does not belong to any category, which spontaneously emerges and remains arbitrary, escaping any order.

Usually we believe that spontaneity can be found only in nature while human activity is conscious, structured, and subordinated to a plan, a rational design. What makes the ordinary so precious is the spontaneity of human actions, the growth of the natural out of the cultural. In the West even islands of spontaneity, such as natural parks and preserves, are carefully demarcated; their very naturalness is the object of cultivation. Russia is the land of boredom, carelessness, and wasting of time whereas in the West even wasting time is usually framed as a form of relaxation or entertainment. Hence the feeling of reality is lost in the West, which is one of the main points of postmodern theory: Everything is culturally produced, semiotically constructed.[5] Reality evaporates with the excess of rationality, which makes life easier and work more effective, and with the complete semiotization of the environment so that even nature is reduced to the sign of nature ("wildlife refuge"). What constitutes reality, however, is the resistance of things to signs, to the categories of cultural classification. The ordinary is that aspect of reality that most thoroughly challenges our semiotic capacity. By walking long distances we feel the reality of the space and of the earth, their dull extension; by driving a car, we substitute the system of signs—road signs, lights, signals, inscriptions—for this experience of the ordinary.

The most exemplary mode of the ordinary in Russia is the queues that arise spontaneously and lead to an enormous waste of time. Standing in long queues you can feel life so ordinary, so slow and empty that reality reveals its authentic substance and duration, something that cannot be rationalized and categorized. Not enjoyment of signs and simulations but a bare courage and patience to be. I do not mean to suggest that the Western world should borrow from Russia this experience of wastefulness, but one can imagine that as Russia needs more structure in its enormous stretches of wasteland and waste-time, the West could benefit from some more spontaneous confusion between labor and leisure, between nature and culture, between doing and not doing, between efficiency and contemplation.

Transculture is an experience of dwelling in the neutral spaces and lacunas between cultural demarcations. Transculture is not simply a mode of integrating cultural differences but a mode of creating something different from difference itself, and one form of it is the ordinary, the formless, the random, the indiscriminate. The ordinary is this excess of existence that does not fit into any existing cultural model, including the opposition of culture and nature, which is also modeled and assimilated by culture. The ordinary is what cannot be assimilated, the "trans-" cultural, "extra-"cultural, the surplus of "just being," something that can be conveyed by such words as "just," "merely," "simply."

Thus we can generalize about at least three transcultural modes: One is exchange, interaction, or integration among existing cultures; another is the creation of imagined or the exploration of potential cultures; and the third is the experience of the ordinary that is extracultural: neither opposed to culture (as nature is) nor inscribed into it.

Notes

1. *The Sociology of Georg Simmel*, trans., ed., and with an intro. by Kurt H. Wolff (New York: The Free Press, 1950): 402–405.
2. Alfred Schutz, *Collected Papers,* II, *Studies in Social Theory,* ed. and intro. by Arvid Brodersen (The Hague: Martinus Nijhoff, 1964): 104.
3. Fredric Jameson, *Postmodernism, or The Cultural Logic of Late Capitalism* (Durham: Duke University Press, 1993): 4, 36.
4. Ibid. p. 48.
5. "Today everyday, political, social, historical, economic, etc., reality has already incorporated the hyperrealist dimension of simulation . . . . Reality has passed completely into the game of reality. . . . The consummate enjoyment [jouissance] of the signs of guilt, despair, violence and death are replacing guilt, despair and even death in the total euphoria of simulation"—such is a typical postmodern discourse on the death of reality as instigated by Jean Baudrillard in *Symbolic Exchange and Death* (1976), trans. Iain H. Grant (London: Sage, 1993): 74.

Chapter 7

The Rehumanization of the Humanities
Mikhail Epstein

Mikhail Bakhtin's late writings assume that the fundamental characteristic of the human is its capacity to be other to its own self. To put it as simply as possible, it is a self-consciousness that splits us into subject and object, and thus makes us other to ourselves. If otherness grows from the very foundation of what it means to be human, this allows us to reinterpret the postmodern paradox of the *dehumanization of the humanities* from Bakhtin's point of view, as a necessary stage of human self-awareness.

One of the general tenets of poststructuralism has been to ascribe the source of our activity to some non-human, impersonal structures speaking through us, a kind of Deleuzian "schizoanalysis" invoking the state of a divided self. But if we reappropriate these alienated sources of our activity and understand them as an indispensable otherness inherent in the nature of human self-awareness, then an entirely new perspective of rehumanization becomes possible. The previous emphasis on dehumanized knowledge, including psychoanalysis, Marxism, semiotics, structuralism, and poststructuralism, may be reinterpreted in new terms as signs of a human self-objectifying or self-othering capacity.

How can we rehumanize formerly humanistic disciplines without reinscribing the limitations of traditional humanism as exposed in the deconstructive critique of metaphysics? How can we get beyond this critique? Which interpretive modes or new epistemologies can form the basis of rehumanization?

Bakhtin's ultimate project (never implemented) was the construction of a philosophical anthropology that would focus on the phenomenon of humanity in a much broader sense than is usually considered by the contemporary humanities. According to Bakhtin, the human being is

> the witness and judge. When consciousness appeared in the world (in existence) and, perhaps, when biological life appeared (perhaps not only animals, but trees and grass also witness and judge), the world (existence) changed radically. A stone is still stony and the sun still sunny, but the event of existence as a whole (unfinalized) becomes completely different because a new and major character in this event appears for the first time on the scene of earthly existence—the witness and the judge. And the sun, while remaining physically the same, has changed because it has begun to be cognized by the witness and the judge. It has stopped simply being and has started being in itself and for itself (these categories appear for the first time here) as well as for the other, because it has been reflected in the consciousness of the other (the witness and the judge): this has caused it to change radically, to be enriched and transformed. (This has nothing to do with 'other existence.')[1]

At this point, Bakhtin's position seems to be directly anthropocentric presuming that the meaning of the world depends on its human cognition and reflection. But what about the world beyond our cognition? Bakhtin further suggests that the existence of human consciousness transforms the entire meaning of the world even if this world is never to be reflected and interiorized by consciousness. This is not the traditional category of humanizing the world, its appropriation and transformation for and by human subjectivity. Rather, the world is radically changed precisely because it remains *unknown* and *untouched,* because now this being unknown and untouched acquires a principally different meaning in the presence of a "witness" capable of knowing and touching.

> Let the witness see and know only an insignificant corner of existence, and all existence that is not cognized and not seen by him changes its quality (sense), becoming uncognized, unseen existence, and not simply existence as it was before, that is, without any relationship to the witness.[2]

In other words, unknown existence is as related to humans and as meaningful in human terms as known existence. Non-knowledge and the non-knowable are humanistic categories related to and derived from knowledge. The Socratic thesis "I know that I know nothing" makes clear that ignorance is the product and object of knowledge: It is impossible to state one's non-knowledge without knowledge of this non-knowledge. If Kant developed a critique of knowledge, Bakhtin's remark suggests a critique of ignorance as a humanly produced form of knowledge. We suppose that the world is what it is insofar as we do not know it, do not intrude and transform it with our perceptions and instruments of knowledge. But this non-knowledge derives from the very possibility of knowledge, which therefore makes the world different from what it would be in the absence of the unknowing person.

Our knowledge always transcends our non-knowledge, because we know that we do not know. The statement "I know that I know nothing" is the axiom of what I would call optimistic epistemology. How could we know that we do not know unless our non-knowledge is an object of knowledge? Even if we do not know "things-in-themselves," this assertion presupposes that we do know that things-in-themselves exist and that we do not know them. Even when we use the disclaimer "only," saying that we can know "only" things as they appear to us, we include a presupposition of another realm of existence beyond our knowledge called "things-in-themselves." The non-knowable is actually an object of negative knowledge.

All knowledge can be divided into positive and negative knowledge, as well as positive and negative non-knowledge; hence the four categories:

1. I know that I know (positive knowledge)
2. I know that I do not know (Socratic knowledge)
3. I do not know what I know (Platonic knowledge)
4. I do not know what I do not know (absence of knowledge)

The first two categories need no further comment; we will discuss the third and the fourth.

That we do not know what we know (unconscious knowledge) is the Platonic principle: Knowledge is anamnesis, or recollection of the forms that we knew before our birth, before any experience, and not through our senses. We know not less but much more than we hope and claim to know because the larger part of our knowledge is hidden from us. "Learning" is recollection of what I know without being aware of my knowledge. Thus, in the Platonic dialogue "Meno," Socrates elicits geometrical knowledge from a slave boy who never had studied geometry.

It is only the fourth statement that can be characterized as the position of non-knowledge in a strict sense. We cannot discuss what we do not know in this last instance since it is beyond our knowledge and never emerges in our thoughts and discourses, even in quotation marks or under a question mark. Number 4 is truly unknown, whereas 3 is unconsciously known and 2 is consciously unknown (is present in our consciousness as an unknown, and we have evidence of its existence, though not of its essence). The place of the unknown is within our knowledge, as "x" is present within algebraic formulations and makes the science of algebra possible. Limitations on knowledge belong to the structure of knowledge, which is the transition between the known and the unknown, and therefore includes both of these domains, as a sign includes both the signifier and the signified. Knowledge is the relationship between the known and the unknown, and therefore the unknown belongs to the very condition of knowledge. The field of knowledge consists of three layers, 1, 2, and 3; it is only 4, the unknowable, that is beyond it.

What of those realms of existence posited in twentieth century humanities as impenetrable to human knowledge, such as the realm of the unconscious, or the realm of language, or the realm of economic production? They are quite meaningful and even more dependent on human knowledge precisely because they are transcendent and exterior to this knowledge. Twentieth-century humanities exalted in the discovery of these superhuman or extra-human determinants that set limitations on human activity, in contrast to the post-Renaissance exaltation of human subjectivity. Now it is time to revise this paradigm of dehumanization, not in order to return to the traditional humanism of the sixteenth through nineteenth centuries, but in order to extend the meaning of this humanistic project and incorporate dehumanization as only one of its indispensable dimensions and unavoidable stages. The human manifests its humanness by positing and transcending its limits and becoming non-human. Non-knowledge is no less a human quality than knowledge.

We may designate a specific prefix in order to display the principal difference between existence as it is in itself and existence as it is in the state of being non-known. This would suggest that being unknown and being non-known are quite different states of being. The "unknown" as expressed in statement four is what has no relationship to knowledge; thus we cannot posit the existence of the unknown in principle because by positing it we still acknowledge it, bring it into negative relationship with the known. The unknown cannot be discussed, indicated, or presented in connection with any human concern—we do not even know whether it exists.

It is the "non-known," as expressed in statements two and three, that is the genuine subject of twentieth-century humanities: the world as non-known to human beings and human beings as non-known to themselves. Now we may recognize that this non-knowledge constitutes part of the very essence and aim of human knowledge, its otherness to itself.

Humanness, as Bakhtin defines this phenomenon, presupposes its otherness to itself. "*Not-I* in me, that is, existence in me; something larger than me in me."[3] There are two different me's: one is "me" in the narrow sense, separate from the other in me; and another is Me who embraces both me and the other. The other, "not-I in me," includes language and the unconscious that are speaking through us, not spoken by us.

This "not-I" is the major theme and stronghold of twentieth-century humanities that explains their anti-humanistic and anti-personal stance. Bakhtin reminds us, however, that this "not-I" is "in me," though it is "larger than me in me" (me in Me). All of these superpersonal entities are larger than "me," but they still belong to the structure of Me in its self-division, self-consciousness, and therefore non-knowledge of itself. This opens for the dehumanized humanities the prospect of rehumanization.

It is remarkable that for Bakhtin, the other, not-I, is more susceptible and open to consciousness than Me. "My temporal and spatial boundaries are not given to me, but the other is entirely given."[4] Therefore, Me is a more complex object for the humanities than "me" or "other." The radical fallacy of the dehumanized humanities was the reduction of Me to me and the belief that "the other" is beyond cognition, in distinction from "me" that is "immediately given to itself," as the sphere of transparence and introspection. Bakhtin paradoxically shifts the perspective: it is "Me" that cannot be fully cognized and objectified, in distinction from the other that "is entirely given." Thus the sphere of the "non-known" in the humanities belongs to their own human subject, to "Me." Humanness, in its capacity of permanent "self-othering," dividing into "me" and the "other," comprises the ultimate concern and enigma of all humanistic disciplines.

The distinction between the three stages in the development of the humanities may now be formulated in the following way. In the first stage, when the very concept of "humanitas" emerged in Renaissance Italy, the humanities were mostly occupied with me in Me, that is, with humanness that separated and distinguished the human from everything else in the world. In the second stage, the phenomenon of humanity was objectified and analyzed as the other in Me. This otherness was interpreted by Marx as the totality of social relationships, as the generic other of alienated material production and economic conditions. Freud interpreted this otherness as the psychological id, as the unconscious, spontaneously determining and mastering the human ego. Saussurian and post-Saussurian developments in semiotics interpreted this otherness as those linguistic mechanisms that predetermine the form and meaning of my speech acts. Tolstoy in *War and Peace* presented Napoleon, who believes in the infinite possibilities of his individual will, as a mere toy in the play of myriads of historical factors and objective conditions. If Renaissance humanists believed that the human being was himself directing the course of his historical destination, then Tolstoy, one of the great historical fatalists, viewed the human being as a child who presses his hands against the carriage and imagines that it is he who pushes it ahead. European humanism, born in the Renaissance, was like this child full of confidence in its creative forces and unbounded activity, whereas Marx, Tolstoy, and Freud looked at this child with the knowing smile of an adult who understands that the carriage is moved by forces that are far from obedient to human will and can easily bring the human to the brink of self-destruction.

Now that this paradigm of otherness has been sufficiently explored and elaborated in the humanities of the twentieth century, we can also locate it in the near past as still another aspect of what constitutes the unity of Me in a human being. The stage "me" coincides with the realm of the traditional humanities, and the stage of the "other" with the "dehumanities" of the late nineteenth through the twentieth century (to suggest a term for that approach to the humanities whose principal message was their dehumanization). This rise of the dehumanities was not a mistake or deviation but a necessary stage of exploration of "otherness" as constitutive of humanness in its capacity of self-transcendence and self-awareness. The entire thrust of Marxist, Freudian, Saussurian, structuralist and poststructuralist thought can be described in Bakhtinian terms as follows: "The *I* hides in the other and in others, it wants to be only an other for others, to enter completely into the world of others as an other, and to cast from itself the burden of being the only *I* (*I-for-myself*) in the world."[5]

Now that the "other" in its opposition to "me" has been theoretically recognized and explored, we are approaching the third stage, when the very phenomenon of Me will become the focus of humanistic knowledge/non-knowledge (since non-knowledge, as we stipulated earlier, is as human a phenomenon as knowledge itself). This new stage of the humanities can be called trans-humanistic since it embraces both human in its narrow, Renaissance sense ("me") and non-human as it was postulated by the dehumanities of the twentieth century ("other"). Trans-humanistic knowledge is addressed both to intra-human capacities and extra-human forces as inherent in the human capacity for self-transcendence, dividing Me into "me" and "other," into "personal" and "impersonal." Me itself, according to Bakhtin, is the "supraperson," or, to follow his original expression, it is "nadchelovek," "transhuman."[6] Bakhtin connects this discovery of "otherness" in a human being with Me's "transhuman" capacity for self-transcendence and self-awareness. "This is analogous to the problem of man's self-awareness. Does the cognizer coincide with the cognized? . . . Something absolutely new appears here: the supraperson [nadchelovek], the *supra-I,* that is, the witness and the judge *of the whole* human being, of the whole *I,* and consequently someone who is no longer the person, no longer the *I,* but the *other.*"[7] Supra-I, or Me, is posited here precisely as the open space of non-coincidence between "the cognizer" and "the cognized" ("me" and "other") and thus as the sphere of humanly creative and responsible "self-awareness" that includes the possibility of self-deception and "non-knowledge."

Semiotic, genetic, economic, and other "unconscious" and "inhuman" structural forces are constitutive of the phenomenon of humanness and comprise the potential field of the transhumanities. Therefore, the otherness that was previously apprehended as a dehumanizing factor can now be reappropriated as the self-transcendence of humanity. In Bakhtin's view, which is maintained here, "this [transcendence] has nothing to do with 'other existence'" ; rather it has to do with the existence of the other. Self-transcendence does not postulate any separate transcendental realm because such an assertion would be a self-contradictory involvement of knowledge in the sphere of the unknown.

Notes

1. Mikhail Bakhtin, *Speech Genres and Other Late Essays,* trans. Vern W. McGee, ed. Caryl Emerson and Michael Holquist (Austin: University of Texas Press, 1986): 137.
2. Ibid., 138.
3. Ibid., 146.
4. Ibid., 147.
5. Ibid., 147.
6. M. M. Bakhtin, *Estetika slovesnogo tvorchestva* (Moscow: Iskusstvo, 1979): 342. The reader should keep in mind that the word "man" in the English transla-

tion often corresponds to the Russian "chelovek" ("human being," without any gender specification).
7. Mikhail Bakhtin, *Speech Genres and Other Late Essays*, trans. Vern W. McGee, ed. Caryl Emerson and Michael Holquist (Austin: University of Texas Press, 1986): 137.

Chapter 8

Nomadic Desires and Transcultural Becomings
Ellen E. Berry

In his essay "Transculture and Society," Epstein delineates three modes within which transcultural dynamics operate: an integrative mode (as a means of unifying existing cultures), an imaginative mode (as a means of inventing new cultural expressions), and an extracultural mode (as a site for the emergence of the ordinary). This chapter explores a fourth, *migratory* modality that emphasizes both the movement of cultural materials between and within cultures (a migratory emphasis suggested by the prefix *trans-*), as well as the nomadic nature of critical thought itself in a postmodern moment. It frames this exploration in relation to some models of the contemporary global system whose radically mobile and interactive nature has definitively altered processes of cultural production and reception.

A number of contemporary scholars have worked on mapping the contours of this still-emerging global system and to specify its multiple effects on cultural production and reception, on social relations, on political processes, and on national economies, among other sites (see, for example, Appaduari, Buell, Featherstone, Harvey, Jameson). There is no widespread agreement on the distinctive features of this global landscape—in part because of its rapidly changing nature and fundamentally mobile character; in part because of the enormity and complexity of any attempts to map its contours; in part because of the range of theoretical and disciplinary perspectives through which various global relations have been conceived. Nonetheless, some specific characteristics might include

(1) large-scale socioeconomic restructurings occasioned by global capitalist investments, communication systems, and information networks; (2) accelerated time-space compressions; (3) violent reassertions of nationalisms and ethnic fundamentalisms on the one hand, and, on the other, crises in the authority of traditional national and ethnic identities; (4) international migrations of intellectuals, labor resources, religious movements, and political formations that confound formerly stable distinctions among first, second, and third worlds and make visible a complex and decentered network of interdependency and interaction, a disjunctive and deterritorialized world of global flows or "scapes" ;[1] and thus, more specifically, (5) a global dissemination of cultures, a "detachment of cultural material from particular territories and its circulation in repackaged, heterogeneous, boundary-violating forms throughout the world."[2] These complex globalizing processes result in modes of cultural homogenization and commoditization on an international scale, such as the global dominance of American mass culture. But they also open unprecedented possibilities for radical new modes of global-local interaction, resulting in, among other things, the emergence of new cultural forms and hybridized knowledges. As Rob Nixon and Wimal Dissanayake succinctly put it, the contemporary world has become both "more globalized (unified around dynamics of capitalogic moving across borders) and more localized (fragmented into contestatory enclaves of difference, coalition, and resistance)."[3] As this brief summary should suggest, the global new world "order" is complex, disjunctive, and unpredictable in its emergence and in its effects. Although no one would deny the disastrous consequences occasioned by the circulation of postmodern global capital, it is equally true that the unevenness of this circulation and its disorganized effects mean that much is contestable within its flows and that no outcomes are guaranteed.

Something of the ceaseless mobility, radical interactiveness, and—what I am emphasizing here—sheer creative possibility of the global landscape is conveyed in this description of "border culture" by the Mexican American performance artist Guillermo Gomez-Peña, a striking—some might say purely utopian—account, but only one of many examples that could be cited:

> Border culture is a polysemantic term . . . [it] means boycott, complot, ilegalidad, clandestinidad, transgression . . . hybrid art forms for new contents-in-gestation: spray mural, techno-altar, poetry-in-tongues, audio graffiti, punkarachi, video corrido, anti-bolero, anti-todo . . . to be fluid in English,

Spanish, Spanglish, and Inglenol . . . transcultural friendship and collaboration among races, sexes, and generations . . . creative appropriation, expropriation, and subversion of dominant cultural forms . . . a new cartography: a brand-new map to host the new project; the democratization of the East; the socialization of the West; the Third-Worldization of the North and the First-Worldization of the South . . . a multiplicity of voices away from the center, different geo-cultural relations among more culturally akin regions: Tepito San Deiguana, San Pancho   Nuyoricco, Miami-Quebec, San Antonio Berlin . . . a new internationalism ex centris . . . a new terminology for new hybrid identities and metiers constantly metamorphosing . . . to develop new models to interpret the world-in-crisis, the only world we know . . . to push the borders of countries and languages or, better said, to find new languages to express the fluctuating borders . . . experimenting with the fringes between art and society, legalidad and illegality, English and espanol, male and female, North and South, self and other; and subverting these relationships. . . . The border is the juncture not the edge, and monoculturalism has been expelled to the margins . . . it also means glasnost, not government censorship . . . to analyze critically all that lies on the current tables of debates. . . . Soon a new internationalism will have to gravitate around the spinal cord of this continent—not Europe, not just the North, not just white, not only you, companero del otro lado de lat frontera, el languaje y el oceano.[4]

Like the object of its inquiry, transcultural studies—as it has developed in the West—is a vitally important, newly developing transdiscipline whose parameters and methods are only beginning to be articulated and mapped. While there is no consensus about the goals of this emerging field or even the meaning of the term transculture, we might say that most generally transcultural approaches, as they have evolved in the Western academy particularly, aim to investigate the history, nature, and effects of complex globalizing processes of interaction, including both the forms of domination they engender and the distinctive new forms of sociocultural life arising from them. Such an investigation has even been called one of the most urgent ethical projects that cultural workers can undertake in our altered world.[5]

What should be the response of Western critical intellectuals in the face of this bewildering globalization of the contemporary world? First, as my introductory remarks have suggested, we can attempt to provide descriptive models, credible maps of emerging global flows that would allow us to make more informed and meaningful interventions within them, in part to provoke their positive potentials. Second, and relatedly, we can generate new methodologies for this cartographic project that move from description to the thought of transformation so as to enable rather than foreclose images of connected but altered spaces in the future. The resistance to closure, the insistence on permanent openness, partiality, and provisionality so evident in many contemporary cultural and political projects might be seen as part of this commitment to opening multiple paths to the future so as not to foreclose it in advance. That is, a critical perspective or a theoretical position may be read simultaneously as a description of what is and—through extrapolation beyond the frame of the theory—as a suggestion of what might become, what Appadurai calls the building blocks of imagined worlds opening to narratives of possible lives or what Raymond Williams, following Ernst Bloch, refers to simply as the resources of hope. All of which indicates that the methods employed by transcultural studies must be as multiple and hybridized as the forms of the transcultural itself, characterized by "weaker" modes of thought rather than the "strong" modes upon which traditional logic depends, by flexible investigative strategies, "a mobile infinity of tactics" that are "contaminated, transgressive, multi-directional, transitive,"[6] as well as by new conjunctive logics "capable of thinking the relations between local, regional, national, and international frames of reference and experience."[7]

With its implicit reference to movements through and across cultural and disciplinary boundaries and its mobility and variety of critical tactics, transcultural studies reflects a tendency common to a range of contemporary cultural theories, even those not directly engaged in the project of theorizing the shifting and disjunctive spaces of contemporary global production. What does this "nomadic turn" suggest about the projects and methods of Western critical intellectuals in a contemporary moment and about how they view their position in this moment? To what degree do globalizing processes implicitly affect styles of critical and political thought?

In an attempt to suggest answers to these broad questions, I first survey a number of influential critics who employ nomadic tropes or strategies in their theories. I do so in order to sketch some general goals and features of a nomadic critical practice as it is currently emerging and to reflect on the various uses to which nomadism as a value has been—and might be—put. Although it should be noted that these critics may differ quite widely in many of their other critical goals, I cite them together as an exemplary group—exemplary first in that they are interesting and important thinkers, and second because they function here as examples of a wider critical tendency within contemporary cultural theory. Next, I put some of Epstein's speculations on Russian transculturalism in dialogue with these Western theorists and extend his speculations in order to propose my own version of a nomadic critical project based upon what I call *a desire to become transcultural*. Finally, I suggest what transcultural perspectives, as I have defined them, might begin to contribute to political thinking in a global postmodern moment.

Toward a Nomadic Critical Practice

Often critical nomadism is proposed as simply a necessary—because more accurate or appropriate—response to the current cultural climate. Whether conceived in global terms or not, this so-called postmodern condition is characterized by such features as the simultaneous presence of multiple conflicting realities emerging in the general breakdown of cultural consensus, by shifting differences within and among subjects rather than stable identities, and by the production of qualitatively *different* modes of subjectivity arising from the expressions of formerly marginalized cultural experiences. As Elspeth Probyn (among others) observes, "the image of the nomad is one response to the critical issue of how to find an adequate symbolic language to describe fractured plural identities in migration and a fractured social world, a messy and disordered geography of plates, continents, or fractal zones slipping, sliding and skidding into, under, and over one another." In a vastly more complicated, perhaps even fundamentally altered, world the critic's goal is to enter into and migrate with a shifting sociocultural geography, to map modes of becoming within "the transversality [not universality] of our times."[8] Critical nomadism is made both possible and necessary by challenges to the Western rationalist, universalist paradigm—with its emphasis on teleological order, hierarchies, oppositional differences, centered subjectivities—by the emergence of postmetaphysical figurations of the subject and affirmations of radical difference that (in theory) act as permanent challenges to established categories of all kinds, and by resulting calls for new critical methods, identities, and styles of thought. That is to say, varieties of critical nomadism are one response to the radical critical and political critiques that have altered understandings over the past thirty years, whether such critiques come from poststructuralist, feminist, queer, or postcolonial perspectives, and whether or not they have done anything more than "simply" expose rather than materially alter the negative consequences of Western logics.

The critic as nomad practices hybrid methodologies and engages in transdisciplinary borrowings designed not simply or even primarily to produce answers but rather to provoke previously unforeseen possibilities. Thus in her effort to describe a feminist theoretical project responsive to the multiple demands of a contemporary moment, Rosi Braidotti speaks of a strategic deterritorialization of critical methods and cultural materials, a "becoming nomad of ideas," and a relocation of these materials through a process of "nomadic networking" that moves terms into alternative discursive constellations thereby confounding traditional logics and knowledge claims while generating potentially new ones.[9] Elspeth Probyn calls for an account of social relations as a series of mobile lateral "surface belongings" that "compel connections, producing themselves as other" as a means of generating a "more vibrant rendering of the social field" and capturing those local ephemeral experiences that may elude large-scale systems of explanation.[10] And Elizabeth Grosz proposes that we redescribe all sociocultural relations in terms of "'bodies, energies, movements, inscriptions rather than in terms of ideologies [or] . . . the transmission of systems of belief or representation."[11] All seek a method capable of capturing the diversity, mobility, and complexity of contemporary social reality, including those experiences that have been denied representation within it.

Nomadic critical aesthetics are irreducible to a single strategy or point of view. They result from incomplete encounters between, and permutations, transformations, and realignments of, previous theoretical and disciplinary modes that are disassembled and reassembled in fluid, strategic, situationally specific ways. This is something nomadic critical practices share with a contemporary politics of affinity or coalition. Such a politics is based not on mobilization of stable identity categories such as race, class, and gender but on local and temporary alliances among all those marginalized and disempowered by the social construction of difference. Within this politics there no longer are fixed universally true ideological positions but rather shifting constellations of meaning, identities, possibilities. Coalitional models have developed out of local political necessities as well as out of recognitions of our specific positionings as global subjects; that is, we participate in a number of diverse, disjunctive, sometimes mutually interrupting communities, each of which may generate a different mapping of the global. As Appadurai points out, our global boundaries are different for each context, and none of us inhabits only a single context. Thus to attempt to draw clear boundaries as a means of authorizing large-scale projects for social change would be to simplify world complexity and to suppress many of the contexts through which one is constituted.[12]

Nomadism as critical strategy and goal also tries to mobilize new schemes of thought, ones that might potentially provide directions out of our current "political stasis and critical deadlock," as Braidotti puts it,[13] by permitting reimaginings that might lead to the "contestation or even subversion of the imagined worlds of the official culture," in Appadurai's terms.[14] In particular the production of alternative—even fantastical— figurations of the subject itself is seen as a necessary precondition for transformative thinking ("there cannot be social change without the construction of new kinds of desiring subjects," as Braidotti succinctly puts it). These new versions of the subject typically are produced in a heterotopic space between what is (emerging) and what might become.[15] And, unsurprisingly, the contemporary search for lines of becoming other than what we are is most often conducted by those subjects who have benefited least from dominant constructions or have historically been rendered invisible within them. For example, in her effort to construct a queer desiring subject that would move beyond the restrictive formulations of identity categories, Probyn, borrowing from Deleuze, speaks of "becoming-horse," a phrase also meant to animate desire itself as a form of transformative movement and to detach it from psychoanalytic notions of lack. Donna Haraway proposes the boundary-violating figure of the cyborg as the subject of her ironic political fable of postmodern transnational feminism. And Sue Golding invents an "impossible spatiality" and an impossible sociality, described as a "space between the 'that' and its other," an "excess *to* the other, a possibly not-other." She does so as a means of excavating a place for queerness and for the "as if" of possibility emerging from the space of the "excluded middle" that exists between stable categories, a space perceived as empty from the perspective of dominant modes of rationality.

In part, this production of fantastic subjects and heterotopias also may be viewed as one means to conceive of a global subjectivity or a way to theorize from a larger global perspective without resorting to essentializing models that would repeat previous errors of exclusion and would be inaccurate anyway. Such fantastic subjects and spaces also reflect the fundamental difficulty if not the impossibility of thinking the global "totality," composed as it is of multidimensional, often radically discontinuous, realities in constant evolution. By global subject I mean in part those new versions of subjectivity proposed as emerging in response to the global postmodern condition; that is, identity formations resulting from the increasingly fragmented, mobile, and interactive nature of contemporary life and from a recognition of the global dimensions of our interactiveness. Probyn refers to this simply as "production of qualitatively different modes of subjectification and new arrangements of populations"[16]; Chambers sees it as the effort to describe a sense of the third world interpenetrating with the first, while Ernesto Laclau views it as "the multiplicity of new—and not so new—identities as a result of the collapse of the places where the universal subject spoke."[17]

Homi Bhabha takes the radical discontinuity of the global as a point of departure for his counternarrative of the postmodern constructed from the perspective of the postcolonial, diasporic subject, "those other postmodern subjects who remain unrepresented in the vaster invisibility of the transnational totality." For Bhabha, what must be articulated from within these new global spaces of discontinuous historical realities is "the problem of signifying the interstitial passages and processes of cultural difference that are inscribed in the in between, in the temporal break-up that weaves the global text." According to Bhabha, the disjunctive intersections of global, national, and local cultures that characterize postmodernism converge most dramatically in the postcolonial subject whose existence on multiple cultural borderlines involves the negotiation and translation of incommensurable differences that, in their continual unfolding, their irresolvability, expose the limits of any claim to a singular, autonomous, or stable identity whether it be cultural, racial, national, or sexual. "Difference" in Bhabha's sense exceeds Western binary logic; it is "neither one nor the other" but like Golding's "impossible spatiality" is an interstitial zone of "excess," a thirdspace that, by way of its very implausibility, becomes the figure of a larger possible cultural praxis, "the site of a possible politics-of-the-future-as-open-question."[18]

Similarly, in her essay "La Conciencia de la Mestiza," Gloria Anzaldua posits the queer and mixed-race subject as an alien consciousness, belonging simultaneously to no one culture and to all of them. Born out of the collision of several cultures, mestiza subjectivity refuses oppositional stances and instead embraces permanent ambiguity and transformation as its values. Anzaldua does not minimize the pain of this struggle to straddle cultures; it is, as she says, "an act of negotiation that makes us crazy constantly, but if the center holds we've made some kind of evolutionary step forward."[19] Like that of the nomad, the cyborg, or the thirdzone subject, mestiza consciousness, born out of the radical disjunctures of cultural hybridity and the breakdown of binaries, may be a prelude to the discovery of new imaginative territories that in turn might generate new political stances and ethical values. Examples such as these could proliferate. In the last section, I will return to this question of new political possibilities arising from what I will call a politics of mobility.

Within the nomadic critical aesthetics I have been piecing together here, the critic is redefined as a mobile, flexible subject who follows the flows of the contemporary world; he/she is also a desiring subject who migrates along the trajectories of desire itself. Here, the critic no longer is disinterested, noncontradictory, or even necessarily logical in a traditional sense; desire, too, is mobilized and made productive. An emphasis on the nomadic, affirmative nature of desire represents a significant departure from psychoanalytic framings of the term and serves also as a powerful critique of them.[20] Many of the most useful recent efforts to refigure psychoanalytic conceptions of desire have come from gay and lesbian theorists—often by way of Deleuze and Guattari—who attempt to "queer" desire as a means of producing more expansive notions of lesbian and gay subjectivity than those found within psychoanalytic frameworks. Writers such as Elspeth Probyn and Elizabeth Grosz in particular begin by refocusing Lacan's conception of desire as an unfilled and unfillable lack endlessly and compulsively circling around a missing and forever unattainable object and therefore endlessly frustrated. Instead of emphasizing lack, absence, and rupture, their theories unfix desire from the Lacanian pursuit of an object, and redefine it as movement itself, an affirmative activity of "pure" productivity that refuses to be reduced to only sexual terms or even to be anchored to an object or an individual. As Deleuze puts it, "desire does not have, strictly speaking, an object, but merely an essence that spreads itself over various objects." It aims at nothing beyond its own proliferation or self-expansion without reference to any exterior agency. Desire circulates in an unpredictable, anamorphic movement of flows and energies "capable of being linked or severed in potentially infinite ways."[21] It compels connections, touches off and sets into motion different possibilities, produces new relations and transformations, short- circuits categorical orders. Herein lies its socially transformative, even revolutionary, potential.

Deleuze and Guattari's theory of desire is radically antihumanist (as well as antipsychoanalytic) focusing as it does on intensities, flows of energy, lines of becoming rather than individual personalities or discrete objects. Because their rhizomatic project envisions networks with no priorities other than their own unfolding, it (theoretically) circumvents any politicization of desire that would simply redirect it into new dichotomies. Clearly, Deleuze and Guattari generate the most extreme of the contemporary refigurations of desiring nomadic "subjects" explored here, and in most cases go a good deal beyond them. The unpredictable movement of desire creates what Deleuze and Guattari call assemblages or multiplicities, which "never make up a whole" and are "defined not by [their] abiding identity over time or by any principle of sameness but through [their] capacities to undergo permutations, transformations, and realignments."[22] This description approximates the decentered space of the global postmodern condition itself and the chaotic movement of cultural, critical, and other flows within it.

Nomadic Transcultural Desires

As philosophers of the twenty-first century (as Foucault called them) who use fantastic fictions to launch a serious philosophical critique of Western logics and power dynamics, Deleuze and Guattari have proven remarkably useful in various critical projects to imagine alternative subjectivities and heterotopias as a prelude to transforming the contemporary world. Inspired by their example—and by the work of the other critics cited here—I want to propose one version of a nomadic critical project by positing the existence of what might be called a desire to become transcultural and by speculating on the transformative political potentials arising from this desire (a desire, not often articulated in precisely these terms, but one that, I would argue, nevertheless pervades contemporary critical consciousness).

As I suggested at the outset of this chapter, the unstable transnational shiftings and cross-cultural flows of the global postmodern may give rise to ever more effective processes of commodification and cultural homogenization or, sometimes as a reaction formation, to desires to retreat into violent assertions of cultural and national purity/singularity. But the boundary breaks that characterize this same global condition may also engender unanticipated progressive affinities, leading to new cultural formations as well as to shared projects for social change. A transcultural approach to this global situation would encourage and work within these affinities by providing a model in which individual cultures and individual subjects maintain their integrity and at the same time interact with differences inherent in other cultures, especially as these differences speak to gaps within the knowledge/experience base of one's own culture. The goal becomes to "mutate" beyond any singular or bounded mode of cultural identity—even a hybridized identity—in order to "become transcultural." This ultimately would mean to inhabit a decentered imaginary space on the border of all cultures—encompassing yet distinct from any of them. Here transculture refers to a space within or among cultures that is equally open to all of them, that embraces all existing cultures as well as all potential cultures, as well as to a kind of consciousness that liberates us from the authority or dominance of any one cultural tradition, from its national, racial, political, or other limitations.

Transcultural thinking aims to broaden an individual's (or an individual culture's) framework of identification so that one may imaginatively inhabit a range of cultural identities that are themselves shifting and mutable. Like Western multicultural perspectives, transculture as it is defined here seeks to move beyond the hegemony of any single dominant culture by recognizing the existence of a multiplicity of distinct cultures within a single national tradition. Transculture shares a desire to dislodge a vision of culture as unitary and monolithic, but it does so by attempting to theorize, work within, even provoke and intensify the interactions and interdependencies arising among cultural differences. Within multicultural frameworks, differences often are promoted for their own sakes or are essentialized and kept resolutely distinct. This can result in a kind of cultural leveling in which differences may in fact be transformed into their exact opposite. As Epstein puts it:

> Pure multiplicity is as sterile as pure totality. There are two kinds of indifference: one is totalitarian and suppresses everybody who is distinct, singular; the other is tolerant, accepting all people who are distinct as if everybody is the same. Pluralism often kills the charms of difference and in the end makes us indifferent. Active differentiation—feeling myself different from others and feeling others different from myself and all strong emotions that proceed from these differences—is the most valuable achievement of culture; in fact I would define culture in its broadest sense as compensation for our being incomplete entities. . . . A person at the bottom of his or her soul wants to belong to all cultures, share all possible experiences. This makes every person a potentially transcultural being who not only gravitates toward his or her own culture but also tries to counteract its limitations.[23]

In recognizing the contingency of every culture, especially one's own, a person also begins to have access to the nonrelative transcultural space of total cultural potential.

In some ways similar to Bhabha's third-zone subject, who exists in the midst and as a result of multiple and non-equivalent cultural differences, the transcultural subject would be produced in and through an experience of cultural dislocation and an encounter with radical difference.

Such an experience is motivated by an active desire to escape the limitations of a singular culture through immersion in others not as an experience of tourism (a dominant Western model) or as a forced imposition (a colonial model), but rather as a fundamental means of self construction, even evolution. Epstein, following Kristeva, suggests additionally that the transcultural experience may function as a form of social psychotherapy, becoming a means whereby we

> live out and decipher our unconscious by progressive interactions with other cultures. It is not easy to interact with people of other races, ages, or mental capacities since it means to invoke other, potentially alien identities within our own self. There may be something frightening, irritating and ghostly in such a contact: a young Western white male finds within his own self an old Asian woman. But this is no more difficult than to interact with our own unconscious if it is really unconscious and not the projection of our consciousness. Perhaps if we could reach the limits of transcultural consciousness and embrace the mentalities and sensibilities of all other people, we, by the same token, could eliminate our own unconscious and make pure consciousness out of it.[24]

Within this framework, transcultural consciousness inhabits a border zone outside of yet equally accessible to all cultures. This is an imaginary space of exchange and excess to all others (to paraphrase Golding), encompassing yet exceeding the productions of any single culture, where many cultural modes of belonging converge, become entangled, and thereby produce ever new belongings. Thus we might say that Epstein posits a global culture of a different sort—figured as a free multidimensional and "nontotalitarian totality" of cultural possibilities—culture as "the totality of alternatives rooted in human freedom."

Epstein's conception of the space of transcultural consciousness also resonates in many ways with Deleuze and Guattari's notions of assemblages and multiplicities, the flows of desire, and the trajectory of a line of becoming. A line of becoming "is not defined by the points that it connects or by the points that compose it [here, by distinct, already-constituted cultural differences]; on the contrary it passes between points [cultures], comes up through the middle, runs perpendicular to the points first perceived . . . it has neither beginning nor end, departure nor arrival, origin nor destination—only a middle—in fast motion . . . a line of becoming is neither one nor two nor the relation between the two, but the relation in between, the border or line of flight—a shared proximity in which the discernibility of the two points disappears."[25] This shared proximity or space of the middle represents the potential for becoming of any culture as it confronts its cultural others, its constitutive outside, as well as the transcultural space of desire where the absolute distinctions between cultures disappear in a sort of immense cultural archive of potentially infinite combinations, what I call in a later chapter the transcultural imaginary. Transcultural space opens outward, creating momentary new cultural syntheses that exceed any recognizable location; it is a space where desires for all other cultural belongings may be enacted.

Within this model the task of the transcultural critic would be to engage in processes of interference, to map negotiations between the "object" of analysis—say, another cultural identity—and the critic's own desire to progress toward it. Through this process the transcultural critic becomes a new kind of desiring subject. Transcultural interferences would involve mapping the multiple "escape lines" by which an individual cultural or critical identity is dislodged through the transcultural desire-to-become-other, and following the logic of a deterritorialization of individual cultural identities through which each identity is radically relativized, transformed, and interpenetrated by the others. Also generated in the process would be a transculturalized critical subjectivity born through the recognition of a fundamental cultural being-in-common, to borrow from Jean-Luc Nancy. Here, subjectivity would be seen as fundamentally intercultural in its construction as well as intersubjective, and community would be based on multiple possible combinations of nomadic cultural interactions.

Against Lacan's notion of desire as unfilled and unfillable *lack*, pursued futilely in relation to others, a transcultural perspective acknowledges the desire for and the potential existence of a profound connection, one that positions us as transcultural global subjects but remains unacknowledged in dominant discourses, functioning instead as a kind of transcultural unconscious—to extend Frederic Jameson's term—or as a yearning for other belongings, to borrow from bell hooks. Lack arises because consciousness of our specific national and cultural positioning—however multiple or hybridized—disrupts recognition of our deep shared cultural contingency and our deep desire for other cultural connections, connections that already are (potentially) in place as conditions of our contemporary existence. In the transcultural interaction—to rewrite Jean-Luc Nancy's statement about the nature of subjectivity—I experience the other's cultural difference together with the alteration *in me* produced through this experience that sets my cultural distinctness outside me and infinitely delimits it, showing it as always partial, in a process of becoming, and thereby desirous of connection. Within the experience of transculturalism the subject is inclined outside its cultural moorings and experiences a "ravishing" of its cultural being, to use Nancy's phrase, that does not cross over into cultural annihilation. Such a "ravishing" allows us to experience our cultural finitude, the limits of our cultural intelligibility, in the presence of the other's cultural difference and desire.

The transcultural model decisively contrasts with those models that would divide the world into a speaker and a spoken-for—models based on the presumption of the subject's rationality, self-mastery, internal coherence; a subject that cannot abide the fact of its own (inevitable) nonmastery of the world. Such a subject thus fears cultural others for concretizing its own specificity and limits, and it seeks to reduce otherness at every opportunity to a form of sameness—as an immanent feature of the subject itself—or to forms of absolute difference that it exoticizes, abjects, and seeks to expel. A transcultural model begins from the assumption that an individual or a cultural identity is never complete in itself because of its relation in a field of differences. There will always be contradictions within and a constitutive outside of identity that undermines the fiction of completeness/autonomy even as it marks the conditions of the subject's existence from moment to moment. The transcultural relation foregrounds this constitutive outside, foregrounds a desire for difference *as* difference, and suggests that pleasure itself arises from the confrontation. Desire is redefined and reaffirmed as a positive relational force that compels cultural connections across multiple forms of cultural belonging.

A Politics of Mobility

Transcultural spaces as elaborated here resonate with a number of other efforts in contemporary theory to describe paradoxical new locations of possibility. Foucault's previously mentioned heterotopias are a notable and widely influential example. Unlike utopias, heterotopias are "counter-sites, a kind of effectively enacted utopia in which . . . all the other real sites that can be found in the culture [or among cultures] are simultaneously represented, contested, inverted. Places of this kind are outside of all places, absolutely different from all the sites they reflect and speak about."[26] Postmodern geographer Edward Soja names these heterotopias "thirdspaces," "real-and-imagined" places created through the breakdown of binary logics. The first space is that of the real material world; the second space "interprets this reality through imagined representations of spatiality." The thirdspace—more than just a combination of the original two—subjects the binary to "a creative process of restructuring that draws selectively and strategically from the two opposing categories to open new alternatives," a critical "other-than" choice.[27] In his effort to elaborate a "creatively critical postmodern practice" Soja explores the logic of thirdspace in the work of a number of contemporary writers, including Henri Lefebvre and Michel Foucault; postmodern feminist geographers such as Gillian Rose, Sue Golding, and Barbara Hooper; postcolonial critics including Homi Bhabha, Edward Said, and Gayatri Spivak; and critical race theorists such as Cornel West and bell hooks, whose concept of marginality as choice, as space of radical openness, forms a cornerstone of Soja's thinking.

As hooks notes in her book *Yearning,* "the metaphoric and the literal don't belong in separate worlds. . . . To imagine is to begin the process that transforms reality . . . our living depends on our ability to conceptualize alternatives."[28] Transcultural spaces occupy ground among what is actually happening in the globalized postmodern world, what is emerging as potential, and what might become. They are constructed through the intersections of materiality, representation, and imagination. They are evident in localized micro-geographies such as the Laboratory of Contemporary Culture, which overstepped the outmoded signs of Soviet official culture in an attempt to form new utopian collectivities and imagined communities as well as in the textual spaces of this book, where processes of interference provoked by the differences of a Russian context have generated new thinking. They are evident in Probyn's description of balcony life in Montreal, where lines of class, gender, sexuality, generation, and nationality intermingle to become a symbol of "ongoing inbetweenness," a "cohabitation that goes beyond tolerance."[29] They are manifested in Peña's giddy description of border culture (the border culturalizing of the world) cited earlier and in Iain Chambers's complex meditations on global migrancy, culture, and identity in his book of the same title.

The transformative logic of transcultural thinking also is apparent in Iris Marion Young's attempt to describe a model of postmodern community based on radical difference or "inexhaustible heterogeneity," as she puts it. She sets this attempt against older models based on a logic of identity, a "desire for selves that are transparent to one another, relationships of mutual identification, social closeness and comfort," a mode of community that must exclude difference as the very condition for the existence of the community itself. In her vision of an ideal community (yet) to come, she proposes a model of the "unoppressive city" in which "persons live in relations of mediation among strangers with whom they are not in community." The city is refigured as an environment and a kind of relationship among people marked by aesthetic and social inexhaustibility, the "being together" of strangers, the accessibility of public space, and an openness to unassimilated otherness. Young describes an actual perspective on and revaluation of the possibilities of contemporary metropolitan life. The "unoppressive city" also is an imagined place awaiting material embodiment.[30] Similarly, Epstein's imagination of the global transcultural both borrows from the realities of an inherited Russian tradition and the contradictory possibilities opened by a unique and fleeting historical moment—perestroika—and expands that model in relation to a newly emerging transnational imaginary that is also in part awaiting material embodiment, as I discuss in a later chapter. These descriptions share a desire to sustain in progressive ways the encounter with and the proliferation of differences—to keep the desire for "unassimilated otherness" ongoing—along with an ethical commitment to what might be called a politics of becoming or mobility.

What of the charge that the project to construct and proliferate transcultural desiring relationships is merely a utopian exercise abstracted from materialist analyses of global relations of inequality and programs for social change? What is the political utility of transcultural thinking? The beginnings of an answer might be found by searching for a thirdspace within established political models.

In her widely influential article "From Redistribution to Recognition? Dilemmas of Justice in a 'Post-Socialist' Age," Nancy Fraser attempts to reconcile two competing paradigms of justice operating in a contemporary moment. The first involves struggles for recognition of cultural difference and specificity mobilized under identity categories such as nationality, race, gender, and sexuality; these are the so-called new social movements. The second, borrowing from older Marxist models, calls for economic, social, and political equality brought about by redistribution of resources and restructuring of inequitable power relations. These two analytically distinct paradigms of justice have conflicting aims since the former is based on calls to end cultural injustice through recognition and revaluation of cultural and symbolic differences while the latter is based on calls for socioeconomic equality that undermine difference as such.[31]

In addition, Fraser posits two broad approaches to remedying injustice. Affirmative remedies aim to correct inequality without disturbing the underlying structures that generate it, while transformative remedies aim to correct inequitable outcomes by radically restructuring political, social, economic, and symbolic structures. Thus an affirmative remedy for cultural injustice—most often associated with mainstream multiculturalism—would revalue devalued groups while maintaining individual group identities and differences among groups. Transformative remedies, on the other hand, would change cultural-valuational structures themselves by deconstructing existing group identities in such a way that everyone's sense of belonging, affiliation, and self would be altered, not just those of devalued groups. Similarly, affirmative remedies for economic injustice—typically associated with the liberal welfare state—would leave intact larger inequitable political-economic structures while transformative remedies—most closely associated with socialism—would restructure relations of production and the social division of labor so that everyone's conditions of existence would change. Since justice requires *both* redistribution and recognition, Fraser attempts to reconcile the two paradigms of justice and the two remedial strategies by conceptualizing forms in which each type of claim would maximally support—or minimally interfere with—the other.

She concludes that, in theory, the most promising scenario would consist of simultaneously pursuing transformative remedies to the problem of both redistribution and recognition. This would result in forms of socialism in the economy plus deconstruction in the culture, generating a "utopian image of a culture in which ever new constructions of identity and difference are freely elaborated and then swiftly deconstructed in an atmosphere of social equality." However, in order for this scenario to be "psychologically and politically feasible" people must be "weaned from their attachment to current cultural constructions of their interests and identities."[32]

How can nomadic thinking and the notion of transcultural desire—as they have been defined here—help to provoke the changes in our cultural imaginaries that Fraser's scenario demands? First, transcultural thinking suggests the necessity of assuming a global perspective on the issue of recognition versus redistribution so that, for example, redistribution of resources in the so-called first world would not produce inequity in other parts of the globe. The conceptual mobility associated with what I've called critical nomadism is necessary to begin to apprehend the complex and multiple relations among local, regional, national, and international frames of reference and circumstance. Moreover, mobility in a more literal sense is an important category of analysis, a significant site through which contemporary relations of power may be grasped within these complex global flows. That is, one's relative freedom and privilege may be understood in terms of access to and control over mobility since movement itself is a highly complex social differentiation with different degrees of access and initiation. Secondly, transcultural desire, as I've defined it here, is above all predicated on a desire for difference *as* difference. It is to be distinguished from the respect for or tolerance of difference that recognition claims demand, a stance that keeps us at one remove across our differences. The process of actualizing Fraser's utopian deconstructive model of difference "freely elaborated and swiftly deconstructed" must begin through an active *encounter* with difference, with a desire for difference itself. Finally, the model of transcultural desire sketched here insists on the importance of maintaining and elaborating a transformative, extrapolative impulse within our theories, one that would make the project of generating possibilities a political one. Soja's thirdspace combines the levels of reality, representation, and imagination; these would correspond to calls for redistribution of material resources, for recognition of the power of cultural representations, and for interventions in the imaginative realm, of which models of transcultural desires and becomings are one.

Notes

1. Appadurai offers the concept of "scapes" as a way of describing those fluid, irregular, and disjunctive relations among global flows. Scapes are "not objectively given relations which look the same from every angle of vision, but rather . . . they are deeply perspectival constructs, inflected very much by the historical, linguistic and political situatedness of different sorts of actors: nation-states, multinationals, diasporic communities . . . sub-national groupings . . . and even intimate face-to-face groups. . . . These landscapes . . . are the building blocks of . . . imagined worlds, that is the multiple worlds which are constituted by the historically situated imaginations of people and groups spread around the globe." Arjun Appadurai, "Disjuncture and Difference in the Global Cultural Economy," in Mike Featherstone, ed., *Global Culture, Nationalism, Globalization and Modernity* (London: Sage, 1990): 296–297). Appadurai identifies five kinds of "scapes"—ethnoscapes, mediascapes, technoscapes, finanscapes, and ideoscapes—although he acknowledges that there are many more that could be described.
2. Frederick Buell, *National Culture and the Global System* (Baltimore: The Johns Hopkins University Press, 1994): 42.

3. Rob Nixon and Wimal Siddanayake, eds., *Global/Local, Cultural Production and the Transnational Imaginary* (Durham: Duke University Press, 1996): 1.
4. Quoted in Edward Soja, *Thirdspace, Journeys to Los Angeles and Other Real-And-Imagined Places* (London: Basil Blackwell Publishers, 1996): 132–33.
5. Buell, 343.
6. Iain Chambers, "Cities Without Maps," in Jon Bird et al., *Mapping the Futures* (New York: Routledge, 1994): 188–198.
7. Fredric Jameson, "On Cultural Studies," in John Rajchman, ed., *The Identity in Question* (New York: Routledge, 1995): 290.
8. Elspeth Probyn, *Outside Belongings* (New York: Routledge, 1996): 34, 13.
9. Rosi Braidotti, *Nomadic Subjects, Embodiment and Sexual Difference in Contemporary Feminist Theory* (New York: Columbia University Press, 1994): 37.
10. Probyn, 35.
11. Elizabeth Grosz, "Refiguring Lesbian Desire," in Laura Doan, ed., *The Lesbian Postmodern* (New York: Columbia University Press, 1994): 59–60.
12. Appadurai, " Disjuncture and Difference," in Featherstone, 308.
13. Braidotti, 75.
14. Appadurai, 297.
15. Foucault speaks of heterotopias as places where radical differences coexist. "Heterotopia juxtaposes in one real place several different spaces, several sites that are in themselves incompatible or foreign to one another" ("Of Other Spaces," *Diacritics* Vol. 16, No. 1 [Spring 1986]: 22–27). Probyn goes on to describe heterotopias as spaces that designate "the coexistence of different orders of space, the materiality of different forms of social relations and modes of belonging" (*Outside Belongings,* 10). Both descriptions resonate strongly with some descriptions of the global postmodern condition.
16. Ibid., 147.
17. Ernesto Laclau, "Universalism, Particularism, and the Question of Identity," in John Rachman, ed., *The Identity in Question* (New York: Routledge, 1995): 94.
18. Homi Bhabha, *The Location of Culture* (New York: Routledge, 1994): 217–219.
19. Gloria Anzaldua, "La Conciencia de la Mestiza: Towards a New Consciousness," in Linda S. Kaufman, ed., *American Feminist Thought at Century's End* (Cambridge, MA: Blackwell, 1993).
20. Most of these contemporary efforts to rethink desire outside of a psychoanalytic framework are indebted to the work of Deleuze and Guattari (especially *Anti-Oedipus: Capitalism and Schizophrenia,* trans. Robert Hurley, Mark Seem, and Helen R. Lane [Minneapolis: University of Minnesota Press, 1983] and *A Thousand Plateaus: Capitalism and Schizophrenia,* trans. Brian Massumi [Minneapolis: University of Minnesota Press, 1987]); and Foucault (especially *The History of Sexuality,* Vol. 1 [New York: Vintage, 1990]). In addition to work by Grosz and Probyn in the field of queer theory (including their

edited collection *Sexy Bodies: The Strange Carnalities of Feminism* [New York: Routledge, 1995]), see Teresa deLauretis, *The Practice of Love: Lesbian Sexuality and Perverse Desire* (Bloomington: Indiana University Press, 1994); in the field of postcolonial studies see, for example, Robert Young, *Colonial Desire: Hybridity in Theory, Culture, and Race* (New York: Routledge, 1995) and Ann Stoler, *The Education of Desire: Foucault's History of Sexuality and the Colonial Order of Things* (Durham: Duke University Press, 1995); in the field of cultural geography see Pamela Shurmer-Smith and Kevin Hannam, *Worlds of Desire, Realms of Power: A Cultural Geography* (New York: Routledge, 1994); in virtual geography, A. R. Sandy Stone, *The War of Desire and Technology at the Close of the Mechanical Age* (Cambridge, MA: MIT Press, 1995) and Claudia Springer, *Electronic Eros: Bodies and Desire in the Postindustrial Age* (Austin: University of Texas Press, 1996); in queer approaches to geography see David Bell and Gill Valentine, eds., *Mapping Desire: Geographies of Sexualities* (New York: Routledge, 1994).
21. Deleuze and Guattari, *A Thousand Plateaus* . . . : 154–155.
22. Ibid., 9.
23. Epstein, unpublished interview with the author, May 1995. Cf. Mikhail Epstein, *After the Future: The Paradoxes of Postmodernism and Contemporary Russian Culture* (Amherst: University of Massachusetts Press, 1995): 301–303.
24. Epstein, unpublished interview with the author, May 1995.
25. Gilles Deluze and Felix Guattari, *A Thousand Plateaus: Capitalism and Schizophrenia*, trans. Brian Massumi (Minneapolis: University of Minnesota Press, 1987): 277.
26. See note 15.
27. Soja, 4, 5.
28. bell hooks, *Yearning: Race, Gender, and Cultural Politics* (Boston, MA: South End Press, 1990): 149.
29. Probyn, 3.
30. Iris Marion Young, "The Ideal of Community and the Politics of Difference," in Linda J. Nicholson, ed., *Feminism/Postmodernism* (New York: Routledge, 1990): 300–323.
31. Nancy Fraser, "From Redistribution to Recognition? Dilemmas of Justice in a 'Post-Socialist' Age," in Cynthia Willett, ed., *Theorizing Multiculturalism* (Malden, MA: Blackwell, 1998): 19–49.
32. Ibid., 38, 39.

B. Infinitions

Part One of "Theory" was devoted to defining some of the more stable transcultural principles in the context of existing theories and categories. This section introduces a range of more speculative concepts that at this stage are subject to in-finition—infinite dispersal of their meaning—rather than definition. To infine is to suggest the infinity of possible definitions of a certain term or concept and therefore to problematize its meaning and the possibility or advisability of defining it. If definition circumscribes a specific conceptual area, then infinition releases the concept from restrictive demarcations and places it in an indeterminate zone. Infinition is for the humanities what for mathematics is a transcendental number with its "infinite decimal expansion" expressed by a nonperiodic decimal fraction: an endless approximation to and escape from a discrete definition.

Chapter 9

How Does Newness Enter the Postmodern World?

Ellen E. Berry

The Temporalities and Temperamentalities of Postmodernism

Although discontinuous histories and multiple temporalities surely coexist within the restless landscapes of the global postmodern, the term postmodernism itself, and therefore its temper, remain curiously static. It is forever mired in definition by negation, in belatedness—as an afterthought to modernism—or, as Fredric Jameson memorably puts it, in "an eternal present and much further away an inevitable catastrophe."[1] We find ourselves alive after the end of history, philosophy, and metaphysics; the death of the subject, the author, and the book; the waning of the historical avant-gardes, the bankruptcy of Enlightenment promises of progress through rationality. We affirm our suspicion of metanarratives, foundational assumptions, totalizing theories, utopian ambitions, large-scale pronouncements of any kind. Art speaks in pastiche, repeating the forms of the past since, as Raymond Federman puts it, "imagination does not invent the SOMETHING-NEW we often attribute to it but rather now . . . merely imitates, copies, repeats, proliferates, plagiarizes . . . what has always been there."[2] Few of us actually believe in the progressive possibilities arising from our "new" world order, and we lack a sense of agency; therefore, pursuing what might be genuinely new becomes increasingly impossible. Within the condition of postmodernity, the future presents itself as foreclosed if it presents itself at all; the year 2000 has already happened.

In pointing to this postmodern sense of an ending, of living after the future or suspended in a perpetual present, I in no way wish to suggest the fundamental illegitimacy of any of the positions characterized here. The postmodern critique has been vitally necessary and, arguably, socially transformative (at least in its intentions). But I do want to explore further *why* it has become so difficult for contemporary progressive thinkers to posit the new—in exact inversion of their modernist counterparts and in absolute contradiction to a self-identity *as* progressive—and, perhaps more importantly, to speculate on some of the consequences arising from this refusal.

First, postmodern challenges to the Western rationalist universalist paradigm have been widespread—affecting virtually all branches of knowledge—broad-based, and impossible to ignore, if not utterly devastating. Whether such critiques emerge from post-structuralist, feminist, queer, neo-Marxist, ethnic, or postcolonial critics, and whether or not they have materially altered the negative consequences of Western logics, the radical critical and political analyses of the last thirty years have, among other things, fundamentally redefined the intellectual project of Western critical thinkers. They have succeeded only too well in demonstrating that we are blocked by ethically bankrupt systems whose horizons we cannot think beyond, systems that have failed but perhaps cannot be overcome. In part, these critiques have emerged from a recognition that some of the bloodiest carnage of the twentieth century has been carried out in the name of bringing newness into the world. The disastrous legacy of "utopian" ambitions in this century has rendered the term itself highly suspect, simply a synonym for the will to power, the intellectual fantasy of total control, or the desire to escape history itself.

Secondly, the very concept of newness has been commodified by postmodern consumer culture to such an extent that genuine innovation seems increasingly difficult to imagine. In the face of a steady supply of new and improved cars, dish detergents, (fill in the blank), newness itself becomes a ruined word, only a repetition of the *idea* of newness in which nothing actually is novel. Fredric Jameson regards this as one of the fundamental paradoxes of postmodernism and one of the greatest problems for contemporary thinkers:

> ... the equivalence between an unparalleled rate of change on all levels of social life and an unparalleled standardization of everything ... that would seem

> incompatible with just such mutability. . . . The supreme value of the New and of innovation . . . fades away against the steady stream of momentum and variation that at some outer limit seems stable and motionless. . . . [W]here everything now submits to the perpetual change of fashion and media image, nothing can change any longer . . . the persistence of the Same through absolute Difference . . . discredits change . . . absolute change equals stasis . . . a disorder after the end of history."[3]

Our current cultural preoccupation with difference—manifested in everything from Benetton ads to identity politics—masks the fact of a "universal weakening and sapping of difference on a global scale," according to Jameson.

Despite what may be its ultimate homogeneity, however, the bewildering surface complexity of the postmodern landscape, its anarchic ontological pluralism, makes any meaningful intervention within it, any real alternatives to it, difficult to imagine, let alone act upon. Thus, as Ernst Bloch writes of his own historical moment, "this world is a world of repetition or of the great Time-And-Again. . . . What-Has-Been overwhelms what is approaching, the collection of things that have become totally obstructs the categories Future, Front, Novum."[4] As a consequence, we lose a sense of "anticipatory consciousness," the spirit of "venturing beyond" what currently exists, a spirit without which, as Bloch says, "the New is inconceivable" and the desire for an encounter with genuine difference, with *unassimilated* otherness, is blocked. The same and the different remain in a state of nonrecognition or static confrontation rather than mutual interaction in the absence of any imaginable change, in the absence of what Jameson calls "the immense unthinkable Difference of an impossible future."[5] That is, being able to encounter difference *as* different, rather than as a version of what one already knows, is predicated upon the assumption that newness may enter the world.

Jameson argues that contemporary intellectuals experience fear and anxiety before the idea of radical change (Bloch would say the refusal of hope itself) for the following reasons: We fear projecting only a repetition of our own sullied world under the guise of the new, and we cannot distinguish between the rhythms of change inherent in and programmed by the system of late capitalism and a change that might actually displace this system by a new one altogether. Thus we remain stuck either celebrating the products of postmodern culture, thereby replicating the giddy rhythms of postmodern "change" itself; endlessly diagnosing the problem, thereby critiquing a system whose failures are by now well known; or enclosing genuinely new situations and problems in past narratives or paradigms of understanding, thereby failing to understand accurately their uniqueness.

Approaching Newness

In *The Seeds of Time,* Jameson explores what he calls the "antinomies of postmodernism"—positions within the postmodern that seem radically incompatible and utterly contradictory—and shows that these apparently oppositional positions in fact are mutually implicated. The paradoxical relation between identity and difference, the same and the new, that I have described is one such antinomy. Another is the apparent opposition between utopia and anti-utopia. Jameson shows that while critiques of the evils of the utopian impulse have become a "Boom industry" among postmodern critics, the most powerful arguments against utopia in reality are themselves utopian. In a similar vein, David Harvey discusses contemporary history as producing the *negative* conditions for and thus potentially the motivation to set into motion something not yet conceived or named, which opens society to a transformation whose outcome is unforeseen—the conditions for a sort of experiment.

The critical paralysis or impasse described at the end of the previous section is one response to the culture of postmodernity. Yet this same set of conditions also has generated different responses: attempts to set into motion the not-yet conceived or named as a means of opening room for the possible, for potentially new thinking. I argued in a previous chapter that some postmodern critics' resistance to closure and insistence on partiality and provisionality in their theories might be considered part of a commitment to opening multiple paths to the future so as not to foreclose it in advance through imposition of a singular narrative. In this section I wish to explore through the work of a range of exemplary critics a number of other sites of and strategies for generating newness. These include newness that emerges a) out of relations forged or attempts to construct bridges between two or more radically different terms; b) through a process of extrapolation from an original site or problematic; c) from the break-up of old totalities or solidities; and d) from alternative, previously marginalized or illegitimate perspectives, including especially here the practices of everyday life. This exploration will act as a prelude to my larger discussion of improvisational practices that appears in part III, in which these practices are promoted as another modality of the transcultural imagination and a virtual space for the emergence of the new.

One of the controlling metaphors of this book is the concept/process of interference. We noted earlier that interference and difference derive from the same Latin root but (in good deconstructive fashion) have come to connote precisely opposite processes: "Differ" means to diverge or move apart from while "interference" means to bridge, to intervene between. The process of interference produces newness by generating unique transcultural patterns formed through the encounter between two previously opposed terms, perspectives, worldviews, ideologies, etc. just as a metaphor explodes into newness through combining terms whose relationship was previously overlooked or seems strange (the principle behind collage aesthetics as well).

Deconstruction—especially in its feminist and postcolonial variants—is, of course, the most recent "logic" or (anti-)system through which to articulate relations between binary oppositions. Far from being neutral pairs, such oppositions most often are revealed through the deconstructive operation to be a hierarchy with one term valued above or even forcibly suppressing the other. In this case, newness enters when the fundamental incommensurability (difference) between the two terms is disclosed and the previously silenced term (woman, postcolonial other, etc.) begins to speak. It does so in a language that seems incomprehensible or nonsensical from the perspective of the dominant term and that therefore forever "troubles" its former stability and sense of self-sufficiency, setting in motion a process of differentiation that permanently displaces the original problematic, if not necessarily the tendency of systems in general to (re)constitute themselves as power hierarchies.

In an essay from which the current chapter draws its title—"How Newness Enters the World: Postmodern Space, Postcolonial Times, and the Trials of Cultural Translation"—Homi Bhabha explores this process of deconstruction and reinscription from the doubled or split perspective of the postcolonial subject in the heart of the metropolis. He does so in part as a means of capturing the historical originality (and thus the "cognitive obscurity") of contemporary global culture with its multiple, discontinuous local histories and its new modes of subjectivity (whether these are called postcolonial, postcommunist, postnational, or simply postmodern). The attempt to negotiate between the "non-synchronous temporalities" of global and national cultures, between two distinctly different national cultures, or among the components of thoroughly mixed identities (that is, the space between two formerly opposed terms), creates a tension "peculiar to borderline existences," destroys the original structures of reference and sense-making, and opens historically unique thirdspaces that Bhabha calls "forms of the future-as-open question."[6]

The temporality of the future-as-open question also discloses new modes of performative agency ("the agency of foreignness") created through the process of deconstruction, displacement, and reinscription of the original system. Indeed, as Bhabha notes, the immigrant's survival *depends* on discovering how to perform newness in the face of—how to translate—radical cultural (in)difference. At least momentarily revealed in this process of translation—through which an incommensurate residue always remains—are genuinely alternative practices and values embedded in "the indeterminate temporality of the in-between" : in the newly unstable linkages between previously opposed terms that must be "engaged in creating the conditions through which 'newness comes into the world.'"[7] However, actually recognizing and engaging with the alterity of these alternative practices and holding open this thirdspace of indeterminacy are difficult challenges for many of the reasons I have elaborated, including the tendencies to assimilate, commodify, or misrecognize difference and otherness. One way of beginning to confront these difficulties is to try to keep ongoing the processes of differentiation and self-differentiation set in motion by the intrusion of foreignness or by the attempt to negotiate in the territory of a newly reinscribed problematic.

In a previous chapter, I argued for the importance of including an extrapolative impulse within our cultural theories that would make the project of generating possibilities part of the political agenda of cultural studies. To extrapolate means to carry something beyond an established framework through intensifying particular features of it. Extrapolation is related to the process of conjecturing or speculating; it operates in the modality "What if?" or in Bloch's realm of the possible. The possible, defined as the capability of "doing other" and "becoming other," constitutes a basic feature of human consciousness, according to Bloch. It is "that which can be directed and re-determined in all determinations." All situations contain the possibility of existing—being configured—otherwise; contain "the constant plus-ultra of essential possibility;" and are "illuminated by it at its leading edge," which is also the limit of what is currently thinkable. Active capacity, agency as such, belongs to the realm of possibility whose function is to develop anticipatory consciousness, defined as "a directing act of a cognitive kind" pointed toward the future. Thinking itself means "venturing beyond" for Bloch; it is a mode not just of conceptualizing but of actually grasping the new as "something that is mediated in what exists and is in motion," something that directs itself toward or uncovers the not-yet-conscious, the goal of which is to provide imaginative encouragement to feel and act differently.[8]

The extrapolative or anticipatory impulse also requires acts of radical imagination or what Bloch calls daydreaming (as distinct from fantasy), which is the "actual space of receptivity of the New and production of the New."[9] Jameson and other postmodern critics, such as Baudrillard, often imply that the imaginative faculty itself has atrophied in a postmodern era so thoroughly has it has been colonized by the media spectacles of consumer culture with its theme-park mentality. In *Modernity at Large*, his study of the various ways in which locality emerges in a globalizing world, Arjun Appadurai argues just the opposite. He claims that within contemporary culture, the increased dissemination of media and migrations of people globally actually have "transform[ed] the field of mass mediation because they offer new resources and new disciplines for the construction of imagined selves and imagined worlds." Instead of purely colonizing forces, the media allow for the production of "communities of sentiment"; they thus become "resources for experiments with self-making in all sorts of societies, for all sorts of persons."[10]

In short, Appadurai argues that the imagination functions as a *constitutive* feature of contemporary subjectivity that plays a new and expanded role in social life itself since it no longer is confined to special persons and preserves, "the expressive space of art, myth, and ritual." Instead it assumes an unprecedented role in the social practices of everyday life for wide groups of people, whose imaginative acts create "new mythographies" that may become "charters for new social projects and not just a counterpoint to the certainties of daily life," "staging grounds for action and not only for escape." As Bloch does, Appadurai claims that the imagination has a projective and futural sense about it, the sense of being a prelude to expression and action: "No longer mere fantasy . . . no longer simple escape . . . no longer elite pastime . . . and no longer mere contemplation, . . . the imagination has become an organized field of social practices, a form of work, and a form of negotiation between sites of agency and locally-defined fields of possibility. . . . The imagination is now central to all forms of agency, is itself a social fact, and is the key component of the new global order."[11]

Despite his enthusiastic claims for the role of the imagination in the new global order, Appadurai does not regard it as a purely emancipatory force (just as it is not entirely disciplined). Instead, imaginative acts disclose and create spaces of active contestation within contemporary media spectacles in which "individuals and groups seek to annex the global into their own practices of the modern."[12] That is, acts of the imagination—of creative interaction and recombination—generate new modes of opening within presumed totalities; they are small interventions from the future, a space/temporality defined by Bloch simply as "what has never been like this . . . the nature of the future is only in this possibility."[13]

The undeniable fact of global late-stage capitalism has created one totalized master narrative of the postmodern. Yet dissolution of old totalities also is a constitutive feature of the postmodern moment and represents another site of emerging newness: When old systems break up, what had previously been obscured by the totalized structure (whose nature is to contain difference) is dislodged from old calcifications, surfaces, and is freed to circulate in potentially new combinations in a transformed arena. The emergence of distinctly new post-communist cultures from the ruins of the Soviet empire is perhaps the most striking recent example of this process of disintegration, liberation, and recombination. The surprising end of the Soviet Union itself confirms that the postmodern world perhaps is not quite as predictable as we thought. As Dick Hebdige puts it, "When the Berlin Wall fell, in a sense it fell on all of us, though one of the formations it fell directly on top of was that whole formation of hopelessness represented by that fatal version of postmodernism which saw the end of everything everywhere in everything. . . . Nothing but nothing is ever *bound* to happen."[14]

The relocation of previously unofficial communities of intellectuals within the new quasi-official spaces opened by the transitional moment of perestroika and their creation of new modes of cultural reinvention in these spaces is one example of this process. The need of these communities to acknowledge newly emerging cultural histories that had been exiled by the Soviet system and to confront newly imported ideas from outside that system is another example. This process also finds a correspondence in the new histories being told in the West from those (women, ethnic and sexual minorities) previously excluded from the official story, resulting in a widespread recognition that the world contains plural histories, diverse cultures, and particularities that were (sometimes forcibly) excised from Western modernism's universalistic project. Both examples illustrate Bloch's contention that new thinking and fresh synthetic combinations can be discovered in the thinking of the past; precisely *because* it remains incomplete, material from the past becomes available for succeeding ages to "refunction" in new ways. Moreover, the circulation of ideas, terms, tendencies from within newly mobilized systems as well as importations from outside their (newly permeable) boundaries create actual and potential(ly infinite) combinations in an ever-evolving transcultural archive—the site of a transcultural imaginary and a repository for cultural possibilities.

As a prelude to my discussion in the final section of this book—which will elaborate the role that improvisational practices might play in the U.S. academy—I want to explore the previous claims in relation to academic disciplines as totalizing structures of knowledge production and the practices of interdisciplinarity as one response to these totalities. While interdisciplinary work has existed in the U.S. academy for a number of years, it has become much more common recently, in part perhaps because its border-crossing hybridized nature reflects the nomadic predisposition of postmodern thought more generally.

Disciplinary formations are the "composite set of claims, activities, and institutional structures that define and protect, create and maintain, [particular kinds of] knowledge practices." Because they are hierarchical structures that attempt to consolidate themselves as totalities, they are also "the locus of struggles to determine the conditions and criteria of legitimate membership" in the discipline. Interdisciplinarity begins when the solidity of a discipline starts to break down through recognition of a gap or a disturbance in its existing organization of knowledge, through its inadequacy to accomplish a given task, or through a challenge arising from outside the discipline. This destabilization may manifest itself as an uneasiness in classification, or a sense that new languages are required to describe emerging concepts, or even as a mutation of an existing concept or method (Roland Barthes calls this an "epistemological slide"). As Julie Klein points out in her study of theories of interdisciplinarity, such newness may initially be experienced as noise or nonsense (interference), but later comes to be understood as the intersection of a new system with the first. "Interdisciplinary cognition is located in the attempt to construct meaning out of what initially seems to be noise." In the process of making sense of this noisy intervention, and at the point of intersection between old structure and new, a hybridized space is created where new knowledge may begin to emerge. Klein describes interdisciplinary cognition at its most basic level as a boundary-crossing phenomenon characterized by heterogeneity, intellectual mobility (nomadism), even chaos, in terms and methods: "The boundary work of interdisciplinary studies is threefold. They detach a category as subject and object from existing disciplinary frameworks, thereby loosening boundaries and stimulating trading zones [zones of interaction]. They fill gaps in knowledge from lack of attention to the category, thereby developing new pidgins and creoles in hybrid communities. And ... they [may] redraw boundaries by constituting new knowledge-spaces and new professional roles."[15]

Despite the capacity of interdisciplinary activity to stimulate the formation of new knowledge, Klein makes clear that interdisciplinary fields—especially when they are consolidated as "proper" fields—don't escape the rules and procedures of legitimation operating within disciplines, which again involve an ongoing process of breaking, reconstituting, and most importantly enforcing boundaries between legitimate and illegitimate knowledge. Klein's analysis provides a useful reminder that the process of creating the conditions for new thinking to emerge in a postmodern world is a difficult, ongoing, and always temporary one. The final section of this book, which is devoted to some concrete experiments in transcultural thinking, embraces the challenging search for newness. While it acknowledges the necessary provisionality of such a search, at the same time it also, we hope, provides resources for "venturing beyond" our current modes of thinking, and the "imaginative encouragement to feel and act differently."[16]

Notes

1. Fredric Jameson, *The Seeds of Time* (New York: Columbia University Press, 1994): 72.
2. Raymond Federman,"Imagination as Plagiarism [an unfinished paper ...]," *New Literary History* 7, No. 3 (Spring 1976).
3. Jameson, 15–19.
4. Ernst Bloch, *The Principle of Hope,* Vol. 1, trans. Neville Plaice, Stephen Plaice, and Paul Knight (Cambridge, MA: MIT Press, 1986): 6–8.
5. Jameson, 61.
6. Homi Bhabha, *The Location of Culture* (New York: Routledge, 1994): 218–19.
7. Ibid., 227.
8. Bloch, 232, 238, 12.
9. Ibid., 116.
10. Arjun Appadurai, *Modernity at Large* (Minneapolis: University of Minnesota Press, 1997): 4.
11. Ibid., 4, 5, 6, 8, 31.
12. Ibid., 4.
13. Bloch, 228.
14. Quoted in Jon Bird et al., *Mapping the Futures: Local Cultures, Global Change* (New York: Routledge, 1993): 271.
15. Julie Thompson Klein, *Crossing Boundaries, Knowledge, Disciplinarities, and Interdisciplinarities* (Charlottesville: University of Virginia Press, 1996): 1–2.
16. Ibid., 84, 36–37.

Chapter 10

The Permanence of Newness and Spaces for Difference: From History to Geography

Mikhail Epstein

From Time to Space

The category of newness seems to disappear from the postmodern world. Not because there is less newness than there was before, but because there is more newness and it no longer takes us by surprise. We are prepared for newness and thus it fails to impress us as strikingly or distinctly new. We have a different horizon of expectation as compared with more traditional societies in which newness happens as an overwhelming break with the past. All experience of modernity, as highlighted by the revolutions of the eighteenth to the twentieth centuries, was dichotomous in terms of the new being opposed to the old, innovation opposed to tradition. However, innovation itself is a mode of the status quo in postmodern societies. There is nothing more permanent and habitual than innovation. If you look at the news rubric on your computer screen and suddenly find it empty, then you are really shocked. The absence of news may be a sign of the Apocalypse coming. This is abnormal. Maybe CNN or Reuters has a problem with their satellites? It is easier for us to imagine a mechanical break in the flow of news than a stoppage of news altogether.

Now we can rephrase Ecclesiastes: There is nothing old under the sun. Nothing that would not be new; nothing that can escape renovation. The "new" no longer stands as a discrete category in binary opposition to the "old." Both of these categories become fuzzy through interference, the new becoming the "old" permanent condition of things and the old becoming just a useful resource and point of reference for ongoing innovations. Not only has innovation become a factor of stability, a part of the postmodern status quo, but the old has also lost its peaceful repose in the past as it is intensively manipulated and transformed from the present. Mikhail Bakhtin wrote that any word and meaning of the past will have its feast of resurrection in the future. What happens now is not so much the feast of resurrection as the routine of renovation. Indeed, the meaning of the past is increasingly determined by the interrogations and solicitations of the present. The postmodern addiction to citations and intertextuality brought the past to the brink of extinction through the expanding dialogue with the present. The electronic web in particular brings the past preserved in texts to the fingertips of our contemporaries who cut, copy, and paste the past according to their own projects and constructive needs.

The political regime of postmodern societies may be defined as a kenocracy—"the power of the new" (Greek *kainos*). A kenocracy is a regime that gives priority to the new on the basis of its newness and almost automatically destroys or invalidates old things only because they are old. A kenocracy is always selective. For example, in the United States, kenocracy applies only to big rulers and not to big rules (new presidents—old constitution). The time span in which a new entity moves to the category of the "old" also can vary: for example, eight years for the presidency, one year for fashion, several weeks for movies in the theaters. But even the old itself is permanently assimilated and reintegrated with the new under the name of contextualization, reconstruction, rereading, rethinking, reevaluation, reinterpretation, and all kinds of "re" -actions. Essentially, a kenocracy is a totalitarian rule of newness, which means that the sharp taste of novelty inevitably disappears. In a Marxist state in which everything is Marxist, including science, literature, newspapers, songs, and movies, there is no longer respect or feeling for Marxism as a distinct system of ideas. In the same way, under a kenocracy the new becomes dull because there is nothing around except newness.

How is it possible, then, to express one's originality if newness is no more a marker of difference? Territories and spaces come to measure difference instead of epochs and periods.

The postmodern emphasis on cartographies and geographies is a reconceptualization of newness in space rather than in time. History has demonstrated its dangerous totalitarian ambitions inherent in the very fact of its unidirectionality. Not only is time totalitarian, it is the source of all totalitarianisms because it forbids movement in all but one direction. There were attempts to overcome this unidirectionality of time by constructing alternative cyclic (nonlinear) models of history, as in Oswald Spengler's *The Decline of the West*. However, cyclic models, though distinct from models of forward progress, still cannot escape the unidimensionality of time within a given cycle. The proliferation of cyclical models in the historical thinking of the twentieth century (Spengler, Arnold Toynbee, Lev Gumilev[1]) was an indicator of the exhaustion of historicity and of the imminent transition to spatial and geographical models.[2] Paradoxically, cultural geography gains momentum at the very moment when physical geography becomes effectively a discipline of the past. The rise of cultural geography occurs now in post-historical space and eliminates the time of history in the same way as the rise of modern history gradually eliminated the territories of geographical exploration. Physical geography has the full extent of its subject matter at the point where history has not yet begun; but the time of history gradually cuts across the physical surface of the earth and, through the discovery and exploration of new lands and continents, turns physical geography into an outdated discipline, or, more precisely, transforms it into cultural geography. This process of super-historization of everything now backfires, eliminates time, and makes history an obsolete discipline. Cultural geography takes revenge on behalf of physical geography, and space, whose physical aspect was consumed by historical time, now regains its dominance as a cultural reality.

Already in the 1960s, with the advent of structuralism, culture was defined as "anti-time," as a machine for the destruction of historical time (Claude Lévi-Strauss). In Russian culturology of the 1960s and 1970s, the concept of culture was clearly opposed to the concept of history. If, according to Marxist and any other type of historicism, culture is the product of history and is dependent on the parameters of historical time and specific gradations of epochs and periods, then, according to culturology, history captures only one flat dimension of the multidimensional phenomenon of culture. In culture, the present is as dependent on the past as the past is dependent on the present. They influence and reinterpret each other and actually exist in one time, which therefore is not "time" any longer but rather the space of time, time as a spatialized pattern. The cultures of all epochs and nations coexist in one trans-historical continuum on which ancient Greece, for example, acquires its cultural meaning not only through the fact that it is Greece but also through the fact that it is ancient from the standpoint of modernity.[3] Each cultural entity acquires its meaning only through its relationship to other cultures in other times.

French structuralism and Russian culturology were only two anticipations of the spatial reconfiguration of history that is now taking place in cultural geography and imaginative cartography. The imaginary component of the new geography corresponds to a place that, in the traditional historical view, was assigned to the future. But the imaginary character of this space or territory is clearly distinct from those utopian or eschatological implications that the future acquired in the historicist world view. The difference is that the future is common to all of humankind and is as imminent and inexorable as the flow of time, whereas an imaginable territory is located in space and presents one of many coexisting alternatives in the search for cultural identity. Territory is a safer notion than epoch, because territory can be navigated in many directions; it confers freedom of choice and orientation, whereas "epoch" "arrives" and "attacks" you from one side (in Russian, the future "*nastupaet*" means both "comes" and "is on the offensive").

One can suggest, however, that in the course of time this geographical paradigm will exert a counterinfluence on the historical vision, and the concept of the future will be restored, although reconfigured in spatial terms. The future will be understood as a variety of futures in the same way as a map represents a variety of territories.

Culture and the Future

The future must be possibilized in order to avoid predicting it. To "possibilize" means not only "to make something possible" but to "introduce multiple possibilities" that cannot be realized simultaneously and therefore keep the future open. As Steven Connor says, what is important is not predicting the future but finding ways in which it might be possible to talk about it at all.

The problem of the future as it is formulated in this statement already contains part of its solution. Finding ways in which it might be *possible* to talk about the future presupposes at least one way: to talk about the future as if it were only *possible,* not imminent, not so much arriving as receding before the present, escaping any prospect of definition. Traditionally the future has been regarded as a blank slate available for majestic inscriptions; every letter in this empty space could be capitalized, since the future was imagined as an infinitely elastic tissue capable of enfolding any far-reaching project and bringing it to accomplishment.

After the future failed to cooperate with master thinkers in their all-encompassing revolutionary projects, thinking lost its interest in the future, as if its love for this capricious beauty remained unrequited. This is where we live now, turning our back to the future that reneged on its promises to us. But this resentful gesture of disinterestedness still accommodates itself to the pattern of the recent futurist or the futurological model of thinking about the future. After the lover is rejected, it is natural for him to heap contempt on the former object of his love. These anti-utopian visions or post-utopian nonvisions of the future are still part of the revolutionary romance that by now has psychologically outlived itself. Instead of a romantic affair with the future we should rather engage in a much more distanced and casual but nevertheless meaningful and mutually respectful relationship. The future is not a place for inscription; it is rather an eraser that eliminates those inscriptions that we leave on the slates of our present.

Now, while we may still accept the inevitability of time's progression, we also may perceive within temporality a force that counteracts this progression, and this is the future itself. The future does not escape the one-dimensionality of time; rather, it is the internal irony of one-dimensionality. Irony permits us to negate the meaning of a word while still using it. If you have no other language to criticize the language of time you can still employ the language of time in order to undermine its validity. Thus the future still speaks the language of time since there is no other language given to us, but it uses it ironically. All our pronouncements in this language—historical facts, chronological entries, accomplishments, projects, and predictions—are rearticulated by the future in such a way that our present and our past begin to sound ironic and sometimes self-defeating. Thinking now about Lenin and Stalin, who in their time were indeed "the conquerors of the future," we cannot but feel the deep irony that the future held in store for their invincible deeds.

Culture is an attempt to create a multidimensional language, a spatial language in order to transcend the one-dimensionality of time. The simplest definition of culture would be "an experiment in immortality conducted by mortal beings." We attempt to transcend our mortality by inscribing our transitory beings onto paper, into stone, into temples, into cities, etc. That is why the word "culture" still has the root "cult" in it. Like cult, culture transcends the realm of mortality, but, unlike cult, it does not project any separate transcendental realm. Transcendence differs from the transcendental in that it needs the future, not eternity. It needs space in time, not beyond time. The inherent paradox of culture is that it escapes the one-dimensionality of time and simultaneously is reinscribed in it again and again, to spatialize time itself. The most glorious monuments are doomed to destruction because immortality is sought within time, not beyond it. That is why culture is inevitably self-ironic in its own endeavors to survive in the substance of dying, to build an eternal palace on the sands of time.

Therefore culture and the future have much in common, both disclosing time's self-irony. If history is related to the seriousness of existence in this world and religion is related to the seriousness of existence in another world, then culture reflects the irony of the existence of one world within the other, worlds that can never merge and never separate. Accordingly, history embraces what happens in time and religion, what abides in eternity, while culture embraces the zone where time aspires to eternity and eternity ridicules time. This *time beyond time* (not time within time, nor eternity beyond time) is the future—the proper time of culture, its self-defeating super-temporality. Books are written to be read and laws are established to be fulfilled in the future. What culture creates must paradoxically exist both in time and beyond time, and this surplus of time, again, is the future.

Utopian visions of the future, including obsessions with the future in the futurism of the 1910s and the futurology of the 1960s, underestimated this cultural meaning of the future because their dominant tendency was to historicize and theologize it. The utopian vision of the future represents an intersection of theological and historical dimensions: The eternal, transcendental world is bound to arise from the flow of time, like an ocean with its eternal swaying and ebbing arises from the influx of rivers. Utopias were twice as serious as historical and theological outlooks were in themselves. Actually, the overlapping of these models of seriousness should produce an ironic effect since typically only one seriousness is possible; two seriousnesses, those of a theologian professing the millennial kingdom and of a historian investigating the conditions of specific epochs, can combine only as a pastiche or parody of each other. That is what was misunderstood in Marxism: By overlapping historical and theological discourses, it produces a surplus of seriousness that is fraught with farce, with its own ironic refutation.

The future is not eternity since it still belongs to the dimension of time, but within this temporal dimension it represents a denial of time. There is only one past and one present, but the future itself should rather be used in the plural since it exists in a subjunctive, not in an indicative or imperative mood. We should speak about "past, present, and futures," emphasizing the asymmetry between these temporal dimensions. While time is still unidirectional, it nonetheless engenders a variety of futures whence the entire idea of creative pluralism may be derived.

Potentiation

Transculture has its own ontological dimension: potentiality. The foundational concepts of ontology are actuality and potentiality as they have been elaborated in philosophy since Aristotle. Aristotle himself gives priority to the actual over the potential, and this predetermined the forms of European thinking about these categories. "[I]t is clear that actuality is prior to potentiality. . . . [F]or that which is in the primary sense potential is potential because it is possible for it to become actual, e.g. I mean by 'capable of building' that which can build, and by 'capable of seeing' that which can see, and by 'visible' that which can be seen."[4]

That which abides in a state of potentiality was considered to be ontologically inferior, imperfect, and in need of actualization or realization—a process through which it ascends to the highest level of being. Reality is thus the ultimate horizon and justification for all possibilities. In his comparison of actuality and possibility, Hegel, like Aristotle and Thomas Aquinas before him, establishes the priority of the former: "[A]ctuality is the more comprehensive, because it is the concrete thought which includes possibility as an abstract element. And that superiority is to some extent expressed in our ordinary mode of thought when we speak of the possible, in distinction from the actual, as only possible."[5] Thus the typical trajectory of historical change and innovation could be viewed as a transition from the imaginary to the real, as the realization of projects, intentions, dreams, plans, utopias, intellectual and imaginative aspirations, and other forms of potentiality.

However, this scheme seriously underestimates the emotional, moral, and intellectual value of potentiality, which is fundamentally irreducible to the state of actuality. For example, the three supreme virtues as they are described in the Christian tradition—faith, love, and hope—are states of potentiality that can never be fully realized, reduced to actual facts or actual knowledge. If hope could be fully realized, then the permanent condition of humans would be absolute satisfaction—but we know that this is not true. If faith could be fully realized, then humans' permanent epistemological condition would be absolute knowledge—but this is not true. The same holds true for negative feelings, such as fear and anxiety, which reveal the potentiality of pain and death rather than their actuality.

Potentiality is not only a central aspect of our moral and psychological life but also of social conditions. The history of the twentieth century gives evidence for a growing potentialization of the entire system of economic and political life in developed societies. The systems of credit and insurance, for example, are based not on actuality but on the potentiality of certain occurrences. Social life in the West was dominated by the state of potentiality for decades without properly recognizing and interpreting this neglected ontological dimension.

Two models have been in competition throughout the twentieth century: the realization of the potential and the potentiation of reality. The Soviet model was the last utopia of actuality that attempted to preserve the priority of the actual by projecting it into the future as a culmination and realization of all potentials contained in the present. A radical way of reversing the Aristotelian system of categories is proposed by the Western model in which reality itself is increasingly potentiated, converted into a state of possibility as having value and dignity in itself.[6]

With the arrival of so-called virtual reality, this ontological revolution acquires a new technological dimension. What is virtuality and how is it related to the actual and the potential? I would define the virtual as *the actuality of the potential* as such. Potentiality has its own actual existence not when it is realized—at which point it is not potential any more—but when it preserves its quality of the potential. On the material of American political life, including polls, primaries, and all forms of "virtual elections," Slavoj Zizek comes to the conclusion that, "The status of possibility, while different from that of actuality, is thus not simply deficient with regard to it. *Possibility as such exerts actual effects which disappear as soon as it 'actualizes' itself.*"[7]

Virtuality is potentiality functioning as actuality, without the need of actualization. For example, the concept of "university" refers to the system of educational practices, to the potential of multidisciplinary training in all realms of knowledge, and to a system of buildings and facilities designed to actualize this potential in a certain time and place. When the potential of the university is enacted without reference to actual places, times, buildings, etc., we encounter the phenomenon of the virtual university—potential in its purest form, which works to satisfy our needs for education. Prior to the end of the twentieth century, social functions and physical entities, or "potentialities and acts," were believed to coincide, but now it has become possible to divorce or at least separate functions from substances, effects from facts, potentialities from actualities.

At the end of the twentieth century, culture has to assimilate consciously those ontological dimensions of potentiality that have already been exploited and utilized in economics and technology. Paradoxically, the humanities so far have failed to recognize the value of potentiation as a mode of interpretation of texts and artistic invention. The method of potentiation has been applied mostly in critical procedures, such as in deconstruction, which demonstrates the potentiality of several meanings where traditional interpretation recognized only the actuality of one. Deconstruction usually aims to expose the problematic nature of all "centered" discourses, those claiming an affiliation with eternal principles or authentic facts and relying on the concepts of truth, presence, and origin. As an instrument of criticism, deconstruction questions the unexamined foundations of such discourses and demonstrates the falseness of their truth claims and the fundamental ambivalence of their messages.

However, deconstruction, as Jacques Derrida emphasizes, should not be interpreted as an instrument of criticism, the opposition of one better reading to another less relevant one, but rather as the potentiality of many readings. Deconstruction, at least in its conventional form of academic poststructuralism, is mostly understood as "the undoing, decomposing, and desedimenting of structures," though, according to Derrida's own intention, it "was not a negative operation. Rather than destroying, it was also necessary to understand how an 'ensemble' was constituted and to reconstruct it to this end."[8] To this definition of deconstruction by its founder, I would juxtapose the definition of potentiation as *reconstruction of potentialities contained within a given cultural ensemble as a multiplicity of alternative ensembles.*

The concept of "deconstruction" has its own logic of negativity; as Derrida further remarks on this term, "the negative appearance was and remains much more difficult to efface. . . . That is why this word, at least on it own, has never appeared satisfactory to me. . . ."[9] I suggest that the term "potentiation" would better accommodate positive aspects of deconstruction: not merely criticism of a given practice or discourse by demonstrating its logocentric pretensions and misconceptions, but construction of alternative readings and interpretations, future projections that might never be actualized as "the present." Such a "positive deconstruction" celebrates the proliferation of interpretive possibilities and unrestricted semantic play set free from any one signified, not by negating the "signified" as such, but by the potentiation of new *signifiables*.

The Place of Utopia

The term "utopia" has to be rearticulated rather than simply eliminated in view of the multiplicity of the futures. Rather than invent new terms, like "anti-" or "post-utopia," in order to negate the totalitarian, historical-theological implications of utopianism, I would suggest a return to the original meaning of this term: U-topia means no-place, the place that does not exist. It was a radical distortion of the initial meaning of the term to treat u-topia as a place that should be found and colonized. The epoch when Thomas More proposed his vision of utopia was the time of geographical discoveries; the *Utopia* (1616) was written only twenty-four years after Columbus unveiled the great topos of the New World. If a real place—America—could become in the course of centuries the promised land for millions of disenfranchised people, why should "no-place," an ideal space of social harmony, not become a real future for all of humanity? The idea of utopia historically has had a career similar to that of America: A topos came to be idealized in the same manner as u-topia had to be realized. Both processes were indispensable for the historical reinscription of geographical discoveries, real or imaginable. Both Columbus and More launched their territories into history. That is how the hyphen in the word "u-topia" was erased by the logic of historical adventure, and a geographical no-place was transformed into the place to be achieved in the future. The future implicitly contains this negation "u" since it negates the stability of the present. This is why utopia as a no-place became associated with the future.

Relegating the notion of utopia from the geographical to the historical dimension, from space to time, from nowhere to the future was in fact an attempt to spatialize the future rather than to temporalize an ideal space. The inspiring example of pure space temporalized and historicized was the colonization of the real place of America, though even this process of historicization had to dis-place the native inhabitants of this place. Historicization of geography can never be accomplished peacefully and bloodlessly because time and space are not completely compatible. If we imagine that the problem of squaring the circle could be solved, it would mean that the inhabitants of the corners would be erased and exterminated in the ideal shape of the circumference, and vice versa. If such a bloody confrontation could occur within geometrical configurations of space, how much more violent would be (and was) the solution to another problem—temporalization of space, historicization of geographical discovery? But when historical parameters are applied not to a real Columbian space, which can function as the present, but to More's imaginative discovery, to no-place, which can function only as the future, the number of potential victims increases in geometrical or, let us simply say, historical progression. Unlike the topos of America, which grew from a geographical into a historical dimension, utopia became the obsessive ideal projected in the future, annihilating the present.

The only dignified way to dispense with utopianism would be not to oppose it with the anti-utopian visions of the over-structured, oppressive future, but rather to return u-topia to the place where it belongs and from which it departed: to transform it into a part of imaginative geography. Ideal places dispersed in space do not present this totalitarian danger, which comes from their location in the time of the future. Whatever the future may be and however diverse the number of futures, only one of them will become the present. This attempt to follow the unidirectionality of time and to implant the future in the present is the source of ontological violence hidden in the very nature of time. Space is pluralistic, and its imaginary islands, hidden corners, distant territories extend the scope of pluralism instead of reducing it to one actuality that is solely compatible with the course of time. Utopia should withdraw from history and reclaim its place on a geographical map, thus expanding the limits of geography to include imaginary spaces not visible on the physical map. As utopias become cartographic projections, even futures can be seen as multiple territories dispersed in the realm of time.

What happened in the last half of the millennium, from Columbus to Lenin, can be summarized briefly: Whereas humankind colonized America, utopia colonized humankind, and that is how two superpowers emerged in one world. Now that one of them no longer exists, it should join other territories on the imaginary map of the world: Utopia, Atlantis, Eden, Civitas Solis, Ultima Thule, the USSR . . .

Notes

1. Lev Gumilev (1912–92)—influential Russian historian, ethnologist, and philosopher of culture.
2. Hence the rise in the 1990s of what is most conventionally called "cultural geography," which studies places and their symbolic representations; the spatiality of cultural institutions; textual, metaphoric, and imaginative landscapes,

etc. For example, see *Inventing Places: Studies in Cultural Geography,* ed. Kay Anderson and Fay Gale (Melbourne [Australia] and New York: Longman Cheshire, Wiley, Halsted Press, 1992); Fred M. Shelley and Audrey E. Clarke, *Human and Cultural Geography: A Global Perspective* (Dubuque, IA: Brown Publishers, 1994); Pamela Shurmer-Smith and Kevin Hannam, *Worlds of Desire, Realms of Power: A Cultural Geography* (New York: Routledge, Chapman, and Hall, 1994); *Place/Culture/Representation,* ed. James Duncan and David Ley (London and New York: Routledge, 1994); Paul Cloke et al., *Writing the Rural: Five Cultural Geographies* (London: P. Chapman, 1994); Terry G. Jordan, Mona Domosh, and Lester Rowntree. *The Human Mosaic: A Thematic Introduction to Cultural Geography* (New York: Longman, 1997).
3. M. M. Bakhtin, *Speech Genres & Other Late Essays,* trans. Vern W. McGee, ed. Caryl Emerson and Michael Holquist (Austin: University of Texas Press 1986): 6.
4. *A New Aristotle Reader,* ed. J. L. Acrill (Princeton: Princeton University Press, 1989): 329–330.
5. Hegel, *Encyclopedia of Philosophical Sciences,* Vol. 1, "Science of Logic." Second Subdivision. The Doctrine of Essence. C. Actuality, paragraph 143 n.
6. On the category of potentiality in contemporary culture see my article "K filosofii vozmozhnogo. Vvedenie v postkriticheskuiu epokhu" (Toward the Philosophy of the Possible. An Introduction to the Post-Critical Epoch), *Voprosy Filosofii* (Moscow, 1999).
7. Slavoj Zizek, *Tarrying with the Negative: Kant, Hegel, and the Critique of Ideology* (Durham: Duke University Press, 1993):159.
8. "Letter to a Japanese Friend" (1983), in *A Derrida Reader: Between the Blinds,* ed. Peggy Kamuf (New York: Columbia University Press, 1991): 272.
9. Ibid.

Chapter 11

The Ethics Of Imagination
Mikhail Epstein

Three Levels of Ethics

Transcultural theory needs to articulate its own ethics, which can be called an ethics of the imagination. Traditionally, imagination was considered to be the capacity least bound to ethical responsibility, incompatible with or even antagonistic to ethical imperatives. The longstanding debates between ethics and aesthetics targeted exactly this opposition between moral norms and free imagination, between duty and desire, between reason and fantasy.

However, if we look at the most common and established ethical rule as it is inscribed in the heritage of many cultures—Christian, Chinese, Greek—we find an implicit call for imagination as expressed in the requirement that we "do unto others as we would have them do unto us." This presupposes a kind of commonness between ourselves and others that cannot be found in actual existence and empirical experience—we are all different. Without imagination a person would be unable to put herself in the position of others or to put others in her own position. One has to be imaginative to be righteous. One has to imagine what other people may need, dream of, and aspire to in order to respond adequately to their needs. Percy Bysshe Shelly has expressed succinctly this link between morality and imagination in his "A Defence of Poetry" : "A man, to be greatly good, must imagine intensely and comprehensively; he must put himself in the place of another and of many others; the pains and pleasures of his species must become his own."[1]

But there is much more to this imaginative aspect of ethics than just identifying oneself with others. Two modifications may be added to the golden rule to embrace those aspects of ethics that are not reducible to a commonness between myself and others, between the subjects and objects of ethical actions.

The first addition would refer to the uniqueness of the ethical subject as distinct from the ethical object. "Do unto others as we would have them do unto us . . . *but as nobody else could do unto them except for us.*" The uniqueness of the ethical subject would be crucial in cases when among the many needs of others are those to which the given subject is uniquely or exclusively qualified to respond. The action that will be ethically preferable is that which no one can accomplish except for me and that which no one can do better than me. Since I am different from the other, the ethical relationship between us should be based on our mutual irreducibility. The basic rule of *differential ethics* thus can be formulated in this way: *Do what no other person in the same situation could do in your place. Act in such a way that your most individual abilities meet the most individual needs of the other.*

This is also true for our expectations from other people. Not only what we do to others, but what we expect them to do for us, is an ethically marked position. A totalitarian politics that forced a violinist to take an ax and cut wood to provide heat during an energy shortage was ethically reprehensible though it claimed to be truly humanistic as expressing equal concern about the needs of all people. From the standpoint of the ethics of difference, the musician should not only be allowed but encouraged to respond to those specific needs of people that he is in a unique position to answer. Reduction of individual abilities to the more general needs is what underlies the crude, politically dominated ethics of "mass societies."

Thus an ethical subject has to imagine not only what makes other people similar to him but what makes them different, which is a more complex task for the imagination. It is easier to imagine that other people need heat and food in the same way as you do than to project their specific intentions and expectations, which might completely escape the range of your interests. This second level of ethical concern involves imagining the other as *the other,* in his or her irreducibility to any common model of humanness.

Finally, the third level of ethics involves not *others as myself* and not *others as others* but *myself as other.* This capacity to be a stranger to oneself, to go beyond one's inborn or socially constructed identity is not just a creative possibility but also an ethical responsibility. Without being different from oneself one can never find points of commonality or dialogical interaction with people of different cultures and ways of life. As Jacques Derrida rightly observes, "it is because I am not one with myself that I can speak with the other and address the other."[2]

Judeo-Christian ethics is focused on the notion of "neighbor," the nearest and closest one; but what about love of, or at least responsiveness to, the distant ones? Nietzsche attempted to introduce this imperative—"love to a distant one"—into ethics but his anti-Christian stance caused him to ignore love for those nearest and actually grew into contempt toward his own "neighbors"—contemporaries, compatriots, colleagues, cohumans, and others in proximity. It is interesting that although Soviet ethical doctrines never explicitly acknowledged Nietzsche's influence, they were based on a similar principle: The distant ones were privileged over neighbors in the value hierarchy of a typical Soviet citizen. He had to love his comrades, his class brothers, and the exploited toiling masses all over the world but was required to denounce his family members on the basis of their disloyalty to the state. Soviet ethics was devoid of imagination and did not recognize the right of model citizens to multiple identities or alterations of identity.

In fact, love for distant ones or at least the ability to interact with them depends on the capacity of a given subject to be different from himself to embrace an unlimited range of virtual or potential identities. In distinction from the ethics of commonality, as prescribed in the golden rule, and in distinction from the differential ethics of uniqueness, the third level can be posited as an *interferential ethics* of multiplied identities and transformational possibilities that is certainly most appealing to the capacities of the imagination.

Ethics in the Subjunctive

Though ethics is usually presented as a set of rules and norms of behavior, this does not imply that the contents of ethics should be as normative and prescriptive as its forms are. Ethical prescriptions include the freedom from prescriptions. This paradoxical element of ethics cannot be fully eliminated. When Christ said, "Know the truth, and the truth will set you free," He expressed in prescriptive form the freedom from all prescriptions.

If we look at the most elementary forms of ethics, such as politeness and courtesy, we find that even these most routine models of morality are based on the presumption of human freedom. If you need somebody to give you a glass of water, the polite way to express this need will be not an imperative or a command but a suggestion, "Would you please be so kind as to bring me a glass of water?" "Would it be possible for you to do this or that?" The politeness is implied in the modality "would," which transforms the action from the actual or imperative modality to a subjunctive mode. My need has to be transformed into somebody else's possibility or opportunity in order to be presented ethically (politely). The imperative "Do this" is applied only between parents and children or officers and soldiers, thus marking the relation of power or authority. But insofar as ethics challenges this power relation, it has to transform any command into a suggestion, every imperative into a subjunctive.

If this is true on the level of elementary politeness, how much more important it must be on the level of the higher moral initiatives that are addressed to others. Even in the most fundamental and global issues of war and peace, power and freedom, authority and equality, discipline and responsibility, ethics should appeal to possibilities rather than impose necessity and constraints. Often the same person who uses the subjunctive "Would you" when asking for a glass of water would use a categorical imperative, demanding that humanity obey his grand ethical schemes and prescriptions. Almost all our discourses and the procedures of teaching and writing are imbued with the imperative mode: Do as I do, do as I say, do as I write. Every interpretation avers its conclusive truthfulness instead of suggesting itself as just a possibility, a discourse in a subjunctive mode. All disciplines of scholarship and interpretation would benefit by incorporating these zones of politeness, potentiality, and imagination, which are not only an "excess" of aesthetic subjectivity but are first of all modes of ethical responsiveness that multiply the levels of freedom in our readers, students, interlocutors, instead of forcing their minds into our own persuasions.

Ethics is the domain of requests rather than commands, the domain of imagination rather than obligation. The commandments pronounced by God cannot help but be obligatory if we identify ourselves with the people of God and recognize the hierarchy that connects heavenly Father and earthly children. However, if ethics should be understood as a specific domain regulating the relationship between brothers and sisters and distinct from the religious domain regulating the relationship between Father and children, we should formulate the principles of this ethics in a noncommanding mode, as a system of requests and proposals appealing to the freedom of the other person, to his "maybe or maybe not." Certainly, this ethics "in the subjunctive mood" is much more favorable to the work of the transcultural imagination than an ethics that prescribes us to obey already established laws.

Thus, in addition to the golden rule of commonness, we need a differential and interferential ethics based on imagining others as different from ourselves and imagining ourselves as possibilities for others.

Notes

1. *Critical Theory Since Plato,* ed. Hazard Adams (Fort Worth, Philadelphia: Harcourt Brace Jovanovich College Publishers, 1992): 519–520. From a different perspective, the connection between ethics and imagination was recently discussed in Mark Johnson's book *Moral Imagination: Implications of Cognitive Science for Ethics* (Chicago: University of Chicago Press, 1994). The author of the influential books *Metaphors We Live By* and *The Body in the Mind,* Johnson extends his views on the cognitive role of metaphors and develops an alternative conception of moral reflection—one that is imaginative and constructive rather than rational and based on universal laws.
2. Jacques Derrida, *Deconstruction in a Nutshell: A Conversation* (Roundtable on 2 October 1994 at Villanova University) ed. with commentary by John D. Caputo (New York: Fordham University, 1997): 14.

Chapter 12

A Transcultural Imaginary
Ellen E. Berry

The concept of a transcultural imaginary has been invoked a number of times and in relation to a number of contexts throughout this study, although the term itself has not always been employed directly. As it is a concept centrally important to the overall argument of this book, it may be useful at this point to clarify some of the multiple meanings the term has accreted, to elaborate on these meanings a bit more systematically, and to situate the term within some contemporary discussions of the nature and possibilities of sociocultural imaginaries in a global postmodern moment. For the sake of clarity, I want to explore here the term "transcultural imaginary" in three conceptually distinct senses, although such distinctions fail to capture the ways in which all three senses are mutually informing and dynamically interconnected.

In the first sense, explored extensively in the chapters "How Does Newness Enter the Postmodern World?" and "Nomads At Home: Improvisation in the Academy," emphasis falls on the creative power of the imaginary as a force of cultural recombination or improvisation, those surreptitious creativities of reuse, central to the social practices of everyday life, through which people interact with and reorder their worlds. Arjun Appadurai in particular argues that, within a global postmodern condition, the imagination—in this active, transformative sense—plays a new, more expansive role in social life. It is in fact "central to all forms of agency . . . and is the key component of the new global order," the primary way in which "individuals and groups seek to annex the global into their own practices of the modern." Through such practices of imaginative interaction, the imagined worlds projected by locally or globally dominant official cultures are symbolically reworked (and thus potentially contested) to become "resources for experiments in self-making," resources for the construction of potentially new imagined communities and narratives of global cultural identity.[1]

In a second sense, emphasis falls on the imaginary not as a concrete practice but as a general locus of cultural potentiality by its very nature ongoing and always incomplete and thus never fully realizable or totalizable. This sense of the term links it to my earlier discussion of the nature and trajectories of transcultural desire as well as to Bloch's notions of the possible and of anticipatory consciousness. The transcultural imaginary in this sense refers to a hypothetical or virtual space containing all actually existing cultures in their discreteness from one another, *but also* in their actual and potential overlappings, mergings, interferences, becomings, and resulting new mutations. The transcultural imaginary would embrace the entirety of global cultural possibilities available at any given moment, by which I mean the as-yet-unfigured horizon of contemporary cultural production, the totality of micro- and macro-cultural flows dynamically circulating and interacting on a global stage. Included here would be those cultural expressions currently realized in some form as well as those not yet having cultural form and therefore existing only as transcultural potential within an immense global archive consisting of potentially infinite combinations of cultural materials. As Deleuze and Guattari say of the flows of desire or the movements of the rhizome, these cultural materials are defined not by a discrete abiding identity persisting over time, but through their capacities to undergo permutations, transformations, and realignments. The modes of cultural interference enacted in this book, which involve the dynamic being-in-common of our cultural differences as well as our potential to generate new cultural and critical expressions as these differences interact, are but a pale shadow of this immense archive.

In this sense, the transcultural imaginary might be compared to the sublime, which produces feelings of awe engendered by confrontation with an experience of infinite vastness or dramatic lack of containment. One instantiation of this is what I called in a previous chapter the "postcommunist sublime." This term was used to refer to the experience of Soviet intellectuals in the moment of perestroika when confronted with the vastness of their own unknown cultural history—which was being made available for the first time—as well as with a recognition of those surplus cultural values and potentials that, historically, had been denied expression within a narrow and repressive cultural system. The postcommunist sublime also refers to the euphoria emerging out of the recognition that, at a moment of unprecedented cultural openness, all cultures—past and present, Soviet, post-Soviet, and global—were now available for engagement and interaction.

My notion of the sublime here bears some similarities to Fredric Jameson's description of attempts to confront the immensity of multinational capitalism in a postmodern moment, what he calls "the incapacity of our minds, at least at present, to map the great global multinational and decentered communicational network in which we find ourselves caught as individual subjects." Contemplation of this enormity and complexity results on the one hand in euphoria and on the other in an experience of dread or doom, a large "virtual nightmare," in Jameson's formulation, in which "psychic fragmentation is raised to a qualitatively new power, the structural distraction of the decentered subject now promoted to the very motor and existential logic of late capitalism itself."[2] Recently, Jameson has emphasized more positive cultural features arising from contemporary processes of globalization especially for those of us in the United States, an emphasis that more closely approximates my sense of the transcultural sublime and the nature of transcultural desire. Jameson notes that, among other things (such as the development of a global corporate culture of standardization), postmodern globalization has engendered an ever-greater decentering and proliferation of cultural differences thereby enabling eclectic contacts and borrowings that encourage the development of new hybrid cultures. He envisions this process resulting in "an immense global urban intercultural festival without a center or even any longer a dominant cultural mode," an image that he calls "ammunition" for "the most vital utopian visions of our own time."[3]

Such a vision of the progressive possibilities emerging from an attempt to think through and in relation to a transcultural imaginary also has been suggested as a basis for potential new political visions of transnational solidarity. In these visions, Benedict Anderson's imagined community of coherent modern identity developed in relation to the autonomous nation-state becomes multiple transnational imagined communities constructed in relation to an ideal cosmopolitanism or mode of transnational citizenship. As Bruce Robbins uses the term, "cosmopolitanism" refers to two things: (1) actually existing "habits of thought, feeling, attachment, and belonging shaped by particular supranational or translocal collectivities," styles of practical consciousness, or actually existing practical stances, and (2) a not-fully-realizable ideal. This ideal cosmopolitanism is predicated on development of a kind of global empathetic and ethical capacity to extend ourselves imaginatively in relation to cultural others. Robbins refers to this as "the variable power of sympathetic imagination to define collectivities of belonging and responsibility," a mobile and reciprocal interconnectedness or accountability at a distance. Such a capacity is a precondition for the development of a transnational mode of citizenship free from the associations of rationalist universalism within which the term cosmopolitan historically has been entangled. Instead of an ideal of Olympian detachment—the basis of this older cosmopolitanism—a contemporary version depends upon ongoing "(re)attachment, multiple attachment, or attachment at a distance" and, I would add, on imagined or imaginary attachments. As James Clifford stresses, current efforts to rethink the term cosmopolitanism are located "not in its full theoretical extension where it becomes a paranoid fantasy of ubiquity and omniscience," what Donna Haraway calls a godlike view from nowhere. Rather, this reworked cosmopolitanism emerges only in specific local instances "where the unrealizable ideal produces normative pressure." This is a pressure to aspire to some future or ideal set of ethical norms for transnational citizenship, norms that undoubtedly require us to think and be other than we currently are, to mutate beyond our present capacities. They form part of the skills needed to produce a politics of the future as open question, what I called elsewhere a politics of mobility.[4]

A postmodern cosmopolitical and ethical capacity also require a kind of psychic mobility and flexibility, and this raises a third sense in which the term "transcultural imaginary" is being used: to refer to a process of engagement with our own cultural unconscious—that within us which is most racially different or strange—and, by extension, with various other cultural differences that exist outside of us. Of course, in a psychoanalytic sense the term "imaginary" has most often drawn on Lacanian definitions. In this framework, the imaginary refers to one of three stages in the construction of the subject. It is a pre-Oedipal, pre-linguistic dimension of images in which the infant constructs a fundamentally illusory sense of itself as whole and unified as it is "captivated" by its own specular image. This construction is a fundamentally narcissistic *mis*recognition that exerts a profound influence over all future relations between self and other, which are forever haunted by it. In the Lacanian scheme, although the subject believes itself to be a coherent whole, it is in fact characterized by a fundamental lack, a primordial alienation arising in part from a retrospective understanding of the misrecognitions that characterize the imaginary stage. For Lacan, then, all subjects live an imaginary, narcissistic, misrecognized selfhood; absence is at the very center of subjectivity, and the imaginary is simply an effect of disguising this constitutive absence, which nonetheless continues to haunt the subject. As Anthony Elliott puts it in his study of relations between contemporary social theory and psychoanalysis, for Lacan, "the self is thus located from the beginning within a damaging imaginary space, inserted into a radical split between an illusory sense of selfhood and something profoundly other."[5]

Elliott criticizes Lacan's account on a number of points—most importantly for our purposes, his notions of the imaginary as only producing blank fictions or misrecognitions and his conception of the subject as based only on lack. Elliott draws more directly on Freud's account of the primary unconscious and stresses instead the creative capacity of the imaginary realm; its ability to organize representational forms, drives, and affects; and its constitutive role in establishing dynamic interpersonal spaces between self and other. The imaginary is viewed as a foundation of human subjective and social life, "a dimension through which the subject opens out to the self, others, reason, and society." The productivity of the imaginary forms one basis for the subject's active reworkings of received meanings, its critical reflections on society, and thus its capacity to potentially transform—even as it lives within—social relations of domination and power. As Elliot puts it, "Systems of domination, no matter how apparently total, cannot contain or exhaust the individual subject's unique representations ... the possibility of *disinvesting* from particular ideological forms can only happen through the imaginary reorganization of the self and its related objects."[6]

Elliott's scheme also suggests that the imaginary is basic to a recognition of another's difference and independence from the self; it is fundamental to the very acceptance of difference as such and is one source for the creation of new relations between self and others. The imaginary exists as both a source of radical difference or nonidentity within the self and a source of innovation and self-renewal; it is inscribed within sociosymbolic forms in both repressive and liberatory ways. And, Elliott concludes, "it is in seeking to understand the relative other of the unconscious—what is nonidentical in ourselves and others—that subjectivity, autonomy, and desire may be more fully realized and transformed."[7]

The search for nonpathological ways of confronting radical differences within ourselves and, by extension, between ourselves and others forms the basis of Julia Kristeva's meditation on the psycho-cultural role played by the figure of the foreigner, *Strangers to Ourselves*. Historically, foreigners have provoked radical destabilizations in our own cultural and psychic identity because they dramatically remind us by their very existence of our own fundamental incompleteness, our own non-knowledge. The foreigner's appearance "signals that he is in addition," "riveted to an elsewhere as certain as it is inaccessible" to us.[8] Confronted with the radical difference of foreigners, Kristeva says, we historically have either domesticated them, by welcoming foreigners within a system that obliterates their difference (the melting pot, for example), or we have sought to exorcise them by destroying them completely (the Holocaust, contemporary ethnic cleansing). Both relations betray the fundamental difference of the foreigner, although of course these relations are not materially equivalent in their effect on the foreigner.

The solution to the problem, Kristeva argues, is to recognize and accept that essentially we all are foreigners, all strangers to ourselves. "Freud brings us the courage to call ourselves disintegrated in order not to integrate foreigners and even less so to hunt them down, but rather to welcome them to that uncanny strangeness which is as much theirs as it is ours. . . . It is with the help of that sole support that we can attempt to live with others." In other words, it is not simply a matter of our being able to accept or benignly tolerate the other; rather, more radically, we must put ourselves in his place and "this means to imagine and make oneself other for oneself." It is through this fundamental act of imagination and psychological displacement that Kristeva envisions and challenges us to construct a cosmopolitanism of a new sort, one that would be founded on a consciousness of its unconscious. In today's global situation a paradoxical community is emerging, consisting not only of attempts to form imaginative attachments across our differences but also composed of "foreigners who are reconciled with themselves to the extent that they recognize themselves as foreigners."[9]

The transcultural imaginary *is* this coming community based on the conscious copresence and constant circulation of radical destabilizing differences. It is built on an acknowledgment of our capacity to pathologize and obliterate otherness, but it also holds out a belief in our capacity to move into historically new modes of relation. These would honor the difference of others by recognizing our own difference from ourselves, which includes our potential to become radically different than we currently are. As such the transcultural imaginary forms the basis for new modes of individual and collective social psychotherapy, if you will. Understood in this sense it is a precondition for more fully approximating the ideal cosmopolitanism to which Robbins and others aspire. It also is a necessary basis for Nancy Fraser's "utopian image of a culture in which ever new constructions of identity and difference are freely elaborated and then swiftly deconstructed in an atmosphere of social equality," an image that depends, Fraser argues, on our being "weaned from [an] attachment to current cultural constructions of [our] interests and identities."[10]

Notes

1. Arjun Appadurai, *Modernity at Large: Cultural Dimensions of Globalization* (Minneapolis: University of Minnesota Press, 1996): 31, 4.
2. Frederic Jameson, *Postmodernism, Or the Cultural Logic of Late Capitalism* (Durham: Duke University Press, 1991): 44.
3. Fredric Jameson, "Notes on Globalization as a Philosophic Issue," in Fredric Jameson and Masao Miyoshi, eds., *The Cultures of Globalization* (Durham: Duke University Press, 1998): 66.
4. Pheng Cheah and Bruce Robbins, eds., *Cosmopolitics: Thinking and Feeling Beyond the Nation* (Minneapolis: University of Minnesota Press, 1998): 9, 3, 260.
5. Anthony Elliot, *Social Theory and Psychoanalysis in Transition: Society from Freud to Kristeva* (Oxford: Blackwell, 1992): 140.
6. Ibid., 46.
7. Ibid., 272.
8. Julia Kristeva, *Strangers to Ourselves*, trans. Leon S. Roudiez (New York: Columbia University Press, 1991): 5.
9. Ibid., 191, 170, 13, 195.
10. Nancy Fraser, "From Redistribution to Recognition? Dilemmas of Justice in a 'Post-Socialist' Age," in Cynthia Willett, ed., *Theorizing Multiculturalism* (Malden, MA: Blackwell, 1998): 19–49.

Part III

Practice

Chapter 13

The Lawlessness of Genres
Ellen E. Berry

Transcultural practices have always existed in some form as a consequence of cultural interactions both large and small. Arguably, however, these practices have multiplied and become more complex in the contemporary moment, accelerated by the increasing dissemination and interpenetration of cultural flows on a global scale, a process aided in part by the circulation of new technologies such as the World Wide Web. This difference in the degree of cultural interpenetration, this transcultural speed-up, also has produced different *kinds* of cultural practices, ones that we still are in a process of delineating. An ongoing project of contemporary cultural critics is to locate and describe the effects of the dizzying array of hybridized cultural forms that are emerging as a consequence of complex globalizing processes of interaction and admixture.

The final section of this book contains examples of some transcultural practices that are also experiments in thinking transculturally. They have developed out of Russian cultural traditions as these traditions are refracted through the poetic philosophy of Mikhail Epstein particularly. They are thus highly idiosyncratic expressions and as such may seem an unlikely site both for suggesting what we mean by transcultural practices in a general sense and for offering the reader a blueprint of sorts for ongoing transcultural experiments. Nonetheless, this brief introduction means to survey the features these multiple practices have in common and, by extrapolating from them, to argue for the value—both personal and political—that transcultural practices such as these might have in encouraging more expansive and creative modes of engagement across multiple kinds of difference.

The inventive writings that follow in this section clearly reflect and in some cases grow directly out of the revisionary cultural agendas promoted at the Laboratory of Contemporary Culture and allied institutions whose history was mapped in section I. Among other things, these institutions took as a goal the restoration to public consciousness of exiled ideas and expressions with an aim of reinventing culture after the death of one extremely powerful cultural system. As Epstein says of the "Book of Books," these practices share an impulse to conduct "encyclopedic investigations of lost or unsolicited ideas," "to restore the imaginable books of the past and . . . stimulate their writing in the future." Such processes depend on the imaginative ability to generate alternatives or to discover that which can be redirected in all determinations, to paraphrase Bloch. This alternative or "other" thinking describes a more general habit of mind (and a survival strategy) of intellectuals during the late Soviet period, a moment when, according to Epstein,

> the totalitarian system was already losing its grip on the social consciousness and growing relatively weak but at the same time remaining strong enough to doom any direct opposition or counter movement. Thus the system underwent a series of oblique and fuzzy metamorphoses, mutating towards all possible alternative theories and practices that were marginalized in the field of social consciousness without splitting or breaking it. . . . Alternative thinking clung to each ideological slogan, philosophical postulate or politico-economic term imposed by the official system and thought it differently, multiplied its possible interpretations.

A desire to proliferate the alternatives embedded in any idea or system, to encourage thinking in a speculative or anticipatory mode, is reflected in all of Epstein's transcultural practices and has been postulated throughout this book as a general feature of—indeed a prerequisite for—transcultural thinking. Alternative thinking as a habit of mind may lead in a number of directions and assume a number of forms as in Epstein's redefinition of common terms or concepts. In his essay "On Genres" for example, Epstein follows Bakhtin to redefine genre as a broad cultural category rather than a narrowly aesthetic one comprised of hierarchies of devices and sets of conventions. Unlike Derrida—whose emphasis on transgression and the law has the effect of returning us to the law—Epstein insists that genre be redefined as a principle of generativity (lawlessness) that is spontaneous; whimsical; paradoxical; arbitrary; and, crucially, given to constant proliferation, to the ongoing generation of new genres throughout the terrain of everyday life. "The generic is born everywhere and instantly as a caprice in the form of repetition . . . victimized by 'the law of genre' spontaneity revenges itself in producing genres out of every single whim of a pen or a brush." Thus, genre is that form or perhaps angle of vision that liberates our ability to imagine in the genre of genre, leading to an aestheticization of everyday life and the construction of alternative cultural worlds (ones in which there could be a Nobel Prize for fog writing). Similarly, in "Poetry as a State of Being," Epstein describes a type of poetry deliberately designed to be common, average, or mediocre and thus generic in another sense—without a distinctive stylistic or temporal location. This is an anti-genre meant to be impersonal and, in being so, to give everyone (anyone) access to what Epstein calls a poetic state of being, which the selection goes on to describe eloquently.

Epstein's transcultural practices also permit and encourage a revaluation of that which has been considered marginal or trivial—the everyday or, what is crucial for former Soviet citizens, the individual, whose perception is registered in all its uniqueness and eccentricity, in all its singularity and difference. InteLnet journals in the humanities, for instance, take as their purview "those realms of thinking that haven't yet crystallized [and are unlikely to crystallize] into special disciplines" such as "Quiet Life," dedicated to a micrology of the ordinary. Similarly, the catalog aims to capture those possibilities that other genres must exclude. Since "a thought always occurs in the form of two or three different thoughts" and authors typically must choose just one, it is only the catalog that may fix all of these thoughts simultaneously, only the catalog that rescues and preserves the unnecessary. The catalog also asserts the importance of—redeems, if you will—individuality of perception in that multiple particularities and differences are juxtaposed and coexist rather than being resolved into greater unities or posed in conflict with one another. Every item in the catalog's list proliferates but does not exhaust the number of articulations that an item ultimately may have, and thus it constitutes "a multiplicity of voices meeting each other without confrontation," a model of the transcultural interaction itself. Similarly, hyperauthorship encourages simultaneous pursuit of mutually exclusive modes of thought that would be incompatible within a single discipline or genre or under the sign of a single proper name.

Transcultural practices, as Epstein imagines them, are both synthetic or integrative and particularistic and individualistic. An impulse to combine the integrative and the particularistic into a single practice grows out of twin goals that may seem at first incompatible: on the one hand, to prevent the fragmentation of culture into a host of separate, often competing differences, a situation in which communication among differences becomes impossible (a danger that Epstein sees in American culture); on the other, to prevent forcing culture into a homogeneous whole, a situation that destroys difference and individuality in the name of constructing cultural totalities that could become totalitarian. For example, the essay, as Epstein defines it, is the quintessential transcultural genre. It is a hybrid form in which all other genres are assimilated and glimpses of what more mainstream literary forms must exclude are included. At the same time, it is also the mode most open to the "eternal flow of everyday life, the vagaries of thought, and the personal idiosyncrasies of the writer." This combination of what Epstein calls "audacity [comprehensiveness] of vision and awesome respect for things themselves" also characterizes the catalog with its unattainable goal of complete enumeration of all possible propositions about a given object and its simultaneous valuing of maximal diversity and particularity.

Although concrete transcultural practices appear in this section, one should regard them not as aesthetic objects, complete in themselves, still less as prescriptions; instead they might best be considered as generating environments that solicit the performance of transcultural desire. That is, their primary goal is not to encourage production of accomplished works of art but rather to stimulate a proliferation of possibilities for their own sake, ones that need not necessarily lead to completed expression. Such an interpretation is reinforced by the fact that all of these practices share a feature that one might call simply "ongoingness." Because they lack a definitive principle of closure, a "stop" convention, they remain always open to more writing, more improvisational "riffs" on an initial proposition; in this sense, they simulate the unfinalizability of the world itself or of any one person in it as well as the inexhaustibility of writing and its tendency always to stray outside its proper place.

Transcultural writing practices share with nomadic critical practices a search for methods able to capture the diversity, complexity, and mobility of contemporary social reality. They provide a training ground in flexible improvisational styles of thought, one aspect of a transcultural epistemology. Appropriately, these practices often operate through digressions that move laterally across many surface directions rather than deepening or developing a single thought. Epstein asserts that in the essay "only the digressions matter." It retains its essence (its "bad pedigree") only when it remains in motion, partaking of other genres but never becoming them; it is a genre of loose ends and unfinished surfaces that await further inscription. Each thought in a catalog generates two or three others, which in turn generate others, ad infinitum. And each catalog "can be completed only relatively"; its "end becomes the beginning of the next catalog." Perhaps because these practices are unfinished by their very nature, they actively invite linkages with (m)any other proposition(s); their movement is rhizomatic and they compel connections across multiple differences. For instance, Epstein's InteLnet projects attempt to stimulate the potentially infinite conceptual combinations that are theoretically possible on the World Wide Web. Thinklinks in particular have as their goal the conjunction of ideas that ordinarily would remain in separate disciplinary domains or in distinct taxonomies on the current Web organization. And hyperauthorship refigures the author not as a single discrete personality but rather as "a wave, going across times, places, personalities."

Because transcultural practices open possibilities that remain ongoing, they also leave room for multiple inhabitants. Because they solicit the other within us (other perspectives, other personalities, more radical others), they might be considered a training ground in new modes of encountering difference, including our own difference from ourselves, our own cultural unconscious. They surely are among those powerful resources for experiments in self-making that Appadurai identifies and calls for. The potential of these practices to awaken those multiple other selves that lie dormant within us, thereby displacing us from our own bounded cultural identities, is perhaps most clearly evident in the selection on hyperauthorship. Epstein calls this practice "writing in the mode of otherness," a state in which we actively solicit and transcribe the virtual authorial selves or the "ethereal bodies" of others that exist in all of us. Hyperauthorship might be thought of as a kind of positive cultural schizophrenia, in marked contrast to the negative postmodern schizophrenic subject that Jameson describes in *Postmodernism, or the Cultural Logic of Late Capitalism*. In "Poetry as a State of Being," Epstein deconstructs the opposition between producers and consumers of culture by reimagining all writing as a kind of double authorship in which millions of anonymous readers rise to the ranks of Pushkin, for example, by inscribing themselves in his texts and thereby transfiguring freely the object of their desire—a symbiotic relationship of mutual exchange, as Epstein imagines it, "where I 'other' myself" and "where I 'author' another."

This surplus of vision, this dynamic interpenetration of self in relation to the other and of other in relation to the self, finds its most concrete manifestation in collective improvisations. Here familiar topics are made strange and wondrous (the metaphysics of frogs!), and the unpredictability of the other's response is matched only by the unpredictability of the improviser's own: "An improviser encounters an otherness, a strangeness in the object of her thought, in the co-subjects of her thinking process, in the others surrounding her, and finally in herself. It is as if I take the others' positions of expectation and surprise towards myself, and this 'unknown in the other' who I am for the others generates in myself the effort to create this 'otherness' that is the aim of improvisation. I transcend myself because I am the 'other' for the others."

As Epstein explains it in the first section of this book, Russian culturology both analyzes the constructive potentials of culture and actively seeks to broaden and multiply these potentials in order to expand the realm of culture itself, partly as a response to a particular cultural heritage. While a Russian variant of transcultural thinking—as exemplified in the experimental practices contained here—is similarly a historically, culturally, and personally specific set of responses, it also means to offer to others (other persons, other cultures) imaginative encouragement to develop and theorize a multitude of different transcultural experiments. These would similarly be both historically and culturally embedded as well as partaking of the transcultural itself—meaning in this sense that which would transcend, throw us beyond, any singular cultural context.

The specific transculturalizing strategies suggested here and throughout this book would include the following:

- Creative and critical practices that encourage alternative thinking, the ongoing pursuit of those alternatives embedded in any idea or system, including especially what these systems omit or deem unworthy of serious scrutiny. Among other things, such thinking prevents any system from promoting itself as definitive and thereby leaves it open to futural significations as well as to other ways of knowing and being. It also may help to restore to our theories the importance of the speculative or imaginative faculty and thereby contribute to promoting mobility, flexibility, and generativity in critical thought.
- Creative and critical practices that train us actively to desire multiple differences rather than simply to tolerate them or view them as objects of analysis. Such practices would be unpredictable, perfor-

mative, and deliberately incomplete, thereby leaving room for the other. They would "hail" us in ways that enable us to enter into relation with the other even as we forego full comprehension of him/her. As hybridized, not pure, forms, transcultural practices also would encourage us to unite ideas that seem most disparate, thereby compelling connections across multiple differences. In short, these practices would seek in multiple ways to deliberately dislocate or displace us from the known. In so doing, they might help to bring about the development of historically new modes of relation by cultivating our empathetic and ethical capacities to extend ourselves imaginatively to multiple cultural others.

Chapter 14

On The Birth Of Genres
Mikhail Epstein

The concept of genre as a cultural (rather than a narrowly literary) category was developed by Mikhail Bakhtin in his works of the 1920s and 1930s. For Bakhtin, a genre is a stable, conventional form of social communication that does not depend on the individual message or intention of interlocutors. "Certain features of language take on the specific flavor of a given genre: they knit together with specific points of view, special approaches, forms of thinking, nuances and accents characteristic of the given genre."[1] The same mechanisms of "generic," interpersonal communication transmit a cultural heritage from generation to generation. As is an archetype, a genre is a reservoir of a cultural unconscious, and it transcends the limits of personal meaning and individual creative imagination. A novelist invests her work with personal vision, but the genre of the novel possesses its own experience and world view that is communicated to the reader beyond any authorial intentions or efforts. Bakhtin and some of his disciples and followers, such as Georgy Gachev, analyzed the specific super-personal contents of such genres as the epic, the novel, and the tragedy. For example, the novel constructs a specific "experimental" status for the hero who "generically" oversteps all social, ethnic, and psychological boundaries. "One of the basic internal themes of the novel is precisely the theme of the inadequacy of a hero's fate and situation to the hero himself. The individual is either greater than his fate, or less than his condition as a man. . . . An individual cannot be completely incarnated into the flesh of existing sociohistorical categories."[2]

However, this interpretation of genres as preexistent forms that dictate their artistic will both to the author and to the reader should be significantly revised in the postmodern era. What is at stake is not the survival of genres through succeeding epochs and individual authors, but the possibility of producing deliberately new genres here and now. The very phrase "new genre" may appear to be oxymoronic since genres from a traditional perspective are never new; what makes them genres is their cultural inheritance and rootedness in the past. However, what is needed for a work of art or for any sign system to become generic, to represent a genre, is the minimal requirement of repetition. For example, if I produce a spontaneous gesture it can convey the meaning peculiar to the specific moment and psychological or social context of its production. But if I repeat this gesture deliberately and vary it to produce several interconnected meanings, it becomes a genre of this specific gesture—refers not just to its singular moment or context but to its reproducible form. What is reproduced at least once becomes reproducible in principle. Even an instinctive, "raw" manifestation of an individual, such as a cough, can be serialized into a generic succession of "coughs" producing various semantic and social effects. Sometimes it is sufficient for somebody to cough once in an audience to provoke a series of imitations with effects ranging from irony to anger. A cough may be not just an arbitrary physiological reaction to dust in the air, but a genre of social behavior.

The problem of the genre becomes especially loaded for the epoch of mechanical reproduction of works of art, to use Walter Benjamin's idiom. Although the work of art loses its originality through the series of its reproductions, simultaneously through this series of reproductions a new original genre comes into existence. In fact, it is only through reproduction that the creation of a new genre becomes possible; thus the "mechanical" epoch is favorable for the formation of new genres. An original genre arises exactly when and where the uniqueness of a work of art becomes questioned. Thus the very relationship between the individual work and its genre becomes reversed.

Traditionally genre is the form of repetition and variation; what is unique is an individual work created in this genre. In twentieth-century aesthetics, the focus is shifting from individual works to the generic laws of repetition—and then to the individuality of genres themselves. After the experimental excesses of originality in the historical avant-garde of the 1900s and 1910s, the late modernists of the 1920s and 1930s, especially those influenced by Marxism, underwent a crisis of originality, and as a result the problem of genre and of the generic came to the forefront.

In this sense, Bakhtin and Benjamin are contemporaries: Both theoretically extend Marx's critique of individualism; both conceptualize the loss of an original "aura" and uniqueness in the work of art through the search for its organic "popular" roots, its generic nature (in the living past) or through the analysis of its mechanical reproducibility (in the technological present).

Postmodernism challenges this modernist commitment to the social and technical dimensions of art with the understanding that the mechanical and the generic are themselves based on deviation and caprice. According to Jacques Derrida, each genre potentially exceeds its own boundaries, and as such signals its own madness; the law of genre is the deviation from the law.[3] This madness, however, has another implication: The most whimsical, paradoxical, arbitrary things and occurrences have a tendency to mature into genres, to acquire regularity through repetition. Not only are genres "mad," but madness itself has a proclivity to become "generic." Deviation is more insistent and repetitive than regularity which easily diffuses in the ordinary, loses its constructive principle and form. In fact, the novel and the essay, the two most productive genres of modernity, are generated by the personal whims and deviations of the hero and the author, respectively, from regular patterns of epic or mythic narrative.[4] It is not only that an individual work is ready to betray its own genre, but that genre itself arises from a betrayal. The generic is born everywhere and instantly as a caprice in the form of (self-)repetition. This is a twofold process: Victimized by the "law of genre," spontaneity avenges itself in producing genres out of a single whim of a pen or a brush. What a contemporary artist usually pursues is not the production of still another work of art but the creation of a new genre, a new form of repetition. It is important to emphasize genre, not method or style. Method is a narrow and transitional category loaded with historical meaning, whereas genres are truly nomadic forms of trans-historical value. Sentimentalism or critical realism are methods long dead; the novel is a genre ever new.

Seriality becomes indispensable for postmodern creativity: Only through repetition of the same device in two or more works does an artist achieve a new status as the creator of a genre. This reproductive capacity that previously came from the cultural traditions of the past (Bakhtin) or from the technical facilities of the present (Benjamin) now is addressed to the future, to the artist's capacity to create a precedent in the very act of production, which becomes potentially reproductive not after but even before the work of art is produced. For example, Ilya Kabakov in the

1970s produced a genre of albums in which the status of a unique painting was sacrificed to a series of very similar pictures reproducing the same object with a slightly changed pattern in each successive frame.[5] In order to vanquish the mechanical force of reproduction, an artist had to assimilate and incorporate it into his own act of painting or writing. Thus works of art become intentionally repetitive whereas original genres proliferate at a rate unknown to previous centuries. In the late twentieth century each artist worthy of this name has to author a new genre in order to maintain his/her creative status.

Any single act, gesture, or discourse is capable of instituting a new genre, if this act creates a precedent, contains a premise of possible repetition or variation, generates a series of similar acts. For example, one can write a word or draw a pattern on a frozen or fogged surface of a window. It is an individual gesture, but it can also be treated as a new genre of writing or painting. It does not matter that the products of this art are ephemeral and short-living, often disappearing momentarily without a single viewer to evaluate the performance. It is necessary, however, that these acts be made deliberately and in some articulate relation to each other, as a matter of repetition or variation. Then the act of leaving traces on the fogged window glass will become generic and may produce masterpieces, inspire great artists, competitions, awards, a Nobel Prize in "capturing fog." Photo-museums, virtual galleries, hordes of people changing their residencies to northern cities to be able to exercise their favorite genre for the largest part of the year possible. . . .

Another example. A sculptor invited friends to see his new works, but on that night an electricity outage occurred. In order not to lose the time and opportunity, friends decided to touch the statues with their fingers. "Isn't that beautiful?" said one. "It's so palpable that one can see it with one's fingers," said the other . . . Then it occurred to them that for the first time in their life they were able to perceive the statues in the very same way they were shaped—by touch, by fingers. Why don't we perceive sculptures in a way adequate to the mode of their production? Are not they designed to stimulate our skin sensibility, to stir up our sense of touch? Seeing kills the immediate power of feeling. Why not create special art objects for touch alone, and let them be contemplated in darkness? Thus a new genre can be born, called "night vision," or the "art of palpability."

Thus crystallization of new genres, "generization" (to distinguish it from it "generalization"), is an absolutely open process that may be improvised here and now, with any single act produced consciously and inviting repetition and variation.

Notes

1. M. M. Bahktin, *The Dialogic Imagination,* ed. Michael Holquist, trans. Caryl Emerson and Michael Holquist (Austin: University of Texas Press, 1981): 289.
2. Ibid., 37.
3. "The genre has always in all genres been able to play the role of order's principle: resemblance, analogy, identity and difference, taxonomic classification, organization and genealogical tree, order of reason . . . Now, the test . . . brought to light the madness of genre. Madness has given birth to, thrown light on genre in the most dazzling, most blindering sense of the word." Jacques Derrida, *Acts of Literature,* ed. Derek Attridge (New York and London: Routledge, 1992): 252.
4. See the next chapter "An Essay on the Essay."
5. On the constructive meaning of repetitions in Kabakov, see Mikhail Epstein, "Emptiness as a Technique: Word and Image in Ilya Kabakov," in his book *Russian Postmodernism: New Perspectives on Post-Soviet Culture* (with Alexander Genis and Slobodanka Vladiv-Glover). (New York and Oxford: Berghahn Books, 1999): 304–306, 320–324.

Chapter 15

An Essay On the Essay[1]
Mikhail Epstein

The essay is part confession, part discursive argument, and part narrative—it is like a diary, a scholarly article, and a story all in one. It is a genre legitimated by its existence outside any genre. If it treats the reader as confidant to sincere outpourings of the heart, it becomes a confession or a diary. If it fascinates the reader with logical arguments and dialectical controversies, or if it thematizes the process of generation of meaning, then it becomes scholarly discourse or a learned treatise. If it lapses into a narrative mode and organizes events into a plot, it inadvertently turns into a novella, a short story, or a tale.

The essay retains its character only when it violates the laws of other genres, interferes with them, and breaks their coherence. It is driven by a spirit of adventure and by the desire to attempt everything without yielding to anything. As soon as the essayist tries to take a breath, to come to a stop, the nomadic and transmigratory essence of the essay crumbles to dust. If sincerity threatens to cross a limit, the essayist intervenes with abstractions. If abstract reflection threatens to grow into a metaphysical system, the essayist unexpectedly throws in a peripheral detail or anecdote in order to undermine its systematicity. The essay is held together by the mutual friction of incongruous parts that obstruct one another. At the heart of the essay is an uneven and discontinuous intonation—that of the sad exile and the brazen vagabond, combining a lack of self-confidence with an extremely casual demeanor. Not knowing from moment to moment what he will do next, the essayist can do almost anything. He is in a permanent state of need or lack, but he releases, in a single line or page, enough riches to potentially fill an entire novel or treatise.

A good essayist is not a completely sincere person, nor a very consistent thinker, nor an extraordinary and imaginative story-teller. The writer who cannot successfully construct his plot or argument, and who consequently loses out as a novelist or philosopher, gains as an essayist. This is because in the essay only the digressions matter. The essay is thus an art of compromises, of surrenders. In the essay, the weaker side wins. The founder of the genre, Michel Montaigne, declares his creative and intellectual weakness on almost every page of his *Essais* (1571). In the essay "On Books" he complains to the reader about his inability to create something striking, polished, and generally useful due to his lack of philosophical and artistic talent. "If someone exposes my ignorance, he will not insult me because I do not take the responsibility for what I am saying even before my own conscience, let alone before others. Any form of self-complaisance is alien to me. . . . Even if I am able to learn a few things occasionally, I am definitely incapable of committing it firmly to memory. . . . I borrow from others what I cannot express well myself, either because my language is poor or my mind is weak."[2]

The essay is the offspring of the "ménage à trois": poor unsystematic philosophy; bad and fragmentary literature; and an inferior and insincere diary. However, it is just this sort of hybridized and bad pedigree that has given the essay its flexibility and its beauty. Like a plebeian who is not burdened by traditions of nobility, the essay easily adapts to the eternal flow of everyday life, the vagaries of thought, and the personal idiosyncrasies of the writer. The essay, as a conglomeration of various deficiencies and incompletions, unexpectedly reveals the sphere of a totality normally hidden from the more defined genres (such as the poem, the tragedy, the novel, etc.); determined by their own ideal of perfection, these genres exclude everything that cannot be encompassed by their aesthetic model.

We can now clearly see that the essay did not originate in a void. Rather, it came to fill the space of that integral verbal form that once belonged to myth. Because its roots run so deep into antiquity, the essay's second birth in the sixteenth century, in Montaigne, appears to be without origins and without tradition. In fact, the essay is directed towards that unity of life, thought, and image, which in its early syncretic form was at the origin of myth. Only at a later stage did this original unity of myth divide into three major and ever-proliferating branches: the sphere of facts and historical events, the sphere of the image or representation, and the sphere of concepts and generalizations. These three spheres correspond to three broad categories of genre—the documentary-descriptive, the artistic-imaginary, and the theoretical-speculative.

Essay writing, like a weak and somewhat sickly growth, found a place for itself in the gap created by the branching-out of myth into those three major directions. From there, this thin branch grew vigorously to become the main offshoot of the great tree of myth. The essay thus became the central trunk of that totality of life, image, and thought, which split into the various branches of knowledge that have become further specialized over time.

In our own times, which have seen a renaissance in mythological thinking, the experience of spiritual totality finds expression more and more frequently in the essay. With Nietzsche and Heidegger, it is *philosophy* that becomes essayistic; with Thomas Mann and Robert Musil it is *literature;* with Vasily Rozanov and Gabriel Marcel it is the *diary*. Henceforth it is no longer only peripheral cultural phenomena that acquire qualities of the essay but central ones as well. The pressure of mythological totality can be felt from all directions. In the essay, however, this totality is not experienced as a given, as accomplished, but as a possibility and an intent, in its spontaneity, immediacy, and incompletion.

Almost all the mythologemes of the twentieth century have their origins in the essayistic mode: Camus's Sisyphus, Marcuse's Orpheus, Miguel de Unamuno's Don Quixote, Thomas Mann's Doctor Faustus and "magic mountain," Kafka's "castle" and "trial," Saint-Exupéry's "flight" and "citadel." This kind of essayistic writing is in part reflexive, in part fictional, in part confessional and didactic. It attempts to derive thought from image and to lead it back to Being. Major trends of literature, philosophy, and even scientific thought of the twentieth century have acted as tributaries to this mainstream of *essayism*. Among its exemplars are Sigmund Freud, Carl Jung, Theodor Adorno, Albert Schweitzer, Konrad Lorenz, André Breton, Albert Camus, Paul Valéry, T. S. Eliot, Jorge Luis Borges, Octavio Paz, Yasunari Kawabata, Kobo Abe, Henry Miller, Norman Mailer, and Susan Sontag. In Russia, too, outstanding poetry and fiction writers, philosophers, and literary scholars expressed themselves as essayists: Lev Shestov, Dmitry Merezhkovsky, Marina Tsvetaeva, Osip Mandel'shtam, Victor Shklovsky, Joseph Brodsky, Andrei Bitov, Andrei Sinyavsky, Georgy Gachev, and Sergei Averintsev.

Essayism is a considerably broader and more powerful trend than any single artistic or philosophical movement, broader than Surrealism or

Expressionism, Phenomenology or Existentialism. It is of this interdisciplinary scope precisely because essayism is not a trend of one of the branches of culture or a method of one of its disciplines but a distinctive feature of contemporary culture in its entirety. Essayism tends toward a neo-mythological wholeness, a merging of image and concept inside culture, but also a merging of culture with Being itself and with the sphere of raw facts and daily occurrences that are usually considered beyond the limits of culture.

Essayism is thus—like its earlier counterpart, mythology—an all-encompassing mode of creative consciousness. Essayism functions as a metadiscourse in relation to all the artistic, philosophical, and documentary modes of representation that feed into it and that originated in mythological wholeness.

However, there is also a profound difference between mythology, which was born before cultural differentiation, and essayism, which arose out of these differentiations themselves. Although essayism unites the disparate—fact, image, and concept; or the sensible, the imaginary, and the rational—it does so without destroying their autonomy. This is how essayism differs from the syncretic mythology of earlier epochs as well as from the totalitarian mythologies of the twentieth century. The latter tend to unite by force what was naturally not subject to differentiation in antiquity. Thus totalitarian mythology requires the ideal to be treated as factual; possibility or even impossibility to be treated as real; an abstract idea to be treated as material force, the prime mover of the masses; and one individual to be treated as a model for all other individuals. Essayism, too, unites fragmented portions of culture. But in so doing, essayism leaves enough space between them for play, irony, reflection, alienation, and defamiliarization. These are definitely antagonistic to the dogmatic rigidity of all mythologies based on *authority*.

Essayism is a mythology based on *authorship*. The self-consciousness of a single individual tests the limits of its freedom and plays with all possible conceptual connections in the unity of the world. In an essay, individual freedom is not negated in the name of a myth, with its tendency for depersonalization, but flourishes in the right to individual myth. This authorial, mythopoetic freedom, which includes freedom from the impersonal logic of myth itself, constitutes the foundation of the genre. The essay thus constantly vacillates between myth and nonmyth, between unity and difference. Consequently, the particular intersects and sometimes merges with the universal, image with concept, being with meaning. However, these correspondences are not complete: Edges protrude, creating uneven surfaces, disruptions, and discrepancies. This is the only way in which the contemporary vision of the world can come to fruition: Aiming for wholeness, it at the same time does not claim to overcome difference of its constituent parts.

Literally "essay" (from French "essai" and Latin "exagium") means "weighing," "testing," an "attempt," an "experiment." This is its indispensable quality. The essay is *experimental mythology,* the truth of a gradual and unfinalizable approximation to myth, not the lie of a totalizing coincidence with it. Essayism is thus an attempt at preventing the fragmentation of culture, on the one hand, and the introduction of a coercive unity, on the other. Essayism is directed against the plurality of disconnected particulars as well as against the centripetal tendencies of a dictatorial totality. Essayism is an attempt at stemming the tide of narrow disciplinary particularization at work in contemporary culture. But it is also a bulwark against the petrification of culture into cult and ritual, which becomes all the more fanatical the greater the discrepancy between the extremes of fantasy and reality grows (which makes it all the more difficult to force them into the immutable dogmatic unity of faith).

Essayism is an attempt at unification without violence, an attempt at projecting compatibility without compulsory communality. It is an attempt at leaving intact, in the heart of a new, nontotalitarian totality, the experience of insecurity and the sphere of possibility, the sacred Montaignesque "I cannot" and "I do not know how," which is all that remains of the sacred in the face of the pseudo-sacralizations of mass mythology. "I speak my mind freely on all things, even on those which perhaps exceed my capacity . . . and so the opinion I give of them is to declare the measure of my sight, not the measure of things"[3] Two conditions must be met in the essay: audacity of vision and awesome respect for things themselves. Or, to put it differently, *boldness of propositions* and *meekness of conclusions.* Only by fulfilling these two conditions, inherent in the essay, can something of true worth be created in our age: an open wholeness.

The present essay has transcended the confines of its topic—"the essay"—and entered the wider sphere of "essayism," which carries a new hope for contemporary culture. But it is only by departing from its topic that the essay remains true to its genre.[4]

Moscow, 1982

Notes

1. Translated from Russian by Slobodanka Vladiv-Glover.
2. *The Complete Works of Montaigne*, trans. Donald M. Frame (Stanford: Stanford University Press, 1957): 298.
3. Ibid., 298.
4. For a more systematic exploration of this genre see Mikhail Epstein, "At the Crossroads of Image and Concept: Essayism in the Culture of the Modern Age," in his book *After the Future: The Paradoxes of Postmodernism and Contemporary Russian Culture* (Amherst: University of Massachusetts Press 1995): 213–253, and "Esseistika kak nulevaia distsiplina" (Essayistics as a Zero Discipline), in his book *Bog detalei. Esseistika 1977–1988* (Moscow, LIA Elinina, 1998): 225–240.

Chapter 16

The Catalog of Catalogs
Mikhail Epstein

Preface

The genre of the catalog is pertinent to transcultural experimentation by virtue of its paradigmatic structure that juxtaposes various judgments on the same subject. Such discourse is released from the order of time or the relationship of cause and effect.[1] In contrast, the syntagmatic structure, in which one proposition is deduced from another, one event succeeds another, is subject to the restrictive and oppressive effects of logical or narrative sequence.[2] Transculture is a metaparadigm, a set of elements (cultures, canons, traditions, epistemes, worldviews) that coexist in a structured space rather than succeed and displace each other in time.

In Japan there existed a special literary genre, *suihitsu* (literally, "following the brush"), that enumerated various attributes of one object—or various objects that possess one attribute. Classical samples of this genre can be found in the *Pillow Book* by Sei Shonagon (966/7–1013?). In some sections, she lists things that most attract or annoy her, or things that distract in moments of boredom. This genre, which can be called the "catalog," arises at the intersection of abstraction and factuality, of the generic and the unique. In its simplest form, the catalog presents the diversity of things that belong to one general category, or the diversity of categories within which a single thing may be located. The beauty of the moon, the beauty of snow, the beauty of pearls . . . The beauty of the moon, the coldness of the moon, the deceptiveness of the moon . . .

Similar compositions are used in structural studies in which a strictly defined object is consecutively described in its various aspects. Wittgenstein's *Tractatus Logico-Philosophicus* is an example of such metaphysical investigation through enumeration of various propositions. A quite different example is provided by the contemporary Russian poet-conceptualist Lev Rubinshtein, whose catalogs, sometimes rhymed, include model rejoinders of colloquial speech with a swiftly changing focus of conversation.[3]

My catalogs follow the middle way between those of Wittgenstein and Rubinshtein: They are neither logico-philosophical nor literary-poetic but rather belong to the fuzzy intermediate zone between them. "The Catalog of Trifles," "The Catalog of Freckles and Birthmarks," "The Catalog of Smoke," and "The Catalog of Catalogs" are experiments in restoring the ancient genre as a model for contemporary culture's self-description. Differing opinions and views do not conflict in these catalogs but rather coexist independently, succeeding each other on the vertical axis (the Greek word "catalog" literally means "words going from top to bottom"). Of these catalogs, which were written in July 1982 in Moscow, only the last one is reproduced here: "The Catalog of Catalogs," which attempts to describe this genre by means of its own structure.[4]

The Catalog of Catalogs

0.0 Everything can be described in a catalog, even a catalog itself.
0.1 A catalog is written and read not from left to right and not from right to left but from top to bottom.
0.2 Such an order means that things do not follow each other but are given simultaneously.
0.3 A catalog simply enumerates everything that is present.
1.0 A catalog is good for the description of things but is still better for the description of thoughts.
1.1 Things emerge and disappear and therefore are narrated in the temporal order in which they succeed each other.
1.2 Ideas are always present as if they were kept in a storehouse where they cannot be lost and damaged.
2.0 The meaning of an object is the totality of all ideas related to it, or of all propositions that can be pronounced about it.
2.1 A catalog permits us to pronounce all propositions that can be pronounced about an object.
2.2 A catalog includes both true and false propositions.

2.3 A proposition becomes true or false through its relationship to an external reality while in itself it simply is, takes place.
2.4 A catalog includes both serious and ironic propositions.
2.5 A proposition becomes serious or ironic through its relationship to the person who pronounces it, but in itself it simply is, takes place.
2.6 A catalog includes the propositions of both the author himself and of other people.
2.7 A proposition becomes original or trivial in its relationship to the previous propositions but in itself it simply is, takes place.
2.8 A catalog is the common place for all possible propositions about a certain object.
2.9 True propositions in the catalog differ from false propositions no more than they differ from themselves, and this also concerns serious and ironic, original and trivial propositions.
2.10 A catalog is valuable not because it contains true, serious, and original propositions but because it is as full as possible.
3.0 The catalog is not a literary or philosophical genre. There is more similarity between a folk song and a scholarly dissertation than between the catalog and all other genres.
3.1 The catalog meets neither scientific criteria of truth nor aesthetic criteria of beauty but only formal criteria of order.
3.2 The catalog is a form that itself takes care to produce its contents.
3.3 The catalog narrates nothing, expresses nothing, and persuades us of nothing. It enumerates like a dictionary.
3.4 As distinct from a dictionary of words, the catalog is a dictionary of propositions.
3.5 Like the words in a dictionary, the propositions in a catalog are not pronounced by anybody. They cannot be personally attributed. They have no author. They do not express anybody's opinion.
3.6 A dictionary and a catalog contain everything that can be said and thought, but the speaker who is speaking in them is language itself, and the thinker who is thinking in them is mind itself.
4.0 A catalog forms an antipode of a text, for a text moves in time while a catalog exists in space. They relate as actuality and potentiality.

4.1 A text is always complete even if it consists of one word; a catalog is never complete even if it includes all existing propositions.
4.2 The critique of a text constitutes a text different than that which is criticized. The critique of a catalog constitutes a part of the catalog itself.
4.3 There is no catalog that could not be extended and that would not need extension.
4.4 A text has an author while a catalog has a compiler. The author is responsible for the truth of his own propositions, whereas the compiler is responsible for the diversity of all possible propositions.
4.5 A compiler is a person to whom thoughts occur when he is not thinking; that is why he does not consider them his own thoughts.
4.6 A thought always occurs in the form of two or three different thoughts. An author fixes only one of them. A compiler fixes simultaneously all thoughts that come together. Each of them is also born in the form of two or three thoughts. This is why a compiler can never complete his work.
4.7 For example, the thought that one has to love one's motherland is born in the form of the thoughts "I have no motherland," "I am not able to love," "My motherland does not love me."
4.8. The thought "My motherland does not love me" is born in the form of the thoughts "The more I love my motherland the less it loves me" and "How many motherlands do I have, if my motherland has so many sons?"
5.0 The catalog contains the folklore of the present epoch, that is, of the time after the time.
5.1 "The time after the time" is the space where all texts become lines in the growing catalog.
5.2 Folklore has performers, catalogs have compilers; both are distributors of the material, not its creators.
5.3 Prehistoric time generates folklore, posthistoric time generates the catalog.
5.4 Folklore accumulates similar, homogeneous ideas characteristic of primitive society, whereas the catalog combines different and heterogeneous ideas characteristic of contemporary society.
5.5 Folklore is produced in the form of a text that conveys one common proposition, whereas the catalog is produced in the form of a dictionary that juxtaposes diverse propositions.

5.6 The catalog revives folklore on the stage of cultural differentiation where the totality of all propositions is reinstated, not in the form of one impersonal proposition but in a collection of many personal propositions.

6.0 While reading a catalog one cannot understand what its compiler is actually thinking. But one can understand what is generally thought and what can be thought in principle.

6.1 A thought in the catalog is not attached to anything beyond itself. It is not issued on behalf of any subject; it does not describe any object; it is not addressed to any interlocutor. It exists only because it is possible for it to exist.

6.2 A thought in the catalog exists as evidence of its possibility. Its existence testifies to the fact that it can exist.

6.3 A thought in the catalog does not explain the world and does not change the world but testifies to the multiplicity of possible worlds.

6.4 A catalog sets up the boundaries of what is possible, of what can be thought.

6.5 The impossible and the unthinkable are conveyed in the continuation of the catalog.

7.0 Each catalog can be completed only relatively, and its end becomes the beginning of the next catalog. Thus, the catalog of trifles passes into the catalog of entertainments; the catalog of smoke passes into the catalog of sky; the catalog of the universe passes into the catalog of catalogs; and the catalog of catalogs passes into the catalog of silence.

7.1 Each of the existing catalogs is a fragment of a larger catalog, and the largest catalog is a fragment of the Catalog which has no title.

7.2 Since a catalog never ends it can be finished at any point.

7.3 Each sentence in a catalog can be the last; therefore, it must be conclusive.

Notes

1. A paradigm can be defined as "a class of elements that can occupy the same place in the syntagmatic string, or, in other words, a set of elements each of which is substitutable for the other in the same context." A. J. Greimas and J. Courtés, *Semiotics and Language: An Analytical Dictionary,* trans. Larry Crist et al. (Bloomington: Indiana University Press, 1979): 224. The sequence "I love

you" is syntagmatic. The sets "love, hate, adore, despise" or "I, we, he, they" are paradigmatic.
2. On the totalitarian effects of time's unidirectionality see the chapter "The Permanence of Newness and Spaces for Difference."
3. On conceptualism in general and on Lev Rubinshtein in particular, see in Mikhail Epstein's books: *After the Future: The Paradoxes of Postmodernism and Contemporary Russian Culture* (Amherst: University of Massachusetts Press, 1995): 29–37, 60–70; *Russian Postmodernism: New Perspectives on Post-Soviet Culture* (with Alexander Genis and Slobodanka Vladiv-Glover). (New York and Oxford: Berghahn Books, 1999): 105–118.
4. The first publication of all these catalogs was in Russian: Mikhail Epstein, "Katalogi," *Dar. Kul'tura Rossii* 1 (1992): 68–71.

Chapter 17

Improvisational Community
Mikhail Epstein

The goal of collective improvisation is to encourage interactions among different disciplinary perspectives, life experiences, and worldviews. It can also be identified with the task Richard Rorty has set for thinkers of the future: "They would be all-purpose intellectuals who were ready to offer a view on pretty much anything, in the hope of making it hang together with everything else."[1] Improvisations might be thought of as metaphysical "assaults" on ordinary things, experiments in creative communication, or exercises in the creation of Rorty's "all-purpose intellectuals."

1. Creativity and Communication

The word "improvisation" derives from the Latin "providere" and literally means "unforeseeable." Improvisation opens the unpredictability of creation for the creator himself. Any kind of creativity, however, shares this feature; otherwise, our mental activity would be better characterized as "knowledge," "scholarship," "erudition," "exercise," "training." What is it that makes improvisation different from creativity as such, which to a certain degree is also improvisational?

Typically in creativity the unforeseeable is contained in the mind of the creator himself. Isolation and self-concentration is a precondition for creative self-expression: A person meditates and converses with himself, therefore, conversations with others become irritating and counterproductive for him.

Quite different is the case in which the unforeseeable is contained in the consciousness of another person, beyond the competence and horizon of the improviser. The topic of improvisation is given to me by somebody else, or it can be also an exchange of topics. Improvisation is a type of creativity that evolves between the poles of the known and unknown, which are contained in *different consciousnesses*. This is why improvisation, as distinct from self-centered creativity, necessarily includes the process of communication: Somebody suggests a topic, unexpected for the improviser, whose task is to elaborate this topic unpredictably for the one who suggested it. Thus, two unpredictabilities arise from the improvisation as the encounter of two consciousnesses. The specificity of improvisation originates in the fact that it is creativity via communication.

But if improvisation is impossible without communication, how does it differ from communication as such? Regular modes of communication presuppose that one interlocutor communicates to another what is already known to him. Even news communicated in such typical situations is news only for the listener but not for the speaker. Typically, communication only reproduces those facts and ideas that existed before and independently of the process of communication. Communication aims to diminish the unknown and to transform it into something known, extending it in a horizontal dimension from one person to another. The psychological value of communication arises from the fact that its participants are united in their thoughts and feelings, and the content of one consciousness is transferred to another.

Although improvisation is impossible without communication, it pursues quite different goals. What is communicated in response to the proposed topic is unknown to the improviser himself. Here the unknown generates something still more unknown. Having received an unpredictable topic, the improviser further elaborates it in an unpredictable way.

Thus, improvisation is distinct from creativity in that it incorporates communication with a different consciousness, and it is distinct from communication in that it includes an act of creativity, the production of something unknown and unforeseeable. Typically, communication with another person distracts from the act of creativity, and vice versa, the act of creativity inhibits or impedes the process of communication. In improvisation, however, creativity and communication reinforce rather than neutralize each other. Improvisation unites creativity and communication as two vectors transcending one's own consciousness. In creativity, this transcendence acquires a vertical dimension, since it is addressed to a higher plane of oneself, whereas communication operates through horizontal transcendence, relating one individual to another.

Consequently, improvisation combines the horizontal and vertical modes of transcendence. Through improvisation, the otherness of another person gives an impetus to my creative self-transcendence. It is as if I take the others' positions of expectation and surprise toward myself, and this "unknown in the other" who I am for the others, generates in myself the effort to create this "otherness" that is the aim of improvisation. An encounter with the consciousness of another and the discovery of otherness in one's own consciousness are the two mutually stimulating processes in improvisation.

2. The Existential Event of Thinking

The improviser creates something different than what he ever could invent and imagine alone, because he is confronted with an unfamiliar topic that requires immediate elaboration, which mobilizes all of his intellectual potential. This resembles a situation of mortal danger in which a human may develop instantly supernatural capacities that leave him as soon as the danger recedes. The mind attacked by a problem feverishly looks for an escape, for a creative solution, and is quickly mobilized in response to the threat of intellectual failure, blankness, and stupidity. There is no other situation that is intellectually as challenging and stimulating as improvisation. Writing an essay for an exam or participating in a brainstorming session always involves some elements of preparation and preliminary specification among expected tasks and topics (the subject of the university course, the agenda of professional discussion). Only at an improvisational session is the range of possible topics absolutely open, extending to all existing disciplines, discourses, and vocabularies.

Improvising presupposes the ability to apply one's intellectual capacities to any realm of human experience. Everybody knows about frogs, but does anybody give attention and effort to thinking about them, except for zoologists, specializing in amphibians? This is the point: We think that we know, but how can we know if we do not think? The majority of people never exercise their thinking abilities beyond the very narrow field of their specialty (if it requires thinking at all). We may have had a passive, sensual experience of seeing, hearing, or touching frogs, but we do not have the active, intellectual experience of thinking about them, and therefore, we are not really self-conscious humans in this aspect of our existence: in relation to frogs—or in relation to trees and bees, for that matter. In relation to almost everything in the world.

To think means to conceptualize a certain entity, to define its general and distinctive properties, its place in the world, and its place in our life. What are frogs? Why do they exist? How are they different from toads, lizards, and snakes? How do they feed the human imagination and mythology? Why did they inspire storytellers and Aristophanes? How have they been viewed in the past and in the present? What is their symbolic role in my native and foreign cultures? What is my personal attitude toward these creatures and how do they fit into my picture of the world, relate to my psychology and metaphysics, my fears and fantasies? *We are not fully human if something present in our sensual experience is absent from our intellectual experience. We have to think what we feel and feel what we think, not because these capacities coincide but precisely because they are so different and one cannot substitute for another.*

Thinking is usually regarded as a means to some palpable practical goal: Technological thinking serves to create machines and tools; political thinking, to create effective social institutions, etc. But thinking is a capacity that does not need any external justification because, more than anything else, it makes humans human. The question "Why think?" is ultimately as unanswerable as the questions "Why feel?" "Why breathe?" or "Why live?" The ultimate reward for thinking is thinking itself.

Collective improvisation is one way to immensely expand the realm of the thinkable and to re-live our experience in a conscious, discerning, articulate manner. All things that appear to be familiar, as components of routine knowledge, suddenly become estranged and deautomatized, become targets of inquiry and interrogation, potential objects of intellectual labor.

Improvisation permits not only an estrangement of objects, but also an estrangement of subjects. People whom we may have known for years now for the first time appear in the existential, "liminal" situation of creativity. We do not know who they really are, as at this moment they are equally unfamiliar to themselves. Creativity is the most mysterious and intimate moment in the life of personality, and this makes improvisation a truly existential experiment and revelation about oneself and others. Usually creativity is presented to others in premeditated and generically predetermined forms, as paintings, poems, dances—as results from which the creator has already distanced herself even if she is singing or acting on the scene. *In improvisation, the mystery of creativity is revealed most intimately and spontaneously, as the self-creation of a personality here and now.*

An improviser encounters an otherness and strangeness in the object of his thought, in the cosubjects of his thinking, and finally, in himself. Therefore, improvisation is not only a social but also an existential event, or, more precisely, the rarest case of *existential sociality,* in which sociality and existentiality do not exclude but presuppose each other. Do we ever think together—not just talk about what we already know, not just socialize, but create a social event of cothinking where each participant is as unknown to others as he is unpredictable to himself?

3. Improvisational Communities: Distinctions between Professional And Folkloric Improvisations

Collective improvisation differs essentially from a traditional public or professional improvisation, which typically takes place in poetic readings or musical concerts and competitions. A professional improviser performs before the audience, which has a purely passive role, and he is opposed to it as an active creator. The audience can participate only in the first moment by setting a topic for improvisation. The act of communication here is incomplete because one of the participants acquires a privileged role and is divided from the audience by the stage. In a collective improvisation, by contrast, each participant enters a reciprocal relationship of questioning and answering with all the others.

The next question is, how does this collective and spontaneous creativity differ from folklore with its oral tradition? In folklore, the performer, as a bearer of mass consciousness, is not separated from his audience; he is one among many singers or storytellers. Improvisation indeed plays an important role in folklore because creativity and communication here have not yet been separated. There is no division between the creation of art and communication through art, between composing and performing: both are enacted in one setting, in one moment of time. This includes what can be called intellectual or philosophical improvisation, such as the dialogues of Socrates: creativity in the process of communication.

The comparison with folklore makes clear that the concert type of improvisation is the result of a disintegration of the initial syncretic creative community. Improvisational community has degenerated into a unidirectional communication from the creator to a passive audience. The professional improvisation, in which the performer is distanced from his silent audience, is a curious hybrid of ancient folkloric and modern individual creativity. What remains from folklore is the immediate process of creativity amidst people; what persists from individual creativity is separateness from the audience. In Plato's dialogues, it is not only Socrates who improvises but also his interlocutors. This is the prototype of improvisational community that avoids the division into performer and passive audience.

It is important to understand that although the improvisational group resembles a commune, its communality extends only to ideas, not to bodies and property. It is in the sphere of thinking that collectivity is not destructive for individuals. Bodies and things are separated by their own spatial nature; a violation of their boundaries can lead to aggression and violence, as in the communist utopia of the twentieth century. The attempt to extend community to material, sexual, economic aspects of life may lead to those repressive excesses of unification that have engendered some of the most bloody conflicts, wars, and revolutions of modernity. Improvisational community does not confuse these two spheres as was done, for example, in hippie communes where the communality of ideas was extrapolated to include property and sexual relationships. A human being must remain a full master of her body and material possessions, but ideas do not belong to her exclusively since by their very nature they are fluid and nomadic, freely traveling from mind to mind. Collective improvisation aspires to that kind of communality which never oversteps the boundary of what has a potential and propensity for commonness.

Such restrictions on commonality have not only an ethical, but also a historical rationale. In folklore, the same oral tradition is shared by all performers, and a single work of verbal art, impersonal and anonymous, belongs to everybody and to nobody. Such folkloric rites cannot be reproduced now in their original form: Collective improvisations, if they wish to be contemporary, must incorporate—not eliminate—the individual mode of creativity. The aesthetics of communality constitutive of folklore cannot fully prevail over the aesthetics of difference that is constitutive of modern creativity. But these two aesthetics have a potential to interact in such a way that communality accentuates rather than destroys individual differences. The commonness of the topic, the unity of time and place, the equality in the conditions of improvisation serve to emphasize, not to efface individual differences.

At some sessions, different roles are distributed among the participants in advance; for example, one might accentuate heroic aspects of the topic, another, tragic motifs; the third will modify it in a baroque style, the fourth in a romantic key, and so forth. The result of collective improvisation is a "postindividual" community of minds that presupposes highly individual contributions of all participants. Unlike folklore, collective improvisation is not a pre-individual form of creativity; nor is it a solely individual creativity, as in a concert-type performance. Instead, it is transindividual creativity that embraces the diversity of interpretations manifested in individual texts.

4. Why Writing?

Why is it necessary for improvisation to have a written character? In front of a sheet of paper or a computer screen, a person experiences the full measure of her individual responsibility as a creator. Without writing, improvisation tends to dissolve into conversation, exchange of opinions; that is, pure communication. To be truly creative, communication must incorporate moments of privacy, isolation, and meditation.

The dialectics of these two factors, isolation and communication, is rather complex. Improvisations are conducted in several stages, in which the periods of speech and silence alternate: discussing and choosing the topic, then writing, then reading and discussing again, then (sometimes) jointly writing summaries of the discussions. Thus, creative minds are joined, disjoined, and rejoined in the process of improvisation, which displays the dialectics of individual and collective.

To a certain degree, collective improvisation, as a genre born in Russia, combines the experiences of public eloquence characteristic of the West and silent meditation characteristic of the East. It is writing that solves the dilemma of speech and silence. The silence of writing allows all participants to coexist in one mood, one mode of intellectual activity, while pursuing different interpretations of the same topic. In the community of writing, there is no division into subjects and objects, which is practically inevitable in oral communication. We know how one person's insatiable "will to speak" can easily transform an entire community into a submissive audience. Collective writing is a silent communication in which the unidimensional time of speaking (one speaker at a time) submits to the multidimensional space of co-thinking. No one's thought is imposed on another's until these parallel flows of thinking are fully mature, ready to be individually expressed.

Between the rhetorical orientation of Greek antiquity and the Far Eastern culture of silent meditation is located the Near Eastern love of books, literacy, and writing, simultaneously silent and self-expressive.

The figure of a scribe and copyist is cherished and even sanctified in "bookish" Judaic, Babylonian, Egyptian, Islamic, Byzantine cultures, as distinct from the Western exaltation of a public orator and the Eastern cult of a silent sage, "Zen master," or "yogi."[2] In Russia, with its geographical location between Europe and Asia, and with its cultural habits inherited from Byzantium, writing is also traditionally considered the supreme kind of intellectual activity, which may partly explain the preference for writing as it developed in Russian improvisational communities.

Writing is a much more intellectually obligating and binding activity than speaking because its result is immediately fixed. Unlike an oral utterance, the written word becomes "immortal" at the very moment of its birth. Thus the Russian proverb: "What is written by a pen, cannot be cut out by an ax." To write creatively (not pragmatically) in the presence of other people is a rather unusual and apparently uncomfortable occupation, especially as there is no chance to revise or polish the text (except for several minutes of purely technical editing at the end of the session). The presence of other people intensifies the course of thinking; since each word written is the last one, the process itself becomes its own result. The responsibility grows as writing must be completed in the given place and span of time.

An improviser is an intellectual soldier who has to fulfill his duty wherever he finds himself. He does not have the privilege of a general in choosing the place of the battle, the topic for meditation. He must be prepared to engage with any topic, to start an intellectual battle over any circumstance or facet of human experience.

As the acquisition of this nomadic way of thinking, a variety of ideas are spontaneously generated in improvisation that would never occur if participants had been working in the seclusion of their offices and had the support of many books, dictionaries, preliminary notes and plans. Many participants later confessed that improvisation allowed them to break through the stupors and impasses of their thinking and provided germs for subsequent, more substantial scholarly or literary works. Of course, improvisation is not a substitute for the professional work of a writer, scientist, scholar, etc. On the other hand, no other intellectual activity, however fruitful it might be, can substitute for improvisation. Improvisation relates to other avenues of creative thinking as the whole is related to its parts. It integrates not only creativity and communication but also theoretical and artistic genres of creativity, private and public forms of communication.

5. The Integrative Mode of Intellectual Activity: Essay and Trance

Improvisation is an integrative mode of intellectual activity in the same way as the essay is an integrative genre of writing. The products of improvisation usually belong not to purely scholarly or purely artistic genres but to experimentally synthetic, essayistic genres. As I have already indicated, an essay is partly a diary, journal, intimate document; partly a theoretical discourse, treatise, article; partly a short story, anecdote, parable, small fictional narrative. The immediate result of improvisation is a highly associative but structured and conceptualized meditation on a specific topic that unites facticity, generalization, and imagination. An improvisation and an essay are related as the process and result, act and product, but both are integrative in their generic model. *The integration of factuality, conceptualization, and imagery in the essay corresponds to the integration of cognition, communication, and creativity in improvisation.*

As was mentioned in the chapter on the essay, the integrity of this genre is of a post-reflexive quality: The three constituents must be consciously articulated, in distinction from a pre-reflective mythology, in which image, concept, and fact are presented as a syncretic unity. In the same way, improvisation differentiates its constituents—creativity, communication, and cognition—in contrast with syncretic practices of religious meditation and contemplation, such as Zen. In collective improvisation, the topic is articulated differently from its interpretations; individual approaches are stated clearly, and participants are working separately on their contributions.

Improvisation does share some similarity with various contemplative states, but here the object of intellectual contemplation does not dissolve into an all-embracing absolute. Rather, it is conceived in its absolute uniqueness, through a series of definitions and specifications. The psychological state of an improviser is not completely self-centered and self-enclosed but produces a tangible entity, a system of signs, a text as a part of the external world that is subject to rational evaluation and discussion. Improvisation intensifies the experience of vertical and horizontal *transcendence* inherent in creativity and communication, but nevertheless it is not identical to a *trance* state. Improvisation has nothing to do with sacramental ecstasy, mystical agitation, or quiet resignation, which resist any objectification and analytic judgment. Improvisation is a self-reflective trance that transcends the boundaries of trance itself, making it an object of rational negotiation and communication.

Improvisation relates to trance in the same way as the essay relates to myth. The essay is the truth of an approximation to myth, not a lie of total coincidence with it. Improvisation is an experience of approximation to trance, not the exaltation of collective ecstasy, or quasi-folkloric community, or a hypnotic and dreamlike state of mind.

6. Un-ity: Claims and Disclaimers

The practice of improvisation raises the socio-epistemological question of how one cohesive whole can be created spontaneously from the multiplicity of individual voices without resorting to the external will of one all-encompassing authority. This inductive "unity from diversity" contrasts with the more typical deductive model in which the author divides himself into separate characters and ideological positions. Both Plato in his philosophical dialogues and Dostoevsky in his polyphonic novels were unitary authors who produced a diversity of voices from the unity of one creative consciousness. The question is, Can voices be united from within, without the anticipating and dictating will of the "transcendental" author?

Only at the peak of the liberal development of individualism and at the threshold of a post-individualist culture can we consciously and cautiously approach this problem. When personality has come to full self-realization, it has no other ways to develop further than to give itself to others. This sacrificial task formulated by Fyodor Dostoevsky as an ethical imperative becomes a methodological principle of improvisation. The goal is to reintegrate oneself in an intellectual community not in its syncretic elementary form that preceded the birth of individuality, but in a fully articulated, synthetic form that issues from the self-transcendence of a conscious individuality.

Thus "unity" as the basis of collective improvisation should be understood both deconstructively and constructively. In the very word "unity" we can detect not only its conventional meaning ("oneness, totality") but also the hidden disclaimer "un" which as a root means "one," and as a prefix, the negation or the reversal of the implied action ("undo," "unknown"). Let the word "un-ity" haunt us with this prefix-disclaimer that problematizes the very meaning of unity. Collective improvisation is a small laboratory of such problematic integration that is both the disintegration of primitive, folkloric unities and a prototype of some fluid communities of the future.

Certainly one should not expect from improvisations those literary masterpieces that are created only by the continuous and sustained efforts of an individual mind. As a rule, improvisations are inferior in their literary or scholarly quality to the output within established genres or disciplines. In the same way, there are no essays comparable in their value and grandeur to the tragedies of Shakespeare, the epics of Homer, or the novels of Dostoevsky. But this is not because the essay is an inferior genre; on the contrary, it integrates the possibilities of other genres: philosophical, historical, fictional. The very range of these possibilities complicates the task of their complete realization because the discrepancy between actual performance and potential perfection is deeper in the essay than in more specific and structured genres. There are perfect fables and sonnets, maybe short stories, but even the best novels impress us mostly with their "colossal failures" (according to William Faulkner, Thomas Wolfe was the best novelist of his generation precisely because his failure was greater than that of other authors). To achieve prominence in the essay genre is even more difficult because it is generically so fluid and indeterminate and lacks the strict rules provided by the narrative structure of the novel or by the logical structure of philosophical discourse.

In the same way improvisation does not achieve the depth and breadth of individual creativity, the sincerity of personal communication, or the rigor of scientific research. Both essays and improvisations are forms of cultural potentiality that in every specific case, with each particular effort, remains unfulfilled. Improvisation fails to compare with literature, art, science, scholarship . . . But improvisation combines all these elements that, in their ideal combination, produce a work in the genre of culture itself. There are no words in existing vocabularies to designate a creator of culture. There are artists, writers, scientists, scholars, engineers . . . but at this point culture has not become the site or genre of creativity (we do not count political and financial management of culture, or educational popularization of culture, which themselves are not culturally creative). Such creativity in the genre of culture is the ultimate possibility of transcultural thinking, which finds in collective improvisation its very tentative experimental model. The deficiencies of improvisational works reflect the unrealized potentials of culture as a whole. The forms of the novel or tragedy, of treatise or monograph are more narrow and definitive than this polyphonic and polysophic orchestra that resonates in the ensembles of co-thinking individuals.

Collective improvisation is a microcosm of cultural activities where speech and silence, writing and reading are articulated in their difference and simultaneously compressed into one time and one place. That is why the process of improvisation is so intellectually and emotionally intense: The poles of creation and perception, writing and reading, reading and discussing, which in the symbolic system of culture are usually divided, delayed, complexly mediated, separated by years or centuries, are condensed into the several hours of an improvisational session, here and now.

One cannot adequately understand improvisation without being an active participant in it. Reading the texts produced by an improvisational session does not provide a quite adequate impression. The main product of improvisation is the expansion of consciousness that may find its expression in texts written individually months or years after the session. The text, as a fixed result of an improvisational session, is only a way to the goal, which is collective thinking itself, an experience of intellectual brotherhood.

The texts of a given session cannot be regarded as self-sufficient products also because the integral work should be considered the totality of texts produced in the course of the existence of a given improvisational community. One page or one chapter of a novel does not constitute a separate work simply because it was created in one sitting and separated from another by temporal intervals. The improvisational community has its history, which is reflected in the sequence of improvisations that should be read like chapters of one novel. Only with the disintegration of the given community can its work be considered complete.

But the improvisational community can find another fate: Gradually expanding from generation to generation, it may incessantly integrate new individuals, communities, and societies. The collective improvisation can become one of the most creative forms of interaction among the intellectuals of the future. The growth of the Internet makes a collective improvisation that will involve thousands of the most active minds of humanity quite feasible.[3]

Notes

1. Richard Rorty, "Pragmatism and Philosophy," in *After Philosophy: End or Transformation?* ed. Kenneth Baynes, James Bohman, and Thomas McCarthy (Cambridge, MA, and London: The MIT Press, 1991): 56.
2. In his influential book *Poetika rannevizantiiskoi literatury* (Moscow: Nauka, Glavnaia redaktsiia vostochnoi literatury, 1977), Sergei Averintsev articulates this cultural difference. As opposed to the Western intellectual, who has the luxury of freedom of expression traceable to liberal ancient Greek oratorial modes, a Russian intellectual finds himself in the position of the bent and harried scribe of the ancient Near East, who had to survive political oppression by

delivering his innermost thoughts, not in open speech to his contemporaries, but in writing to an audience in posterity. This accounts for the gravitation of Russian culture, among others in Eastern Christianity, to the "mute word," while Western culture favors oral and visual modes.
3. This is the task and the hope of my next project, the InteLnet (Chapter 22).

Chapter 18

Sample Sessions at Universities

Improvisation at Bowling Green State University
Compiled by Ellen E. Berry[1]

In this section are samples from the two improvisational sessions held at Bowling Green State University on October 19, 1996, under the sponsorship of its Institute for the Study of Culture and Society. Individual participants responded to an invitation that was distributed widely to the university community as well as to selected individuals in the local community:

The flyer read:
We invite you to participate in either of two Collective Improvisation sessions led by Mikhail Epstein (Russian Studies, Emory University) and Ellen Berry (English/Scholar in Residence, ICS). These sessions occur in conjunction with a talk the previous night by Epstein and Berry titled "Experiments in Transculture: Rethinking Russian and American Creative Communication." You are encouraged to attend the talk, but attendance is not required in order to participate in the sessions.

Collective Improvisations were group writing experiments pioneered at the innovative Moscow Center for Experimental Creativity in the last years of perestroika. Their goal was to liberate thinking from predictable channels and encourage interactions among vastly different disciplinary perspectives, life experiences, and worldviews.

Each session began with an introduction by Mikhail Epstein in which he briefly explained the history, rationale, and procedures of improvisations to the assembled group. The four examples that follow are from the morning session, where the topic selected was "The Possibilities and Limitations of Technology."

Technology and Spirituality, Vida Penezic, Department of Popular Culture. There is a computer hard disk in Iowa on which is stored all of our deleted revisions and drafts, all our spelling mistakes and grammatical errors, all the personal thoughts we wrote and then decided we would rather die than show to anyone. Except that instead of disappearing from the face of the earth, they are forever preserved on that hard disk in Iowa. While there are people who still claim that all our deletions go directly to God, the fact remains that they go to Iowa after all.

What happens when we introduce the idea of technology—or, more precisely, the idea of a technological device—into our search for the absolute? If I am looking for the secret of the universe, will computer technology help me to find it? Can I search the Internet for the answer? Or does technology just stand in the way of my search? Technology would seem to be completely outside such an ancient or primitive quest, which can only be conducted by a primitive tool such as the brain. But are our brains ancient at some level or do they simply travel along and change as we—the species—travel through history, changing? Does technology loom so large on our horizon that we now believe it alone might reveal the secret of the universe?

Walkman and sunset. Internet and meditation. There are probably good reasons why these pairs of terms should not be considered polar opposites, but for the moment, let's assume that they are. Their role in my life is that they compete for my attention, for that limited number of minutes every day that I give myself permission to use however I choose, to do whatever pleases me. Walkman and sunset. I try to take a walk several times a week. Do I wear my walkman or do I pay attention to the beauty of my surroundings—leaves on the lawns, the sky, the sunset? Which will take me close to the secret of the universe? Internet and meditation. The same thing. Every morning I have time only for one. Am I going to sit down and meditate to have my mind less noisy, less cluttered; try to draw on some inner channels, perhaps? Or should I travel the Internet, reach out into the world, fill my mind with thousands of new images and messages? I guess the question for me is, Do I have to choose or should I let both—all of it, all of everything—into my world?

In lieu of a conclusion: One good thing about having written this out by hand is that it won't end up on that hard disk in Iowa—unless someone types these improvisations on their computer. Sunset and meditation, on the other hand, are not a part of this system unless, of course, they are directly hooked up to God. Then they are search engines for the secrets of the universe.

The Social Consequences of Technology, Francisco Cabanallis, Department of Romance Languages. The social consequences of technology are simultaneously favorable and unfavorable. Like other social constructs, technology is an expression of power. As a form of rhetorical propaganda, technology is defined as a problem-solving entity; it is supposed to make existence better. And, to a large extent, it does so. But it also creates other problems, which new technologies must resolve. Technology creates a great deal of our social existence; it determines most of our social patterns. Favorable technology articulates itself in the social fabric with more than technological premises; it needs to accommodate its propositions within ethical premises too. Unfavorable technology disregards ethical concerns; it is usually driven by narrow economic interests.

Some of the social consequences of the latest technologies include a simultaneous interplay between promoting social interaction and promoting social alienation. As the current ultimate expression of technology, computers can do both. They can connect individuals with the rest of the world, but they can also isolate those individuals from physical contact. Virtual reality is both social and antisocial.

Some of the negative consequences of the latest technologies involve the ability of the state to accumulate information about individuals and to use it to repress the individual or a social group. Technologies always have had this effect. The main difference with the latest technology is that such surveillance has become even easier.

Another negative consequence of technology has to do with the way in which businesses take advantage of it; individuals are monitored in terms of their consumption, so their public identity runs the risk of consisting of nothing more than their consumption habits to the exclusion of any other traits. Technology thus can redefine identity.

An important social consequence of technology, which I have heard in both directions, consists of the possible elimination of cities (or the reduction of their importance), given that technology will make concentration of individuals in one physical space obsolete. I have also encountered some economists who say the opposite: Cyberspace will increase the vitality of cities. Only in the first instance would high technology have a profound social impact in that it would be reproducing a pretechnological form of society based on country—not city—existence.

Another important social consequence of technology (particularly computers) is that it increases reading and writing—which television decreases. However, it is feasible to think that, given the pragmatic nature of technology, reading and writing are stimulated only in terms favorable to consumer society.

Technology can have positive social consequences in certain societies; however, overall I don't believe that technology is universally good. Ultimately, the instability of technology suggests that people outside the field of technology should monitor it. What I mean is that if we are to ensure that technologies are used in positive ways, we should always keep in mind the ethical consequences of them and should try to articulate them in the broadest and most democratic terms—nationally and internationally—which technologies such as the Internet are in a position of doing.

Everyday Technology and Communication, Patrick Alexander, American Culture Studies. In an age defined by technology, questions are often raised concerning the intimate role of the machine in the life of the user. A transcultural perspective can be especially helpful in this respect, as different cultures have various tools that they take for granted (imagine chopsticks juxtaposed with forks); although they may use similar technologies, it is likely that every culture uses them in different ways or has a different way of expressing a personal relationship with the technology.

The subject of our personal relations with technology can be a difficult topic to elaborate on due to the clichés established in contemporary culture concerning the personal-technological dichotomy. There is a tendency to imbue our technologies with spiritual or maybe simply human characteristics, for instance.

In this we can see the personal relationships we take on with our machines. People name their cars, even their computers, and other objects. We want to coax our technologies into functioning properly by caressing them, patting them, or goading them on with soft sweet talk: "C'mon now, that's it, load that program" or "Start for me, c'mon, Bob." However, isn't this just simple anthropomorphism, the same way we explain to ourselves in our own terms the ways in which animals behave? Through personalizing our technologies, we can better justify their integral role in our daily existence.

If we just label them all as machines we put a uniform quality onto them, generalizing them as one thing that functions in one uniform way. Perhaps through our anthropomorphic attitude we are aiming to recognize the differences and diversity that characterize machines. I can personally attest to having gotten involved in personal and distinctive relationships with seemingly identical machines. Since I teach in three different places, I became acquainted with three different Xerox machines. For each individual machine, I was forced to adopt a particular attitude if I wished to successfully interact with it. So in many ways it was no different from having to interact and modify my behavior with three separate colleagues. The most superficial, in that it is the most commonly trivialized, aspect of "the question of technology" and at the same time the most little discussed and most pressing is not just the relationships we form with machines but how these relationships affect our communications with other people.

It is interesting to consider the almost imperceptible process through which a technology moves from being a strange novelty to being an item of great centrality and unimaginable importance to our daily lives. I recently bought a laptop computer. When I picked this item up at the shop, the salesman said, "After this you won't be able to imagine how you lived your life before." And this certainly seems to be the case. We assimilate technologies into our daily routines quite readily. Even the most trivial appliances—such as a coffee grinder or a food processor or a remote control—become so much a part of our daily lives that the thought of being without them seems the ultimate in deprivation. And this is where a real difference can be seen between cultures. What about cultures in which items such as these are not universally available or owned by all? What about people who operate within our own culture without these trinkets? In cases such as these, *can* disparate experiences translate? Can people who speak different technological languages communicate?

This is the part of the essay where I fear I will fail in my goal of shedding some new light on the topic of everyday technology and communication for all I can do is to restate the commonplaces—but perhaps this too can be helpful. Does the use of the telephone facilitate communication or do people meet less face-to-face and fail to seek one another out? Does a television (or ten) in every pub inhibit real conversation or serve as a stimulation and launching pad for discussion? Does video isolate everyone in their homes, preventing them from venturing out to the cinema, or serve as an excuse for them to convene with others, view a film together, and then discuss it? Does the Internet link millions of people or only accelerate and facilitate misinformation, misinterpretation, misunderstanding? Perhaps we should ask, Does a solid community have to exist first, which can later be enhanced by technology, or can technology really create community, really generate true—and new—forms of communication?

Tools and Art, Ellen E. Berry, Department of English. Any technology is a tool, and tools are prosthetic devices, ways of extending the capacities of the body and moving us beyond our physical limitations. So a rock becomes a hammer to protect the hand, which would otherwise be incapable of pounding corn into cornmeal. Human consciousness and behavior are undeniably altered through the intervention of technology. In fact we might claim that the history of civilization is inseparable from the invention of various technologies, whose purpose has always been to extend the capacities of the human body over time and place.

Was there a second use of technology present from the beginning? Did our ancestors use rocks not only to pound corn into cornmeal or to kill animals but also to decorate their huts with small piles of stones that became sculptures? When and how did tools move from pragmatic instrumental objects to become conduits of creative expression? What can we learn about the complex and multiple histories of human creative expressions by looking at the technologies through which creativity ultimately had to be expressed? Do particular technologies open specific kinds of creativity, and thus do genuinely new art forms only arise when new technologies are developed? What is the sequence here?

The computer is perhaps the most recent example of a dramatically new technology, one originally invented for purely instrumental uses (and military ones at that; violence and the exercise of power through technology would be another angle on this topic). Yet the computer has, almost from the first, been used for artistic purposes as well. Computer art has had to go through the same process of acceptance that other new art forms have had to. I am reminded of how people considered photography and cinema to be illegitimate art when they first were invented. Their invention also raises the question of relations among the development of new technologies, the emergence of new art forms, and the resulting impact of these new technologically assisted arts on our perception of older art forms. Walter Benjamin wrote about the waning of the artwork's "aura" (a kind of unique artistic presence) in the face of the possibility that art could suddenly be reproduced mechanically, made in multiple copies—the emergence of Xerox-consciousness and the loss of absolute, one-of-a-kind artistic uniqueness. The shock of these new art forms—photography and cinema—has long passed, and the computer—computer-generated art—is now the site where we are working through these issues and anxieties concerning relations between the human and the technological—the human enhanced. The artist is now "assisted" by the computer, or the computer actually generates the art. Where is the artist in all this? Has the human element disappeared in creativity to be replaced by the machine itself? With the computer, have we invented a technology that—because it is a model of the human mind—will ultimately usurp the human as creator?

All these techno-fears and science-fiction scenarios. Can thought go on without a body, as Lyotard asks? Can artistic expression? Or has the human creative capacity always been so dependent on technology that it is inseparable from it, and in our demand to be recognized as individual creators, have we repressed and ignored this fact?

Improvisations at Emory University
Compiled by Mikhail Epstein[2]

Invitation

"On Saturday, February 28, 1998, the Center for Language, Literature, and Culture of Emory University is sponsoring a Collective Improvisation or 'experiment in dialogical thinking.' Such experiments were conducted in the 1980s in Moscow by our colleague Mikhail Epstein at the Center for Experimental Creativity; Mikhail has since staged them at other universities in this country. The CLLC would like to bring this unique form of interdisciplinary exchange to our own campus.

We are seeking between seven and fifteen participants willing to devote several hours to the following exercise. Each member of the group will propose a topic, out of which one will be chosen by negotiation. An hour or so will be devoted to individual writing on the chosen topic, followed by individual reading and group discussion of each essay. Participants should be prepared to improvise on any topic, including the trivia of everyday life, from the angles of their professional discipline, personal experience, or philosophical worldview. They are also invited to become specialists in alternative, virtual, or nonexistent disciplines. We plan to include graduate students as well as faculty, once we hear back from those of you who are interested.

This improvisational session is what might be called a metaphysical assault on everyday things. It can also be identified with the task Richard Rorty has set for thinkers of the future: to be "all purpose intellectuals . . . ready to offer a view on pretty much anything, in the hope of making it hang together with everything else."

Protocol

Topics suggested:

frogs
food
bridges
dreams
ocean and islands
email and typos
wilderness
tragical and comical elements of one's profession

Selected by the majority: Frogs.
Duration of writing: one hour.
Duration of the entire session: 10 A.M.-4:30 P.M.

The Royalty of Frogs, Walter L. Reed, Department of English. When I was young, maybe thirteen, and in that awkward, amphibious stage of development known as adolescence, I was cast by my mother in a neighborhood play called *The Frog Prince*. It was an adaptation of the fairy tale, whose source I don't remember. My mother had abandoned a fledgling career as an actress in New York when she got married and started having children, and she was beginning to exercise her theatrical talents on those children and their friends.

I will leave on the psychoanalyst's couch the confusion of feelings evoked by my mother's directing me as the hero in a play in which I was to be kissed into human form and royal inheritance by the girl next door (well, a mile or so away—we lived in the country) on whom I had my first teenage crush. What I would like to present to this gathering of stand-up intellectuals is my sense that the myth or legend or metaphor of the subhuman frog becoming the highest form of humanity (assuming that you are not too radical a democrat to deny the metaphorical appeal of kingship) is an interesting one. I guess I'd like to say that it seems to have spiritual implications. The frog-in-waiting was once the legitimate heir; he got turned into a swamp creature by that ubiquitous figure of evil, the evil step-mother (if I remember the plot); and he could only be restored to his original condition by a non-wicked helper (of the female persuasion) willing to overcome a deep-seated human revulsion and extend an act of creaturely charity, so that he could be retransfigured.

I have the feeling that I'm still back on the psychoanalyst's couch, but never mind. I will persist in my project of spiritual allegory, in the medieval Christian tradition of "Ovid Moralisée." I'm firmly resisting the temptation to the modern absurdist tradition of Kafka's rewritten legends, in which the would-be deliverer would be magically transformed into the frog princess and the couple would live disconsolately ever after in the petit-bourgeois swamp. Resisting, I say, the gravitational attraction of the Kafkaesque version, I want to offer a lighter and brighter interpretation. To wit:

The frog prince—or princess (we can surely allow more inclusive language here)—may be said to represent the human soul, which knows that its inheritance and its destiny are more aesthetically appealing than its present green and slimy condition.

The princess—or prince—redeemer represents another human soul, its otherness perhaps simply figured as a difference in gender, who is willing to descend from its higher plane in an act of charity that requires an experience of the unpleasant or the disgusting.

The restitution and happy ending represent the psychic community or fellowship on which psychic identity depends.

Here endeth the lesson.

Though if I were Percy Shelley, the English romantic poet I have been reading too much of recently, I would probably want to add another chapter. (Shelley finished his great closet drama *Prometheus Unbound* in three acts, but couldn't resist adding a fourth act, which has not usually been greeted with acclaim.) Act IV: Inspired by the example of Prince Froggie Unbound, the whole swamp community joins in the amphibious human-potential movement. Everything, from the methane gas bubbles in the mud to the white egrets perched on the top of the branches of the cypress trees festooned with Spanish moss, breaks into song, grows legs, and begins a joyful line dance heading toward the royal palace.

Tune in next week, when we will hear the prince call out, "Dear, I think you need to set a few more places for dinner."

Any resemblance between characters in this work of fiction and actual creatures living or dead is purely coincidental.

* * *

Frog Wars, Rosemary M. Magee, College of Arts and Sciences. I despise frogs.

In fact, even more seriously, I object to frogs. Admittedly I know little about them. For instance, what is the difference between a frog and a toad? For some reason I tend to think of a frog as green and a toad as brown. But it has got to be more than that.

I don't want to know.

As much as I would like to meet a prince, it is important to state: I would never, never, never kiss a frog. Although I did eat frog legs one summer night. It was a time of wild abandon. Despite their many interesting qualities, I do not wish to live with frogs or be one in another life. I stayed out sick from school the day we were to dissect frogs in biology. For all these reasons and more, I am intending to inaugurate an anti-frog campaign. We will stamp out frogs, eliminate them from the face of the earth by putting them all in a spacecraft and blasting them into the next galaxy.

This effort will be interdisciplinary and international in scope. Physicists, biologists, psychologists, and mythologists will unite in a worldwide attempt to evacuate frogs from this planet. Naturally, in opposition, there will be a pro-frog contingent: environmentalists who wear green baseball caps and argue for the critical place of frogs in the ecosystem, animal rights advocates who maintain the individual sanctity of frog life, and little boys all across the land who regularly conspire with frogs. The dawn of the twenty-first century will bring with it the first of several frog wars.

You may wonder why it is I object so strenuously to frogs. As you would expect, these feelings are deeply embedded in the early stages of my cognitive and emotional development.

As a child I learned to avoid those little boys who put frogs down the backs of the dresses of little girls who wore their hair in braids and read books at lunchtime about adventurers: stories about Laura Ingalls, Pippi Longstocking, Jo March, Anne of Green Gables. These heroic girls also had their own frog trials and tribulations. Like them, I felt certain I knew the kind of men the frog boys would become. They were the ones who tricked people, who scared women. With frogs, they invaded other people's private spaces, somehow wanting to hold them in their power. Bill Clinton was among them, no doubt their leader. Thus frogs seem part of a masculine world I don't fully understand. They occupy a mysterious cosmos, although not necessarily a mean-spirited or ugly one.

These strong feelings are hard for me to reconcile in my life right now because I have a little boy who would like nothing better than to covertly install a frog on his big sister's pillow. I know he contemplates his strategy daily. He observes her feminine ways, her nocturnal habits, her state of mind, to determine just the right time and place to strike with frog in hand. He knows there will be serious repercussions, but he is prepared to live with the threat of retaliation for that one brief moment of joy her outraged shriek will provide.

This boy, who forgets to bring home his science book the night before a test, who cannot find his shoes in the morning and thereby misses the schoolbus, has focused the full powers of his concentration on the task before him. He searches for frogs in the creek behind our house by day. He reads up on their life cycles by night. He arranges frog-jumping contests with neighbors. He hops around in odd ways as if to get in touch with his own frog essence.

I am afraid to enter my son's room as I never know what I might find there. Possibly petrified frog droppings. The skeleton of a starving or heartsick frog, bereft of his frog family and natural niche. Or a nest of baby tadpoles who will expect me to care for them in ways I do not understand. And cannot fulfill.

These frogs are otherworldly, possessed of mythical attributes, engaging in amphibious antics. They do not belong in a civilized, structured, orderly world. Through their otherness and unpredictability, they shake my sense of who I am and what is supposed to happen and how life is to unfold. We have nothing in common, these frogs and I. And that is why they should go and I should stay. I will win these frog wars. With this triumph will come much satisfaction and a sense of accomplishment. A job well done. Order restored in my household and on the planet.

And what about my little boy, you ask. How will he cope? What new possibilities will capture his energy and imagination? As his mother I will teach him about the ways of the world. Life and his place in it. He is something much greater and better and larger and more majestic than a lowly, warty, scaly, gnarled, hyperactive frog. We've already had this conversation once at the breakfast table. Along with Pop Tarts and Lucky Charms, I fed him a logical discourse on the fallacies of frogs. To which he simply replied "ribbet" and happily hopped away.

Frogs On The Go, Raymond C. Ganga. Frogs don't move quickly over land for a long distance. In Britain nature lovers got highway engineers to change plans for a road by constructing tunnels and bridges to allow for frog and toad migrations because frog road kill not only was loathsome but became a traffic hazard.

One reason it seems to me that the Budweiser commercials are amusing is the contrast between a normal frog's movements and what happens when the frog's tongue sticks to a passing beer truck and doesn't let go. The frog takes flight, to our delight—a possible metaphor for our own liberation from being earthbound—a common if not universal dream.

In the water, however, frogs assume more grace. The limbs elongate after each kick to accentuate the hydrodynamic shape of the whole body, a shape at once aesthetic and functional. This shape, of course, evokes a frog's tadpole beginnings, appearing perfectly streamlined. This ability to move from one medium to another gives a freedom to frogs but at the potential price of multiplying predator enemies—snakes and raptors, for example—who would like nothing better than a frog meal.

In the rural south, particularly, young boys, perhaps the premier frog predator, spend a lot of time "gigging" frogs, i.e. planting a spike in the end of a stick to jab into a frog's spine just in back of the head to see how many can be spiked on one nail at a time. The ostensible reason is for food—frog legs—but the real reason is probably deeper, with many levels, not least some relationship to the wilderness in all of us.

But it is in the transitions of a frog's life that the notion of movement and change are most evident—beginning life as an egg, which hatches (as a reptile or bird might); emerging as a tadpole with gills and a tail, prey to his neighbors; and finally going through a metamorphosis into a creature capable of living and moving on land, sans tail, and now a recognized predator in its own right, of insects. These transitions match the movement from water to land, from "oceans to islands," as it were, and in this sense a frog leads a picaresque kind of life.

One can see in all this both the "tragedy and comedy" of a frog's existence—a cute, bumptious, awkward, nubbly, green creature that can evoke both humor and interest, on the one hand, and fear and loathing, on the other when, you suddenly meet up with a frog where it is least expected. Frogs are also thought of as slimy and as vectors of disease, a gross calumny more characteristic of their toad cousins. And, of course, the ultimate transition in frog fairy tales is the transformation of the frog to a prince, a perfect change from ugly to handsome. It might be possible to recast the riddle of the sphinx with a frog in mind—what goes on no legs when young, four legs in middle age, and ends up as road kill or prey? And not only as road kill or prey because in our world of increasing pollution and global warming, frogs are also now becoming a universal symbol, like songbirds, of the coming crisis. Frog populations and species are declining throughout the world, a possible harbinger of our own fate.

I don't know if I could imagine life as a frog. The Beatles sing, "I'd like to be / Under the sea / In an Octopus's garden in the shade," and I can imagine frog neighbors stopping by for tea in this kind of a world. But my imagination is necessarily human-bound, and lends itself to metaphors more like those of Lewis Carroll, whose frogs are messengers for the Red King and Queen. To actually know the cool green underwater life as a frog (even for the kind of underwater navy personnel formerly known as "frogmen") or to know the hopping, lurching life on land, warming a cold-blooded body on a rock and looking up at the bottom of leaves in the same way as those bulging frog eyes do, is forever beyond us. We could only grope toward this experience as toward some Platonic ideal of frogginess. The achievement of such an exercise is in the effort; the being is the doing, and the benefit, ultimately, is in what we learn about ourselves.

To be judgmental and personal, I also know I'd rather not be a frog. Frogs don't do email, a metaphor for a wider range of experiences frogs can never know. I heard Gary Snyder, a noted poet, give a commencement address at Reed College in Portland, Oregon, in which he used the "wilderness" as a theme and urged respect and love for animals and stressed the need to develop "trans-species eroticism," a theme that he did not elaborate, but I'm sure he was not referring to baser instincts but more to a true love of nature. This is something we can achieve.

In the end, though, when I think of frogs I return to death as a theme. A classic underground short film known as *The Trouble with Fred* is based on increasingly close pictures of a wooded pond with reeds and rocks. As we get closer we see a frog on one rock, and as we get closer yet we see the frog is dead and shriveled in the sun. The final caption reads, "The trouble with Fred? He's dead!" The audience all laughs, of course, which once again underlines the comic and tragic nature of frogs. In that sense, I suppose, they are exactly like us.

Frog In a Well, P. Venugopala Rao, Department of Physics. I have always asked myself this question many times—why I am confined to this place full of water, weeds, worms, and whatnot? I confronted everyone I've met with this question and no one seems to know the answer. These vertical walls surrounding me sometimes scare me. I remember the little one that tried to climb along the walls, hanging desperately with its legs and hands holding on to the slippery surface.

The old green frog spoke to me one day and told me an interesting story. I still think it is a story, but the old frog thinks that it is the truth and what really happened. "In the beginning it was all water, pure and distilled, surrounded by smooth vertical walls of infinite height. Then a disturbance appeared mysteriously in the waters. Its source is a tiny speck. The speck grew immensely in size, for how long we do not know. After a long time it became a huge thing. As it lay motionless in the waters it began to think and dream. It decided to divide into smaller parts, each small part becoming a different kind of thing, of different size and color. We are all descendants of that great one. We call it Frog, because it gave us the life we have. It sacrificed itself by dismemberment so that we can all 'become' and 'be.' Its spirit lives in us. We live and think because of its existence that exists in us. There are no frogs here that are not part of that primordial Frog. We are like the Great Frog except we do not dismember ourselves to multiply. One of our ancestors made a great discovery. It showed us that all we have to do to multiply is to lay eggs and let the eggs become frogs. It was a moment of great excitement in our frog world. That discoverer is the one whom we remember whenever floods come. We call him Creator. We save as many eggs as possible in the nooks and corners, here and there."

I interrupted the old frog and asked it why we have floods and how often they come. It got annoyed a little bit. It did not want to answer that question. It simply mumbled, "They come now and then." As an afterthought it added, "Maybe the Great Frog knew." It appeared to me that the old frog is afraid of the flood.

One of the frogs that spends most of its time in a hole in the wall above the water line told me about a flood it had witnessed. "There was a sudden rush of waters pouring down from all sides. Before anyone realized, the waters rose so high that many of our frogs began to be washed away. Only the few that were able to hang on to the walls survived. After that flood I found it safer to live in this hole."

I never liked the frogs who live in their holes. I am young. I jump up and down a lot. I spend most of my time above the water surface. Several seasons ago, a tiny frog fell among us from up above. It must have jumped or flew in from someplace. Nobody understood what it said. It could not survive. The waters were too much for it. The old frog who was there when it happened thought that the tiny frog was trying to tell us something to the effect that there are a lot of frogs like it out there. The old frog, of course, dismissed the idea that there is anything called "out there."

The old frog is a good friend of mine. But I do not like its attitude. I am scared by the way it talks sometimes. If there is no where else, we are trapped forever in this place. But why do I get the feeling that we can leave this place? The images of that tiny frog that fell in our place haunt me. If only I can jump out!

The old frog says, "This is our universe. We have everything we need here". I do not think so. Certainly this place does not have everything I want, because I feel that I want something more. Why do I feel like wanting something else? I cannot explain this feeling.

There must be other universes. I call this place a "well." I joke about it a lot. I tell all my friends, "We are frogs in one well." There may be many more wells in a big universe. The old frog one day overheard this joke, got angry, and shouted at me, "Prove it, if you think so." But how can I, if I cannot get out of this place? Maybe one day somebody will discover how to fly away or maybe a great flood will come and carry me away into the universe out there. I pray for a flood.

All the other creatures that live among us seem to have no sense of feeling. No intelligence. They lead a dull and routine life. I think a superfrog will be born among us to create a new sense of being and connect us to the rest of the universe.

I think that is what the old frog secretly wishes too. It meditates a lot. Only the Great Frog knows what it does or thinks. But I keep praying for a flood. Isn't it wonderful to think that we live in a well, inside a well, inside a well . . . in a big universe. Awesome!

Notes

1. More extensive samples of various sessions are presented on the Web site devoted to collective improvisations: http://www.emory.edu/INTELNET/impro_home.html.
2. I want to thank Professor Walter Reed of the English department for organizing and chairing this session.

Chapter 19

Nomads at Home: Improvisation in the Academy
Ellen E. Berry

Improvisation as a Practice of Everyday Life

As do certain aleatory or chance techniques, the improvisational has had a long history in twentieth-century avant-garde art—from surrealist and dada experiments to the situationists to the music of John Cage—and may be considered part of an avant-garde commitment to joining art and everyday life in a process of mutual interaction and transformation. This improvisational tendency also may be considered part of a performative modality that defines reality in terms of process, flow, interaction, play, and participation, and that has been called the unifying mode of the postmodern. As a root metaphor or model, performance finds parallel expression in a variety of art forms and in the boundary breaks between forms. Performative works promote the values of immediacy, spontaneity, change, openness, transitoriness. They are less aesthetic objects than generating environments or open-ended fields of action that promote the intrinsic value of the improvisational experience itself rather than any product or object that may result from it.

But improvisation also is one of the practices of everyday life, what Michel deCerteau calls simply "ways of operating or doing things," the commonplace or taken-for-granted practices that form the "obscure background of [all] social activity." In *The Practice of Everyday Life,* deCerteau studies not cultural artifacts themselves or the systems that produce them, but rather the "dispersed, devious, silent" ways consumers improvise with the building blocks of culture that are given to or imposed on them: "Users are bricoleurs who make innumerable and infinitesimal transformations of and within the dominant cultural economy in order to adapt it to their own interests and their own rules." deCerteau's study illuminates the procedures, bases, effects, and possibilities of these collective, nearly invisible, transformations that constitute the arts of the powerless: "the clandestine forms taken by the dispersed, tactical, and makeshift creativity of groups or individuals already caught in the nets of 'discipline.' "[1]

He studies as well the ways these ordinary practices insinuate themselves into philosophical thought, analytic techniques, and systems of all kinds (and in the process work to undermine their solidity). Official culture operates according to strategies that produce things (knowledge, people, products) for profit and power. It is rational, expansionist, spectacular. As deCerteau puts it, a strategy refers to "the calculation . . . of power relationships. . . . It postulates a place that can be delimited as its own and serve as the base from which relations with an exteriority composed of targets or threats (customers or competitors, enemies, the country surrounding the city, objectives and objects of research, etc.) can be managed. . . . [Strategies involve] an effort to delimit one's own place in a world bewitched by the invisible powers of the other. . . ." For deCerteau, strategies constitute a specific kind of knowledge and power that is rational, empiricist, and scientific; they also are actions that, because they operate from an established place of power, engender theoretical systems and totalizing discourses capable of being deployed from the array of physical places in which forces are distributed.[2]

Whereas strategies are organized by the postulation and dissemination of power, tactics are defined by the absence of power. They lack a proper, legitimate place that would act to delimit them; instead, they are calculated actions that find myriad ways and opportunities to use, manipulate, and divert the omnipresence of official places and power. Strategies function in this way partly because the arts of everyday life operate according to different styles of social exchange, technical invention, and moral resistance than do the dominant orders that enclose them: "an economy of the 'gift' . . . an esthetics of 'tricks' (artists' operations), and an ethics of *tenacity* (countless ways of refusing to accord the established order the status of a law, a meaning, or a fatality)."[3] They introduce excess and waste into systems designed for efficiency; they reject profit as a motive for action; they fail to respect the sanctity of private property.

As a result, these multiple, mutable ruses of everyday life, their countless ways of using systems, constitute for deCerteau an invisible history of resistance to the law that has persisted through the institutions of successive political orders. Because these practices introduce a certain play into official institutions and create spaces for the manipulations of unequal forces, they become, for deCerteau, utopian points of reference. Consistent with Appadurai's findings about uses of the imagination in contemporary global culture, deCerteau predicts that the continued expansion of technocratic rationality will lead not to a diminishment but to an explosive growth in the circulation of these tactics, precisely because the space of global capitalism is becoming at once more homogeneous and more extensive: "Cut loose from the traditional communities that circumscribed their functioning, [these tactics] have begun to wander everywhere in a space which is . . . too vast to be able to fix them in one place, but too constraining for them ever to be able to escape from it and go into exile elsewhere. There is no longer an elsewhere." And, because the essence of the tactics of everyday life resides in their mobility, flexibility, and adaptability (which they share with the critical nomadism outlined in a previous chapter), deCerteau predicts an endless proliferation of them over an ever-wider sphere: "myriads of almost invisible movements, playing on the more and more refined texture of a place that is even, continuous, and constitutes a proper place for all people."[4]

Although deCerteau focuses in *The Practice of Everyday Life* primarily on the "arts of the weak," in the end he calls for us all—whatever our institutional location—to become tricksters, gift-givers, and *les perruques* (those who disguise their own work as work for their employer, who "put one over" on the established order on its home ground). *Les perruques* practice forms of economic diversion that, deCerteau argues, mark in reality the return of a sociopolitical ethics into systems that have abandoned them:

> Let us try to make a *perruque* in the economic system whose rules and hierarchies are repeated, as always, in scientific institutions. In the area of scientific research (which defines the current order of knowledge), working with its machines and making use of its scraps, we can divert the time owed to the institution; we can make textual objects that signify an art and solidarities; we can play the game of free exchange, even if it is penalized by bosses and colleagues when they are not willing to 'turn a blind eye' on it; we can create networks of connivances and sleights of hand; we can exchange gifts; and in these ways we can subvert the law that, in the scientific factory, puts work at the service of

the machine and, by a similar logic, progressively destroys the requirement of creation and the 'obligation to give.'⁵

Practicing the arts of everyday life in the heart of an institution would result in a return of the ethical, of pleasure, and of free invention within that institution. Ultimately such practices might act to transform the intellectual practices through which we have come to operate and to reorganize the place from which official discourse is produced.

Nomads at Home: Improvisation in the Academy

In this section, I want to draw on deCerteau's theory in order to extend previous discussions of the nature, uses, and effects of improvisation. (Because it combines creativity and communication, improvisation, as Epstein defines it, might be seen as a conjunction of art and everyday life—though not precisely in the sense meant by the historical avant-gardes.) I will do so by taking the contemporary U.S. academy as a site within which improvisational practices might intervene if not as a wholly subversive force then at least as disruptive of "business as usual"—the corporate economy through which the academy as an institution increasingly has come to function.

Of course, the original Russian context of intellectual production within which improvisational techniques first developed differs markedly from the current context of intellectual production in the United States (and undoubtedly from the current Russian context as well). As Epstein recounts it, improvisations developed among intellectuals who were neither part of official cultural institutions nor pointedly opposed to them as in dissident culture. Instead, these groups were composed of intellectuals from among the many loose, decentered, unofficial communities that had for years worked in the margins of official culture, those brilliant dilettantes most of whom had been unable to exercise their talents in a professional application. Moreover, the perestroika moment during which formation of semi-official institutions such as the Laboratory of Contemporary Culture became possible was itself a transitional, liminal moment, an improvisational moment if you will, in which official culture began to crumble from the weight of its own internal contradictions, and it was anybody's guess what might come next so anything seemed possible. Finally, it is perhaps understandable that improvisation as something of a privileged method would have developed in the Soviet Union since the arts of making do, of tricking the system, of improvising with the materials one found available, were so much a means of day-to-day survival. As Svetlana Boym states in her brilliant study of Russian everyday mythologies and rituals of ordinary life, *Common Places,* "In Russia the history of relations between culture and nation, art and life, society and individual, public and private, commodity and trash, often diverges from familiar Western European or American versions of modernity." In demonstrating this thesis, she elaborates those many unwritten laws of everyday existence, everyday aesthetic experiences, and alternative spaces carved on the margins of official discourses in Russia.[6]

By contrast, the United States academy increasingly produces knowledge as a commodity sold for profit to customers (our students) whose business must be retained in an ever-more-competitive academic marketplace. Students demand that ideas have pragmatic applicability, a demand expressed immediately in terms of individual classes ("Will this be on the test?") as well as in terms of translatability into long-range cash value ("Will this major get me a good job?"). The ideals of knowledge pursued for its own sake, intellectual play, and speculation seem like quaint anachronisms that become harder and harder to justify even to ourselves—not to mention to our students, to academic administrators, to Boards of Regents, and to the general public, all of whom demand that we be ever-more-narrowly accountable for the work that we do and ever more efficient in producing it. Competition for increasingly scarce resources often serves to discourage cooperation and may also reinforce disciplinary hierarchies. Even if we possess the inclination, there rarely is either the time or the opportunity for anything like a free exchange of ideas with our peers (perhaps this is why many of us are nostalgic about our graduate school experience); intellectual community is something we must go to conferences to experience, if it occurs there at all.

The commodification of our labor presupposes the commodification of our time. As Steven Connor puts it, paraphrasing Lyotard, the goal of the current system is literally to store up and control time: "In the economic structure of thought which dominates the world [including the world of the academy], any activity, event . . . in the present is considered as a form of loan, or investment, which must be paid back, or include within itself the fact of its economic return. . . ." (hence, the emphasis on "accountability" in the academy today). "Value, therefore, comes to consist . . . not in specific yields or products but in the very speed of the economic process itself—literally the 'rate' [time] of exchange rather than the objects of exchange." Anything that interrupts smooth operation of this principle of reason—"to rush to its goal with a minimum of delay"—is considered wasteful, nonproductive, a space in which "time remains uncontrolled, does not give rise to work, or at least not in the customary sense of the verb 'to work.' "[7]

Within the U.S. academy we are theoretically free to write and publish whatever we wish, and academic freedom is a value we vigorously defend (rightly so) as the very essence of our professional lives; however, our intellectual labor is also traded for profit, whether it be in the form of an annual merit raise; publication in a prestigious journal (the precondition for the raise); or, for the very few, a chance to compete in the academic star system (where bidding wars for hot "properties" sometimes begin to rival those involving professional athletes). At the very least, the growing corporatization of the academy and the knowledge-for-profit model make it increasingly unlikely that we actually will produce new ideas that stray outside dominant paradigms of what sells in the knowledge industry. This includes critiques of that industry; however radical or transgressive ideas may appear to be in print, however trenchant the critique of the knowledge-for-profit model itself, such ideas are easily recontained. It might be argued that the mechanisms I describe have always been in operation. While this may be true, I would claim that never has the gap between our ideals (what we say we profess) and the reality of our daily lives in the academy been more nakedly transparent. Never has the knowledge industry functioned more vigorously or efficiently, and never has the academy operated more as a hierarchized class system.

Insinuated into the space of the academy, improvisational practices may offer one way to disrupt—temporarily—the rules by which its dominant cultural economy currently functions. This is so in part because the goals and the results of these practices, as well as the interests and desires of those who participate in them, differ from the fundamental goals of the academy (to maintain competitiveness, profitability, and prestige through exchange of a product; to make time productive). The practice of improvisation does not produce consensus (a precondition for things moving forward) but rather activates and intensifies differences among participants, whether these be differences in disciplinary training, ideology, class position in the academy, etc. Since the improvisational setting and act conjoin creativity and communication (as Epstein discusses), improvisation also dismantles more fundamental divisions between public and private acts/spaces, performer and audience, individual and community, speech and silence, body and mind, known and unknown, intellect and emotion, spontaneity/immediacy and contemplation/deliberation, self and other. Improvisational practices of cothinking also introduce newness and unexpectedness into the academic setting—a kind of distance or estrangement from business as usual—since they do not work to transfer a known product from one consciousness to another (as in a lecture, a scholarly article, a committee report) but rather introduce the unpredictability of creativity (imagination) into a communicative situation. Because they operate using modes of communication and models of intellectual production that differ from those currently in operation within the academic system, because participation in improvisations is freely chosen with no apparent gain (profit), and because they take place within but to one side of proper academic spaces, they encourage formation of new intellectual identities (not experts or specialists but all-purpose intellectuals, as Epstein, paraphrasing Rorty, puts it) as well as new models of community—becoming, if you will, a therapeutics for deteriorating social relations within our intellectual communities.

Moreover, because improvisations typically take as their focus topics from ordinary life "belonging" to no one/everyone, they disrupt the rules of intellectual property rights or the individual ownership of ideas, a (perhaps the) cornerstone of the academic system. No one owns the products of the improvisation because they are trans-individual, radically collaborative texts with no proper place and no legitimate value in the academic system of exchange. In this respect, they make no sense; they are excessive and wasteful since they reject the profitable use of time as a motive for action. The ideas circulating in the improvisational setting are perhaps best thought of as gifts that participants freely exchange with one another according to a wholly different economy and ethical system (the "requirement of creation and the obligation to give," in deCerteau's words). Such an exchange—a kind of economic diversion—encourages pleasure in the wasteful time of speculation, what deCerteau calls "casual time," that causes a lapse in production and creates a "play in the machine by interfering with it."[8] In this regard, improvisations produce neither disciplinary nor interdisciplinary knowledge (despite the fact that participants do inevitably write from the perspective of particular backgrounds).

Improvisations share some features with the "epistemological slide" identified by Roland Barthes as a symptom and precondition of one (inter)discipline arising from within the limitations of another. But whereas even interdisciplines must limit this slide in order to constitute themselves, improvisations keep the slide ongoing, potentially infinitely. Thus, to some extent, improvisations make evident the arbitrariness of the boundaries that demarcate both disciplines and interdisciplines; they produce nondisciplinary or perhaps superdisciplinary knowledge (although they do take place within productive constraints). The ongoingness of improvisations is the ongoingness of thinking itself, which is also the inexhaustibility of writing and its tendency always to stray outside its proper place.

Places, Doreen Massey says, should not be understood as areas with boundaries but as "articulated moments in networks of social relations and understandings. . . . Places like people [may] have multiple identities."[9] Within the "proper" space of the academy, improvisations introduce new kinds of "articulated moments," new "networks of social relations," and, in the process, multiply the kinds of identities the academy might have. In making these claims for improvisational practices, however, I do not mean to suggest that they escape altogether the system of exchange and future utility through which the academy typically operates. Since practices of improvisation—as I've discussed them here—are resolutely situated within an institutional location, at the most they introduce a temporary delay into the system, "a kind of extension of the moment of uncertainty at which value is in the process of being decided . . . keeping open a space between present and future."[10] However, precisely because of this fact, introducing these practices into the classroom could be one method of questioning—collectively—the means by which knowledge is produced and valued both within and outside the academy, and how things might be configured differently. One could imagine such questioning taking place in a number of different types of classes: composition or creative writing classes, classes in the sociology of knowledge or on avant-garde practices in a postmodern moment or the history of the academy and its institutional validation of particular kinds of writing practices.

Improvisation as an approach to knowledge production also might serve as a basis for new models of structuring courses. Several years ago, for example, I organized an experimental graduate seminar that invited faculty from all over my university to offer one class lecture on some facet of the general topic "Cultural and Critical Spaces." Fifteen faculty members from eight different disciplines chose to participate, and thirty graduate students from six different majors enrolled in the class (which was cross-listed in each of eight "home" departments). Each week in the seminar a different aspect of the topic was introduced and elaborated by means of a lecture; these ranged from surveillance on the Internet, to the space of the Holocaust Museum in Washington, D.C., to Quebec as an emerging national space, to public memorials and spontaneous shrines in Northern Ireland. One goal of the class was to proliferate the number of meanings that "cultural and critical spaces" could have as a concept. Because of this there was—by design—no closure to the class, and the concept was even more nebulous (rich) at the end of our fifteen weeks than it was at the beginning. This lack of neat summation posed a problem for some of the students, chiefly because they felt—rightly so—that our evaluation of them by means of a traditional graded seminar paper seemed to violate the spirit of open experimentation through which the course had been organized. The difficulties raised by many participating faculty were—predictably—lack of time to attend all of the lectures (everyone was involved in the course in addition to their regular teaching load—no release time) and lack of institutional recognition and reward in terms of "credit" for their participation. Despite their difficulties, many students have since requested that such a course—with different topics—be offered on a regular basis; because of their difficulties, few faculty are willing to commit themselves to another round of the seminar—despite their enthusiasm for the idea behind it.

Improvisational practices also might be used in a more directed way as a problem-solving method. Having served on more "University Task Force on X" committees than I care to think about, I know that committee work (university service) is the academic site most resistant to innovation, perhaps because it is most nakedly concerned with perpetuating the institutional status quo (here we're in the heart of the beast, so to speak). Rather than follow typical committee procedure, however, the task force could function as an improvisational community with aspects of the "charge to the committee" forming the basis of multiple improvisational sessions. It might even be interesting to submit a collection of all the improvisations as the task force report, thereby signaling a refusal to tidy up complex thinking into the typical bulleted list of recommendations. Even as I write this, however, I am reminded of Jameson's comments concerning the ways in which a rhetoric of innovation is used in a postmodern moment as a cover for reproduction of the same, for lack of substantial change. Despite this fact, it remains true that the American university system is changing in significant ways at this moment in history, is being forced at the risk of obsolescence to move "outside the box" (as our provost puts it in a wonderful and glaring translation of market speak), to adapt to the changing conditions of a global information economy with its constant demand for highly skilled workers. Because the university system is in a state of flux, however, this historical moment presents one of the best opportunities to intervene within that system. Improvisational techniques and practices as I've presented them here suggest one small means of intervention since they are tactics that create modes of opening—pliable, fluid, and yet shaped through an organizing structure—modes that might act as counters to institutional solidities and strategies.

Resources of the Transcultural Imagination

The method and practice of improvisation involve nothing more and nothing less than the production of possibilities: Given sufficient time, opportunity, and people, potentially endless variations on a single theme are possible. In this respect, the process of improvising is more important than any of the actual products that might result from this process. What seems most essential at this moment in cultural history is that we find ways to engage with the modality "What if?," with Bloch's realm of the possible, that which can be redetermined or done otherwise in all determinations. In doing so, we enter into a process of becoming in relation to others, and our intellectual communities become spaces of free experimentation, spaces that are opened to their own unfolding rather than to a particular goal or telos. And participating in this process of becoming is perhaps one conduit to *what* is becoming or approaching (Bloch's terms for the future, for newness). As thinkers, we need imaginative encouragement to feel and act differently; we need modes of opening in our critical thinking, ways of animating possibilities within current structures of knowledge and the critical impasses they so often lead us to. The improvisational—as a practice that borrows from everyday life—generates intellectual movement, mobility, and flexibility. It positions us in a heterotopic space between what is emerging and what might become. As such, improvisation—as I have elaborated it here—is one other aspect of a nomadic critical practice and one vital resource of the transcultural imagination.

Notes

1. Michel deCerteau, *The Practice of Everyday Life,* trans. Steven F. Randall (Berkeley: University of California Press, 1984): xi, xii–xiv, xiv–xv.
2. Ibid., 35–36, 38.
3. Ibid., 26.
4. Ibid., 40–41.
5. Ibid., 27–28.

6. Svetlana Boym, *Common Places: Mythologies of Everyday Life in Russia* (Cambridge, MA: Harvard University Press, 1994): 2–3.
7. Steven Connor, "Between Earth and Air: Value, Culture and Futurity," in Jon Bird et al., eds., *Mapping the Futures: Local Cultures, Global Change* (New York: Routledge, 1993): 233.
8. deCerteau, 30.
9. Doreen Massey, "Power-geometry and a Progressive Sense of Place," in Bird et al., 66.
10. Connor, in Bird et al., 234.

Chapter 20

Hyperauthorship: The Case of Araki Yasusada[1]
Mikhail Epstein

Preamble

If collective improvisation is a project of spontaneous interaction and the integration of many minds, then hyperauthorship presents an opposite vector of creative communication: the splitting of one author into many potential authorial personalities.

The work of Araki Yasusada (1903–72) has appeared in numerous publications lately and has provoked a good deal of discussion in the world of poetry. I say "world" because poets and critics are avidly speculating about the work in the United States, England, Japan, Russia, Italy, Australia, and Mexico, where selections and critical commentary started to appear in the 1990s. It is understandable why the Yasusada phenomenon has caused such fascination and controversy, for it is, without doubt, one of the most enigmatic and provocative authorial mysteries of twentieth-century poetry.[2]

Originally presented in various journals as translations from the posthumously discovered notebooks of Yasusada, a purported survivor of the bombing of Hiroshima, the writing has recently been revealed by its "caretakers," Kent Johnson and Javier Alvarez (two individuals whose existence is empirically verifiable), as the creation of their former and now deceased roommate, Tosa Motokiyu, who has been credited in all previous publications as the main "translator" of Yasusada's work. Johnson and Alvarez assert that Tosa Motokiyu is the hypernym for an author whose actual identity they are under instructions never to reveal.

I came into contact with this work through two fortuitous occurrences, first in 1990 and then in 1995; but it was in January of 1996 that I became more intimate with it, when I received a letter and a package of Yasusada materials from Motokiyu, who explained that he had been urged by "our mutual friend" Kent Johnson and his own interest in my recent book, *After the Future,* to write to me. In this letter he acknowledged himself to be the empirical writer of the Yasusada materials, and he asked for my thoughts on the implications inherent in such a scrambling of authorial identities. I wrote him back a lengthy reply, only to learn from Kent Johnson in the summer of 1996 that he had died not long after receiving my letter.

1. *A Letter to a Japanese Friend*[3]

To Tosa Motokiyu
from Mikhail Epstein
February 6, 1996

Dear Tosa Motokiyu:
Thank you for your letter and rich materials that I will certainly go through with great interest. I've been so inspired by some of your suggestions that I don't want to delay my response.

Why couldn't we establish an International Society (or Network) of Transpersonal Authorship? We could invite for membership those people who feel themselves overwhelmed by different (and multiple) authorial personalities who wish to be realized through their transpersonal creative endeavors. This writing in the mode of otherness is not just a matter of a pseudonym, but rather of a hypernym. We don't produce our own works under different names but we produce works different from our own under appropriate names.

This is a crucial issue in contemporary theory and writing. Poststructuralism has pronounced a death sentence for the individual author(ship), but does this mean that we are doomed to return to a pre-literary stage of anonymity? One cannot enter twice the same river, and anonymity in its post-authorial, not pre-authorial, implementation will turn into something different from folklore anonymity. What would be, then, a progressive, not retrospective, way out of the crisis of individual authorship? Not anonymity, I believe, but hyperauthorship.

There is so much talk about hypertexts now. But what about hyperauthors? This question has not even been raised. Hyperauthorship is a paradigmatic variety of authors working within the confines of one (allegedly one) human entity. A hyperauthor relates to an author as a hypertext relates to a text. Hypertext is dispersed among numerous virtual spaces that can be entered in any order, escaping any linear (temporal or causal) coherence. Hyperauthorship is dispersed among several virtual personalities that cannot be reduced to a single "real" personality.[4]

As thinking is always thinking "of," without necessary specification of the object, writing is always "writing by," but this "by-ness" of writing cannot be reduced to any biological, or historical, or psychological subject. To follow Husserl who called this "of-ness" of thinking "intentionality," we can call this "by-ness" of writing "potentionality" that does not need to be biographically actualized or can be actualized in multiple figures and persona. The same writing can be potentially ascribed to various authors, which intensifies the play of its meanings and interpretations. In traditional literary theory, the author is a real individual or a group of individuals, but this is an outmoded way of thinking that can be compared with the conceptual framework of physics before the advent of quantum mechanics. The latter showed that we cannot pinpoint a particle with any specificity in time and space; it is a fuzzy phenomenon, embracing the aspects of discreteness and continuity, a particle as well as a wave. What I am discussing now is precisely the concept of "fuzzy," or "continuumlike" authorship, which refers not to a discrete personality but rather to a wave going across times, places, and personalities. Tosa Motokiyu and Araki Yasusada are some of the observable locations of this hyperauthorial wave that can reach the shores of other epochs, countries, and strange personalities. Hyperauthorship is virtual authorship in which real personalities become almost illusionary, while fictional personalities become almost real. This "almost" is what allows them to coexist on the same continuum in the imaginations of readers. Leo Tolstoy said, "In art, the 'almost' [*chut'-chut'*] is everything." This concerns not only the matter of artistic representation, but also its mode of authorization.

Previously the author was interesting to the degree that his/her personality could illuminate the text and be instrumental in its understanding. This tendency culminated in the widely announced "death of the author" by virtue of which the text became a self-sufficient and self-enclosed entity. Now I am inclined to think that a text is interesting only inasmuch as it manifests the multiple, infinite possibilities of its authorship. What we should enunciate, perhaps on behalf of several authors, like Tosa Motokiyu, Araki Yasusada, and Ivan Solovyov, is the resurrection of authorship after its death, this time in the wavy, misty, radiant flesh of prolific hyperauthorship, no more coinciding with the mortal animal flesh of a separate biological individual.

We have moved far beyond the concept of biological parenthood which is now recognized as only one of many forms of parenthood. Now let's have done with the reductive concept of authorship as only "biological" authorship limited by the input of the author as a living individual. There are many sorts and degrees of nonbiological—psychological, intellectual, inspirational, magical—authorship. The question is how to differentiate these numerous authorships related to a single piece of writing, without hierarchical subordination of one to another. In what sense and in what respect are Yasusada's pieces authored by Tosa Motokiyu, and in what respect are Motokiyu's pieces authored by Araki Yasusada? This is the adequate way to question post-individual or transpersonal authorship, not just to ask, Who is the real author of this work, Motokiyu or Yasusada?

There is a principal asymmetry and disproportion between living and writing individuals in the world. It's evident that not all living individuals have either the inclination or the capacity to become authors. Some individuals cannot write or can only write checks and holiday cards. This renders quite plausible the complementary statement: not all authors have either the inclination or the capacity to become living individuals. There are many authors who, for certain reasons (which need further exploration), have no potential for physical embodiment, as there are many individuals who for some related reasons have no propensity for becoming authors. This implies that some living individuals, who have a potential for writing, must shelter or adopt a number of potential authors within their biological individualities. What awaits actualization in the writing of one individual is the potentiality of many authors—those creative individuals who have no need or taste for living, in the same way as many living individuals have no need or taste for writing.

The deficiency of previous theories was to confuse these two aspects of writing, a biological individual and an authorial personality. Poststructuralist theory contributed to the solution of this question only negatively, by denying the attributes of a creative author to a biological individual. What logically follows is that we should also deny the attributes of a biological individual to a creative author. We have to split these naive equations of the naturalistic fallacy. But we also have to proceed beyond the limits of this twofold denial. Now the question has to be solved in a more constructive way, by positing hyperauthorship as the potential for an infinite self-differentiation of an (actual) individual, as well as the creative integration of different (virtual) individuals in the process of writing. The deconstruction of authorship opens the way for the construction of hyperauthorship.

The basic principle of writing is the excess of signifiers over signifieds, which generates synonyms, metaphors, paraphrases, parodies, parables, and other figurative and elliptical modes of writing. Furthermore, this principle applies to the surplus of interpretations over the primary text, which, again and again, becomes a single signified for proliferating critical discourses. What has not yet been discussed is the extension of this principle to the sphere of authorship. The excess of authorial personalities and their unlimited proliferation is the final surplus of creative signification. The author who was believed to produce the excess now becomes its product.

I believe that in the course of time hyperauthorship will become a conventional device not only in creative, but also in scholarly writing since it becomes impossible for a postmodern intellectual to adhere strictly to one position or one methodology in matters of his/her profession. The need for the development of new, hypothetical methods of research (and which method is not hypothetical?) will bring about hyper-scholars who would pursue several alternative ways of argumentation that are mutually exclusive and complementary in the expanded universe of virtual knowledge.

Let me share with you one secret. When you confided to me that it was not Yasusada but you who actually wrote his poems, I remained hesitant about the meaning of this statement, perceiving it as a possibility for still another round or level of interpretative play between these two probable authorships. What is essential here is not the difference between Motokiyu and Yasusada but their mutual interference. Finally, do we know, following the famous parable of Chuang Tzu, whether Chuang Tzu sees a butterfly in his dream, or whether it is the butterfly who dreams of herself being Chuang Tzu? Are you absolutely sure that it's you who invented Yasusada, not the other way round?

Let us leave this divination to critics and literary historians, and let's proceed with the fact that both of these potential authorships are maintained on the level of "hyper"—are mutually interchangeable without determination of the "origin," which is impossible, as you know, according to the theory of the trace. There is a trace of Yasusada in you, and there is a trace of Ivan Solovyov in me, but the origins of these traces are lost and irrecoverable, or perhaps never existed. What is important to discuss is the relationship among these traces, not their relation to the "pseudo" origin. What becomes "pseudo" under this new mode of writing is not the name of the fictional author but the identity of the "original" author. Biologically and historically, I am Mikhail Epstein, but as an author, I am a complex amalgam of several authorial personalities (some of them remain unknown even to myself), among whom Mikhail Epstein has no authorial privilege on the grounds of the simple fact that he has some extra-textual body.

I also can imagine a journal (an annual?) inviting the contributions of transpersonal authors and elaborating the theory of hyperauthorship. The title might be *TBA,* meaning "trans-biological authorship" and at the same time "To Be Announced," an abbreviation for something that has not yet and perhaps never will be determined.

Cordially,

all of us, including Mikhail Epstein

2. The Russian Identities of Araki Yasusada

As some other critics and scholars have done, I have reflected on the matter of Yasusada, and certain curious coincidences and parallels have emerged. Is it possible that I have a more personal connection to this work that I was not initially cognizant of? Is it possibly the case that the author whose hyper-identity is Tosa Motokiyu already knew of me many years ago, when we both were citizens of the bygone Soviet Union, and that his announced "death" is meant as a metaphor for his "death as an author"? I write now to offer the following two hypotheses concerning the authorial origins of Yasusada. I do so not to try to "solve" the matter (for paradoxes are not to be solved), but rather to suggest possible layers of hyperauthorship whose consideration may enrich the further interpretation of Yasusada's texts (and his life as a potential megatext).

The intriguing scholarly controversy, in fact "author-mania" that erupted over the issue of Yasusada's identity(ies), gradually focused on the potential authorship of Dr. Kent Johnson, poet and college professor of English, who published and annotated the majority of Yasusada's works. I find this attribution no more persuasive and no less hypothetical than the two others that I would like to present. It is worth pointing out that Emily Nussbaum's discussion in *Lingua Franca* (Nov./Dec., 1996) regarding the presence of Yasusada poems in Kent Johnson's doctoral dissertation does in no way settle the question of the Yasusada authorship.

In fact, as my remarks will suggest, it is quite feasible that Johnson placed this work in his dissertation at the request of its actual author. Such a gesture would have been perfectly consistent with the "conceptualist" aesthetic of one of the writers I discuss later. I might further say, in regards to this matter, that I happened to be a guest lecturer in Bowling Green, Ohio, in the spring of 1990, and was invited to attend Johnson's dissertation defense. As he began, in front of a table full of solemn professors, to speak about the poems of Yasusada, two other graduate students seated on the floor behind him began (carefully following notations set down in copies of Johnson's lecture) to exclaim loudly certain utterances in English and Russian, and to blow, strike, and drum on an array of Asian musical instruments. This they did for the next fifteen minutes or so, while Johnson presented a collage of theoretical and poetic propositions. Although the professors on Johnson's committee seemed perplexed, I can attest that this was truly an inspiring and memorable event, one very similar in flavor to a conceptualist poetry evening in Moscow.

This parallel was all the more vivid to me because my lecture at Bowling Green and the subsequent conversations with Kent Johnson and his colleagues Ellen Berry and Anesa Miller-Pogacar was devoted in a significant part to conceptualism and the construction of multiple authorships. Of this conversation, published later, I will cite only one passage that relates directly to the current discussion on the authorship of Yasusada's poetry:

> After deconstruction comes an epoch of pure constructivism. Anything can be constructed now. As one of my philosophical characters says—most of my recent works are constituted not by my own thoughts, but by those of my characters—a word cannot be exact, cannot be precise, so it must be brave. Deconstruction demonstrated that a word can't be precise, it can't designate any particular thing. But what remains to be done with the word? To be brave, to use it in all senses that are possible to it. This [is] the new domain of construction which comes after the deconstruction. . . .[5]

Included in this domain is, first of all, the construction of authorship, as implied in those philosophical characters (conceptual persona) in my own work about whom and on whose behalf I am speaking. This explains why I became so intrigued by the phenomenon of Yasusada and now attempt to look into the enigma of his origin. It is up to the reader to decide if the following hypotheses pursue the goal of deconstruction of Yasusada or rather can serve as an example of critical constructionism.

Hypothesis #1

The manuscript "Doubled Flowering: From the Notebooks of Araki Yasusada" was originally composed in Russian by the famous writer Andrei Bitov and then translated by Kent Johnson and at least one Russian-speaking informant into English. I'll try to substantiate this version with irrefutable facts.

Bitov, born in 1937, is Russia's major novelist, a founder of postmodernism in Russian literature. His work generated a number of famous hyperauthors, among them Lev Odoevtsev, a literary scholar and the protagonist of Bitov's major novel *Pushkin's House,* and Urbino Vanoski, a writer of mixed Polish, Italian, and Japanese origin, the hyperauthor of another of Bitov's novels, *A Professor of Symmetry,* which is annotated as "a translation from English without a dictionary."

I have maintained friendly ties with Bitov since the late 1960s and have firsthand information about the following. In the mid-1960s, Bitov—by that time already one of the leading figures of the so-called youth prose—received an invitation to visit Japan through the official channels of the Soviet Writers' Union. However, he was denied an exit visa by Soviet authorities, who claimed that he was too ideologically immature for such a responsible trip to a capitalist country (he was suspected of being a hidden dissident, probably rightfully, as presumably 80 percent of the Soviet intelligentsia were at that time). One can easily imagine both the excitement and disappointment of a young writer who spent two or three subsequent years reapplying for this trip and reassuring the authorities of his "maturity" in vain. This bitter experience inspired him to write a novel *Japan (Iaponiia),* about the country he never saw but tried to invent in his imagination. Two planes alternated in this novel: The bureaucratic trials of a young author haunting the thresholds of high Soviet authorities, and imaginary landscapes and poetic visions of Japan, including fragments of an imaginary anthology of contemporary Japanese poetry. Incidentally, though Bitov never considered himself a real poet, he has hyperauthored several brilliant poems allegedly written by some of his characters (in particular, Aleksei Monakhov, the protagonist of Bitov's "dotted" novel *The Days of a Man*).[6] I assume that Bitov's novel *Japan,* which would be more properly titled "Dreams about Japan," was a kind of symmetrical response to the eighteenth-century Japanese masterpiece *Dreams about Russia,* written by Kodayu Daikokuya (1750 or 1751–1828), a treatise that mixes pseudo-ethnographic description with lyrical visionary passages.[7] This book was translated into Russian, and I have no doubts that Bitov was intimately familiar with it.

With the coming of glasnost', Bitov intended to publish his novel *Japan* after some additional stylistic elaboration. I was very intrigued by this plot, especially after Bitov's other book *A Professor of Symmetry* came out, a monumental stylization of a contemporary multi-ethnic Western author, slightly in Conrad's or Nabokov's vein (English was not Vanoski's native language; hence Bitov's alleged translation from English into Russian of a novel that itself was presumably translated from his mother language into English, at least in the bilingual imagination of the imagined author). I expected that Bitov's *Japan* would again induce a case of "doubled authorship," now with a Japanese hyperauthor. According to Bitov's account, *Japan* was almost finished. But gradually all rumors about its pending publication disappeared, and my direct questions addressed to Bitov failed to receive any definite answer. Bitov complained that he was burdened with numerous urgent literary projects and administrative responsibilities. Indeed, since the early 1990s he has been the president of the Russian division of International PEN (a worldwide organization of writers). Thus, the publication of *Japan,* with a poetic anthology as its supplement, was postponed for an indefinite period.

The last time I saw Bitov was December 11, 1995 when he visited Emory by my invitation to give a lecture on Russian postmodernism. In our conversation he confirmed again, with a visible reluctance, that *Japan* will be published in due time, but probably "in a modified form" (he did not go into detail). On December 29 of the same year, in downtown Chicago, at the annual convention of the Modern Language Association, I met by chance Kent Johnson, whom I had not seen for several years. He shared with me news of the rising posthumous star of Araki Yasusada, and gave me some copies of Yasusada's publications. Not immediately, but with an increasing feeling that I had guessed rightly, I recognized Bitov's stylistic charm in these English verses allegedly translated from Japanese. But why not directly from Russian?

The fact is that Kent Johnson, as the compiler and editor of a well-known and critically acclaimed anthology of contemporary Russian verse, *Third Wave: The New Russian Poetry,*[8] had more of a first-hand familiarity with Russian poetry than with Japanese. Is it possible that there is a connection between Kent Johnson, who is now prominently connected to Yasusada's legacy, and Andrei Bitov, a master of hyperauthorship and the author of the still-unpublished novel *Japan*? Let me explain further.

I first met Kent Johnson in St. Petersburg (then Leningrad, the native city, incidentally, of Bitov) in 1989, at a conference on contemporary Russian culture. Kent was then busy collecting materials for his English anthology of the newest trends in Russian poetry of the 1970s through the 1980s. This anthology came out, with my afterword, from University of Michigan Press in 1992, and had a significant success, particularly in the world of Slavic literature: It was the first book in English representing the "new wave" of Russian poetry, and, most valuably, it contained, in addition to verses, theoretical manifestoes from the poets. Kent Johnson and his coeditor Steven Ashby managed to make a superb choice of authors and their representative works, as well as of skillful translators, for this unique collection. This project by itself would have justified Kent's trip to St. Petersburg, but, as I suspect now, it was in Russia that he got the impetus for the preparation of another anthology, this time a Japanese one, subsumed under the name of a central hyperauthor (Yasusada), but including two of Yasusada's *renga* collaborators, Ozaki Kusatao and Akutagawa Fusei, and their three contemporary translators, Tosa Motokiyu, Okura Kyojin, and Ojiu Norinaga. I am amazed by the subtle skills that were employed to translate this anthology from Russian to English in order to finally present it as originally Japanese. Now I can also understand why Bitov withdrew his intention to publish *Japan* under his own name. To become part of a foreign culture is a more inspiring, generous, and at the same time ambitious enterprise than just to add still another piece to the treasury of one's native language.

Yasusada's work is conceived not just as a poetic collection, but as a novel with its own plot (the editorial piecing together of the fragmented record of a Hiroshima survivor), cast in the multigeneric form of diaries, letters, verses, comments, etc. The meta-genre of "novel in verses" is deeply rooted in the Russian literary tradition, with Pushkin's *Eugene Onegin* as its prototype—the major source of Bitov's inspiration throughout his creative search and especially in his major novel *Pushkin's House*. No wonder that the novel *Japan* proved to be not just a novel with a "poetic supplement," as was intended initially, but "a novel in verses," or, more precisely, "a novel with verses." Every reader of Yasusada's texts will agree that verses constitute only one aspect of this larger literary whole, which, like both Pushkin's and Bitov's novels, includes numerous self-commenting pages, lyrical digressions, and critical reflections. This is truly a poetic novel of Yasusada's life, a novel in the tradition of Russian literature that now, through Kent Johnson's mediation, again invests its inspirations into the treasury of Japanese literature, but now in the even more palpable and congenial form of "a newly discovered author."

Such Russian authors as Pushkin, Dostoevsky, Tolstoy, and Chekhov were for a long time the moral and artistic authorities for Japanese literature; now, with Bitov-Johnson's contribution, Russian literature becomes an indispensable part of Japanese literature, of its novelistic flesh and poetic blood. As a scholar of Russian literature, I can only rejoice at the fact of this transcultural interaction and the resulting synthesis.

Hypothesis #2

This, I believe, is the least hypothetical of the two, being merely a combined statement of several well-known facts. Among Russian authors presented in Kent Johnson's anthology of contemporary Russian poetry, one of the most preeminent figures is Dmitry Prigov, a close acquaintance of Bitov and a central proponent of Russian conceptualism who is known for his poems and whole collections written on behalf of various characters and mentalities belonging to different cultures. As Prigov puts it in his manifesto published in Johnson's anthology,

> the heroes of my poems have become different linguistic layers. . . . A shimmering relationship between the author and the text has developed, in which it is very hard to define (not only for the reader but for the author, too) the degree of sincerity in the immersion in the text and the purity and distance of the withdrawal from it. . . .The result is some kind of quasi-lyrical poems written by me under a feminine name, when I am of course not concerned with mystification but only show the sign of the lyrical poem's position, which is mainly associated with feminine poetry. . . .[9]

In 1987 or 1988, Prigov circulated a collection of verses on behalf of a Chinese female poet, thus helping to fill the gap of female authorship in the highly developed but almost exclusively male-oriented Chinese classic tradition. Further, he planned to expand the cultural geography of his hyperauthorship by introducing a collection by a Japanese poet with "a rather unusual but universally comprehensible fate and sensibility." This collection was never published under the name of Prigov himself, and I submit that in this case the project of hyperauthorship underwent a further mysterious expansion to acquire an international set of hyperauthors, hypereditors, etc., along the lines of a global poetic plot (imitating and parodying the "Zionist-masonic conspiracy" as exposed in *The Protocols of Zion*). Prigov once, in the spirit of "new sincerity," confessed to me his "masonic" conspiracy for the triumph of creative impersonality throughout the world of art.

Precisely at the time Prigov's Japanese collection was due to be finished (1989), Kent Johnson came for his first and only visit to Leningrad to meet with Prigov and other poets participating in the future Russian anthology. From my continuous personal talks with Prigov at this time (we even spent a rather "sincere" night of discussions and confessions in the apartment of our common friend, poet Viktor Krivulin), I could conclude that along with the poems he passed to Kent for this anthology, there was an additional set of materials large enough to form a separate collection that, it is easy to conclude, came to be known as *Doubled Flowering* by Araki Yasusada.

I want to underscore once more that everything aforesaid is only a hypothesis, though all mentioned facts are true. I daresay this kind of hypothesis does not need a further factual verification, inasmuch as the true identity of the person named Tosa Motokiyu (who, as I mentioned earlier, is now claimed by Johnson and Alvarez to be the "real" author of the work) is never to be revealed, according to his own last will. A question poses itself: Whose will is this, if its author refuses to accept attribution of its authorship? This is the same kind of paradox that we find in the most famous of logical paradoxes of "liar's type": "The liar says that he is always lying. Is it a truth or a lie?" If we believe Motokiyu's testament that his true name is not to be revealed, then this is not Motokiyu's testament.

A vicious circle? But is not the same circle inscribed into the most glorious and suspicious declaration of authorship? Is Shakespeare Shakespeare? Let us suggest that whoever Shakespeare was he succeeded in producing, in addition to *Hamlet* and other classical plays, the most enigmatic of his creations—the author named "Shakespeare," the one who wrote both prophetic *Hamlet* and his own, almost illiterate will. The enigma of Motokiyu, who authorized the eternal suspense and concealment of his authorial identity and who claims to be behind Yasusada without revealing who is behind Motokiyu himself, is not only a deeply parodic reinstatement of the "Shakespearean question," but a subversion—or rather endless and deliberately vicious multiplication—of the very phenomenon of "authorship."

The vicious circle is a creative one. An author's imperative: to create an author. How can we trust a doctor who is permanently sick? There is a biblical saying: "Physician, heal thyself." How can we trust an author who limits himself to inferior characters, like kings, generals, adventurers, etc., and cannot create an author?

Thus we should be grateful to Motokiyu, who succeeded in creating Yasusada and, even more, his friends, translators, editors, and executors. But who created Motokiyu? And who created his creator? The answer is infinitely deferred, to use the deconstructionist cliché, but what is more important and goes beyond the realm of deconstruction is the construction of infinite authors in the place of the absent single one. By this I do not mean to imply that the quest for an original authorship should be qualified as a critical fallacy; the point, rather, is that the dispersion of creative origins is inscribed in the very act of creativity and brings forth the possibilities of infinite answers. Is not the goal of creativity the excess of meanings over signs, and therefore, the excess of authors over texts, since each additional authorship is a way to radically change the overall meaning of the text and to extend the scope of its interpretations? Each text is allowed to have as many authors as it needs to have in order to become maximally meaningful.

Vladimir Nabokov once remarked on what makes literature different from the "true story" or "the poetry of testimony": "Literature was born not the day when a boy crying 'wolf, wolf' came running out of the Neanderthal valley with a big gray wolf at his heels: literature was born on the day when a boy came crying 'wolf, wolf' and there was no wolf behind him."[10]

A friend of mine with whom I shared this observation, remarked pessimistically: "In our wretched times, when the boy runs in crying 'wolf, wolf!' no poetry is born whatsoever — he will simply be dragged to court for 'making false statements' and 'disturbing the peace' of the pedestrian-minded." Some will regard such a view as overly gloomy, but it does suggest why, in our times, the boy might do well to disappear together with the ghostly wolf he dared to herald so bravely. In other words, the author is drawn to become fictitious in the way fiction is itself; the author shares the destiny of his characters and becomes one of them, like a chameleon—a grand illusion among illusions. Perhaps a new kind of literature is being born these days—one in which neither the wolf nor the boy are found to be real, even though the heart-rending cries go on echoing in the villagers' ears.

But wait, object the villagers, for in the meantime rumors about the wolf and the boy who supposedly are "never present" become more insistent and repetitious. Isn't this play of language without wolf and even without boy behind it exactly what we know as "postmodernism"? If the wolf in this little parable represents the objective truth of realism, while the boy is the subjectivist pathos of modernism, then the vanishing of both of them constitutes the effect of postmodernism.

Is it not a blasphemy to "post-modernize" such a deeply tragic experience as conveyed by Yasusada's poetry? Theodor Adorno, with even deeper pessimism than my friend whom I mentioned above, famously proclaimed that there can be no poetry after Auschwitz. We might likewise conclude that there can be no poetry after Hiroshima. But is this true? Could it be, instead, that poetry has to become wholly different from what it used to be in order to fulfill its human calling after Hiroshima? If so, then the work of Yasusada points toward one possible form of renewal: *dissemination of authorship*. With Yasusada, poetry reaches beyond the individual's self-expression, beyond the original testimony, beyond the "flowering" of one person, to become "multiple flowering," a shared imagining and expression of potential Japanese, American, Russian authors, of all those who are capable of sharing the tragedy called "Hiroshima" and co-authoring the poetry called "Yasusada." Yasusada's fragments, letters, and poems become, through the generosity of a person or persons we call Motokiyu, an appeal for a transpersonal—and thus selfless and in a sense authorless—empathy.

Perhaps we can say this: In Yasusada's poetry there exist as many potential authorships as there are individuals in the world who are aware of Hiroshima and can associate themselves with the fate of its victims and survivors. In our quest for the genuine author of Yasusada's works a moment of truth arises when each of us is ready to ask, Could it be me?

In conclusion, I must state again that all foregoing facts concerning real names, persons, and historical circumstances, are true. It is only the interpretation of these facts that can claim the higher status of a hypothesis.

Postscriptum

On November 15, 1996, my path crossed with Andrei Bitov's at a Slavic conference in Boston. I told him very briefly about Yasusada and shared with him my hypothesis about his potential authorship. He thought for a while and then noted, "The more hypothetical is one's approach to an author, the more truthful it may finally prove to be." "Does this relate to this specific case?" I asked directly. He evaded the answer and continued: "The value of a hypothesis is to predict a thing which cannot be observed. The value of an author is to make palpable what is impossible. A critical hypothesis about an author is just a retroactive projection of his own creative work and does not need any further justification. As you know, some of my characters are literary scholars, which presumes that some literary scholars ..." Did he mean to add "are my characters"? At this moment—we were strolling around the book exhibition—an acquaintance of Bitov approached him and distracted us from the conversation. Unfortunately, later on in the day we had no opportunity to talk privately, and neither of us wanted to bring this topic to public attention.

Two details of this short exchange need to be emphasized: (1) Bitov did not ask me what Yasusada's works were about; (2) anyone familiar with Yasusada's style cannot but recognize its echoes in Bitov's manner of coining paradoxes.

Notes

1. "A Letter to a Japanese Friend," was first published in *Denver Quarterly* (University of Denver) 31, No. 4 (Spring 1997): 100–105. "The Russian Identities ..." was first published in *Witz* (Studio City, CA) 5, No. 2 (Summer 1997): 4–13.
2. See the most complete collection of Yasusada's works and critical interpretations: *Doubled Flowering: from the Notebooks of Araki Yasusada*, ed. Tosa Motokiyu, Ojiu Norinaga, and Okura Kyojin (New York: Roof Books, 1997). The materials on Yasusada were published in *Grand Street, Conjunctions, Abiko Quarterly* (Japan), *First Intensity, Stand, The American Poetry Review, Countermeasures: A Magazine of Poetry and Ideas, Lingua Franca* (November 1996), *Boston Review* (Summer 1997), and many reputable journals all over the world. Forrest Gander wrote in *The Nation*: "[T]he most controversial poetry book since Allen Ginsberg's *Howl* ... [T]he pages of *Doubled Flowering* are stunning as poems and failures as the historical documents they turn out not to be. They are alternately funny, ironic, irreverent, bitter and passionate."
3. I consciously repeat here the title of Jacques Derrida's famous piece in which he elaborates in a "Japanese," "negative" manner the undefinability of deconstruction. Perhaps it is more than a simple coincidence that the reconstruction and "hyperization" of authorship was also inspired by the work of a Japanese author.
4. The meaning of the prefix "hyper" is a combination of "super" (excess) and "pseudo" (illusion). The proliferation of authorial personalities makes each of them less "real." This simultaneous evolution of cultural phenomena, including authorship, in two directions, "super" and "pseudo," resulting in the

triumph of "hyper," is one of the most salient traits of postmodernism. "Unlike the prefixes "over-" and "su[pe]r-", it ["hyper"] designates not simply a heightened degree of the property it qualifies, but a superlative degree that exceeds a certain *limit*. (The same meaning is found in words like "hypertonia," "hypertrophy," "hyperinflation," "hyperbole".) This *excess* of the quality in question is so great that, in crossing the *limit,* it turns into its own antithesis, reveals its own illusionary nature. The meaning of "hyper," therefore, is a combination of two meanings: "super" and "pseudo." 'Hyper' is the kind of 'super' that through excess and transgression undermines its own reality and reveals itself as 'pseudo.'" Mikhail Epstein, "The Dialectics of *Hyper:* From Modernism to Postmodernism," in *Russian Postmodernism: New Perspectives on Post-Soviet Culture* (with Alexander Genis and Slobodanka Vladiv-Glover). (New York, Oxford: Berghahn Books, 1999): 25.

5. Ellen E. Berry, Kent Johnson, and Anesa Miller-Pogacar, "Postcommunist Postmodernism: An Interview with Mikhail Epstein," *Common Knowledge* (Oxford University Press): 1993, 2, No. 3, 110.

6. The first collection of Bitov's poems *V chetverg posle dozhdia* (St. Peterburg: Pushkinskii fond) was published in 1997.

7. The original Japanese title is *Oroshiyakoku Kodayu hyoryu nikki noutsushi.* Russian translation: *Sny o Rossii.* (Izdanie teksta, perevod, vstypitelnaia statia i kommentarii V.M. Konstantinova; pod. red. N.I. Konrada. [Moscow: Izd-vo vostochnoi lit-ry, 1961]). See also the historical novel under the same title of the contemporary Japanese writer Yasushi Inoue (1907–1991), *Dreams about Russia,* also translated into Russian: *Sny o Rossii,* (perevod s iaponskogo B. V. Raskin. [Moscow: Nauka, 1977]).

8. *Third Wave: The New Russian Poetry,* ed. Kent Johnson and Stephen M. Ashby (Ann Arbor: The University of Michigan Press, 1992).

9. *Third Wave,* 102.

10. *The Writer's Quotation Book: A Literary Companion,* ed. James Charlton (New York: Penguin, 1986): 9.

Chapter 21

Poetry as a State of Being: From the Notes of Ivan Solovyov[1]

Publication and Preface by Mikhail Epstein

Ivan Igorevich Soloyov (1944–90), philosopher, essayist, theorist of literature and art, lived in Moscow. He graduated from the philological faculty of Moscow State University, but he chose not to compromise himself with the ideological establishment of Soviet academia and preferred the life of independent scholarship and writing; he also taught high school Russian language and literature. He did not succeed in publishing any of his many works during his lifetime. Some of his writings appeared posthumously and are available in English translation.[2]

In the following pages Ivan Solovyov shows himself occasionally as a versemaker and, more typically, as a theoretician of contemporary poetry and culture. Over the length of his entire life, Ivan Solovyov wrote only twelve short poems, all in all no more than a hundred lines. It is necessary to forewarn the reader: In poetry Ivan Solovyov does not have his own voice. At the same time, it is impossible to find in him the explicit repetition of other poets, the parodic borrowings and the unconcealed citations so fashionable in the epoch of Russian conceptualism (1970s through 1990s). His poetry is rather "no-poetry," the "zero-degree of writing." The verses of Ivan Solovyov resemble the compositions of many other poets, and at the same time they do not resemble each other: Among them it is impossible to isolate a unique stylistic principle marking authorial individuality. They resemble poetry in general, even though they are not genuine poetry. It might be possible to conclude that Ivan Solovyov simply failed to mature into a true poet, had he set himself such a task. But more probably he created simulations of poetry, typical samples of what poetry could represent for a common reader. Such a genre of "a-creative" activity Solovyov himself defined as "poems without author or sense, without addressee or soul." Perhaps his experiments were extensions or illustrations of his theoretical work on "impersonal states of poetry." No one knew that he wrote poems, no one heard him recite them. In general he rather painstakingly maintained his archive, but the poems were found on carelessly torn random pieces of paper. Were it not for correction marks, they might be mistaken for someone else's poems, which they were designed, perhaps, to be.

As Ivan Solovyov did not intend his verse experiments for print, I would not dare to bring them to the reader's attention had he not proved to be a forerunner of some important tendencies in the Russian poetry of the late twentieth century. The debates from the 1970s through the beginning of the 1990s between the meta-realists, conceptualists, presentists and others have almost died out.[3] It is now clear that poetry has not chosen the path of high or low style, not the path of myth or parody, metabole or concept, but the path of a middle style or even "no-style": not an elegant middle nor an expressive middle, but precisely the average, the intentionally mediocre. That which can be called "unauthorial poetry" finds a direct precursor in Ivan Solovyov: His papers even provide theoretical notes upon which it is possible to ground a style of "poeticality without poetry" (to use one of his expressions). This relates to a tendency in contemporary writing not so much to construct a new poetic work as to reconstruct a common—"nobody's"—poetic state of being. Thus, it is possible to find in Note #4 ("The ecstasy of reading") an allusion to the genre of the "shriek" created by Dmitry Prigov.[4] The catalogue-verses of Lev Rubinshtein and the pastiche lyrics of Timur Kibirov, which bring others' speech in congruence with the author's own and, therefore, irritate the admirers of purely authorial poetry, may be, if not justified, in part explained by a theory of a poetic state of being. As I. Solovyov wrote in one of his unpublished notes, "In verses there should be neither originality nor imitation, because the very difference between one's own and another's is irrelevant [*nesostoiatel'no*] as long as we are talking about the state-of-being [*sostoianie*] of poetry and not about individual poetic acts."[5]

Ivan Solovyov's poems are rhymed and composed in classical Russian meters—trochee and iamb (the last poem)—which is not observable in the translation. I provide the titles to the theoretical sections as well as the footnotes.

—Mikhail Epstein

Poems

***

Verses without author or sense,
Without addressee or soul . . .
They are hanging like a rainbow over the desert,
Why should they be written at all?

They can never be memorized,
But they are composed every day—
Such is a crazy man
And providential laziness.

Only in these weak and poor verses
I've grasped the voice of a moment.
It is a whisper of our mind
  (unfinished)

Cicada

A loud cicada in the garden.
What a bizarre ability
To repeat itself without procrastination,
Without fatigue, without doubt,
Without divinity, without inspiration . . .[6]
Will this not prove helpful in hell?

***

Night, Russia, I and Pushkin.
I and Pushkin? Wait a moment!
Only the dark tops of a forest
Are seen ahead.

Only ringing sounds are heard.
Only bitter smoke in the nostrils . . .
Pushkin. White columns.
And Russia's fine and final dust.

Theoretical Notes

Poetry without Properties

In his old age Valentin Kataev[7] invented "mauvism"—bad art—as a stylistic trend. This is clearly an avant-garde invention: Perhaps he was recalling friends of his youth, the Odessa circle, or the LEF circle.[8] Avant-gardism tried to create the antithesis of "good" style—regulated, precise, elegant, polished—and this scandalous antithesis succeeded. There was much "mauvism" in futurists, in *Oberiuts*,[9] and now in the conceptualists[10] (incidentally, Kataev himself wrote well). "Dyr bur shchil ubeshchur" (A. Kruchonykh[11]). "Man cannot live, if he does not have!" (L. Rubinshtein). Nonsense, roughness, disarticulation, tooth-grinding . . . But it seems that the next step will be in a different direction. Not from good to bad. And not from bad to good. But from good and bad to the median, the inarticulate, nothing at all.

What is it that people need? They need poetry, all that is good and bad in it, the great and the banal. They will receive this poetry in "not-at-all" poems. Some people need good poets; some people relish "bad" poets; but the majority, perhaps, requires average poets, who aspire to be neither better nor worse than poetry as a whole. "Not-at-all" poetry is written not on behalf of a certain poet; it is devoid of an authorial element, idea, purpose: It is written as if it were just poetry, without the specification of genre, style, time, or place. It is poetry as an abstraction that takes the form of concrete poems.

Of course, by traditional standards, this would not constitute poetry at all, but rather graphomania. It is precisely the graphomaniac, however, who tries to make his mark, to be original and innovative, to write unlike anyone else, to create great poetry, outstanding poetry. Unauthorial poetry is not graphomaniacal, but necessarily anonymous, like folklore. This is not to say that some rough folk verses, "tittle-tattle," are greater than Pushkin or Pasternak, but that folk verses can satisfy the poetic demand of the masses more fully than Pushkin or Pasternak. Now that poetry has gone through various styles, both good and bad, classical and avant-gardist, and has succeeded in producing every kind and quality, now comes the time of "any-ness" and "no-ness," the time for "not-at-all" poetry. Like folklore, this poetry is free of the mark of individuality. But it is not the preliterary folklore of primitive society. This is the postliterary and postindividual folklore of cultured people who have read Pushkin and Blok, Mandel'shtam and Tsvetaeva: In their soul all impressions from all poets have simply merged and mixed, and all that remains is love of poetry as such, or rather the physical need for it.

This is a most novel and frightening state, when culture becomes a physical need, a second nature. Already we cannot go to the table without a newspaper. Nor to the bathroom. Already we cannot walk through the forest without humming something autumnal to ourselves: "I love nature's sumptuous fading, the woods clothed in purple and gold; the golden grove has ceased to speak in the gay language of birches; and life, as autumn stillness, is deep in detail . . ."[12]

Poetry after Poets: Neofolklore

As it is, there is too much poetry: It is like unending rain on a window; its noise is permanently in the ears. It sings and murmurs and whispers to us even when we are not thinking of it. But this poetry that is everywhere and nowhere has not yet found its textual expression. There are many verses of genius, even more of talent, and so on; but these are all works of literature. The other poetry, however, the one that rustles in our ears like rain or leaf-fall, is no longer a literary work, but a state of being of culture, its most elemental, spontaneous, impersonal, and unconscious condition. And every cultured person from time to time, perhaps reluctantly, falls into this poetic state of being. All the words and lines one has ever heard or read make background noise, inarticulate speech in one's soul.

But how to express it? How to convey poetry, not in the form of a separate work, but in the mode of a sticky, dull, viscous substance, which it is impossible to separate from the soul, because this poetic murmur is itself the soul, or, in any case, something many mistake for the soul? Poetry as a state of being will in time replace individual poetic works and will acquire its own representatives and exponents, probably anonymous or heteronymous. In contrast with ancient, preliterate folklore, this neofolklore will arise on the basis of written language, as the blending of everything that was once literature—the blending of styles and epochs, the dissolution of the best in the worst. The drops will blend, and the rain will fall. It will no longer be important which lines come from Pushkin, which from Blok, which from Solovyov, or from Ivanov, Petrov, and Sidorov[13]: Only taken together do they constitute poetry as a state of being.

How to convey this poetic noise into which separate sounds blend and disappear? How to convey the bittersweet feeling caused precisely by noise, its inarticulate sound, deafness, slowness? How to present the overall poetic pattern in which distinctions between Pushkin, Esenin, and Pasternak dissolve and disappear? Sometimes it seems to me that I already hear the noise of this new poetry, but maybe it is just the rain on the window.

It Is Rainy, It Is Versy

I imagine a poet who will want to incarnate poetry as a state of being. This will hardly be a real poet, a poet by vocation, because he will be devoid of authorial individuality. He will resemble all other poets and will not resemble himself. He will write not poems, but nonpoems: They will relate to poems only to the extent that they negate the latter's discrete quality. There is a seductively fine line, however, between this "non-" and that which it negates, especially when the connection is made not across a space but across a hyphen. A hyphen [*chertochka*] has its own diminutive devilry [*chertovshchina*], something tiny, girlish, almost childish, but already cunning and seductive, a grammatical nymphet.[14] "Non-poems" relate to poems as "no" relates to "yes" in the conventional semiotics of flirtation: The very division is evasive; "no" may mean "yes," and vice versa.

"Non-poems" does not refer to bad verses, although by definition they cannot be good verses. They simply have another, conditional mode of existence in one of the possible, though not the best, poetical worlds. Non-poems are poems in the subjunctive mood, written not because someone in fact writes them, expresses himself in them, but because they have the potential to be written. Such a mode of "being written" can be designated only through the grammar of state of being, such impersonal forms as "It is freezing" [*morozit*], "It is cold" [*kholodno*], "It is rainy" [*dozhdlivo*], "It is vers-y" [*stikhovo*]. Yes, "It is vers-y" is an appropriate way to define the poetic state of being, which has grown beyond any reference to individual subjects.

To attribute to such verse-ness [*ctikhovost'*] the presence of a subject, of an author, would be the same kind of anthropomorphic illusion or mythological projection as to consider that "It is raining" [*dozhdit*] or "It is freezing" [*morozit*] represents someone's action. Such impersonal sentences have no grammatical subject, nor can they have one.[15] I go into a fury remembering yesterday's lesson. The students, still spontaneous mythmakers, cannot take a step without the introduction of a subject. Their typical question: "But who did it?" Well, let us agree that in all these dubious cases it was Pushkin who did everything.[16] It is also he who verses [*stishit*]. Not versifies, like a human subject, but verses, like an element of nature. Can you rain, or can anybody in the world? Understand in the phrases "It is raining" [*dozhdit*] or "It is getting dark" [*smerkaetsia*], that it is not someone raining and someone getting dark, but it is the state of being of nature itself. In the same way Pushkin is the state of being of Russian culture.

Language has special verbs and adverbs for the designation of such acts without actors: "It's getting light" [*svetaet*], "It's getting vers-y" [*stikhoveet*]. If a subject appears in such constructions, it is not in the nominative, but in the dative case. Not he acts, but it is given to him to experience these states of being, to be subject to them, to be conditioned by them. "I'm warm" actually means "It is warm to me."[17] This position in language, designated by the dative case, is not yet established in culture: to be a poet not in the nominative but in the dative case—not the one who composes verses but the one to whom it is vers-y.

Do we already have poets in the dative? What lies ahead now is to lead our bearded schoolboys, our gray-haired schoolgirls, and all the respectable literary establishment to the consciousness that, like language, culture and poetry have their own state-of-being categories, and they also demand some new forms of textual "dativity." If, in a country with as saturated a poetic atmosphere as Russia, it constantly verses, then we must be grateful for such heavenly abundance and not substitute for it the individual acts of verse making. It is necessary to define the basis for a new authorless poetics, to inscribe the grammar of impersonal states of being into poetry and culture.

The Ecstasy of Reading

Poetry inspires savagery. Once, poets were physically gripped by the power of this super-personal ecstasy. "As the worshiping Corybantes are not in their senses when they dance, so the lyric poets are not in their senses . . . they are seized with Bacchic transport, and are possessed. . . ."[18] But since poetry became literature, sequences of letters written down on paper—where are the frenzies, the cries, and the rapture that befit the spirit of poetry? In the epoch of individual creativity even the great poets prove to be nothing but men and women of letters who simply write, scribble their compositions.

But with the transition from personal action to the category of state of being, even the physical structure of poetry changes. What poetry has accumulated for centuries as the investments of individual energies now acts with the impersonal strength of a stormy discharge, as if the atmospheric conditions [*sostoyanie*] were saturated with electricity. Poetry [*stikhi*] returns to its element [*stikhia*].[19] Poetry is shouted, cried out, vocalized, glossolalized, ecstatically sung in many voices. The new bearers of the poetic state of being ("non-poets") will intrude in our ears with wails and roars because they are the spokespersons for our common cultural tenor, overfilled with poetry. The lines of *Eugene Onegin* should be performed loudly and ecstatically, as Pushkin himself never imagined his chamber verses composed in the genre of a romantic novel with lyrical digressions. Now, a century and a half later, these verses enter our ears already saturated with dozens of readings, interpretations, commentaries—and our own responses, surprises, and resonances. How many times have we repeated to ourselves, both with and without cause: "My uncle—high ideals inspire him . . ."; "We all meandered through our schooling haphazard . . ."; "He who has lived and thought is certain to scorn the men with whom he deals"; "I write to you—no more confession is needed, nothing's left to tell . . . ;" "Was she the Tanya he'd exhorted . . . ;" "Fortune's jurisdiction has fixed; but for my heart to beat I must wake up with the conviction that somehow that same day we'll meet . . . ," etc.[20] Our heads virtually buzz with *Eugene Onegin,* with the humming of these winged words, familiar expressions, the chirring of these ubiquitous citations-cicadas that never quiet down.[21] Indeed, culture is a powerful dynamic added to the text that increases its volume and resonance and finally overflows our hearing with the peals of multiple echoes. In addition to the endless variation of the text in secondary readings and interpretations, we have our own almost maniacal manner of whispering some citations to ourselves, as if they were recorded on a tape loop that goes round day and night, incessantly rustling in the ear. Culture deprives us of silence and converts even the most peaceful moments into a garrulous babble of citations. As for classical works, they are simply the loudspeakers, placed right next to our ears and droning incessantly.

And yet am I expected to read *Evgene Onegin* in a calm voice, with soft breathing, as if conducting an intimate conversation in an intellectual circle? Quite the opposite: I will scream and spew it along with the bits of my own lung tissue that have become attached to Pushkin's rhythms, stuck in his stanzas. I will read poetry not as it is written, but as it resounds in me, as it has reached me through the thickness of culture and through all the resonances of personal and social memory. I will revise the stanza about my uncle's high ideals and intermingle Pushkin's lines with my own impressions of that most ideal uncle whose cockroach moustache I contemplated on the parade portraits from my childhood.[22] In Tatyana's shameless and innocent letter to Onegin, I will insert a couplet about a small girl who, although she never saw the hero of her dreams, is nonetheless ready to conceive with him the whole chosen people of the future.[23] And after the line, "I must wake up with the conviction that somehow that same day we'll meet . . . ,"[24] I will add, "that same day, and tomorrow, and all days of this and next week, and in the afterlife . . ." I will repeat this a dozen times as I used to repeat these lines when they came into my head on appropriate personal occasions.

Those who wish to may listen to me and those who don't may stop up their ears, but screaming, howling, and hallooing at the top of my lungs, I will read to you the *Onegin* that has reached and shaped me. *Onegin*, which has long ceased to be the personal act of the poet Pushkin, instead has become an acoustic state of being of Russian culture, its roaring decibels and alarming, albeit unheard, ultra- and infrasounds. The acoustics already press so heavily upon my eardrums that, in order to even out the pressure differential, all that remains to me is to cry back *Eugene Onegin, Dead Souls, The Brothers Karamazov,* "The Twelve," although I doubt that the value of saving the eardrums is worth breaking the vocal cords.[25]

I am not alone; there are many of us who experience literature as "dativity," as "given to us," and this is the premise of its new folklorization. If at the dawn of poetry, the poets themselves were ecstatic and possessed, then now this ecstatic spirit of poetry overflows into us, the readers. The frenzied muse of reading replaces the once-powerful muse of singing who has lapsed into silence in the epoch of writing. For centuries poetry split into droplets of literary seclusion, authorial contemplation and quiet leisure moments, but, one after another, all these drops overflowed the reader's hearing. Now the voices of Homer and Mandel'shtam float together: a "dark sea thunders, eloquent, and rumbling heavily, it breaks beneath my bed."[26]

Symbiotic Genre

Subconsciously or semiconsciously we assimilate another's music or poetry as if it were our own. The majority of musical and poetic souls have a need to create precisely those works that already have been created by others. Millions of anonymous readers will be inspired by the possibility of recording and performing these assimilated and slightly modified works under the sign of double authorship, as the composition of Pushkin-Solovyov or Pushkin-Ivanov. The division of humanity into creators and readers fails to account for the third and most extensive category: those who want not only to read, but to create others' works. Occasionally, it seems to them that they have actually composed "I remember the wonderful moment . . ." (Pushkin's poem), or "Christ's Appearance to the People" (Aleksandr Ivanov's painting[27]), or *Swan Lake* (Tchaikovsky's ballet). This is the happiest moment of their lives: when they suddenly hear within themselves this poetry or music, or see with an internal eye their splendid canvas; when all that has been repeatedly seen and heard before is born anew in them. In genuine readers and viewers this rebirth is even accompanied by labor and torment.

This is a great unquenchable cultural need: to create another's work; not, God forbid, as a form of plagiarism, but as a modest coauthorship that permits me to change or add maybe one word or one line in ten, something like "Galina" in place of "Leila" (in one of the last Pushkin poems). I cannot concede the authorship of this tiny insertion even to Pushkin, for it is peculiar to myself to be enchanted—and, therefore, disappointed—by Galina. You see, it is my beloved, not his, whose name is Galina.

> In the evening with indifference
> Leila left me.
> —Pushkin[28]

> In the evening not without bitterness
> Galina left me.
> —Pushkin-Solovyov

> I remember the wonderful moment:
> You appeared before me
> Like a fleeting vision,
> Like a spirit of pure beauty.
> —Pushkin[29]

> I remember the bright day in April:
> You appeared before me,
> Amidst the ringing gentle drops of Spring,
> In a mist of fragrant decay,
> Like a spirit of pure beauty.
> —Pushkin-Solovyov

Alexander Pushkin began writing these poems in his own name, and they will end in a thousand names, including even my own, joined and signed together with him.

In his treatise "On Love," Stendhal compares the growth of love to that of a bare branch, which grows brilliant crystals when immersed in rich brine. And so a simple event, an encounter with a woman, grows in our soul with hopes, fears, desires, and doubts, and crystallizes into love. According to Stendhal, love itself is this crystallization—a special activity of the mind, which extracts from everything the discovery that the beloved possesses new perfection. Now, I am speaking not of Pushkin's love for Kern, the heroine of the previously cited poem, but of our love for Pushkin. The encounter with his poetry grows in our souls with crystals of tenderness, hope, and doubt: We make conjectures (about the deeper meaning), we are jealous (of rival readings), we wonder, we wander with his lines through the forest and invoke them during encounters with friends and lovers, we fill them with our experience and our anxiety, we invest intimate meanings into each word uttered by Pushkin. Let our love find fulfillment in the text of our choice, amorously adorning and gently transforming the object of our passion. Let the poem grow with the crystals of new meanings that our love has attached to it, like a living branch, with colonies of polyps, reshaping it into a multicolored coral forest. Let it grow with words that explain and question it, that cling to it, like parasites entering into symbiosis with the main organism and unable to live without it because they derive from it sustenance and protection. This is our greatest cultural necessity: to transfigure freely the object of our desire, to be delirious with it, to spy upon it, to reflect it and be reflected in it, to adorn it with flowers and vignettes of our own imagination.

Yet no one has responded to this necessity, no one has explained its urgency for the overwhelming majority of cultured people. They would like not merely to read and reread, but to love what they read, which means to crystallize their feelings in the text, to give way to their fantasy. It is not enough for them to be simple readers, although of course they do not have an ambition to become creators: they are decent, modest people. But to read, to read, to read, simply to read is unbearable, in fact impossible, for throughout the millennia so much has been written and still each year brings forth unknown masterpieces ... Reading as such is a Sisyphean labor without a tangible outcome. But what if some deliciously mixed genre were found, so that the reader could (re)create what he is reading and thus satisfy at least minimally his coauthorial pride?

It is necessary to legitimize this symbiotic genre in culture, so that readers will not be alienated by the creators' arrogance. The humbleness of the labor of reading cannot be exploited infinitely. Otherwise people will stop reading, and there will be no one to write for. If coauthorship became possible, even in the proportion of one hundredth added to the original text, then how many readers would read anew *The Captain's Daughter* or *War and Peace:* "Well, it is partly my own work; I have to polish this peculiar Tolstoyan roughness and several cumbersome passages, to insert my favorite names, dishes, landscapes ... Then I will not be ashamed to sign such a monumental composition next to Tolstoy." Let the entire Ivanov family, down to their distant relatives and posterity, read the corrected version of *War and Peace* by Tolstoy-Ivanov. And let the critics write analytical articles in the literary journals: "Which is the Better Coauthor? A Comparative Analysis of *War and Peace* by Tolstoy-Ivanov and Tolstoy-Sidorov."

Andrei Pushkin, Pyotr Einstein, and Others

Double authorship involves not only the inspired appropriation of works belonging to someone else, but the no-less-enthusiastic donation of one's own creations. Actually, it is possible to "compose another's works" in two senses: by signing another's property or by signing one's own property with another's name. I do not know which creative need is greater. I sense in myself several unborn authors, with whom I would gladly share some of my writings. Not because these works, designed to be authored by others, are inferior to my own ("take what I don't need"), but because in conception and in style they are not mine, though in reality no one else happened to compose them. For the same reason that it pleases me to compose some of Pushkin's verses, it pleases me that Pushkin should compose some passages from my critical prose. If not Alexander Pushkin—that would be too great an honor for me—then let it be Andrei or Ivan Pushkin. I sense in my womb the stirring of this Andrei Pushkin, who is just about to write a scholarly, slightly structuralist commentary on the compositions of his great ancestor—no, of the great poet bearing the same surname. Or, not too long ago, among thoughts about the physics of ethereal bodies, I heard the voice of my contemporary and, it seemed, even my classmate in elementary school, Pyotr Einstein.

It is not that I want to write about Andrei Pushkin and Pyotr Einstein, to make characters out of them; no, I want to make them authors, so that they will write with me and sometimes in place of me: Andrei Pushkin and Ivan Solovyov, "A Comparative Analysis of Alexander Pushkin's Poems 'The Prophet' and 'Imitation of the Koran.'" Or in a gesture of self-effacement: Pyotr Einstein, "The Cosmology of Ethereal Bodies and the Physics of Dreams." Is it really my business to write about ethereal bodies? But if it pleases me to write such scholarly articles, then I have to realize that in this critical or philosophical state of being [*sostoianie*] I am not alone, but I precisely relate or co-stand [*so-stoiu*] with someone else.[30] This *alter ego* of my writing may be Pyotr Einstein, and, if the agenda turns to the theory of singularities and quantum mechanics, then perhaps Igor Heisenberg.

Of that which I write, only the lesser part belongs to myself, Ivan

Solovyov. The larger part belongs to those enigmatic authors whose ethereal bodies are periodically departing from me, whose voices I hear at an increasing distance, even though they are still linked with the memories of my childhood or youth. All of us, Pushkin, Solovyov, Einstein, are former fellow students or classmates, members of one disappearing generation, one already remote historical formation, disintegrating into separate, though still mutually resonating voices.

In fact, I always begin to write as Ivan Solovyov, but then my writing becomes foreign to me, and it strikes my fancy to put it in quotation marks, as if I were citing from my previous writings rather than writing authentically here and now. And then, conversely, it is my fancy to remove the quotation marks, not in order to reappropriate the text after its temporary alienation, but to transfer it completely into the possession of someone else. Almost always an ethereal body turns up who could with more legitimacy have created that which it was my pleasure to write down. Such is the subtle, gradual replacement of the author, or, more precisely, authorship as the process of substitution. At first I am simply writing, then citing myself, then citing someone else; then someone else is writing instead of me. The otherness of writing comes full circle and returns to me as a potential coauthor. The same writing begins under the name of Ivan Solovyov and ends under the names of Andrei Pushkin or Pyotr Einstein. One beginning and so many diverging ends . . .

This circle is made not only in writing, but also in reading. The same poem begins under the name of Alexander Pushkin and ends under the name of Solovyov, or Ivanov, or Sidorov. This makes for two circles, one in writing, where I distance myself and acquire a coauthor; another in reading, where I assimilate somebody else's work and become his coauthor. Hence the encounter of two circles, smoothly passing into each other, like the figure 8. Like anybody who writes and reads, I stand at the central point of this configuration. One circle demonstrates my otherness to myself and another circle, my oneness with another. I share my authorship in writing, and I become a coauthor in reading. For example, on one end of this double-circle I find Alexander Pushkin, with whom I become one in reading; on the other end, I find Andrei Pushkin, who becomes my "other" in writing.[31]

Such a figure 8 shows that authorship is always othership, whether it is accomplished through the acts of writing, where I "other" myself, or reading, where I "author" another. Now I add my name to that of Alexander Pushkin; now the name of Andrei Pushkin is added to mine. Everything turns out equally, justly, because we are many and poetry is one; it makes use of all our names to reveal its infinite anonymity.

Authorship Donated and Received as a Gift

Such gestures as stolen and given authorship were not unknown to our greatest writer and the most responsive reader, Alexander Pushkin himself. He was able to dip his open hand into others' literary property and to give away his own property with full hands. His daring inventiveness [*predpriimchivost'*] was challenged only by his genius for imitation [*pereimchivost'*]. Many of Pushkin's pieces that appeared to be originals are now revealed as borrowings, stylizations, transpositions, sometimes lacking reference to the original. These discoveries, of course, do not serve to increase Pushkin's honor, and may be attributed simply to the lack of copyright restrictions in that epoch, which was still able to delight in the poetic states of being that stretch across the limits of individual authorship. It was possible to disregard authorial honor, although matters of honorarium are always more complicated. Even "I loved you . . . ," one of Pushkin's most illustrious poems, turns out to be the composition of a certain Frenchman, with whom Pushkin did not wish to share the posthumous glory of the masterpiece, even if in life he shared with him the poetic state of unrequited love. If you read this pearl carefully, you will find nothing except the poetic state of being and the grammar of lyrical persuasion: no force of original creativity, no fantasy, no imagination, no metaphors.[32] Pushkin was a master of "not-at-all" poetry, of quite conventional lyricism to which everyone can apply his own hand and sign his name as an expression of some elusive and common state of being.

On the other hand, Pushkin was not stingy with his own literary property. I am not even speaking of his countless poetic imitators, enviers, and debtors, who, independently of his good will, borrowed from his work without asking. More importantly, Pushkin sensed in himself someone else to whom he was inclined to trust and attribute his work. The camouflage proved to be so successful that literary fame came to a certain Nikolai Gogol, who is most renowned for writing Pushkin's *Dead Souls* and *The Inspector General*. Gogol conceded, in his "Authorial Confession," that it was Pushkin who donated these subjects, these masterful plots that in themselves were quite sufficient to secure Gogol literary immortality.[33] These plots are not any worse than those in Pushkin's own works; in fact, they are better. But Pushkin heard in these bizarre phantasmagoric motifs a voice belonging to another author; and a young man, only twenty-five or twenty-six at that time, with a sparkling sense of humor, who had recently published two collections of folkloric tales, came to Pushkin's mind . . . Previously Gogol had never engaged in anything but operetta-like Ukrainian themes, and even those he had been writing on behalf of a garrulous provincial beekeeper, Rudyi Panko[34]; all of a sudden he engaged in writing a Russian epic . . . Instead of a beekeeper, a much more powerful collaborator appeared to him. Gogol himself confessed: "When I was creating, I saw only Pushkin before me. . . . I undertook nothing and wrote nothing without his advice. Everything good that I have I owe to him. And my current work is his creation."[35]

And so Nikolai Gogol, the author of funny Ukrainian tales up until this point, found himself the author of the Russian epic poem, *Dead Souls*. Subsequently, Gogol regretted that he wrote something other than what he had intended to write; he complained that *Dead Souls* was not quite what he meant and aspired to . . .[36] Indeed, it was rather Pushkin's work enacted through the simulative figure of Gogol. And when Gogol tried to continue *Dead Souls* on his own, he struggled painfully with the second volume and had eventually to give up, to burn the almost-finished manuscript and to die in an agony of self-condemnation. Thus Gogol remains a magnificent dummy in Russian literature, a developer of Pushkin's plots, a Belkin elevated to the status of an honorable classic.

The reverse of all this is also possible: It was Gogol who attributed to Pushkin his works, finding in *Dead Souls* and in *The Inspector General* the presence of a different creative individuality. Something was not right in *Dead Souls*, not entirely Gogolesque, but rather Pushkinesque: the mood of autumn, Russian melancholy rather than Ukrainian humor. That is why Gogol was so astonished by Pushkin's reaction to *Dead Souls:* "When I finished reading, he [Pushkin] uttered in a voice full of anguish: 'God, how sad is our Russia.' I was amazed to hear this."[37] Gogol was amazed to learn that the book he had written was different from what he expected it to be; therefore, he attempted, with hindsight, to attribute its conception and plot to Pushkin. Where could the Pushkinesque quality of his mature works have come from, if not from Pushkin himself?

In the final analysis, it is difficult to determine who gave the idea to whom, whether *Dead Souls* was a blessing bequeathed from Pushkin to Gogol or a gift of respect and reverence offered from Gogol to Pushkin. But it is possible that Pushkin was partly Gogol even before Gogol emerged, and that Gogol was still partly Pushkin after Pushkin's death.

Maybe, in some eternal book of books under *Dead Souls* will be written, "authored by Pushkin and Gogol."

Gogol, however, cannot be fully trusted[38], whereas Belkin undoubtedly shared with Pushkin the highest creations of his prose. Pushkin could by no means have given his authorial name to "Mistress into Maid" or "The Stationmaster:" The style is too naive and abundant with simplehearted sensitivity; the plot is designed for pure entertainment; the narrator is culturally limited and devoid of a truly aristocratic spirit. Thus another author gradually emerged in Pushkin, a provincial petty landowner, of whom there is nothing to say, except that he is a decent fellow, an attentive listener, a kindhearted storyteller. Pushkin recognized that these tales belonged to Ivan Petrovich Belkin (1798–1828), and it is not for us to contradict Pushkin's authorial will, which, in an act of self-effacement, designated a different author to his creation. It is therefore insulting both to Pushkin and to Belkin when their difference and sovereignty are disrespected; when, for instance, in anthologies we read: " 'Mistress into Maid,' a story by Pushkin." Not Pushkin, but Pushkin-Belkin, a diabolical difference.[39] Who is to blame that the name Pushkin, as in the aforementioned proverbial sayings, is attributed to something he did not do? Of course one could object that Pushkin himself attributed his compositions to Belkin; that is, that they belonged to Pushkin. But if I give something to someone, is it still mine? By no means could Pushkin, having made a gift of authorship, ignobly take it back, not even if he discovered later the true worth of such a trinket. No, it is not Pushkin, but we who are to blame, taking from Belkin that which Pushkin gave to him.

Finally, is it not the case that the Boldino autumn of 1830 was so productive[40] because Pushkin found several potential coauthors and wrote on their behalf, hardly having time to dip his pen in the inkwell? William Shenstone (1714–63) wrote "The Covetous Knight," John Wilson (1785–1854) "A Feast during the Plague," and Ivan Belkin "The Tales of the Late Ivan Petrovich Belkin."[41] As for the lyrical poems, who at this autumnal feast of creativity has not put a hand to them—from the real English poet Barry Cornwall[42] ("I drink to Mary's health") to the fictive Turkish poet Amin-Oglu ("The unfaithful now glorify Stambul")? The Boldino autumn, which has become the symbol of a great poetic harvest, is rich not only with works, but also with authors from whom Pushkin inspirationally borrowed and to whom he hurriedly distributed his creations.

8

If I am writing under another's name, it means, in this very moment

(unfinished)[43]

Notes

1. Translated from Russian by Michèle M. Biscoe.
2. To date the following works of Ivan Solovyov have been published: (1). "Razmyshleniia Ivana Solovyova ob Erose," *Chelovek* (Moscow) 1 (1991): 195–212 (in English: "Ivan Soloviev's Reflections on Eros," in *Genders* 22, a special issue, *Postcommunism and the Body Politic,* ed. Ellen Berry [New York and London: New York University Press, 1995]: 252–266); (2) "Poeziia kak sostoianie. Iz stikhov i zametok Ivana Solovyova. Publikatsiia i predislovie Mikhaila Epshteina" (Poetry as a State of Being: From the Poems and Notes of Ivan Solovyov, publication and preface by Mikhail Epstein), *Novyi mir* 8 (1996): 230–240; (3). Ivan Solovyov, "Messianskie rechi" (Messianic Discourses), publication and foreword by Mikhail Epstein, *Oktiabr* (Moscow) 7 (1998): 148–167. Solovyov's treatise on the fate of Catholicism in Russia, "The Triple-Faith and the Mustard Seed," has been prepared for publication.
3. On these major trends in contemporary Russian poetry, see Mikhail Epstein, *After the Future: The Paradoxes of Postmodernism and Contemporary Russian Culture,* trans. with intro. by Anesa Miller-Pogacar (Amherst: University of Massachusetts Press, 1995): 19–101, 193–195, 200–203.
4. Dmitry Aleksandrovich Prigov (b. 1940), Lev Rubinshtein (b. 1947), and Timur Kibiriv (b. 1955)—popular Moscow poets, leading representatives of conceptualism.
5. Russian original expressions that help to make clear the untranslatable wordplay are cited in brackets.
6. This line is from Pushkin's famous poem "To***" ("I remember the wonderful moment . . . ," 1825).
7. Valentin Kataev (1897–1986)—Soviet novelist and a classic socialist realist, who in his sixties turned to the genre of experimental, associative, "modernist" prose.
8. Literary currents of the 1920s and early 1930s. The Odessa circle: writers Isaak Babel, Yury Olesha, Ilya Ilf, and Evgeny Petrov. Lef (Left Front of Arts): Vladimir Mayakovsky, Osip Brik, Nikolai Aseev, and others.
9. *Oberiuts* is a Russian literary circle of the late 1920s-early 1930s that included Daniil Kharms, Nikolai Zabolotsky, Nikolai Oleinikoa, Aleksandr Vzedensky, and others.
10. Avant-gardist and postmodernist movements of the 1910s, 1930s, and 1970s-80s, respectively.
11. Alexei Kruchonykh (1886–1968)—a poet-futurist.

12. A blend of citations from three Russian poets: Pushkin, Esenin, and Pasternak.
13. Ivanov, Petrov and Sidorov are idiomatically used as the most typical Russian family names, symbols of an average Russian (like Jones or Smith in English).
14. Untranslatable wordplay. In Russian, the words "cherta" (line, feature, trait) and "chertochka" (little line, hyphen) are homonymous with "chert" (he-devil) and "chertovka" (she-devil). "Chertochka," according to the semantics of the diminutive suffix "-ochka," would mean not only "hypen," but also "little-she-devil," "devil's little daughter."
15. In Russian, the subject does not need to be stated for a thought to be considered complete. Russian impersonal sentences do not have even the formal subject that is expressed in English by the pronoun "it," the so-called expletive used merely to fill out a sentence.
16. An ironic reference to an idiomatic Russian expression: "Who did this? Pushkin?" or "Did Pushkin do this?" "Pushkin" here means "anybody else," especially in a situation in which a person wants to avoid responsibility for something done wrong and for which he allegedly has to blame "Pushkin." It is interesting that in Russian the name of the greatest poet is used to designate a universal "scapegoat," a ghost-performer of all those actions for which people do not want to take responsibility.
17. Russian expressions of this type (*mne teplo*—"I am warm", *mne kholodno*—"I am cold") are impersonal dative constructions that translate literally as "it is warm (cold) to me."
18. Plato, Ion, 534a, in *The Collected Dialogues of Plato,* ed. Edith Hamilton and Huntington Cairns (Princeton: Princeton University Press, 1994): 220.
19. "Stikhi vozvrashchaiutsia v stikhiiu." In Russian, the approximate homonymy of these two words, *stikhi* ("verses") and *stikhiia* ("element")— (both are derived from the Greek)—accounts for the intuitive perception of poetry as an "elemental" and "spontaneous" (*stikhiinyi*) outburst of spiritual energy.
20. The verses are cited from Alexander Pushkin, *Eugene Onegin,* trans. Charles Johnston (London and New York: Penguin Books, 1979): ch. 1, stanza 1, page 35; ch. 1, st. 5, p. 37; ch. 1, st. 46, p. 55; ch. 3, Tatyana's Letter to Onegin, p. 100; ch. 8, st. 20, p. 215; ch. 8, Onegin's Letter to Tatyana, p. 222.
21. Solovyov alludes here to Osip Mandel'shtam's metaphoric definition of citational art: "A quotation is not an excerpt. A quotation is a cicada. It is part of its nature never to quiet down. Once having got hold of the air, it does not release it. Erudition is far from being the same thing as the keyboard of allusions, which is the main essence of an education." Osip Mandel'shtam, *Selected Essays,* trans. Sidney Monas (Austin and London: University of Texas Press, 1977): 7.
22. Solovyov refers to Iosif Stalin, who died in 1953 when Ivan Solovyov was only seven years old.

23. Stalin was conventionally hailed in his lifetime as "the father of the Soviet people." Solovyov recalls a children's song popular during Stalin's dictatorship: "I'm a little girl, I play and I sing. Though I've never seen Stalin, I love him." In Pushkin's novel, Tatiana saw Onegin only once before she sent him her confession of love.
24. Alexander Pushkin, *Eugene Onegin*, ed. cit., p. 222.
25. Listed are works by Pushkin, Gogol, Dostoevsky, and Alexander Blok. Solovyov implies that the overwhelming acoustic effect of Pushkin and other Russian classics, multiplied by their echoes and resonances in Russian culture, will break his eardrums unless, at the risk of breaking his vocal chords, he releases the pressure in his head by shouting back "his own, internal Pushkin," etc.
26. Cited from Mandel'shtam's poem, "Insomnia. Homer. Tautly swelling sails . . ." Osip Mandel'shtam, *50 poems,* trans. Bernard Meares (New York: Persea Books, 1977): 37
27. Alexander Ivanov (1806–58)—a renowned Russian artist who worked mostly in the genre of monumental religious painting.
28. One of the last Pushkin poems (1836).
29. "K***" ("I remember the wonderful moment . . . ," 1825). *The Heritage of Russian Verse,* intro. and ed. by Dimitri Obolenski (Bloomington and London: Indiana University Press, 1976): 89.
30. In Russian, *sostoianie* (state of being) literally means "co-standing."
31. So far I have not found in Ivan Solovyov's archive any works written on behalf of Andrei Pushkin.
32. That is why this poem of eight lines proved to be the focus of a no-less-illustrious article by Roman Jakobson, "Poetry of Grammar and Grammar of Poetry," in his book *Language in Literature* (Cambridge, MA and London: The Belknap Press of Harvard University, 1987): 121–144.
33. "Avtorskaia ispoved'," in Gogol, *Sobranie sochinenii* v 7 tomakh (Moscow: Khudozhestvennaia literatura, 1986): v. 6, 413.
34. The narrator in Gogol's early collection *Evenings on a Farm Near Dikanka* (1831–32).
35. "Current work"—the first volume of *Dead Souls.* Gogol's letter to M. P. Pogodin, March 1837, in Gogol, ed. cit., v. 7, p. 156.
36. "With great effort I succeeded in publishing the first part of *Dead Souls,* as if in order to find how far I am still from what I was striving for. After that a graceless state again descended on me . . . I thought that the capacity of writing simply was taken from me." (Gogol's letter to Zhukovsky, 10 January 1848, ed cit., v. 7, p. 323.)
37. Gogol, "Four Letters to Different Persons on the Occasion of *Dead Souls,*" ed. cit., v. 6, 248.
38. The famous fact that Gogol received the ideas of his greatest works from Pushkin is supported only by Gogol's own evidence.

39. Ivan Solovyov imitates Pushkin's famous expression: *Eugene Onegin* is not just a novel, but a novel in verses: a diabolical difference.
40. During his sojourn in the village of Boldino (Nizhegorodskaiia province) in autumn 1830, Pushkin created many of his masterpieces, including "Belkin's Tales" and "Little Tragedies." Thus the phrase "Boldino autumn" in Russian literary language stands for the outburst of creativity and inspiration.
41. The reference to Shenstone in the subtitle of Pushkin's little tragedy is purely fictive; the English poet never authored anything like "The Covetous Knight."
42. The pen name of the English poet Bryan Waller Procter (1787–1874).
43. The first publication of this piece in the reputable Moscow journal *Novy Mir* was followed by the editorial comment: "Unfortunately, we do not have any additional information about the life, works and opinions of Ivan Solovyov. Curious readers may address Ivan Solovyov's executor Mikhail Epstein who now lives in Atlanta, USA. 'Executor,' according to the views of Ivan Solovyov himself, is almost like 'co-author,' and, in a certain sense, 'author.' " *Novyi Mir*, 8 (1996): 240).

The first publication of Ivan Solovyov's "Reflections on Eros" in English was accompanied by the following note by the editor Ellen Berry: "This work, written under the name of Ivan Solovyov, contains many conscious allusions and references to the legacy of the greatest Russian philosopher Vladimir Solovyov (1853–1900). Vladimir Solovyov was the founder of the philosophy of 'total-unity,' later adopted by many other Russian thinkers. In the twentieth century, one of its outcomes, ecumenism, became an increasingly influential movement for the reunification of all Christian churches and denominations. Vladimir Solovyov was also the founder of Sophiology, the doctrine about Sophia, the feminine hypostasis of Godhead, the divine wisdom and 'the soul of the universe.' " *Postcommunism and the Body Politic*, ed. Ellen Berry (New York and London: New York University Press, 1995): 264.

A philosophical dictionary states: "Influenced by German idealism, [Vladimir] Solovyov saw development as a progression from primitive unity through differentiation to a higher reintegration. . . . Reintegration requires the establishment of 'all-unity': the reuniting of the world with God . . ." *The Oxford Companion to Philosophy*, ed. Ted Honderich (Oxford and New York: Oxford University Press, 1995): 839. In other words, humankind, according to Vladimir Solovyov, is a single organism that goes through the continuous pangs of individualization and differentiation in order to achieve a state of "free unity," the symphony of fully developed personalities that arises out of their historical struggles and contradictions.

Thus Ivan Solovyov's theory of "symbiotic authorship" and poetry as a superpersonal "state of being" may have been inspired by the great Russian thinker bearing the same surname.

Chapter 22

InteLnet: Web Projects in the Humanities
Mikhail Epstein

http://www.emory.edu/INTELNET/
On the Web since July 1, 1995*

*T*he Social Innovations Award 1995 from the Institute for Social Inventions (London) as one of "the most imaginative, feasible and potentially transformative schemes."

The "InteLnet" stands for "Intellectual Network," an interactive site and virtual community devoted to the discussion and promotion of interdisciplinary ideas in the humanities.

What makes the InteLnet special among many intellectual sites on the Internet is its attempt to generate new ideas through electronic communication, to realize new interactive possibilities of thinking opened with the Internet as a whole. Not only does the word "InteLnet" sound like "Internet," but the former is an intellectual replica of the latter. The InteLnet is an intellectual connection among those cyberspaces that can be connected electronically.

For me, the Internet is analogous to the human mind, with its infinite conceptual links and associations. Now, retrospectively, I can interpret our attempts at collective improvisations in Moscow (1982–89) as a search for cyberspace within the more traditional space of a room and a roundtable. The idea of the InteLnet, an electronic community of creative minds, though in essence as old as the world, or at least as old as Plato's Academia, comes from my experience in that late-Soviet intellectual milieu. Together we tried to create integrated, "polyphonic" descriptions of certain cultural phenomena and to work out patterns of "translation" for different professional languages. Our improvisational community was a sort of pre-electronic InteLnet, which can now develop in a technologically more mature, global form.

The Internet can digitally link everything to everything else: ideas, disciplines, civilizations. Our capacity to understand and interpret these potentially infinite links is, however, limited by the traditional division of intellectual labor. For the time being the Internet, as a creation of a technical mind, by far exceeds the conceptual capacities of a humanistic mind. The InteLnet is an attempt to bring the humanistic "message" of the Internet in line with its electronic "media," to elaborate the methodology of thinking adequate to the multidimensionality and interconnectedness of computer networks. The InteLnet is one response of the human intellect to the Internet's challenge, a response of the creative mind to the challenge of the expanding universe of electronic communications. To use a Hegelian expression, the InteLnet evolves through the Internet as its self-awareness, as the conscious manifestation of its own Idea.

The InteLnet sets five goals and accordingly supports five branches:

1. to advance new ideas that reconfigure the paradigms of humanistic knowledge and transcend the borders of existing disciplines ("Bank of new ideas");
2. to investigate meaningful connections of concepts and ideas among the diversity of disciplines ("Thinklinks");
3. to elaborate the methodology of a new humanistic metadiscipline responsive to the demands and possibilities of an electronic environment ("InteLnetics");
4. to designate specific electronic sites for the crystallization of new humanistic disciplines and areas of research ("InteLnet journals"); and
5. to create interactive textual bodies that might grow in time and involve the collaboration of many minds ("Interactive Anthology of Alternative Ideas").[1]

Branch 1. Bank of New Ideas

The InteLnet can take on a role that neither a scholarly press nor an academic institution is able to fulfill—as a channel for connecting society with the work of its most powerful intellects. Any obstacles in this channel can lead to both the intellectual impoverishment of society and the deterioration of the social function of the intellect.

The traditional genre of the scholarly article or review, as it is established in professional journals, does not satisfy contemporary needs in intellectual communication. Articles frequently contain no new ideas whatsoever, or else their ideas are dissolved in the flow of background information that obscures the degree of actual novelty. The result is a kind of scientific folklore, involving a migration of motifs without any creative productivity: The means of synonymous expression in any language are unlimited. Many ideas lack definite authors, and many authors lack definite ideas. It is necessary to create a more flexible system of preservation and dissemination of ideas, one that could reflect the uninterrupted process of producing new knowledge, the continuity of cognitive activity itself.

One could justly point out that the evaluation of new ideas already takes place within academic forums, such as the dissertation defense, but these activities can go on for years: The idea accrues "accountable" supporting material, in which its original message and innovative impulse are likely to drown. In addition, the most innovative ideas are usually found on the borders between various fields, so that they have difficulty "passing muster" with specialized scientific councils and committees and are subsequently lost to that larger science for which they were intended. A truly new idea seldom fits into ready-made spheres of knowledge; rather, it wrenches itself away from the established set of dissertation topics to create its own sphere.

The task of the InteLnet is to present new ideas in the most direct and condensed form and to provide a public forum for their discussion. This is the "interest" that authors gain from their deposits in the Bank of New Ideas. It is not like a conference or a newsgroup where discussion is led by small and usually inconsistent impulses of opinions, remarks, rejoinders and objections. It is not like a professional journal treating some particular problems in a highly specialized language. What is crucial to the InteLnet is a specific genre of "a new idea," so pertinent to the receptiveness and responsiveness of the electronic network.

Criteria

The humanities, as compared with natural and social sciences, remain in a difficult situation as the very criteria for identifying and evaluating new ideas are unclear, yet virtually never discussed. For these reasons I will share the experience of the Bank of New Ideas, which was founded under the auspices of the Image and Thought intedisciplinary association in Moscow in 1986.[2]

The goal of this pre-electronic bank was to preserve and foster the ideas that showed a significant degree of innovation and potential for a productive impact on society. Discussion and registration of ideas was conducted by experts of the Interdisciplinary Council, representing several professions. A system of parameters was worked out for the evaluation of ideas, including the following:

1. Unexpectedness—the capacity to amaze, to disrupt theoretical paradigms and established patterns of thought.
2. Originality—innovativeness, the extent to which the idea differs from others previously put forth in its field.
3. Verifiability—the extent to which the idea is convincing in the light of available facts as well as its logical development from the foundations it proposes.
4. Expressiveness and aesthetic properties of the idea—the inner harmony of its components and levels of argumentation, the proportionality of deductive and inductive elements, its plasticity and clarity, accessibility to intellectual contemplation.
5. Breadth and scope—the volume of material embraced and interpreted by the idea, the range of its repercussions and theoretical generalizations.
6. Productivity—the heuristic potential of the idea to influence intellectual development in areas beyond its own basic material and disciplinary boundaries.
7. Realizability—the practical measure of the idea, as applied to its specific contents and contexts; the possibility of its actualization on various levels of social life.

Such are the principles employed by the Bank for the assessment of new ideas. With further refinement they could serve as a basis for a more extensive storehouse of interdisciplinary ideas and concepts.

Nothing unites one mind with another better than the flash of a new idea. The effectiveness of the InteLnet should consist in rapid dissemination of new ideas in the domain of public consciousness, without any introductions, conclusions, equivocations—just the concentrated essence of innovation. Some of the ideas may well prove fallacious, but the same rule should apply in the sphere of cognition that applies in ethics. It is better to acquit ten guilty people than to convict one innocent. It is better to voice ten fallacious ideas than to silence a single true one. It is likely that there are no fallacious ideas, just more and less productive ones.

Frequently Asked Questions

Q. What makes the InteLnet different from other Internet sites in the humanities?

A. Its interdisciplinary orientation, which does not imply dilettantism or disregard of intellectual rigor and responsibility, but accentuates new ideas rather than professional erudition.

Q. How will the novelty of my idea be recognized?

A. Unlike the technical disciplines, there are no patents for new ideas in the humanities. The Bank of New Ideas provides authors with the best possible certificate: The date of your submission is automatically registered and indicates your priority.

Q. Are there any restrictions on the number of submissions?

A. No. You are invited to deposit as many ideas as you can produce and want to share.

Q. Are there any restrictions on the disciplinary range of ideas?

A. Yes, there are.

Not accepted: ideas in technology, mathematics, natural sciences, empirical social sciences; purely critical or polemical ideas.

Examples of unacceptable ideas: (a) "Writer X borrowed this motif from writer Y, . . ." (b) "The results of this social poll show that . . ."; (c). "The following mistakes can be found in the monograph of Z . . ."

The most desirable ideas are constructive rather than critical and cross-disciplinary rather than monodisciplinary.

Q. Can I deposit an idea that was already published in another form (book, article, conference paper)?

A. Yes, you can, if this idea is presented in a capsule form and meets the demands of originality and transdisciplinarity. However, it is recommended that you use this unique space for ideas that have had no opportunity to be publicized in a more traditional manner.

Q. Is there a copyright for the ideas submitted to the Bank?
A. The authors of new ideas retain the copyright for their submissions (texts) and can use them as they find appropriate.

Q. Can I cite in my work passages from the materials collected in the InteLnet?
A. Yes, you can. References to the source, its author and the InteLnet are obligatory.

Guidelines for the Submission of New Ideas

You are invited to submit to the Bank your original ideas that cross the boundaries of existing disciplines, or lay the foundation for a new discipline, introduce a new paradigm into an existing discipline. Although there are no legal forms for the patenting of nontechnological ideas, the bank suggests the approximation of this procedure by recording the date of submission. The submissions should be limited to two to four pages, with possible links to more detailed sources. What is expected are unexpected ideas capable of creating their own field of knowledge and becoming foundations for new theories and/or practices. Such thinking can be called "paradigmatic" since it does not add a new element to existing paradigms but instead creates the paradigm itself.

Several Suggested Areas:

1. New cognitive concepts and research methods in the humanities
2. New disciplines and fields of scholarship
3. New artistic and literary movements
4. New models of social and professional behavior
5. New spiritual practices and movements
6. New methodological principles and metaphysical systems
7. Theory of everyday life
8. Alternative civilizations
9. Possible worlds

Immediately after the submission of your idea it is placed in the Bank and becomes available for every Web user. See the Repository of new ideas at: http://www.emory.edu/INTELNET/bank_response.html

Branch 2: Thinklinks

This branch of the InteLnet is designed to establish intellectual links among distant and seemingly unrelated spheres of knowledge. Thinklinks is a virtual metaspace where other cyberspaces (subjects, areas, disciplines) can interact and penetrate each other.

For many centuries, human knowledge developed through increasing specialization. This is, in particular, reflected in the hierarchical trees and subject directories on the Web, such as Yahoo. The same Web, however, creates a unique opportunity for remote fields to be instantly connected. Within the existing patterns of specialization, a new tendency is at work: to build interconnected, interlaced hierarchies of knowledge more reminiscent of a forest than of separate trees.

A *thinklink* is a basic unit of interdisciplinary thought, an attempt to connect within coherent logical discourse the concepts of various professional domains. A thinklink is similar to a metaphor in that it unites two heterogeneous images; a thinklink, however, is not a metaphor since it establishes the internal, logical connection of two concepts or phenomena rather their imaginative or associative resemblance.

Eventually, all these thinklinks could be incorporated into those subject areas they mutually connect. The resources and directories on linguistics, for example, will contain links to geology and gastronomy, astronautics and silentology, not only specific languages, grammars, and dictionaries. Thinklinks will constitute another dimension of the Web, making it intellectually what it already is electronically—a web rather than a rigid conceptual grid. In this sense, the InteLnet is a Contra-Yahoo as it interweaves "rhizomatically" distant categories and rubrics of knowledge rather than separating them.

Guidelines for the Submission of Thinklinks

You are invited to insert thinklinks—analytical connections among various subject areas on the Web. Thinklinks are not just an intellectual game or an exercise in creativity, but a new dimension of the Web, a metaspace where other spaces (areas, disciplines) come into interaction.

Please connect two or more subject areas in a single logical discourse or analytical essay. Size is limited to between 1 and 4 pages, or 300 and 1,200 words, with approximately 2 to 8 thinklinks interwoven in the text. Areas must be connected essentially and analytically, not just through personal preferences or idiosyncratic associations. (For example, statements like "I like to read Nietzsche when flying in an airplane," or "Two things I hate most of all are porridge and philosophy" do not constitute a thinklink between aviation, philosophy, and gastronomy). See an example of a "linguistics-gastronomy" thinklink: http://www.emory.edu/INTELNET/tl_lingvo_gastro.html

Branch 3. InteLnetics: Perspectives on Integrative Knowledge

Verbal Epigraphs

> In everything there is a part of everything.
> —Anaxagoras

> Everything exists only because of the argument between those who agree with each other and the love between those who argue.
> —Giordano Bruno

> Individuality contains infinity.
> —Gottfried Leibniz

> About each truth one can say something completely opposite to it and it will be equally true . . . Everything that is thought by a mind and said in words is one-sided. . . . But the world itself, everything existing around us and within us, never is one-sided.
> —Hermann Hesse

> Every thing can be described by means of any other thing.
> —André Breton

Figure II (see p. xi).

This is not a whimsical artistic fantasy, but a fractal picture produced by a computer on the basis of mathematical formulas discovered by an American mathematician of Polish origin, Benoit Mandelbrot. A fractal is a fragmented geometric shape that can be subdivided into parts, each of which is a reduced copy of the whole. Fractals describe many real-world objects, such as clouds, mountains, turbulence, and coastlines, that do not correspond to simple geometric shapes.

Ideal objects, such as concepts, ideas, and minds, can also be described as "fractals," in the sense that every idea potentially contains in itself many other ideas. Philosophers of various epochs, in their attempt to achieve universal knowledge, selected one, "primordial" aspect of the world and deduced from it all existing phenomena. "Water," "fire," "idea," "spirit," "matter," "will," "life," "existence," and other principles served more or less successfully to explain the totality of the world.

According to our epigraphs (both verbal and visual), the "world" as a whole consists not of abstract principles, but of smaller "worlds." Each world contains the previously mentioned principles, and all other possible principles as well. InteLnetics attempts to explain the totality of the world not from abstract particulars, but from their interaction within concrete totalities. The pyramid consists of pyramids, not of lines and points. Lines and points, as abstract units, or "principles," have their role in the construction of cubes, rhombi, parallelepipeds, and other forms, but they cannot explain what makes the pyramid the pyramid. The basic property of the world is "worldness," the capacity to encompass and connect the four basic elements and a number of other substances and properties in one whole.

InteLnetics, as any project of "universal science," could be easily challenged as still another utopian project, a kind of "perpetuum mobile." It is the birth of cyberspace, the all-embracing electronic network, that turns this abstract project into a feasible humanistic one.

A remarkable "coincidence": Cybernetics (now more routinely called "computer science") and what I propose to call "inteLnetics," a humanistic metadiscipline, have one spiritual father, the German philosopher and mathematician Gottfried Wilhelm Leibniz (1646–1716), who elaborated the project of a universal science capable of characterizing not only quantities but qualities. This project of *characteristica universalis* historically split into "technical" and "humanistic" parts, with the first part implemented in the World Wide Web. Now it is time for the two aspects of the "universal characteristic" to come together in a neo-Leibnizean synthesis. Cybernetics is here; it is now the time for inteLnetics . . .

Branch 4. InteLnet Journals in the Humanities

http://www.russ.ru/antolog/INTELNET/zhur_gum.html

These electronic journals take a middle course between highly specialized professional journals that employ only academic discourse, and intellectual journals that are designed for a general educated audience and do not have any thematic specialization or focus. InteLnet journals can be defined as *one-profile* and *multigenre* publications that combine the characteristics of academic and popular intellectual journals. They attempt to cover those realms of thinking and inquiry that have not yet crystallized into special disciplines and therefore need multiple levels of discourse starting with unprofessional observations and documentation, private diaries and correspondence, and ending with genres of articles, critical reviews, and other scholarly discourses. Several of these journals are devoted to ordinary life and to the very concept of ordinariness. Below are statements of purpose for the three journals.

In any useless occupation, one has to attempt to be divine. Or not to engage in it.

—Paul Valéry

Quiet Life

There are many journals devoted to the active forms of leisure: travel, sport, gardening, cooking, etc. This journal is devoted to the purposeless, useless, passive modes of spending leisure time. What do we do when we do nothing? What are the minimal forms of human activity? And how do they reflect personality and humanness? To stare out the window or loiter about the street—is it possible to be a master and expert in these useless activities; to develop a metaphysics of trifles, whims, pranks, tiny occupations, or no occupations at all? This journal deals with the concept of the ordinary because it has thus far attracted no attention from humanistic theory. In the meantime, it is the ordinary and not the political, aesthetic, technical, or mathematical that constitutes the larger part of human life. But is there a theory of the ordinary—Triviology or Ordinarics—that could compare in its weight and significance with mathematics, aesthetics, political science? Epicurus taught us to live imperceptibly or inconspicuously. But this does not mean that what is imperceptible to others should remain imperceptible to ourselves. Each individual is the best theoretician of his or her life. Nobody can replace him or her in the exploration of such a precious and unique material, neither Plato nor Hegel nor Marx nor any teacher of the humanities. This journal invites everyone to become a theoretician of one's own life and of those singularities with which we intimately surround ourselves. One person cannot live without soccer, another without a pipe, the third without his collection of stamps. And no one can live without the experience of breathing, walking, touching a cold windowpane or the rough bark of the tree. What is the significance of these ordinary experiences, and what do they add to our understanding of the nature of humanness?

Quiet life is the resource of our most tenacious unconscious memory, which awakens under the impact of hypnosis, brain trauma, or the threat of imminent death. In his book *Epilepsy and the Functional Anatomy of the Human Brain* (1985), Wilder Penfield demonstrates that such spontaneous flashes of memory, which happen on the threshold of death, invoke only the most mundane images, such as peeling vegetables, washing dishes, or watering the flowers in the evening. None of the patients he discusses remembered anything connected with strong emotions, generalizations, complicated professional tasks, or responsible decisions. What is remembered is the uneventful background that surrounds our ordinary life without provoking any noticeable response, that part of existence that escapes the consciousness and, as Proust remarked, due to forgetfulness is preserved in its untouched freshness.

It is true that the task of this journal is to introduce the quiet life into the field of consciousness and therefore to remove at least a tiny part of it from this storehouse of unconscious memories. But the imperceptible life extends into infinity, and it is possible to recover only one drop of it to lay the foundation for *the micrology of the ordinary,* for the investigation of its smallest forms, noneventful facts, microbes and viruses of daily existence.

Genius

Practice random geniality!

In the context of this journal, genius is not a permanent quality of special individuals but a certain state—mostly short-lived and transitory—that is familiar to many people. In Roman mythology genius is a deity of the momentary, the ephemeral. The journal publishes materials devoted to flashes of genius in diverse spheres of science and art, in everyday life, personal relationships, in love, in friendship, in leisure, in madness . . . The journal's motto presupposes that geniality (like kindness) can overstep all established boundaries (professional fields, ethical norms) and become a spontaneous, improvisational way of living. One can be a genius of silence, a genius of idleness; there may be geniuses of parenthood and housecleaning. In a mediocre text there may be glimpses of genius. The journal explores the nature of extreme capacities in the most ordinary conditions of their manifestation.

Scientiae Desiderata *(Desirable and Imaginable Sciences)*

This journal is devoted to nonexistent disciplines that have a certain epistemological potential and value, in particular, as bridges between science, desire, and imagination. Many sciences, like aesthetics or genetics, had individual creators and were first imagined on the basis of some preliminary experience, experiment, or intuitive knowledge before they were elaborated into separate disciplines. Though the nomenclature of institutionalized research includes already thousands of established disciplines, the process of their proliferation is unlimited and requires new investments of desire and imagination.

In his famous classification of sciences, Francis Bacon placed under the heading "Scientiae Desiderata" such disciplines as the theory of machines, the history of arts and sciences, and others that developed centuries later and now are firmly established. Almost all blank spots in Bacon's table of sciences came to be filled in the course of time, as empty rubrics in Mendeleev's periodic table of chemical elements did.

Scientific knowledge does not suppress human desires; on the contrary, it is moved by the force of desires and in its advancement realizes them more fully. In this sense Bacon's *Scientiae Desiderata* is probably the first conscious synthesis of science and desire, the expression of such deep and socially meaningful desires that determined the future of science.

On the eve of the twenty-first century, as the power of the imagination more and more insistently intervenes into the structure of scientific knowledge,[3] it is appropriate to concentrate our attention on the methodology of imaginable sciences. It is advisable that the essays on imaginable sciences (and also intellectual occupations and vocations) offered to this journal include at least some of the following components: (1) methodological introduction, rationale for the creation of a certain discipline, and perspectives on its practical application; (2) position of this discipline in the networks of knowledge and its relationship to other existing and imaginable sciences; (3) elaboration of the conceptual system of the given discipline and definition of its principal terms in their interconnection, including the possible interpretations of these terms on behalf of various scientific schools and trends within the discipline; (4) short illustrations of the definitions, excerpts from the major works and papers—the texts can be as imaginative as the discipline itself but they must demonstrate its categories and ideas in action; (5) the general situation in this discipline—its main contradictions, complexities, problems, challenges, perspectives, tendencies, debates, and confrontations; and a (6) bibliography, including short annotations and evaluations of the most fundamental and noticeable studies that can prepare the rise of this discipline and make it practicable in the future.

The role of the imagination in sciences is not limited to the task of their popularization but belongs to the very core of cognitive activity. In addition to *popular science* (such as popular physics or biology) and *science fiction*, which applies artistic fantasy to scientific subjects, there is a place for what can be called *imaginative science*, which elaborates those metaphoric and poetic potentials that are inherent in conceptual thinking as such. Along with the classification of sciences there is a need for an experimental branch of the philosophy of science that would deal with the construction of sciences. In fact, it was the father of modern experimental science, Francis Bacon, who initiated also the constructive methodology of sciences. Accordingly, Bacon's famous aphorism, "Knowledge is power," can be rephrased: "Imagination is the power of knowledge." Albert Einstein, however, expressed this epochal shift even more resolutely: "Imagination is more powerful than knowledge."

Other InteLnet Journals Include:

New Movements and Sects

The Theory of Voids (empty forms in nature and culture: holes, cavities, grids, webs . . .)

Russian Spleen: The Journal of Melancholy and Consolation

Northern Web: The Virtual Worlds of Russian Culture (WWW and Traditions of Communal and Apocalyptic Spirituality)

Hyperauthorship: The Journal of Virtual and Trans-Biological Authorship

The fifth branch of the InteLnet is the most voluminous and will be described in the next chapter.

Notes

* Founded and developed by Mikhail Epstein, the InteLnet received the Social Innovations Award 1995 from the Institute for Social Inventions (London) as one of "the most imaginative, feasible and potentially transformative schemes."
1. There is also the sixth branch, "Collective Improvisations: Experiments in the Communicative Generation of New Ideas." It was described in the previous chapters. See the electronic site devoted to collective improvisations: http://www.emory.edu/INTELNET/impro_home.html

Branches one through three and six currently exist only in English, branches four and five only in Russian.
2. On the history of this association and the pre-electronic forms of the Bank of New Ideas, see the chapter "Collective Improvisations and Transcultural Consciousness," in the "History" part of this book, pp. 48–51.
3. The ground-breaking works of Gaston Bachelard in the poetics of material elements and of George Lakoff and Mark Johnson on the role of metaphors in cognition, helped enormously to substantiate the connection between science and imagination.

Chapter 23

The Interactive Anthology of Alternative Ideas: An Introduction

Mikhail Epstein

http://www.russ.ru/antolog/INTELNET/kniga_knig.html

The Interactive Anthology is a collection of alternative ideas in various fields of the humanities: philosophy, ethics, aesthetics, linguistics, history of religions, and theory of culture. Fragments from many books serve as illustrations for these ideas that challenge established theories and concepts in the humanities. That is why the anthology is also called "Book of books," or "Book^2." Alternative thinking is different from negation or opposition: It does not require the removal or destruction of what already exists but rather adds another dimension or option, posits a new alterity.

For example, linguistics, a crowning discipline in twentieth-century humanities, is formed around words and sounds that break the silence, not around the silence from which the units of language and speech are extracted. Silence sets the boundaries for the activity of language and creates the possibility and background for its articulation. Thus a new alternative discipline may come into existence—the linguistics of silence or, more precisely, silentology, the exploration of pauses and ellipses, of "sils"— units of silence that form speech both phonetically and semantically and create subtext, ellipsis, aposiopesis, all kinds of figurative meanings. Accordingly, under the rubric "silentology," the anthology offers representative fragments from several books, such as *On the Borders of Language: Introducing the Linguistics of Silence*, *The History of Silence in Russian Culture*, and others. The IAAI is an encyclopedia of alternative thinking, a compendium of strange, suspicious, condemned, and exiled ideas that for various reasons were denied entry into the history of the humanities but with the anthology have a chance to be realized in the future.

Positive Deconstruction

The *Book²* is an attempt to deconstruct those concepts and theories that determine the identity and self-consciousness of the contemporary humanities. However, this is not the critical type of deconstruction that, following the initiatives of Michel Foucault and Jacques Derrida, became so widespread in Western academia. *The Book²* is a deconstruction through the creation of multiple variants, alternatives, competing models of conceptual systems. This is a *positive* deconstruction, or what we earlier called *potentiation,* designed to demonstrate that alongside each discipline, theory, concept, and term there exists its "shadow," which, from a different perspective, could appear as a primary object of consciousness. Positive deconstruction does not simply shatter the foundation of some system of concepts, exposing its vacillation and relativity and confronting a reader with an ironic "naught": no signified, no presence, no truth, no origin. Positive deconstruction deploys a series of constructive alternatives for a concept or theory; instead of focusing critically on the given discourse, it potentiates new ones, inscribes each concept into a broader framework where it can be posited as only one in a whole family or cluster of possible concepts. This is a logical potentiation of a term, multiplication of its possible meanings, the process of building it into a larger field of consciousness. The logic behind alternative thinking is not deductive or inductive but *abductive,* suggesting that a certain phenomenon can be abducted from the conceptual network to which it belonged for a long time. I would define abduction as a method of reasoning from which one infers an alternative explanation or conceptualization of the same fact.[1]

I think that new historical foundations for the abductive logic of potentiation were laid in Russia in the 1970s and 1980s, when the totalitarian system was already losing its grip on the social consciousness and growing relatively weak but at the same time remaining strong enough to extinguish any direct opposition or countermovement. Thus the system underwent a series of oblique and fuzzy metamorphoses, mutating toward the variety of alternative theories and practices on the margins of social consciousness without splitting or breaking it. Political dissidentism (*inakomyslie*) was only a small, visible island of this powerful vibrating other-thinking (*inomyslie*) that dissolved the solid foundation of the regime but surfaced much later. Along with the political Archipelago that Alexander Solzhenitsyn made famous, there was still another, intellectual Archipelago of silenced concepts, entrapped theories, and darkened corners of thinking that may only now emerge into the light of consciousness.

The metaphor of an archipelago perfectly fits these scattered islands of alternative thinking that resisted totality on each small conceptual plot of its aggression. Alternative thinking clung to each ideological slogan, philosophical postulate, or politico-economic term imposed by the official system and thought of it differently; multiplied its interpretations; potentiated from it different, equally relevant terms and postulates. If the official slogan was, following Marx, that "religion is the opium of the people," then, watching the ubiquitous alcoholism among the citizens of the first atheistic state, it was fair to conclude that "when religion is abolished as the opium of people, then opium becomes the people's religion."

Now all these islands of intellectual resistance come together to present an unknown configuration on the intellectual map of the twentieth century—a different GULAG: *Archipelago of Gonimykh Umov, Logicheskikh Al'ternativ i Gipotez* (Persecuted Minds, Logical Alternatives and Hypotheses).[2]

The *Archipelago GULag,* subtitled "An Experiment in Literary Investigation," is not just a single work; it is a literary genre created by Solzhenitsyn. *The Interactive Anthology* is a variety of this genre, but here the unit of representation is not a human life but a human thought—a manuscript, an idea, a conception . . . The Book^2 is an experiment in the encyclopedic presentation of lost or unsolicited ideas. This is not historical or documentary research, but, unlike Solzhenitsyn's book, it is also not a literary investigation, not a narrative. Rather, it is an imitation of encyclopedic discourse targeting the objects of consciousness: theories, concepts, and terms.

Books in Search of Authors

I have been working on *The Book*^{2} for fourteen years (since 1984), and I will continue to work on it for ten to twelve years more. *The Book*^{2} contains fragments of several hundreds of books on philosophy, theology, ethics, literature, and linguistics written by many authors (still unknown and mostly anonymous) in the years 1950 to 2000 in Russia. It is the Book of Condemned Ideas and Conceptual Provocations and contains

The Interactive Anthology of Alternative Ideas: An Introduction   293

challenges to Plato, Hegel, Marx, Nietzsche, and Heidegger, to all those who had the opportunity to establish their ideas in our civilization and thus, often contrary to their intentions, founded the intellectual Archipelago . . .

I would like to place among the Russian thinkers of the twentieth century those missing figures who never existed but could exist. They had something to think about and wished to share their thoughts with their contemporaries and with posterity. But these potential authors died in a political gulag, or their ideas perished in an intellectual gulag. There are books that have never been written; there are schools and trends of thought that never have emerged as a historical fact but still abide as a logical possibility, and therefore, exist as the reality of thinking. *The Book*[2] embraces this continuum of ideas that earlier or later had to find its entry into historical time. Regrettably, this happened later rather than earlier; still, it is important that logic, though lagging behind chronology, nevertheless could secure its place in the history of ideas.

I look at the *Dictionary of Theories*—"one stop to more than 5,000 theories[3]—or at the *Key Ideas in Human Thought*—"2,500 of the most important terms and concepts that have shaped the modern world."[4] Magnificent compendiums! Even Vladimir Lenin is here: "bolshevism," "vanguard party." And Mikhail Bakhtin is here: "polyphony," "carnivalization," "dialogism." But why can't I find in them the term "theomonism," coined by Yakov Abramov, or "verbject," suggested by Maksim Turnin? Because these thinkers were never given the chance to write, to publish, or sometimes even to exist. We do not discuss here which vicissitudes of social or biological evolution prevented them from becoming major thinkers of the twentieth century. Some were killed or exiled, some were banished from publishing, some fell into depression or madness, some married happily and withdrew from academic careers, some were never born because their potential parents died prematurely or never met each other. But their ideas still have the right to exist. The gaps in existing dictionaries need to be filled. And if the twentieth century was cruel enough to forsake some valuable elements of its intellectual heritage, let the twenty-first century recover them and erect a monument to them at the entry to the new millennium.

I would like to collect in this Book all possible metamorphoses of thought that were solicited by the logic (or absurdity) of our life in Russia towards the end of the communist era, on the crossroads of so many intellectual traditions coming from Judaism and Christianity, from fathers of the church and founders of the Enlightenment, from Plato and

Hegel, from Marx and Nietzsche, from Tolstoy and Dostoevsky, from Solovyov and Fedorov ... My intent is to bring together all those disparate variants and alternatives of thinking over which this epoch wracked its brains searching for the escape from the prison into which Thinking itself, in its most sublime, idealistic, and ideocratic models, incarcerated the being and the lives of all of us.

The books contained in this book are looking for their potential authors not only in the past, but also in the future. Every text presented here is only a fragment that miraculously survived the fire that destroyed our Philosophical Archive ... But each text is also only a rough draft of those books that might comprise the Library of the Humanities in the coming century. This is a book of new disciplines, methods, trends, and paradigms of thought that were never given a chance to be written. The presses that could have produced these books and the stores that could have sold them were banished. *The Book*[2] is not a collection of real books but is an attempt to restore the imaginable books of the past and to stimulate their writing in the future. Their excerpts are obtained from the library of the twenty-first century, where the humanistic archive of the twentieth century would have been preserved.

I wrote the first draft of the book, about fifteen hundred pages, in Moscow in 1984–88. Although it contains no borrowings from other authors, except for those that are explicitly quoted, this book is designed as a collection of many books that have been written by other authors. Which authors, will depend on those creative readers who will volunteer to assume authorial rights and responsibilities.

To Potential Authors

I address here all readers of *The Interactive Anthology of Alternative Ideas*. If, in any of the books that comprise the anthology, you recognize your own voice, please consider it to be your own. Add new chapters, finish this book and publish it under your own name. In relation to these books, all rights of intellectual property are revoked. It is not only permissible but desirable that all fragments be adopted by an author who will take full responsibility for their fate and further embodiment of a given idea. If you feel that an idea is simply stolen from you, that you had been thinking the same way but just forgot to write it down, then please, consider this idea your own, consider yourself the author of any book of your choice and to your taste. Polish and finish it and submit it to publishers under your own name. It depends on you whether the given fragment will take the form of a book, an article, an essay. But don't fail to attend to it if it contains something cogent for your mind—introduce it into the family of your creations.

I would be happy to receive a notice from you about your adoption of a certain fragment. Then I will put under this text your full name, and you will be confirmed as its author. If an editor or a publisher should become interested in this book, he will address you, not me. If at least part of these fragments are adopted and grow into separate books, in two or three generations an entire library will emerge from *The Book²*, whose initial fragments will become scattered and forgotten, as rough drafts that have been many times revised and expanded.

I hope that eventually the Book² will acquire as many authors as there are books in it. As many signatures as there are titles.

I will cite the titles of several books that are sampled and excerpted in *The Book²*:

The Kenocracy of the Future
Introduction to Theolinguistics
A Thing as an Object of Ethics
A History of Penny-Pinching and Hair-Splitting
Morphology of Garbage
How to Collect Nonexistent Objects
Physiosophy of the Itch
Cells and Holes
Poetics of the Dictionary
Minus-Epistemology

All books are open for free authorization, except for the *Book of books* itself, its prefaces and afterwords, which belong exclusively to me. Are foster authors subject to some moral or material obligations? It is desirable that you give an articulate expression to a certain idea, transform it into a monograph, an article, a practical project. But if this does not happen, it's not your fault, it's the fault of the idea itself that failed to be viable and vigorous enough to receive proper embodiment. Hence my only request: If you feel that the adopted fragment is wasted, please return it where it belongs, that is, let me know that you are returning the idea to *The Book²*. No explanations or apologies are needed. Simply from now on the text will be expecting another foster author.

Now it is easy to imagine an American-style advertisement for this Russian intellectual product: *Free selection of texts for all manner of creative uses and intellectual appropriations. A paradise for thinkers and scholars: a collection of new ideas, never signed and cited before. Fragments of books that were never published. Drafts for numerous books that await their authors.*

Virtual Books

The hope of this anthology is that it will find many foster authors who will develop and complete its numerous fragments. But a still deeper hope is that some of these fragments will stay unauthorized and present the books from which they are extracted in their essential virtuality. The term "virtual book" here will refer not to an electronic form of a book but to the virtuality of every book inasmuch as it presents a possibility for reading that rarely comes to fulfillment. Usually we purchase a book not in order to read it immediately but in order to have the possibility of reading it in some imaginable time and space. The majority of books are present in our consciousness as a set of authors' names, titles, and several key ideas and fragments. One hundred lines usually contain about one-half of the entire information that we assimilate from the book even after it is completely read.

The virtual book consists of two or three pages, one of them being the title page and the others containing several short excerpts. The virtual book is an intellectual form of the book without its textual extension. It is a function of a book separated from its physical substance. It is a sign of "book" without the signified. It is the eschatological expectation of the book that never fully comes through but allows us to experience even more sharply the "bookness" of the book precisely as a result of its substantial absence, as a pure potentiality that is not damaged by actualization.

It is important for such a book to have a title in order to function differently from the genres of aphorism or maxim, which speak for themselves, not on behalf of some larger virtual whole. An aphorism does not have margins. It destroys the surrounding space (context) by exhausting the topic in its most condensed formulation, whereas a virtual book institutes broader margins than could be filled by any amount of text. A virtual book may further be divided into virtual chapters and sections citing appropriate excerpts from them and expanding even more its internal space.

Thus, *The Book*[2] is a collection of virtual books that should be partly completed to generate a library of the future, and remain partly empty to demonstrate their pure potentiality.

Reverse Citations

The Book of books not only projects future books but virtualizes existing books, authors, and systems of thought, thus creating virtual spaces and meaningful "bubbles" in the substance of culture. Many sections of the Book are created by the method of the "reverse citation." Direct citation is my use of someone else's words; reverse citation is the donation of my words to another author. Reverse citations are necessary to rethink the heritage of some authors of the past who initiated certain intellectual movements that have not found and will never find their full expression either with these thinkers themselves or with their followers. The potentiality of Hegel's thought exceeds its actuality as fixed in the body of his texts. Hegel continues to think through my own consciousness. In the manner of Hegel one can produce a variety of utterances that relate the potentiality of his thought with the actuality of new historical conditions. For example, we cannot find in Hegel any references to the Bolshevik revolution, World War II, or the Internet though Hegelian thought to a certain degree initiated these historical events and can illuminate them.

"The realization of the Absolute Idea in the period of its post-capitalist development goes through the phase which can be characterized as an attempt at suicide." Are you not familiar with this often-quoted utterance? This is Hegel's inscription on the margins of Lenin's book *State and Revolution*.

Instead of inserting ideas from other authors into *The Interactive Anthology*, we will insert its excerpts into many other books and systems of thought. Sometimes these are unknown works of great thinkers, such as Hegel's unfinished treatise, *History Beyond Logic*, or a draft of Nietzsche's aphorism "Will for Defeat."

If reverse citations are attributed to previously published works, we give a precise reference including the number of the page and of the paragraph where an alternative turn of thought could take place. For example,

»The possible as compared with the real is the being of the first and the third order whereas the real belongs only to the second order because it actualizes some possibilities and potentiates others. The real is only a mediation between two orders of possibilities.«[5]

Of course, do not bother to look for this utterance in the indicated section of Hegel's *magnum opus*[6]; it is inscribed into Hegel from the *Interactive Anthology* and belongs to alter-Hegel, the alternative possibility of Hegelian thought that was never realized in his works but was suggested by them. Accordingly I designate reverse citations with reverse quotation marks.

The reader will discover that a certain sentence could be inscribed into Hegel, another into Plato, a third into Descartes in such a way that if these citations had been assimilated by these authors their thought could develop in a different direction and bring forth a different history. These inscriptions serve as alternative formulations of familiar ideas that reveal their capacity for self-differentiation. The aim of the *Interactive Anthology* is not to criticize or synthesize but to *potentiate* the previous systems of thought through their alternative rereadings and rewritings. If the Hegelian history of philosophy sublates all previous teachings in the final synthesis, then the *Interactive Anthology* unfolds multiple projections of ideas, as an experiment in their transformative interpretation.

I inscribe in Socrates: »I do not know what I know.« I believe that this utterance belongs not to myself and not to the historical Socrates but to an alternative Socrates. The historical Socrates pronounced, "I know that I know nothing," but this capacity to transcend one's own limits of knowledge should be investigated in both directions, as my superiority over my ignorance and my inferiority to my own knowledge. The fact that historical Socrates explored only one of these alternatives encourages us to explore the other, to "abduct" the thought from Socrates and to return to him a different thought.

I indulge in those potentials of thinking that can be revealed at the borders of the historical record both as resulting from and alternative to the original concepts. This is a retroactive history of thought read not from the previous periods to the present but from the present to the past, which will also integrate the openness of the future. For me Socrates, Descartes, and Hegel are thinkers not only of the past but also of the future, still unknown to themselves and to anybody else in the world. The history of philosophy embraces these multiple alternatives, which depart from the past and, making a circle, return to the past in the form of alter-Socrates and alter-Hegel.

I find counterproductive the "anti" genre, such as Engels's *Anti-Dühring,* or Marx's and Lenin's numerous critical works that could be titled *Anti-Proudhon, Anti-Mach* , etc., which is so characteristic of the Marxist classics, masters of short-lived polemics. "Anti-" is a degraded form of "alter-." If you have something to say against a certain thinker, say it for him and on his behalf because even this criticism is provoked by his own thought and should be reinscribed as alternative ramifications and bifurcations in the corpus of his work.

Thus, the Book of books aims to create virtual spaces in the systems that seem to be most solid and esteemed in the history of ideas. This is what I understand by the term "potentiation." Even the actuality of the past still contains those resources of alterity, those potentials for rewriting, not only rereading of history that make the past open to the indeterminacy of the future. Since the twentieth century has more systematically worked in the opposite, utopian direction, trying to impart to the future the determinacy of the past, the potentiation of the past is a post-utopian gesture of compensation with which the century comes to an end.

I would like to further illustrate the range of the reverse citational mode by presenting a collection of responses to the *Interactive Anthology* itself.

Preliminary Reviews

The interactive network InteLnet conducted a poll of outstanding authors from various cultures regarding the *Interactive Anthology* (*Book of books*) on the eve of its first electronic publication. According to the standards of American documentation, the responses are listed in the reverse chronological order of their submission.

> »Announcing the end of the Book and the beginning of the epoch of Writing, one has to admit that the interval between these two epochs is filled with all kinds of "metabooks," which retroactively project the infinity of writing on the discrete genre of the book and therefore explode the latter from within.«
>
> —Jacques Derrida

> »The medieval library was composed of numerous commentaries on a single Book. The postmodern Middle Ages move in the opposite direction: from the scholastic culture of multiple commentaries to a single metatext, to a Book-as-Library. That is why the second millennium ends with the Interactive Anthology.«
>
> —Umberto Eco

> »Russian metaphysics of the Soviet era as presented in this Anthology has reached us only in scattered fragments and is reminiscent of the elusive heritage of the gnostics or the pre-

Socratics. *The works in their entirety were either destroyed or banished from publication by the victorious dialecticians—powerful persecutors of metaphysicians. The genre of the Book reminds me of the ancient doxography of Diogenes Laertius's* Lives and Opinions of Eminent Philosophers. *Unlike the latter, the* Anthology *is almost void of "lives" and contains only "opinions." In this sense, Russian metaphysics of the twentieth century is even more ancient and mythic than Thales and Anaxagoras.«*

—Milorad Pavic

»*This colorful world is split into a multitude of glittering fragments, and, like that of Balzac and Dostoevsky, is also the result of the turbulent invasion of capitalism into the relatively quiet stagnant Russia of the period of rotting feudal communism. This book reflects a gigantic collapse, unexpected collisions of such diverse systems of thought that previously peacefully coexisted in the sleeping consciousness of Brezhnev's epoch.«*

—Fredric Jameson

»*Artistic strategies—estrangement and polyphony—elaborated by Russian theoreticians Viktor Shklovsky and Mikhail Bakhtin now have been transferred into the domain of an imaginative history of ideas. The most conventional schemes of thought that go back to Plato and Aristotle all of a sudden are estranged, de-automatized and reveal their strangeness, whimsical character, and even a touch of madness.«*

—Julia Kristeva

»*It is easier to perceive the nature of a flower from one flower than from hundreds of flowers. This is a book that contains hundreds of books and at the same time does not resemble any of them.«*

—Araki Yasusada

»*This book has an unusual quality: The thoughts that you extract from it are easily forgotten, but when you recall them you cannot find them where they once were. It seems that*

> during your absence, somebody shuffled the pages or rewrote them anew.«
>
> —Michel Montaigne

Notes

1. See a somewhat different explanation of the term "abduction" by Chris Eliasmith in his entry in the electronic *Dictionary of the Philosophy of Mind*: http://artsci.wustl.edu/~philos/MindDict/abduction.html.
2. GULag (*Gosudarstvennoe upravlenie lagerei*) is a Russian acronym for the Soviet government agency that supervised labor camps in Stalin's epoch. Solzhenitsyn used this term as a metaphor for labor camps that were scattered through the ocean of civil society like a chain of islands extending from the Bering Strait almost to the Bosporus.
3. Jennifer Bothamley, *Dictionary of Theories* (London, Detroit, and Washington D.C.: Gale Research International Ltd, 1993).
4. *Key Ideas in Human Thought,* ed. Kenneth McLeish (New York: Facts on File, 1993).
5. Hegel, *Encyclopedia of Philosophical Sciences,* Vol. 1, Science of Logic. Second Subdivision. The Doctrine of Essence. C. Actuality, paragraph 143 n.
6. Actually Hegel wrote: "[A]ctuality is the more comprehensive, because it is the concrete thought which includes possibility as an abstract element. And that superiority is to some extent expressed in our ordinary mode of thought when we speak of the possible, in distinction from the actual, as only possible." The alter-Hegel's utterance belongs precisely to this section on actuality from which it is eloquently absent, because it could subvert the entire system of Hegel's idealism-historicism-actualism.

In Place of a Conclusion: Transcultural Dialogue

Ellen E. Berry and Mikhail N. Epstein

Our individual voices and critical identities have interfered with one another in a variety of ways throughout this book. The introduction merges our perspectives in a fully collaborative attempt at joint authorship written in a more-or-less impersonal mode of critical discourse. In the main sections of the book our voices diverge from and alternate with one another as each of us writes our own individual chapters adopting distinct conceptual strategies, from the analytical and critical to the improvisational and poetic. Here, we return to a fully collaborative effort, but one in which our individual voices are distinctly audible and encounter each other freely. The following "inconclusive" dialogue covers a range of topics and touches on many of the points of commonality and difference that have emerged consistently from our writing. We include subheadings so as to guide the reader more clearly through our conversation, but beyond this we did not wish to constrain the free flow of ideas contained here.

On Marxism I.

BERRY: Marxism is important for me because it's still one of the only systems that has a comprehensive vision of social justice and an analysis of the roots of social injustice. This needs to be qualified by saying that I don't think Marxism as a theory is the same as state socialism as a system of government, so that the "fall" of the Soviet Union doesn't necessarily invalidate Marxism as a theory. My attachment to Marxism in part arises from the way in which it is filtered through feminism. Although these two systems of thought are not wholly compatible in their assumptions or methodologies—as many feminists have shown—I admire the fact that they both try to offer a systematic explanation of the roots of human misery and injustice; in the case of feminism it would be the dominance of patriarchy as a long-standing global system that varies in its individual manifestations. One problem that I find with both Marxism and feminism is in the determinism that each falls victim to. This can lead to reductive explanations and also to paralyses of will and imagination since they can be so rigid in terms of how they explain human intentions and possibilities.

EPSTEIN: Does this represent any evolution in your thinking about Marxism and feminism?

BERRY: I started out as a quasi-Marxist in the early 1970s—the time when my political consciousness was first being formed—because it was the only real political discourse I found available, the only discourse of opposition to the way things were. Those of us who rejected the Vietnam War as an immoral action on our country's part often resorted to Marxist categories of explanation. I became disenchanted with the antiwar movement—as many of my friends did—when I saw how sexist in practice it really was, and many of us formed consciousness raising groups to discuss our evolving feminist awareness. At this point I am much less ready to believe that any one system of explanation—however subtle or powerful—can be the whole answer or can provide a fully useful model of analysis. The problems facing humankind are so much vaster and more complex than either feminism or Marxism or postcolonialism can possibly explain.

On Feminism I.

EPSTEIN: Are there any tensions between Marxism and feminism in your understanding?

BERRY: As I understand it, the "woman question" for Marx was really submerged within larger questions of the class struggle, whereas feminists, broadly speaking, want an analysis that foregrounds the gender struggle; they see gender inequality as prior to class inequality and focus more directly on the realm of the private sphere and forces of reproduction rather than solely on the public economic sphere and the forces of production. It has frequently been the case in third world struggles for liberation, for instance, to claim that the woman question can wait until after the revolution. So women fight right alongside of men and then when the revolution has been accomplished the old gender inequalities return.

The case of women's roles in Russia today is a good example of how existing socialism did very little to alter the fundamental gender inequality of patriarchy even though women supposedly were considered equal under the law. Typically this meant freedom to live within a double standard such as the classic two jobs—one outside the home and the other once the woman gets home. Many Russian women, having spent years on this treadmill, now want to have a domestic life and all the "feminine" refinements—a desire that many Western feminists have trouble understanding. But the desires of many Russian women have to be put in the context of their lives under the Soviet system. Western women must be careful not to judge these women through our own values or to automatically advocate in more postmodern terms the deconstruction of gender differences altogether.

EPSTEIN: Many women participated in Marxist parties. Are there any men participating in feminist movements in the United States?

BERRY: I think that there are many men of genuine good will who would consider themselves feminists. But the fact is that men simply have less of an investment in wanting to see gender hierarchies changed because these hierarchies tend to advantage most men or because many men have a hard time seeing them as hierarchies just as people who are white or able-bodied have a hard time understanding what it is like for others to live in a racist or able-bodied culture. I think the thing that appeals to me most about *transculture* is that it is also a theory of empathy, in which people try to imaginatively inhabit many forms of difference and otherness and therefore develop a greater emotional or empathic range. Until we really understand how forms of systematic discrimination and power imbalances hurt all of us, then things are unlikely to change in any meaningful sense. Perhaps transculture can be one small contribution to helping people live beyond the narrow boundaries of their personal existences and thus to see the open possibilities around and between them. What is your history with Marxism?

On Marxism II.

EPSTEIN: Marxism had such a tragic and bloody history in Russia that my personal history with it was over even before I became a conscious being. The generation of my parents, terrified and silenced, already had ample evidence that social injustice could be even more outrageous in an "egalitarian" society built on Marxist principles. For me Marxism is one of these modernist theories that propagate in increased proportions the same evil that they claim to exterminate. It claimed to be the theory of collective action, but in reality it led to the destruction of any social bonds among people and even between colleagues and relatives. It claimed to be a materialist theory but in fact it destroyed material prosperity and submitted everyday life to abstract ideological constructions. It claimed to be a theory of the most effective economic organization of society but in reality it proved to be catastrophic for Russian industry and agriculture.

I think Marxism is an extremely bright theoretical hallucination that turns into dust and nothingness as soon as you try to realize it, to touch it with your hands. On the surface, it can be blamed for being recklessly reductive, attempting to reduce a personality to his or her class origin, reduce a human being to the totality of social relationships, reduce culture and spirituality to their economic bases and relationships of production. But the danger of Marxism goes far beyond this error (and terror) of reductionism. The point is that classes, societies, economic basis, material existence—all these realities that proclaim their theoretical priority in Marxism—are ultimately not reinforced but annihilated as a result of its practical application. It is not that the restriction of spiritual freedoms and individual rights in Marxist societies leads to the triumph of collectivist economic modes—both are mutually ruined, because one is impossible without the other. No such things as pure materiality or pure sociality exist in a real society; they are abstract ideas posited as hallucinatory visions that lead to the collapse of exactly those entities they claim to sustain and advance. No social relationships exist beyond free human choices and personal ties; no forces of material production exist beyond human intelligence and spiritual capacities. Therefore Marxism not only destroys higher realities for the sake of lower ones—this is the site of reductionism—but also destroys lower, foundational realities since they are converted into pure illusions, abstract essences by the force of overspeculative and self-negating reason.[1] The latter is the site of self-destruction. The result of Marxist praxis is neither burgeoning culture—it was killed by materialistic reductionism—nor material prosperity—it was destroyed by ideological chimeras. Marxism is a theoretical entry into a black hole of history.

BERRY: Why do you think that Marxism has remained such an attractive idea to left intellectuals in this country? What did you think of this phenomenon when you first came to America?

EPSTEIN: When I first came to the United States in 1990, I was struck by the intellectual influence of the Marxist paradigm in this country. Here Marxism did not succeed in its traditional sphere of igniting class struggles, but instead it expanded into those areas where it was hardly applied in the Soviet Union: the theory of multiculturalism, for example. If traditional Marxism reduces all cultural products to class origin, what came to the forefront in the United States was racial origin, sexual origin, ethnic origin as well as physical condition and age group. I felt as if I had been transported back to the 1920s when so-called vulgar sociologism was in its full swing in the Soviet Union and Pushkin was criticized as the mouthpiece for the nobility, though partly excused by the fact that it was only the petty nobility that he gave voice to in his poems. Practically all aspects of human nature, all those inborn qualities like race, gender, health, and so on, were advanced as the final motivation and justification for cultural activity. I can explain this obsession with the nonclass application of Marxism by the fact that its Western adherents consciously or unconsciously still avoid instigating really explosive class antagonism on a Marxist basis.

For some academic intellectuals, Marxism and multiculturalism are ways to expand their transcultural experience, to convert themselves conditionally and temporarily into "oppressed minorities." In prerevolutionary Russia, Marxism also was propagated almost exclusively by the members of the nobility and the intelligentsia although it claimed to express the deepest needs and aspirations of the toiling masses. Therefore, one can distinguish between Marxism as a revolutionary self-destructive practice and as transcultural play, a mode of crossing one's cultural borders that may become quite a positive experience of otherness for an intellectual putting himself or herself in the position of a factory worker or a black mother. This constructive application of Marxism and multiculturalism is possible only if we inscribe it in a transcultural framework and thus limit its intrinsic claims for the revolutionary dismemberment of the society. Certainly Marxism as such would not accept such limitations and would categorize transculturalism as the petit bourgeois play of intellectual transvestism; but then Marxism can be accordingly assessed as a mode of social transvestism, with intellectuals dressing up as proletarians. That's why again I would suggest that the only way to preserve at least a grain of Marxism, if anybody is interested in its preservation today, would be to read Marxism as one of many intriguing transcultural practices, as a form of the transcultural imaginary.

BERRY: Do you think the problem with Marxism primarily arises because it seeks to provide a total explanation, that it is a totalizing system as such, or because it simply is inaccurate, that it fails to explain how human history evolves? Is transculture itself in danger of simply being another—alternative—total explanation?

EPSTEIN: I would fault Marxism not with being a totalizing theory but with totalizing on the basis of a very limited and particular segment of human existence, such as class identity or material production. Totalitarianism is historically connected with the rule of one party; the very meaning of these words indicates the foundational substitution of the part for the whole, party for the totality, *pars pro toto*. Totality as such should not be confused with totalitarianism. Transculture as I understand it is a totalizing approach indeed, but in such a way that it curbs the totalitarian pretensions of any part of culture, any theory and any discipline to advance itself as the whole truth. Transculture is the process of self-distancing, self-estrangement, and self-criticism of one's own cultural identities and assumptions. That's why we should discriminate between (1) totalitarianism that claims the whole to be a privileged possession of one particular historical subject—the proletariat, the Communist party, the Soviet state, or any specific race, gender, church, or doctrine; and (2) totalization that works through incessant self-limitation of our cultural claims and the recognition of the other's ability to produce a more adequate image of us than we can.

Totalization, in this case, is an experience of infinite self-limitation, not self-aggrandizement. I am only this small entity, belonging to a certain gender, time, space, ethnicity, class, age . . . That's why I am in such desperate need of being different from myself. In order to transcend my limits I have to admit my limitations. Cultural humility is the best premise for transcultural totalization.

On Feminism II.

EPSTEIN: In your view, how could feminist topics be rethought from a transcultural perspective?

BERRY: Feminism has suffered from some of the same problems that you identify with multiculturalism. The imperative to recognize differences among women and to honor and respect those differences often has had the consequence of splitting feminists into multiple groups that do not necessarily interact with one another. We are so afraid of misunderstanding each other or of failing to respect the other woman's difference that we tend not to engage with her at all. This is certainly the safest route (no danger of offending if there's no interaction), but unfortunately it has also compromised feminist action and the production of more expansive and adequate feminist theories; it has led to the pluralization of feminism into multiple versions—psychoanalytic, postcolonial, black, materialist, etc. I think feminism desperately needs to find a way to deal more productively with differences among women and to find ways of thinking about feminism as something other than (or in addition to) simply the sum of the many various kinds of feminism that comprise it. Transculture—by providing a model of intersubjectivity and interaction that builds on and for difference—holds great promise for feminist applications.

EPSTEIN: What about the basic difference not within feminist movements but in the relationship between women and men? What kinds of interference between male and female cultures are possible if we presuppose the existence of these separate cultures in the first place?

BERRY: Good question. I'm not sure that I see male and female cultures as wholly distinct. There are certainly more similarities between you and me—as educated writers about culture—than there are between me and a fourteen-year-old pregnant girl who has dropped out of school. What I do share with this young woman is that we both exist in a culture that still divides power and privilege unequally according to gender (among other things!). We also live in a culture that is resisting the attempts to change relations between men and women into more equitable ones—there is, I think, much "backlash" on a cultural level that expresses itself in everything from increasing violence against women to the right's call for a "return to family values." I think we are at an important cultural moment for male and female relations; we desperately need to learn to love each other's differences (wherever those differences come from). And I think the model of transculture at the very least can provide an imaginative space—if not a social space—for us to explore our multiple differences from each other as they would configure themselves along gender lines. This would include an interrogation of our own differences from ourselves—my own maleness or what might exist outside or in between the categories of male and female—some new genders or an escape from gender altogether?

EPSTEIN: Does not love between men and women include love of each other's differences, and is not sexual love in this sense a most powerful transcultural experience?

BERRY: Yes, in its ideal state love should and can mean this, can include this even if it is other than heterosexual. But I think so many expressions that are called love are based on the desire for the other to fulfill my ego, to be my ego-ideal. This automatically cancels out a true recognition of his/her difference. We need ways to approach the other's otherness without fearing it or seeking to tame or distort it. If one accepts a psychoanalytic model one would be fairly pessimistic about this possibility.

On Education and Emotions

BERRY: On a related topic, do you think the transcultural method or perspective can be applied and taught; should it be a part of what we try to bring to our students?

EPSTEIN: The transcultural approach not only can be taught but it underlies the very process of teaching. What I would suggest is not so much to teach transculture as a separate discipline as to transculturalize the process of education. Education should proceed from the assumptions that, first, the teacher and the student belong to different cultural formations at least by virtue of their age, gender, and experience; second, teaching is not simply the transference of knowledge from a full space to an empty space but is an interaction between differently filled spaces; third, the teacher must find a place for students' cultures in his/her own system of values, and therefore can expect that a student will find a place for the teacher's culture in his/her system of values; and fourth, the teacher is the one who initiates and leads such an exchange and this is what makes him/her a teacher.

BERRY: Are the rational and the emotional equally necessary to what might be called transcultural consciousness? We've talked about empathy and love as being necessary states of being. Are there other emotions that would be important to cultivate, say perhaps wonder? What about the darker emotions of rage or jealousy or hate? What role might they play? How would we prevent them from being disruptive of the transcultural bond, of productive modes of interference? This is a question involving both individuals and individual cultures.

EPSTEIN: Emotions are the most precious experience of otherness that is given to us. From a purely rational point of view we can construct any broad, abstract categories submerging all differences into a kind of overarching unity. Emotions, however, keep us within the network of differences and simultaneously work to unite people on the basis of these differences. To give the simplest example, love is what unites people on the basis of their gender difference. Pity or compassion is the emotion evoked by the difference between the weak and the strong or the sick and the healthy.

Is there any criterion for the demarcation between positive and negative emotions? I would suggest that all emotions proceed from the experience of difference, but positive ones tend to transform this difference into unity, whereas negative ones transform it into opposition. Fury, anger, hate, jealousy, envy, resentment, contempt push the differences between people to the level of confrontation and mutual exclusiveness. Also what makes the emotions negative is the closure of our identity, the inability to open oneself as the cause of hatred, contempt, anger. Multiculturalism, though it has a noble intent of recognizing the values of diverse cultures, often degenerates into suspicion and hatred because these cultures are thought to be self-sufficient and self-enclosed. Thus, not only is the experience of otherness mostly emotional, but the character of these emotions indicates the vector of moving from otherness to either opposition or unity.

On Transculture and the Avant-Garde

BERRY: Is it necessary from a transcultural point of view to accept a culture's darkest pathologies as part of transcultural "evolution"? Are evolution, cultural maturity, or cultural balance even terms we should consider using?

EPSTEIN: Yes, I think that transculture should embrace the diversity of cultural experiences, both good and evil, light and dark, inasmuch as these experiences are really perceived as different. If the polarity between good and evil is eliminated then you have no moral experience at all, neither of good or evil. Some of Dostoevsky's characters, such as Stavrogin in *The Devils,* try to extract the greatest pleasure from doing both good and evil to other people; but the sharpness of this pleasure is maintained only insofar as the evil is experienced in contrast to the good. As soon as these two poles are neutralized as sources of equally sharp pleasure, pleasure itself loses its sharpness and the characters, like Stavrogin, are moving toward suicide. Transculture lives by differences that include positive and negative, gentle and cruel, humanist and misanthropic aspects of various cultures. Poles are acceptable precisely in their polarity. Differentiation is what gives sharpness to our experience, and transculture can be seen as the continuum of the most intense cultural experiences due to their differential nature. This position can be formulated, in contrast to the Nietzschean "Beyond good and evil," as "Between good and evil," making the two more contrastive through one's transcultural location between them (rather than beyond them). This is also a way to demarcate decadent immoralism and avant-gardist challenges to morality from postmodern acceptance of moral distinctions as foundational for the intensive play of meanings.

By the way, how would you describe the connection between what you call the "postmodern avant-garde" and transculture?

BERRY: I think the postmodern avant-garde—including collectives like ACT UP, which tries to raise social awareness about AIDS, or certain feminist performance artists—sees art as having a socially transformative mission. But being postmodernists they do not feel that there is a realm apart from everyday life or culture—a utopia elsewhere—that art can take us to. They recognize that all cultural actions or performances are complicit with what they seek to critique. So as I said in my chapter on this subject, there is a doubleness to the postmodern avant-garde: a desire to change society/culture combined with a recognition that it is basically unchangeable beyond very small steps; the Moscow Laboratory had a similar doubleness—a certain utopian goal combined with an absolute suspicion of utopia. Perhaps it is the teleological goal of postmodern avant-gardists that keeps them mired in the doubleness; it strikes me that they are still caught in oppositional thinking rather than the thinking from and through difference that transculture tries to promote. To me that is what's new about transculture. It is a way of thinking about difference not from the point of view of an outmoded modernist (or postmodernist) order but thinking difference from the perspective of difference itself. Transculture would be a perspective in which all cultures look decentered in relation to all other cultures, including one's own. I have some suspicions of my own desire to call transculture "new" because it seems that this is just more of the same utopian search for the better and the new.

On Utopianism

EPSTEIN: In what sense is transculture utopian? Do you imply the impossibility of realization? Is there any difference between utopianism and the spiritual search and striving as such?

BERRY: In one sense transculture is utopian because it assumes that we all want to be more culturally complete or personally complete, that we are lacking in our current modes of thinking and being. It is impossible because I'm not sure that complete fullness of being is realizable except in another order of things, another plane of existence. On the other hand it could be seen as the cultivation of another kind of human capacity, cultural empathy or curiosity, which would not necessarily have to imply an end or a goal—the capacity to accept or encounter difference would be an ongoing process that could by definition never be complete. There is a spiritual element to transculture but I wouldn't privilege the spiritual over other ways of developing. I think transculture is also utopian because it is a mode of thinking or feeling or perhaps apprehending that is located in the future; I don't believe we are currently constructed to think transculturally; I don't think it is seen as a positive value in most cultures.

EPSTEIN: The term "utopian" usually refers to something (a) unrealizable and (b) purposefully pursued to be realized. I think that transculture is not utopian in any of these senses. I think it is realizable though it does not attempt to be realized. It is realizable exactly because it doesn't project a specific goal for realization but is realized in the process of living through various cultural experiences. I agree that fullness of being can be attained only in another plane of existence and that is why transculture stops its movement where the movement of religion starts. There shouldn't be any confusion between transcultural and religious categories since transculture presupposes human acts of self-creation and self-transformation while religion treats men or women as creatures dependent and reliant on the Creator. The cultural and hence the transcultural is distinct from both natural and supernatural; it is a narrow, though infinitely expandable realm where the human being is capable of self-transcendence.

On Russia and America

BERRY: What did the idea of America represent to Russians during the Cold War years?

EPSTEIN: Trapped in the system of state-imposed collectivism, Soviet citizens viewed America as the utopian land of unlimited individualism. What Soviet people misunderstood and why many of them were later so disappointed with the real America is that "unrestricted individualism" presumes, first, a developed system of legislation as a discipline of *mutual restriction* and, second, a system of cultural rituals of *self-restriction*. The price is the apparent (self-)effacement of sharp individualities, including a standardization of personal interactions that permits the society to survive without the forceful limitation of individual freedoms. Americans are scared to impose their individuality on other people. Even in a simple social conversation they try to refrain from topics that could make them morally or psychologically vulnerable or seem provocative to their interlocutors; as a result the most convenient topic of conversation becomes the weather or sports.

In the same vein, Americans perhaps were fascinated with Russian people by the qualities they found in Dostoevsky, Tolstoy, and Chekhov—the spontaneous character, the fluidity of soul, and the freedom of individuality that oversteps social borders and posits metaphysical challenges to all socially established norms of behavior. Russians impress Westerners as sincere, raw, fresh, natural people, as if they were "newly born" at the time of their adulthood and had not undergone restrictive social training. They are not afraid of scandals; they are adventurous and immature, open and provocative, excessively hospitable and frankly malicious. Americans, in their turn, were disappointed in their encounter with Russian and especially Soviet reality to see instead of Dostoevsky's metaphysical scandals utterly oppressed individuals squeezed by a tough system of bureaucracy and enforced collectivist models. It was exactly the tradition of anarchy on "the earth without form and void," this element of unrestrained, uncultivated freedom that provoked in Russia such pressure from the state and an emphasis on collectivism in order to limit the spontaneous outpouring of individual will.

Therefore, along with fascinations and disappointments that both cultures presented for each other during the Cold War, they are progressing toward a more realistic understanding of interconnections between the two poles of each national character. Formal freedom is balanced by deliberate self-restriction in America, and the anarchic individual character is compensated by the strong pressure of the state in Russia. If these two nations understood each other realistically, their utopian visions of each other could be realized more fully than ever before. The vision of unrestricted individuality in the Russian sense combined with socially sanctioned freedoms in the American sense would result in freedom without anarchy, collectivity without compulsion. Sometimes I dream about Russia and America becoming one symbiotic culture.

Russians still have to appreciate the benefits of the American democratic system but they must also realize that this system could be practically implemented only at the expense of ambitious, frivolous, flamboyant characters who had to submit deliberately to boring procedures of mutual legislative limitation. The opportunities of the post—Cold War period come with the appreciation of differences without forcing them into oppositions.

Now I want to ask you: What is it that might attract Americans in post-Soviet Russian culture and what would be the basis for the interference of these two cultures?

BERRY: One thing that Americans might be attracted to is an opportunity to see a culture that had formerly been constituted as our absolute other, experiment with what we tend to think of as our most valuable "export" to the world: democracy. In a simpleminded way some Americans use the "fall" of the Soviet system as automatic justification for the rightness of Western or specifically American ways; we essentially "won" the Cold War. This is unfortunate because it closes down the critical space we might have used to question how we have developed our distinctly American character very much in relation (and in opposition) to the Soviet state. It also renders the concept of democracy static, and even sacrosanct, thereby preventing us from considering the ways in which American democracy is much more a utopian conception, an ideal, than something actualized in this country. In another sense, then, perhaps we hope that the new democracies emerging in Eastern Europe and Russia will discover or embody a more legitimate, more perfect form of democracy.

I think we must have a longing to confront, to know, even to love, the ghostly specter of Russia that for so many years haunted our collective national consciousness. Perhaps the most attractive aspect of Russian culture as I understand it is the sense of shared responsibility that people seem to feel for each other. The American insistence on individualism has led to a great deal of indifference and to what I think of as sometimes unhealthy social units like the ideal "nuclear" family, which becomes the only cultural example of collectivity in American culture. Perhaps it is my romantic idea of Russian community or collectivism that is really being invoked here. What I would like to find is vestiges of community as it has been developed in Russia to answer the great need for collective forms of caring that exists here in the United States. It seems as if we need a national tragedy such as the Oklahoma City bombing or the recent school shooting in Colorado in order to be publicly responsive to each other. We don't even have a national child-care system that would symbolize our recognition that children are everyone's responsibility and not the individual "property" of their parents.

But then in this regard Russia is still being constructed in a compensatory relation to America; we look to (an imaginary) Russian culture to compensate for what we feel to be lacking in this one. How can a transcultural perspective help us to undo the oppositional relations between our cultures even in the case of what we might think of as positive oppositions? Doesn't seeing transculture as compensation for what is lacking in one's own culture still allow this essentially oppositional mode to continue rather than liberating other more complex modes of thought and relationship? And wouldn't looking for solutions to our own limitations in other cultures prevent us from finding solutions to them in our own: Couldn't it lead to a sort of political quietism?

On Compensation and Surplementation

EPSTEIN: Which more complex modes are you thinking of as different from a compensational mode?

BERRY: Modes that would exceed the lack and fulfillment models that imply, to me, binary relations. These more complex modes would have to allow for more multiple responses, perhaps more unpredictable ones. Or maybe I'm not quite understanding compensation, compensatory relations as you mean them.

EPSTEIN: The initial motive for compensation is always the lack of or demand for a certain quality, but the outcome of compensation is unpredictable and cannot be reduced to what was solicited or requested in the beginning. A person can need just one citation from a certain book, goes to the library, reads the entire book, then a shelf of books—and ends with a different way of life, with a new understanding of her vocation. In the time of Peter the Great (the early eighteenth century) Russia needed Western technology, and she got it, but in addition to the art of shipbuilding Russia received literature, science, intelligentsia, revolution, and many other things that completely changed her fate in the coming centuries. Was it just a compensation? And is compensation limited to the assimilation of another culture's elements? What emerged in Russia as a result of her Westernization was as different from the actual West as the West itself is different from Russia. A unique culture without any precedent in the past, neither in the West, nor in pre-Western Russia. The "lack" is only a trigger for producing otherness, which initially may have been charged with egoistic and compensatory impulses but eventually surpasses the binarism of demand and fulfillment.

Perhaps "supplement" would be a more accurate term for this cultural dynamic than "compensation," with its economic and psychological underpinnings. The concept of supplement implies that a structure compensates for its deficiency not exactly by providing the quality that is sought in the other (the missing external reality) but by adding new elements to its own diversity, by further self-differentiation. One can never get a supply just to fill a gap—the result is always some surplus. Not just a supplement but a *surplement,* or *surplementation.* When A borrows something from B, this does not imply that A will become identical to B; A, with the help of B, is becoming C, which is even more different from B than A was. St. Petersburg is an example of such surplementation through compensation. St. Petersburg was designed as a Russian window to Europe and was modeled on Amsterdam, but nowhere in Europe, even less in Holland, will you find anything similar to St. Petersburg. This is the paradox of supplement as surplus.

BERRY: You spoke of an initial "lack" in someone's (or some culture's) identity as the trigger that initiates a search for otherness-as-surplus. At this point of initiation, you said, the search is charged with egoistic impulses revolving around a demand that the lack be fulfilled; but eventually the search leads beyond the binarism of demand and fulfillment. It seems to me that this initial stage of egotism, the demand for gratification, is a pretty dangerous one that could lead (and historically has led) to all sorts of violations of cultural others. How do we get to the point of surpassing this initial stage?

EPSTEIN: If culture in the proper sense of this word deals with symbolic values, then their appropriation or sharing them with others cannot cause damage to any of the participating cultures. Unlike physical substances or material objects that can be possessed by one only at the expense of the other because of their ontologically exclusive properties, symbolic values require an exchange and increase with sharing. A symbol was originally a token, in the form of an object broken in twain, so that identity could be proved by having the two parts match. Only a divided thing, only a shared entity becomes a symbol. A portion of bread dwindles when divided among several eaters but one idea is multiplied when shared with several thinkers. What was a miracle in the multiplication of loaves (Mark, 6) is the routine way in which ideas multiply. The fact that Shakespeare's images resonated and proliferated in so many cultures doesn't empty Shakespeare of his aesthetic value but rather expands his symbolic empire. In this symbolic realm, to "appropriate" means to be appropriated and to "share" means to acquire. For example, as long as Russian culture assimilated German philosophy or French literature it was proportionally assimilated by these Western European cultures. In the course of recent postindustrial developments, the wealth of nations increasingly incorporates informational, symbolic values whereas material property becomes a diminishing constituent of national economies. This provides for "surplemental" exchange between nations as opposed to antagonistic or exploitive modes based on material objects stolen by one culture from another.

BERRY: But what about the legacy of violence between cultures where, for example, indigenous peoples in this country have all but lost their culture through being forced for many years to assimilate to a dominant white culture? How do we forget the legacy of violence that has dominated throughout history in trying to seek a more peaceful and productive means of cultural exchange?

EPSTEIN: We don't forget and we shouldn't forget but in this particular case, strange as it may seem, the mechanism of surplementation is again at work. The idea of openness to other cultures is most characteristic of those cultures that have this experience of violence in the past. Both American and Russian cultures can serve as examples. By violating the borders of other cultures and expanding aggressively to assimilate them, these super-ethnic powers acquired their capacity for self-transcendence that, in the course of time, started to work in an opposite direction, as readiness to let other cultures in and provide them with sites for their own voices and alternative identities.

BERRY: The problem, though, is that this alternative identity has been "purchased" or acquired at great expense—at someone else's great expense. I'm thinking of groups such as African Americans, who have demonstrated that many of the most distinctive cultural forms in America have been produced by blacks but never acknowledged by American culture as a whole as having been produced by them. Or the reassessments of modern art, which have shown that Picasso and others borrowed liberally from African art (and failed to acknowledge it) while Western culture as a whole at the time still regarded Africa as culturally primitive, a heart of darkness.

EPSTEIN: The very fact that you are asking these questions already implies a form of answer to them. You are a white, middle-class, politically liberal, heterosexual American woman who displays such a genuine concern about the use of African masks by a Spanish artist in the early years of the twentieth century. I doubt that Talibs who are so concerned about keeping their national and religious identity as Islamics in Afghanistan would be as worried about this act of cultural stealth or appropriation.

BERRY: And frankly, I think the Talibs have a problem with tolerance—just ask women who live there—and could use a little transcultural therapy! Seriously, I wonder if you're implying some kind of a theory of cultural evolution for humanity: First we steal each other's cultures and kill anyone who is not like us, and then we appreciate all cultures in a kind of pluralistic celebration that ends up being a form of great indifference and disinterest, and then . . . ? I think it's possible that we are evolving toward a truly transcultural world in which radical cultural exchange of the kind we have described in this book becomes a norm, in which a healthy desire for difference is assumed—at least that's been my hope all along. Trying to provide some of the resources for creating such a world has been one of my primary motivations for wanting to write this book—that and the chance to work with you of course! Russian culture gives me much hope and inspiration.

One of the things that impressed me greatly when I first visited Leningrad was how fully involved ordinary people were in producing and participating in culture. I met lots of teenagers who were published poets, painters who were bricklayers, shopkeepers who quoted Pushkin; I attended a poetry reading that was actually crowded, standing room only! It amounted to a full-scale love affair with culture and a deeply held commitment to its preservation, or at least that's the way it seemed to me at the time. I couldn't help but contrast it with the typical indifference to culture that seems to pervade American society; culture may be ordinary—inevitable and all around us —as Raymond Williams said, but not ordinary enough for most Americans. I'm wondering if you also see such a fundamental difference between the ways in which Russians and Americans value culture and if so whether this difference accounts for why culturology as you've described it developed in Russia? It is almost a theory of salvation through culture.

EPSTEIN: Yes, your observation is to the point, though capitals like Moscow and St. Petersburg can create an exaggerated impression of mass infatuation with culture. Culture in Russia is this "surplement" that grows from deficiencies of physical comfort and economic stability. A permanent irritation, frustration, and disturbance caused by poor material and shaky social conditions make people more sensitive and thirsty for symbolic values. But are these symbols only sublimations or substitutions for certain deficiencies? Is a theater spectacle or lyrical poem simply a compensation for being hungry, jobless, unsettled, or humiliated by the authorities? Russia gained her culture through much suffering, but the outcome of this suffering cannot be reduced to its cause. Anna Akhmatova wrote, "If you could imagine from which litter poems grow . . ." This doesn't mean that poems *are* litter or that a rose *is* manure: They grow *out of* this substance, and *over*grow it. Culture is the overgrowth of nature, and transculture is the overgrowth of culture, the totality of supplements.

Culture in Russia, indeed, is endowed with a redemptive mission, and culturology has become a sort of secular theology that interprets culture as a spiritual exercise, as a way to salvation. Perhaps, precisely because the Orthodox Church has not elaborated anything like a theology of culture and hasn't been involved with scientific and aesthetic issues, it became the task of culturology to theologize about culture.

On National Character and Proper Naming

BERRY: Running throughout this conversation has been the assumption that one may speak about such a thing as (the Russian or American) national character, a set of defining characteristics based on one's cultural and geographical origin. Yet we could easily (and rightly) be charged with essentializing what is basically an extremely diverse set of individual traits that become anachronistic in a transnational or even a postnational moment—if they ever have been accurate as a set of descriptors. (Not to mention the recent tragedies that have resulted from asserting a Serbian national character, for instance, or a Bosnian Muslim character.) Do you think there is any validity or value in positing the concept of national character? Is transculturalism as you understand it ultimately a theory of postnationalism or a kind of new cosmopolitanism that would dispense altogether with nation as a foundational means of self-identification?

EPSTEIN: I think the concept of a "national character" still may be useful as a mechanism for semantic provocation and redefinition, especially if this concept serves as an instrument of national *self*-transformation. A person must sometimes say to himself, "I am a coward"—in order to overcome cowardice. Nations, like people, are and are not what they are. Blaise Pascal observed: ". . . We change and are no longer the same persons. . . . It is like a nation which we have provoked, but meet again after two generations. They are still Frenchmen, but not the same."[2] Cosmopolitanism, in the best sense of this word, doesn't forbid us to discuss national characters, because cosmopolitanism is not an indifference to nations, like justice is not an indifference to individuals, but a way to coordinate their different interests.

I agree that naming so many people comprising a nation with one name—"courageous or cowardly nation," "laborious or lazy nation"—is dangerous and unjust. In the same way negative theology challenges the validity of naming God. But without affirmative theology that gives names to God in order that negative theology could question and dispute them, there would be no theology at all. Cosmopolitanism without recognition of distinct national characters would have no ground upon which to exist.

Talking about God is dangerous. Talking about nation is dangerous. But only where there is danger, is there salvation (in Russian, these two words, *opasnost'* and *spasenie,* have the same root). Such is the double effect of any talk: By naming a certain thing, one does injustice to it but simultaneously provokes a search for justice, creates multiple possibilities for renaming. Talking creates a potential for new things to emerge, signification creates the possibility of new signifieds.

That's why I disagree with the radical poststructuralist postulate that the system of signs has no external references, that writing or speaking is an unrestricted semantic play that is not anchored in any signified. A sign does have a signified, which, however, is not merely doubled but initiated or modified by the sign, in the very moment of utterance. The thing named and the thing unnamed are two different things. In fact, an unnamed thing is not a thing at all but only a piece of substance with certain physical characteristics. Something solid becomes a stone when it is named "a stone." The name reveals its similarity to other stones and difference from sand, rocks, and mountains; now it can be used to "stone" a sinner or laid as a "cornerstone" in the foundation for a temple ... A sign does not simply refer to, but infers and interferes with the signified, makes it different from what it is. I would prefer the term "signifiable" to the "signified," to emphasize that signification is also *potentiation*. Naming a thing is a prerequisite for its changing, reveals the range of its possibilities. To say about the people that they are such and such implies the possibility for them to become different than what these names signify. To define does not mean to confine, but rather to destabilize the object of definition, to let it go beyond the scope of its name, to provoke disobedience. Words initiate change, texts create different contexts.

Even most formal and empty logical propositions carry a potential for semantic upheavals and transformations. An example from logic: "Socrates is a man." No doubt, he is, but even such a "tautology" immediately provokes a series of interrogations and redefinitions. Does he continue to be a man now that he is dead? Is he only a man or is he also a thinker, a talker, a soldier, a teacher, a citizen, a victim? How to prioritize these names and identities? Could he be all this being woman, not man? How does his maleness relate to his humanness?

Any definition contains a space for alternative definitions and redefinitions. In the absence of definition, things have no identity and therefore cannot be changed. If there is no border, how can you cross it? If there are no cultural identities, how can you think and work transculturally to surpass them? We do need to care about truthful naming because a false name does not provoke change. I will not react if I am hailed as John or Steve. If we call Russians the most thrifty and rational people in the world, they will not react. Proper names are needed for proper reactions.

Notes

1. For a more detailed treatment of this issue see Mikhail Epstein, sections of "Hypersociality" and "Hypermateriality," in his book *Russian Postmodernism: New Perspectives on Post-Soviet Culture* (with Alexander Genis and Slobodanka Vladiv-Glover) (New York and Oxford: Berghahn Books, 1999): 19–24.
2. "Thoughts," 122, in *The Harvard Classics*, 55th pr., Vol. 48 (New York: P. F. Collier & Son Corporation, 1963): 50.

Index of Names

Abbeele, Georges van den, 72
Abe, Kobo, 191
Abramov, Yakov, 293
Achilles, 36
Adorno, Theodor, 191, 253
Akhmatova, Anna, 319
Akutagawa, Fusei, 249
Alexander, Patrick, 217
Alvarez, Javier, 240, 251
Amin-Oglu, 271
Anaxagoras, 4, 283
Anderson, Benedict, 171
Anne of Green Gables, 223
Anzaldua, Gloria, 128
Appadurai, Arjun, 5, 121, 124, 126, 127, 138n1, 148–49, 169–70, 181, 231; *Modernity at Large*, 148
Aquinas, Thomas, 158
Araki, Yasusada 240–251, 300; *Doubled Flowering*, 251, 253–54, 254n2
Arguedas, Jose Maria, 4
Aristophanes, 204
Aristotle, 50, 158, 159; *Metaphysics* 50
Aristov, Vladimir, 39, 49
Aseev, Nikolai, 272n8
Ashby, Steven, 249
Averintsev, Sergei, 15, 16, 17, 22, 54n6, 191, 212n2

Babel, Isaak, 272n8
Bachelard, Gaston, 289
Bacon, Francis, 287–288
Bakhtin, Mikhail, 15, 16, 17, 18, 22, 23, 24, 25, 27n13, 55n10, 113–115, 117–119, 153, 178, 184, 186, 293, 300
Bakshtein, Iosif, 33, 39
Balzac, Honoré de, 300
Barthes, Roland, 150, 235
Baudrillard, Jean, 58–59, 65, 148
Beatles, The, *Octopus's Garden,* 226
Belkin, Ivan Petrovich, 271–272
Benjamin, Walter, 185–186, 219
Berdiaev, Nikolai, 16
Bergson, Henri, 46
Berry, Ellen, 214, 246, 275n43
Bhabha, Homi, 5, 85, 94, 128, 131, 135, 146–147
Bibler, Vladimir, 15, 22
Bitov, Andrei, 191, 247- 250, 253–54; *The Days of Man,* 247; *Japan,* 247–48; *A Professor of Symmetry,* 247, 248; *Pushkin's House,* 247
Blanchot, Maurice, 67
Bloch, Ernst, 124, 144, 147–149, 170, 178, 238
Blok, Alexander, 248, 250; "The Twelve," 264
Borges, Jorge Luis, 191
Boym, Svetlana, 233; *Common Places,* 233
Braidotti, Rosi, 126, 127
Breton, Andre, 42, 191, 283
Brezhnev, Leonid, 46, 300

324 *Index*

Brik, Osip, 272n8
Brodsky, Joseph, 33, 191
Bruno, Giordano, 283
Buell, Frederick, 5, 121
Bunche, Ralph, 80
Burger, Peter, 57–58, 59, 61
Burroughs, William S., 60

Cabanallis, Francisco, 216
Cage, John, 229
Camus, Albert, 191
Carroll, Lewis, 226
Chambers, Iain, 128, 135
Chekhov, Anton, 250, 313
Chernyshevsky, Nikolai, 88
Chuang Tzu, 42, 244
Clifford, James, 172
Clinton, William (Bill), 223
Columbus, Christopher, 161–162
Connor, Steven, 155, 233–234
Conrad, Joseph, 248
Cornwall, Barry, 271, 275n42

Daikokuya, Kodayu, 247
Danilevsky, Nikolai, 15, 16
Debord, Guy, 59–60, 80
DeCerteau, Michel, 229–232, 235; *The Practice of Everyday Life*, 231–232
Deleuze, Gilles, 80, 113, 127, 129; and Guattari, Félix, 129, 130, 132, 170
Derrida, Jacques, 21, 43, 79–81, 83, 97–8, 160–61, 166, 178, 186, 254n3, 291, 299
Descartes, Rene, 298
Dissanayake, Wimal, 122
Don Quixote, 191
Dostoevsky, Fyodor, 88, 210, 211, 250, 294, 300, 311; *The Brothers Karamazov*, 264; *The Devils*, 311, 313, 314

Eco, Umberto, 299
Einstein, Albert, 288
Einstein, Pyotr, 267–268
Eliasmith, Chris, 301n1

Eliot, T.S., 57, 83, 89n7, 191
Elliott, Anthony, 173
Engels, Fredrich, *Anti-Duhring*, 298
Epicurus, 285
Epstein, Mikhail N, 64–66, 68–70, 74, 75, 121, 124, 131- 132, 136, 177–183, 214, 220, 232, 234, 235, 245; "Letter on Transculture," 36–37, 65
Esenin, Sergei, 260
Evan-Zohar, Itamar, 9–10

Faulkner, William, 211
Faustus, Doctor, 191
Featherstone, Mike, 5, 121
Federman, Raymond, 142
Fedorov, Nikolai, 294
Florensky, Pavel, 15, 16
Foucault, Michel, 60, 88, 94, 130, 134, 135, 139n15, 291
Fraser, Nancy, 74, 136–37, 138, 175
Freud, Sigmund, 118, 173, 191
Fusei, Akutagawa, 249

Gachev, Georgy, 15, 22, 184, 191
Ganga, Raymond, 224
Glinka, Mikhail, 88
Goethe, Johann Wolfgang von, 15
Gogol, Nikolai, 88, 269–271, 274nn33–38; *Dead Souls*, 264, 269–271, 274nn35–37; *The Inspector General*, 269, 270
Golding, Sue, 127, 128, 132, 135
Gomez-Pena, Guillermo, 122, 135
Gorbachev, Mikhail, 31, 54
Grosz, Elizabeth, 126, 129
Groys, Boris, 54n4
Guchkov, Aleksandr, 87, 88
Gumilev, Lev, 154, 162n1

Haber, Honi Fern, 92–93
Hall, Stuart, 22
Hannerz, Ulf, 5
Haraway, Donna, 2, 71, 127, 172

Harvey, David, 5, 71, 121, 145
Hebdige, Dick, 70, 149
Hegel, Georg Wilhelm Friedrich, 40, 46, 50, 94–96, 158, 285, 293, 294, 297–298, 301n6
Heidegger, Martin, 191, 293
Heisenberg, Igor, 267
Hercules, 36
Herder, Johann, 15
Hesse, Hermann, 283
Hoggart, Richard, 22
Holtzer, Jenny, 60
Homer, 211, 264
hooks, bell, 81, 85, 133, 135
Hooper, Barbara, 135
Huntington, Samuel, 2
Husserl, Edmund, 242

Iakovenko, Igor, 39
Ilf, Ilya, 272n8
Ingalls, Laura, 223
Inoue, Yasushi, *Dreams about Russia*, 255n7
Ivanov, Aleksandr, 254, 274n27
Izumova, Elena, 63

Jakobson, Roman, "Poetry of Grammar and Grammar of Poetry," 274n32
James, William, 46
Jameson, Fredric, 2, 5, 66, 106, 121, 133, 142, 143–145, 148, 171, 181, 237, 300; *Postmodernism, or the Cultural Logic of Late Capitalism*, 181; *The Seeds of Time*, 143–144
Johnson, Kent, 240–241, 245–246, 248–251
Johnson, Mark, 168, 289n3
Joyce, James, 57
Jung, Carl, 191

Kabakov, Ilya, 33, 35, 186–187, 188n5
Kafka, Franz, 57, 107, 191, 222
Kaladjian, Walter, 60–61
Kant, Immanuel, 40, 115

Kataev, Valentin, 258–59
Kawabata, Yasunari, 191
Kharms, Daniil, 272n9
Khlebnikov, Velimir, 64
Kibirov, Timur, 257
Klein, Julie, 150–151
Kovalev, Vitaly, 49, 50
Krauss, Rosalind, 76n9
Kristeva, Julia, 84, 86, 104, 132, 174, 300; *Strangers to Ourselves*, 174
Krivulin, Viktor, 54n6, 251
Kroeber, Karl, 93
Kruchonykh, Alexei, 259, 272n11
Kurginian, Sergei, 54
Kusatao, Ozaki, 249
Kyojin, Okura, 249

Lacan, Jacques, 129, 133, 172–73
Laclau, Ernesto, 128
Laertius, Diogenes, *Lives and Opinions of Eminent Philosophers*, 300
Lakoff, George, 289n3
Lefebvre, Henri, 135
Leibniz, Gottfried, Wilhelm, 283, 284
Lenin (Ulyanov), Vladimir, 87–89, 102, 105, 156, 162, 293; *State and Revolution* 297, 298
Lèvi-Strauss, Claude, 154
Lippman, Walter, 80
Longstocking, Pippi, 223
Lorenz, Konrad, 191
Losev, Aleksei, 15, 18
Lotman, Yuri, 15, 22
Lyotard, Jean-François, 7, 71, 94, 220, 233

Magee, Rosemary, 223
Mailer, Norman, 191
Malevich, Kazimir, 64
Mamardashvili, Merab, 82
Mandelbrot, Benoit, 283
Mandel'shtam, Osip, 33, 259, 264, 273n21, 274n26
Mann, Thomas, 191

Marcel, Gabriel, 191
March, Jo, 223
Marcuse, Herbert, 85, 191
Marx, Karl, 36, 117, 118, 186, 285, 292, 293, 294, 298, 303
Massey, Doreen, 236
Mayakovsky, Vladimir, 64, 272n8
Medusa, 36
Mencken, H.L., 26n9
Mendeleev, Dmitry, 287
Merezhkovsky, Dmitry, 16
Mikheev, Aleksei, 39
Miller, Henry, 191
Miller-Pogacar, Anesa, 77n15, 246
Miziano, Viktor, 100, 101n12
Monakhov, Aleksei, 247
Montaigne, Michel, 190, 193, 300–301
More, Thomas, 160–62; *Utopia*, 161
Morgulis, Liudmila, 39
Morrison, Toni, 80
Motokiyu, Tosa. See Tosa, Motokiyu
Mozart, Johann C. Wolfgang Amadeus, 109
Musil, Robert, 191

Nabokov, Vladimir, 248, 252
Nancy, Jean-Luc, 71–74, 133–34: *The Inoperative Community*, 72–4
Napoleon I, 118
Nietzsche, Friedrich, 46, 166, 191, 293, 294, 297
Nixon, Rob, 122
Norinaga, Ojiu, 249
Nussbaum, Emily, 245

Odoevtsev, Lev, 247
Ojiu, Norinaga, 249
Okura, Kyojin, 249
Oleinikov, Nikolai, 272n9
Olesha, Yuri 272n8
Orpheus, 191
Ortiz, Fernando, 4
Osmolovsky, Anatoly, 100

Ostwald, Wilhelm, 26n1
Ozaki, Kusatao, 249

Panko, Rudyi, 270
Parshchikov, Aleksei, 49
Pascal, Blaise, 320
Pasternak, Boris, 33, 259, 260
Pavic, Milorad, 299–300
Paz, Octavio, 191
Penezic, Vida, 215
Penfield, Wilder, 286
Perseus, 36
Peter I (The Great), 316
Petrov, Evgeny, 272n8
Picasso, Pablo, 318
Plant, Sadie, 58–59
Plato, 40, 50, 107, 115, 206, 210, 285, 293, 294, 297, 300; and the Academia 276
Plekhanov, Georgy, 88
Poggioli, Renato, 5, 7, 57
Pol'shakova, Liudmila, 39, 43
Pound Ezra, 57
Pratt, Mary Louise, 4, 5
Prigov, Dmitry, 34, 250–251, 257
Probyn, Elspeth, 125, 126, 127, 128, 129, 135, 139n15
Proctor, Bryan Waller, 271, 275n42
Proust, Marcel, 286
Purishkevich, Vladimir, 87, 88
Pushkin, Aleksandr, 88, 109, 181, 250, 259–271, 275n40–41, 306, 319; *Eugene Onegin*, 249, 262–264; *The Captain's Daughter*, 266; "I loved you . . . ," 269; "K***," 265; "Belkin's Tales," 271, 275n40; "Mistress Into Maid," 271

Rao, P. Venugopala, 226
Reed, Walter, 221, 228n2
Robbins, Bruce, 6, 171–172, 175
Robertson, Roland, 5, 6
Rorty, Richard, 201, 221, 235

Rose, Gillian, 135
Rousseau, Jean-Jacques, 25
Rozanov, Vasily, 191
Rubinshtein, Lev, 196, 257, 259
Russell, Charles, 59–60, 62

Said, Edward, 135
Saint-Exupery, Antoine de, 191
Sardar, Ziauddin, 18
Saussure, Ferdinand de, 118
Schutz, Alfred, 102
Schweitzer, Albert, 191
Sedakova, Olga, 39
Sei Shonagon, 195; *The Pillow Book*, 195
Shakespeare, William, 211, 251; *Hamlet*, 251, 317
Shaw, Carolyn, 4, 5
Shelly, Percy Bysshe, 164, 222; *Prometheus Unbound*, 222
Shenstone, William, 271, 275n41
Shestov, Lev, 191
Shklovsky, Viktor, 23, 300
Simmel Georg, 15, 102
Sinyavsky, Andrei, 191
Sisyphus, 191, 266
Snyder, Gary, 226
Socrates, 114–115, 205, 206, 298, 321
Soja, Edward, 134, 135
Solovyov, Ivan, 242, 244, 256–257, 260, 265, 267–268, 272n2, 274nn23, 25, 31, 275nn39, 43, 294
Solovyov, Vladimir, 275n43
Solzhenitsyn, Alexander, 292; *Gulag Archipelago*, 63, 292
Sontag, Susan, 191
Spengler, Oswald, 15, 154; *The Decline of the West*, 154
Spivak, Gayatri Chakravorty, 80, 135
Stalin, Joseph, 156, 273n22, 274n23
Stendhal, 265; "On Love," 265
Struve, 87, 88
Suliagin, Vladimir, 39

Taylor, Diane, 4
Tolstoy, Leo, 88, 109, 118, 242, 250, 266–267, 294, 313; *War and Peace*, 266
Tosa, Motokiyu, 240–245, 249–253
Toynbee, Arnold, 154
Tseitlin, Boris, 39, 49
Tsvetaeva, Marina, 259
Turnin, Maksim, 293

Ulyanov, Vladimir. See Lenin (Ulyanov), Vladimir
Umnova, Mariia, 39
Unamuno, Miguel de, 191

Vainshtein, Olga, 39
Valéry, Paul, 191, 285
Van den Abbele, Georges, 72
VanLoon, Borin, 18
Vanoski, Urbino, 247, 248
Vergasova, Irina, 39
Vvedensky, Aleksandr, 272n9

Warner, Michael, 74
West, Cornel, 85, 135
White, Leslie, 26n9
Williams, Raymond, 22, 124, 319
Wilson, John, 271
Wimal, Dissanayake, 122
Windelband, Wilhelm, 15
Wittgenstein, Ludwig, 196; *Tractacus Logico-Philosophicus*, 196
Wittig, Monique, 60
Wolfe, Thomas, 211

Yasusada, Araki. See Araki, Yasusada
Yeltsin, Boris, 31, 54
Young, Iris Marion, 72, 135–136

Zabolotsky, Nikolai, 272n9
Zizek, Slavoj, 159

Index of Subjects

Actuality and potentiality, 158–159, 297, 301n6. *See also* Potentiality
Alienation, 107
Alternative(s) (in theory and culture), 21, 132, 178, 182, 290–292, 297–299, 322; alter-Hegel, 297–298, 301n6; alter-Socrates, 298; "alter" and "anti," 298. *See also* Interactive Anthology of Alternative Ideas, Otherness, Thinking
Ambivalence, 40
American and Russian cultures (comparison), 1, 10, 62–63, 75–76, 104–106, 110–111, 232–233, 313–315, 318–320. *See also* Russia (the Soviet Union) and the West
Art, 23, 64, 187, 205; centered, 63–64; dissident, 63; as estrangement, 23
Author, 210, 252; author-mania, 245; and character, 250, 252; and coauthor, 268; death and resurrection of, 242–243; excess of authors over texts, 252; foster author, 294–295 and hyper-author 242; pre-authorial and post-authorial, 241; potential, 294–296; vs. compiler, 198
Authorship, 2, 192, 198, 240–275, 294–296; and anonymity, 241, 259, 269; and coauthorship, 264–269, 271; dissemination of, 253; donation and appropriation, 267–272; double, symbiotic, 264–272; and hyper-authorship,240–245; as othership, 268; as substitution, 268; and text, 242; 294–299; transbiological, 244, 245; transpersonal, 241, 243, 245, 253. *See also* Hyperauthorship
Avant-garde, 2, 6–7, 56–77; historical vs. postmodern, 7, 12, 56–58, 61; and improvisation, 229; postmodern, 56–77, 311–312; and rear-garde, 64–65, 67–68; Russian, 31, 62–64; and social critique, 57–62; and transculture, 311–13; vs. modernism, 57–58

Bank of New Ideas, 49–51, 57, 65, 71, 277–281; criteria of evaluation, 279
Being-in-common, 72, 73, 133
Book, "bookness," 296; virtual, 296
Book of Books (Book^2). *See* Interactive Anthology of Alternative Ideas
Border culture, 122–123, 135
Border subject, 128, 146–147

Case, nominative and dative, 261–262
Catalog (as genre), 179–81, 195–199; vs. text, 197–198
Chinese poetry, 250
Circle, in hyperauthorship, 251–252; in reading and writing, 268
Citation, 263, 273n21; and hyperauthorship, 268; reverse, 11, 297–299

Club of Essayists, 2, 33–34, 48
Collective improvisation, See Improvisation
Commodity, commodification, 106–110; as freedom, 108–110; and knowledge, 233–237
Communication, 31–32, 38, 202–203, 205, 278; silent, 207 See also Creativity
Communism, 45–46, 54
Community, 72–73, 205–07, 212; critiques of traditional models, 72–73; improvisational, 205–06, 276–277; intellectual, 235–238; interdisciplinary, 53; new models of, 3, 72. 74, 135–36, 171–72, 238; postmodern, 135–136; postmodern crisis in, 71, 74
Compensation (cultural), 315–320; unpredictability of, 316–317; vs. surplementation (supplement), 316–320
Conceptive criticism, 3
Conceptualism (in Russian literature), 34–35, 63–64, 68, 246, 250, 256, 259, 272n4
Consciousness, anticipatory, 147, 178; syncretic and synthetic, 51–52
Construction, constructivism: of author and authorship, 244, 246, 252; vs deconstruction, 21, 244, 246, 252, 291. See also Potentiation
Cosmopolitanism, 5–6, 171–175, 320–321; defined, 320; and national character, 320–321
Counterculture, 25, 36, 44–45, 85–87, 106–108; and multiculturalism, 85
Creativity: and alienation, 107; and communication, 31–33, 37–39, 201–203, 205; and excess of signification, 244, 252; in improvisation, 204–205
Critical fatalism, 70, 149
Criticism: conceptive, 3; constructionist, 246; ecological, 93

Cultural studies (Anglo-American), 1–2, 18–23, 25; compared with culturology, 1, 18–23, 69–70; goals and limitations of 69–71. See also Culturology
Culturality, culturalness, 23, 36–37
Culture, 15–27, 35–37, 52–53, 263; branches and constituents of culture, 19–21, 52–53; and commodification, 106–110; and compensation, 131, 315–320; and cult, 16; as dativity, 262, 264; death of, 65–66; defined, 16, 17, 52–53, 83, 110, 131, 156; and estrangement, 10, 23–24; fragmentation of, 46, 180, 192–193; as freedom and liberation, 21–25, 52–53, 166–167, 192; and the future, 157–158; as integrative genre, 36–37, 211; interaction of cultures, 25, 53, 316–318; monoculture, 36; national, 87–89; and nature, 24, 25, 83, 94, 110–111, 259, 319–320; paradox of, 157; and politics, 8, 19–22, 35, 37, 45–46, 52–53, 88–89; "progessive and reactionary," 87–89; reinvention, 56–77, 149; and self-irony, 157; and society, 16, 19–24, 88, 102–110; as state of being, 260–262; and symbiotic genre, 266; as surplement, 316–320; and symbolism, 16, 21, 24, 25, 317; and time, 156–157; as totality, 17, 19, 22, 36–37, 46–47, 52–53; and transculture, 24–26, 82–84; vs. history, 16, 154; vs. ideology, 108–109; and violence, 318
Culturology, 1, 11–12, 15–24, 53, 89, 154; as critique, 21, 23; defined, 15–23, 26–27n9, 36–37, 53; vs. cultural studies, 18–23, 25, 69; vs. Marxism and structuralism, 16–17; as metadiscipline, 15, 23; and morality, 20–21; as secular theology, 319,

320; vs. sociology, 26n9; and transculture, 23–25
Cybernetics, 284

Deconstruction, 2, 21, 79–87, 100, 244; and construction and constructivism, 244, 246, 252; and history, 83–84; vs. multiculturalism, 80–85; positive D., 21, 160, 291–292. *See also* Potentiation
Definition, 141, 321–322; and infinition, 141
Dehumanization and rehumanization (of the humanities), 113–119
Desire, and science, 287–288. *See also* Transcultural desire.
Deterritorialization, 80, 126; and global system, 122, 133
Dialectics (in Hegel and Marx), 91, 95–96
Dictionary, 197, 198, 293
Difference, 7–8, 81, 91–100; as abstract category, 96; active differentiation vs. pluralism, 131; between signs and things, 43; as cause of indifference, 2, 96, 131,147; and emotions, 310; gender, 308–309; vs. identity and opposition, 91–98; and interference, 7–11, 96–100, 308–309; and politics, 92–93; and transcultural imaginary, 173–4; and transculture, 97–100, 131. *See also* Interference, Self-differentiation
Disciplines and interdisciplinarity, 48–52, 225–226, 278–280, 282,285; and improvisation, 39, 225–226; new disciplines, 287–288
Dissidentism, 21, 45, 63, 291–292

East, 207–208, 212n2
Ecstasy (in poetry and reading), 262–264
Eidetics (aesthetics of ideas), 50–51, 279

Epistemology, 6, 50, 115; epistemological slide, 150, 235; optimistic, 115. *See also* Knowledge
Essay, 34, 180–81, 189–193; as experimental mythology, 193; and improvisation, 34, 209–211; and myth, 190–193
Essayism, 191–193; and culture, 192–193; as metadiscourse, 192
Essentialism, 80–81, 94
Estrangement (deautomatization), 10, 23–24, 103
Ethics, 164–168; and culturology, 20–21; differential and interferential, 166–168; in the subjunctive, 166–168; and politeness, 166–168; and religion, 167; three levels (rules) of, 164–166
Everyday, the, 39–41, 67, 110, 145, 285–286; and critical nomadism, 231; deCerteau on, 229–32; and improvisation, 229–32; and institutional change, 231; and les perruques, 231–2; strategies and tactics, 230–1; utopianism of, 44, 231. *See also* Ordinary
Experiment. *See* Transcultural experiment

Feminism, 84, 303–05; and Marxism, 303–304; and newness, 146; and political critique, 125–6, 143; and transcultural perspectives, 308–09
Folklore: and catalog, 198–199; and contemporary poetry, 259; and improvisation, 205–206; neofolklore, 260, 264; scientific, 278
Frogs (topic of improvisation), 220–228
Future, 2, 70–1, 124, 145, 149, 155–158, 161–162; as-open-question, 147, 238; and eternity, 157; future imperfect temporality, 71; and the past, 299

Genius, 286
Genres, 37, 177–183, 184–189, 191; as lawless, 177–83; "new idea" as genre, 278; of culture, 211; production of new genres, 178–179, 186–188; symbiotic, 264–267; and transculture, 37, 46. *See also* Essay, Catalog, Improvisation, InteLnet
Geography, 134–135, 153–155, 161–162; imaginative, 162; physical and cultural, 154, 162n2; vs. history, 153, 161–162
German intellectual tradition, 15, 47–48
Global culture, 25, 66; and cultural "flows", 5, 122, 138n1, 170
Global subject, 127–8, 133, 146, 148, 170–1, 172
Global system, 1, 2; and citizenship, 171–2; and critical intellectuals, 123, 171–2; as deterritorialized, 122; and imagination, 148–9, 169–71; models of, 2–3, 5–6, 121–2; and movement of desire, 130; and multinational capitalism, 5, 231; as nontotalitarian totality, 132; transcultural approach to, 171–172
Globalization, 1, 5, 25
Graphomania, 259
Gulag (political and intellectual), 292–293

Heterotopia, 68, 127, 130, 139; and utopia, 134–5
History, historicism, historicity, 153–154, 161–162; history of ideas, 293; and logic, 293; prehistoric and posthistoric, 198; and theology, 157; vs. culture, 16, 154
Humanists, 47–48, 117–118
Humanities, 16–17, 21, 23, 46, 113–119, 141, 160, 294; and alternative ideas, 290–291; and dehumanities, 118–119; and Internet, 276–289; and otherness, 117–119; and technology, 17277, 284; vs.science, 16–17; web journals, 284–288. *See also* Dehumanization and rehumanization
Humility (in culture), 97, 308
Hybridization, 4, 94
Hyper, 244, 254n4
Hyperauthorship, 3, 11, 181, 240–254, 267–272; defined, 241–242; as process and inspiration, 268; Pushkin and Belkin, 271; Pushkin and Gogol, 269–271; Shakespearean question, 251; and vicious circle of interpretation, 251–252; Yasusada and Bitov, 247–250, 253–53; Yasusada and Motokiyu, 244, 251,253; Yasusada and Prigov, 250–251. *See also* Author, Authorship
Hypertext, 241–242
Hypothesis (in the humanities), 51, 244, 245, 251, 253–254

Idea, 39–40, 50–51, 146, 278–280, 290–294; alternative ideas, 290–291; continuum of ideas, 293; criteria of evaluation, 278–280; genre of "new idea," 278; as gift, 235; and the ordinary, 39–40. *See also* Bank of New Ideas, Interactive Anthology of Alternative Ideas, Thinking
Identity, 81, 84–85, 91–96, 322; as abstract category, 91–96; and hyperidentity, 245; multiple, 84, 86–87,94, 166; and opposition, 91–92
Ideocracy, 105, 294
Ideology, 64, 108–109
Image and thought, 51, 55n9. *See also* Thinklink
Image and Thought association, 2, 48–49, 55, 278
Imagination, 266; and ethics, 164–168, 168n1; imaginable books, 294; and

newness, 148–150; and science, 286–287. *See also* Transcultural imaginary.

Improvisation (collective), 2, 3, 11, 12, 33–34, 37–43, 67, 145, 182, 201–213 ; and avant-garde, 229; and community, 38, 205–206, 276–277; defined, 201–203, 210; and essay, 34, 209–211; examples of, 214–228; history of, 33–34, 37–39; in US. academy, 229–39; as integrative mode of thinking, 209; and interdisciplinarity, 39, 235; and Internet, 212, 276–277; as mode of thinking, 38–39, 203–204; and nomadism, 238; and otherness, 38, 203; as practice of everyday life, 229–32; problem-solving method, 237; psychology of, 38; as social and existential event, 38–39, 204–205; techniques and types, 41–43, 66; topics, 39–41; as transcultural activity, 211–212. *See also* Community, Writing

Indifference. *See* Difference

Individual, 206–207, 210, 242–243, 259, 262; individuation, 38; pre-individual and post-individual, 207, 210, 243, 259

Individualism and collectivism, 313–314

Infinition (vs. definition), 11, 141

Intellect: and society, 277–278; and Internet, 276–277, 282

Intellectual(s), 46, 70, 88–89, 201; critical, 123, 171–2; postmodern, 244

Intelligentsia, 46, 70, 104–106

InteLnet ("intellectual network"), 11, 181, 276–289; as Contra-Yahoo, 282; defined, 276–277; goals, 277, 278; journals in the humanities, 284–288; pre-electronic, 277, 279. *See also* Bank of New Ideas, Interactive Anthology of Alternative Ideas, Thinklinks

Intelnetics (metadiscipline), 46, 277, 283–84; and cybernetics, 284

Interactive Anthology of Alternative Ideas (Book of Books, Book²), 277, 290–301; defined, 290, 294, 296. *See also* InteLnet

Interference (in culture), 1, 3, 7–13, 76, 84, 96–100, 133, 135, 146, 150, 170; constructive and destructive, 99,101n11; defined, 9,11, 12n7, 13n8, 99; and ethics, 166; as hologram,13n9; in hyperauthorship, 244; proto-interferential, 2; vs. difference, 1, 7–11, 99, 244; vs. multiculturalism, 2–3, 7–8. *See also* Difference, Self-Differentiation

Internet, and collective improvisations, 212, 276–277; and human mind, 276–277. *See also* InteLnet

Irony, 156–157

Japan, 195, 240, 247–255

Kenocracy (the power of the new), 153

Knowledge, 20, 114–119, 298; and academia, 233; as commodity, 233–37; division of, 19, 51–52; and improvisation, 233–234; integrative, 283–284; and non-knowledge, 114–119; Platonic, 115; Socratic, 114–115; unknown, 114–116, 119

Laboratory of Contemporary Culture (in Moscow), 2, 52–54, 57, 65–68, 74, 135, 178, 232; compared with avant-garde and rear-garde, 67–68; and cultural reinvention, 66–7; goals of, 65–68; and interference, 11; program of, 53

Literature: birth of, 252; and folklore, 259–260; preliterary and postliterary, 259–260

Logic, 39; abductive (vs. inductive and deductive), 292, 298, 301n1

Love: as crystallization, 265–266; as transcultural experience, 86, 309;
Lyrical Museum, 2, 43–44, 66–67

Majority, 86–87, 103–104
Marxism, 16–17, 22, 72, 91, 95–96, 153, 154, 157, 185–186, 292, 302–03, 305–08; and feminism, 303–304; Marxism-Leninism, 22–23; Marxist-Leninist theory of culture, 87–89; reductionism and destruction, 305; as theoretical hallucination, 305–306; in transcultural perspective, 306–307; Western, 306–307
Mauvism, 258–259
Me (supra-I), 117–119
Metadiscipline, 46
Metaphysics, 40, 82, 100
Middle class, 104–106
Minorities, 85–87, 103
Modality, 229; in ethics, 166–168; in poetry, 261–262; of thinking, 51
Modernism, 56; and avant-garde, 57–8; and postmodernism, 152, 186, 253
Multiculturalism, 2–3, 80–85, 93, 97, 137, 310; vs. deconstruction, 80–85; and Marxism, 306–307; vs. transculture, 2–3, 25, 84–85, 97, 131, 310. *See also* Transculture
Museum. *See* Lyrical museum
Myth, 190–192, 210

Name, naming, 321–322; and potentiation, 321
National character, 1–2, 35, 54n3, 320–322
Neofolklore, 260, 264
New Left, 85, 86, 106
Newness, 2, 142–154; Appadurai on, 148–9; Bloch on, 144; and breakup of old systems, 145, 149–50; and consumer culture, 143–4; and deconstruction, 146; and the everyday, 145; and extrapolation, 145, 147–50; and imagination, 148–50; Jameson on, 143–5; kenocracy, 153; and "noise," 150; permanence of, 152–154; and postcolonialism, 146–47; and postcommunism, 149; and postmodernism, 142–51; and refunctioning, 149; sites of, 145–51; and transcultural practices, 151
New social movements, 60, 126, 136, 149
Nomadic aesthetics and critical practices, 11, 121–40; in the academy, 232–8; and critical identity, 125, 129, 133; and Deleuze and Guattari, 129–30; and globalization, 124–5; goals and features of, 124–30, 133; and improvisation, 238; and interdisciplinarity, 150–1; and new subjectivities, 127; and transcultural desire, 129–34
Nontotalitarian totality. *See* Totality

Of and *by*, 242
Opposition, 21, 91–96, 310, 315; as abstract category, 91–96; binary, 70, 316–317; and unity, 310; vs. transcendence, 21, 36, 45; within culture, 87–89
Ordinary, the, 39–40, 43–45, 51, 110–112, 179, 285–286; defined, 110–112; and the humanities, 285–286; micrology of, 179, 286; and transculture, 39, 110, 112; trivia, 39, 45; triviology, 285; and utopianism, 44. *See also* Everyday, the
Origins and disorigination, 79–80, 83–84, 244
Otherness, othering, 87, 113, 117–119, 203, 306, 309; alterity, 290, 299; and dehumanization, 117–118; and emotions, 310; in the humanities, 117–119; in hyperauthorship, 241,

268; in improvisation, 38, 202–203, 182; positive O., 87; as surplus, 316–317; and transculture, 87, 181. *See also* Alternative(s), Difference
Pan-textuality, 43
Paradigmatic and syntagmatic, 195, 199n1
Paradox, of culture, 157; of postmodernity, 79–82, 145
Philosophy, 46, 50
Pluralism, 97, 131
Poetry, 250, 256–271; after Auschwitz and Hiroshima, 253; as state of being vs. authorial self-expression, 179, 181, 256–271; impersonal and anonymous, 261–262, 269; in nominative and dative, 261–262; nonpoems, 261; no-poetry and not-at-all poetry, 256, 259, 269; unauthorial, 257, 259, 262. *See also* Hyperauthorship
Politeness, 167–168
Politics and culture, 8, 19–22, 35, 37, 45–46, 52–53, 87–89, 93
Possibility, possibilization, 101n13, 145, 147, 155, 158–159, 167, 199, 238, 297, 301n6; and naming, 321. *See also* Potentiality, Potentiation
Postcolonial, critique, 125, 143, 146; studies, 1, 4–5; subject, 128, 146–147
Postcommunist (postotalitarian) culture, 8, 47–48, 52, 63–69, 149; and newness, 146, 149; vs. postmodernism, 63, 68; and sublime, 66, 170–171; Western conceptions of, 75
Postmodern(ism), 1–2, 4, 7, 56, 58–9, 125, 152–153, 253, 255n4, 312–313; and critical paralysis, 142–5, 149; internal contradictions and antinomies, 79–82, 145; ludic, 59; and modern(ism), 152, 186, 253;

and newness, 142–51; performance, 229; of the possible, 71; and resistance, 59; in Russian literature, 247; temporalities of, 142–145; and Western intellectual project, 143
Postmodern avant-gardes, 56–77, 311–12
Poststructuralism, 21, 113, 118, 160, 243, 321
Potentiality and actuality, 37, 158–159, 163n6, 197, 211, 243, 299; of authorship, 194–296; of book, 296; vs. intentionality, 242. *See also* Potentiation, Virtuality
Potentiation (methodology in the humanities), 11, 158–161, 291, 297–299, 321; and deconstruction, 160–161, 291; defined, 160
Power, 109–110, 230; and struggle, 94–96
Pride and humility (as cultural dispositions), 97
Project (as genre), 37
Public: culture, 66, 74; improvisation, 37–38
Pseudo, 245; and *super*, 254n4

Quantum mechanics, 242
Queer, political critique, 60, 125, 129, 143, 311; subject, 127, 129

Reader, as potential author or coauthor, 262–264, 294–296
Reading, 262–264; and writing, 266–269
Reality, 111, 112n5,158–159; and signs, 111
Rear-garde, 64–65, 67, 68
Recognition and redistribution, as political models, 136–138; transcultural approach to, 137–138; utopianism of, 137, 175

Reductionism, 17, 19, 40, 52–53, 82, 89, 305
Reinvention (cultural), 56–77, 149
Religion, 16, 119, 167, 313
Renaissance, 117–119
Repetition (seriality), and new genres, 185–187
Reverse citation *See* Citation
Revolution, 36, 62, 85, 87
Romantics, 47–48
Russia (the Soviet Union) and the West, 1–3, 44–48, 62–63, 70–71, 74–76, 99, 104–112, 159, 207–208, 212n2, 316–317. *See also* American and Russian cultures

Science, and desire, 287–288; experiment 6–7; imaginative science, 288
Self-differentiation, 81, 93, 97–99, 117, 243, 307–308. *See also* Difference, Interference
Signs and semioticity, 43–44, 111, 161, 321; and reality, 111; and the ordinary 111; signifiables, 161, 321; signifiers and signifieds, 244, 321
Silence, 207–208; and language, 290; silentology, 290
Singularity, 43–44, 285
Sociologism (vulgar), 306
Soviet culture (civilization), 34–37, 45–46, 53, 66, 102, 108–109; and other cultures, 35–36, 45, 54n6; and Siberia, 66; and post-Soviet, 34–37
Soviet mentality, 48–49
Space, 134–135, 152–155, 162, 195. *See also* Geography, Time, Thirdspace
Specialization and universality, 17, 20, 51–52, 70, 282; and transculture, 46–47, 179–180
State of being (in grammar, poetry and culture), 261–262, 269
Stranger and strangeness (in society and culture), 102–104

Structuralism, 16–17, 154
Struggle and power, 94–96
Subculture, 8, 86–87,88
Subjunctive, in ethics, 166–168; in poetry, 261
Sublime, 66, 170–1
Suihitsu (genre of Japanese literature), and catalog, 195
Super and *pseudo*, 254n4
Surplement, 11, 316–20
Symbol, 317, 319; in culture, 16, 19, 21, 24, 25; symbolic vs. material values, 317, 319
Syncretic, 205; and synthetic, 51–52, 209, 210

Technology (topic of improvisation), 214–220
Territory and epoch, 155
Text: and authorship, 242, 252; in improvisation, 212; life as megatext, 245; and reading, 263; vs. catalog and dictionary, 197–199
Theology, 320, 321
Thing, 43–44, 111; and word, 43–44
Thinking, 293–294; abstract and concrete, 94–96; alternative, 178, 290–291; in catalog, 198–199; holistic, 51, 75; and Internet, 277, 281–283; in improvisation, 203–205, 207–208; oppositional, 315; paradigmatic, 281; syncretic and synthetic, 51–52; thinklinks, 282–283. *See also* Alternative(s), Idea, Image and thought
Thinklink (unit of interdisciplinary thinking), 282–283; and metaphor, 282; and rhizome, 282
Third culture, 5, 94, 131
Thirdspace, 128, 134–135, 147
Time (temporality), 71, 152–158; asymmetry of, 158; and postmodernism, 142–145; and space,

153–154, 162, 195, 197, 198, 207; and totalitarianism, 154
Tolerance, 97
Topos, 161–162. *See also* Utopia
Totality, 52, 307–308; culture as totality, 17, 19, 22, 36–37, 46–47, 52–53; and essay, 190–191; nontotalitarian totality, 11, 74, 96–100, 132, 193, 307; philosophy of total unity, 275n43
Totalitarianism, 7, 22, 46–47, 52, 95–97, 109, 153–154; and culture, 109; and mythology, 192; and temporality, 154; vs. totalization, 307–308
Transcendence, 21, 24, 33, 36, 82, 87, 107; and commodification, 107; culture as transcendence, 17, 24, 82–83, 107; in culturology, 21; in improvisation, 203, 209; self-transcendence, 17, 24, 107, 118, 119, 203, 210, 313, 318; and trance, 209–210; and transculture, 33, 82–83; vs. opposition, 21, 35, 45
Transcendentalism, 47
Transculture, 2–6, 9, 12n6, 23–26, 31, 33, 34–37, 39 46, 65, 86–87, 89, 94, 97, 100, 103, 131–135, 158, 164, 195, 304, 306–309; and archive, 66, 170; and avant-garde, 311–12; and collective improvisation, 211; and consciousness, 51; and cultural antagonism, 2–3; and cultural appropriation, 318; and cultural estrangement and alienation, 10, 23–34, 37; and cultural evolution, 317–319; and culture, 24–26, 36–37, 82–85, 89; and culturology, 23–25; and deconstruction, 100; defined, 2–3, 10, 23–25, 33, 36–37, 65, 85, 97, 101n11, 112, 131, 195, 307, 312, 313, 320; and education, 232–238, 309–310; and emotion, 310–11; and ethnography, 4; and feminism, 304–305, 308–309; genres of, 37, 46; and global system, 25, 130–131; history of the term, 3–6; and historical ruptures, 47; history of the transcultural project, 31–55; as intercultural, 4; and liberation, 24–25, 82–83; and love, 86, 309; and Marxism, 304–305, 306–308; and moral categories, 311; and other historical epochs, 47–48; and the ordinary, 112; and postcolonialism, 4–5; and religion, 313; as resolution of postmodern antinomies, 79, 84–85; and Russian and Soviet cultural traditions, 46, 102; and strangeness 103–104; and society, 102–112, 121; and sublime, 66; and third culture, 5; three modes of, 112; as transcendence, 24, 33; and transculturation, 4; as transformative, 6; and utopianism, 311–13; and the unconscious, 132; vs. American "melting pot," 2; vs. compensatory relations between cultures, 315–320; vs. counterculture, 25, 36, 85–87; vs. multiculturalism, 2–3, 25, 80–85, 87, 94, 97, 103, 131, 306–307; Western approaches to, 3–6, 75–76, 123
Transcultural desire, 11, 121–140, 182; defined, 129, 138; as liberation from culture, 24–25; as nomadic, 129–134; and politics of mobility, 137–138, 172; vs. psychoanalytic conceptions of, 129, 133
Transcultural experiment: defined, 6–7, 145; vs. avant-garde experiment, 7; vs. scientific experiment, 6–7
Transcultural imaginary, 11, 133, 136, 137–138, 150, 169–75, 307; as cultural potential, 170; and foreigner, 174; as imagination, 145, 169–70; vs. Lacanian imaginary, 172–173; as

sublime, 170–171. *See also* Imagination
Transcultural practices, 24, 31, 177–83, 184–301; as experiments, 177; as generative, 178, 180; as improvisational, 180–181; as nomadic, 180–1; as ongoing, 180–181, 236; as training ground, 180–181
Transhuman, 119; transhumanistic knowledge, 118–119; transhumanities, 119
Transindividual, 207
Transnationalism, 5, 6; and citizenship, 171–172; and imagined community, 171
Transsociality, 102–104

"Un" and "non," 116–117
Unconscious, the, and transcultural consciousness, 132
Universics (metadiscipline), 46–47
University, 159; and improvisation, 232–238
Unity: as "un-ity," 210
Unknown, 114–116, 119

Utopia, 2–3, 7, 64, 67–68, 137, 143, 145,157, 161–162, 231, 311–313; and America, 161–162; ; and heterotopia, 68, 127, 130, 134–135, 139; its death and resurrection, 68, 100; and the ordinary, 44; and topos, 161–162 ; and transculture, 3, 312–313; trans-utopia, 100

Virtuality, defined, 159–160; of book, 296–297; in culture, 297; and hyperauthorship, 242

West. *See* Russia (the Soviet Union) and the West
Wonder (in epistemology), 49–50
World Wide Web, 177, 181, 212, 276–289; web journals in the humanities, 284–288; web vs. grid, 282. *See also* InteLnet, Internet
Writing, 33, 107; creative and scholarly, 244; and hyperauthorship, 242, 244; in improvisation, 33, 207–208; and living, 243; vs. speaking, 207–208